To my Yael

Transforming Terror

in solidarity
Israel / Selva

Jamie
12. June . 2011

Transforming Terror

Remembering the Soul of the World

EDITED BY

Karin Lofthus Carrington and Susan Griffin

with Howard Teich

UNIVERSITY OF CALIFORNIA PRESS

Berkeley · Los Angeles · London

University of California Press, one of the most
distinguished university presses in the United States,
enriches lives around the world by advancing
scholarship in the humanities, social sciences, and
natural sciences. Its activities are supported by the UC
Press Foundation and by philanthropic contributions
from individuals and institutions. For more information, visit www.ucpress.edu.

University of California Press
Berkeley and Los Angeles, California

University of California Press, Ltd.
London, England

Library of Congress Cataloging-in-Publication Data

Transforming terror : remembering the soul of the
world / edited by Karin Lofthus Carrington and Susan
Griffin.
    p. cm.
    ISBN 978-0-520-25102-1 (cloth)
    ISBN 978-0-520-26928-6 (pbk.)
1. Terrorism. 2. Terror. 3. Terrorism—Psychological
aspects. 4. Violence—Prevention. 5. Emotional
intelligence. I. Carrington, Karin Lofthus. II. Griffin,
Susan.
    HV6431.T696 2011
    363.325—dc22   2010041000

Manufactured in the United States of America

20   19   18   17   16   15   14   13   12   11
10   9   8   7   6   5   4   3   2   1

This book is printed on Cascades Enviro 100, a 100%
post consumer waste, recycled, de-inked fiber. FSC
recycled certified and processed chlorine free. It is acid
free, Ecologo certified, and manufactured by BioGas
energy.

In the hope that future generations will live in a more compassionate world, we dedicate this volume to the memory of the many innocent children, women, and men who have perished during violent conflicts.

The world too has something of a spirit or a soul.
Václav Havel

Contents

Foreword

ARCHBISHOP DESMOND TUTU

The book you hold in your hands presents a path through which we might one day meet the challenge of terrorism and bring peace to our troubled world. If we are ever to put an end to the terrible cycle of violence terrorism causes, the use of more violence is not, in the end, the answer. As this book makes clear, in the effort to transform hearts and minds, we need to change the way we think, both personally and on the level of public policy. Yet if we are to do that, we must first enlarge our understanding of what terrorism is and the nature of the suffering it causes. With a wide range of contributions, combining ancient, spiritual wisdom with modern insights and approaches, this collection of essays presents us with new ways to heal the damage terrorism causes and at the same time addresses its complex causes on the deepest level.

Reflecting the premise that underlies this book, which is that collectively we all share responsibility for terrorism, those who have contributed to this volume come from many different cultures, religions, and nations. If we are to create the just and compassionate world in which terrorism cannot thrive, we must all join in this effort.

To transform terror may sound like a tall order. But the future requires it of us. And I speak from experience as a witness to many beautiful and unexpected acts of courage and generosity that this task is well within the realm of possibility.

Acknowledgments

We want to acknowledge Joan Miura for her perceptive, tireless, and generous assistance in the process of completing this collection. Amy Rennert saw the value of this book in an early form and helped us to make it viable. Our editor Reed Malcolm saw us through a long process with patience and a kind intelligence. We would also like to thank Jodie Evans, Nancy Kittle, and John Harris for their contributions. Stacey Pulice with her husband Ron Pulice generously supported this work. Thanks also go to Rita Lustgarten for her support and engagement all along the way. We are grateful for the generosity of many of our contributors and for their work in the world and also for the activists and community organizers who work daily to make the world a safer and more peaceful place now and for generations to come.

Introduction

SUSAN GRIFFIN AND KARIN LOFTHUS CARRINGTON

That gentle and all-knowing sage then kept me from losing
heart, "Do not let terror block your purpose . . ."
—Dante, *The Inferno*

We have called this collection *Transforming Terror* instead of transforming "terrorism" for a reason. If many of the pieces included here address the complex causes of terrorism, this book also explores the dominion of terror itself. Over the last decade, whether in Palestine or Israel, Pakistan or Mumbai, Baghdad or Kabul, Rwanda or the Sudan, the United States, Spain, or Great Britain, we have witnessed a vicious cycle in which terrorism causes terror and the experience of terror seeds acts of terrorism. And yet, though the human emotions we all share—fear, grief, and loss—are so clearly part of this murderous equation, in delineating and defining this violence rarely does society consider the experience of terror that lies at the heart of terrorism.

With this focus in mind, in assembling this anthology, we have used a simple, though broader and ultimately more humanitarian definition of terrorism. Instead of viewing this form of violence according to those who enact it, we believe terrorism should be viewed from the perspective of those who are harmed by it. Thus, we see terrorism as acts of violence against unarmed civilians, no matter who perpetrates them. By this definition, we include attacks that are initiated by underground organizations such as Al Qaeda, by groups such as the Ku Klux Klan, by nations or alliances between nations, and by unaffiliated individuals. Whether acts of violence committed against civilians are purposeful or labeled as collateral damage, if they result in harm to women, men, and children who are not soldiers and are not participating in an armed

conflict, we define them as terrorism. Only when various ideologies, political considerations, power struggles—over legitimacy, for instance, or
the possession of land—are stripped away does the raw emotional truth
of the terror we are all facing emerge. And yet it is only by facing this
emotional reality that we can bring about the transformation peace
requires.

Since the destruction of the World Trade Center and the deaths of over
3,000 civilians on September 11, 2001, there have been many books written about terrorism. Our contribution to this continuing discussion is
unique. We are looking at the way terror damages the human psyche or,
as the ancient Greeks called it, *soul,* and how it is through this damage
that the world enters seemingly endless cycles of violence.

In this regard the subtitle of our book, *Remembering the Soul of the
World,* is also deliberate. If we are to heal ourselves, we must move past
denial to remember what the world is suffering. No re-membering of
the soul can occur if we do not share the weight of terrifying memories
together. Even in those cases where self-defense is necessary, to respond
to violence with force does not by itself heal whatever damage has been
inflicted in each life and to whole nations. Not only physical but psychological wounds must be named, delineated, witnessed, and acknowledged. For this reason, justice is also crucial to peace, not as retribution
but in order to bring the truth into public consciousness as well as assert the right we all have to be free from violent attack.

We include in *Transforming Terror* suggestions regarding ways that
we might work locally and as an international community to escape
from this cycle of violence and denial and transform the effects of terror
into a force for cooperation and peace. We are not arguing in this volume that force should never be used. Nor, except as examples of what is
possible, do we offer a strategy for transforming terror. What we aim at
instead is the first but crucial step of changing the way we see terrorism,
both analytically and emotionally. In this way, we hope to open up new
avenues for understanding events and finding solutions to seemingly
endless conflicts.

Though the last century and the beginning of the twenty-first century
have witnessed devastating violence, this has also been a period in which
our understanding of human psychology has grown immensely. This
collective understanding has lead to countless ways—therapeutic techniques, forms of mediation, and social solutions—that can be and have
been used to heal both individuals and society effectively. Thus, we present contributions from a range of psychological thinkers, cognitive sci-

entists, jurists, poets, writers, spiritual leaders, philosophers, and activists addressing both ideas and emotional processes.

The contributions in this book are organized into two parts. The first part contains a series of chapters that chart the psychological, social, and cultural processes, from trauma to denial, fear and the illusion of power, by which terror and violence lead to more terror and violence. The chapters that make up the second part of the book present insights, approaches, and understandings—from the necessity for justice to the role gender has often played in violence, to the knowledge of interdependence and the experience of compassion—through which vicious cycles of terror might be transformed.

Because, as Pascal wrote in the seventeenth century, "The heart has reasons that reason does not understand," we hope in these pages to awaken the full spectrum of the human capacity for reflection and change, inviting not only intellectual but emotional intelligence and spiritual knowledge to the table. To that end, we have included poems and prayers in this volume.

Though no single volume can be representative of the entire political spectrum on any issue, we have attempted to include a wide range of perspectives here. But we are neither adjudicating nor taking sides in the many current conflicts raging in the world today. Though each of us has our own political opinions on various conflicts, we are not aiming to express those in this volume. We have in fact included some entries from those who may have, in other venues, made statements with which we do not agree. But peace cannot be made among people who already agree with one another. It requires a pluralistic process to find, among our many disagreements, the mutual needs and understandings that we share and that can lead us to sustainable peace and a collective remembering of the soul of the world.

PART ONE

A Deeper Look

At this crucial moment in history, we are facing a formidable challenge. Over several decades, as new incidents of violence continually arise in different locations throughout the world, countless attempts to stop terrorism by force have lead to failure or, with the seemingly endless proliferation of violence, a sense of futility. Yet even if the means we have been using are ineffective, the task of ending terrorism is not insurmountable. What is required of us all, however, is not simple; no single approach or strategy will solve the dilemma. We are being asked by circumstance to undergo nothing less than a profound transformation, both collectively and within each of us; if we are to heal our world of this form of violence, we must enlarge our understanding and begin to see more clearly and deeply what we and others have suffered and how and why this suffering has occurred. If in turn such a change may seem impossible, we have only to remember that with shifting technologies, creative cultural movements, social and political revolutions, many transformations have already occurred in human history throughout the globe.

Instead of drawing a precise profile of the transformation we need here—a profile no one can render until this change has taken place—we have collected wisdom and insights from diverse healers and thinkers that seed the potential for change by opening new paths in consciousness. Because any process of transformation must begin with a radical change in perception, Part I of this volume, called "A Deeper Look," is dedicated to the way that collectively we see terrorism. This part contains three chapters: the first, "Terror and Terrrorism," posits a new, more accurate, and, we believe, just way of defining terrorism; the second, "An Unbearable Heartache," helps the reader to grasp the full emotional dimensions of terror, the cataclysmic emotion that is the goal of terrorism, through accounts from those who have survived to tell the tale; and the third chapter, "Denial, Dogma, and the Heroic Myth," explores psychological habits, such as denial and fanaticism, that underlie and lead to acts of violence that are otherwise unthinkable.

Susan Griffin with Karin Lofthus Carrington

CHAPTER I

Terror and Terrorism

You cannot solve any problem by blowing up innocent
people.
—Chinua Achebe

Terrorism remains a crime against humanity no matter who commits it
or for what reason. As one of the six children who survived the Okla-
homa City bombing, Chris Nguyen, has said, "Terrorism is terrorism, no
matter where it comes from." To be free of violent attack is a primary
human right; yet violence against civilians continues in many forms. In
this light particularly, to limit the definition of terrorism to specific acts
of violence committed in one region, in a single period of history, or by
one kind of perpetrator is to harness the meaning of the term to a po-
lemical purpose and thus reduce its meaning. For over a century, terror
has been used as an instrument of power many times by every political
faction, left, right, and center. The modern use of the word came into being during the French Revolution. In the Soviet Union, Stalin was famous
for using terror to suppress opposition; the Nazi regime used terror, including the Holocaust, to gain and retain power; terror has been used
within the United States in the service of racism, and similarly all over the
world to curtail human rights.

Both the destruction of the Twin Towers on 9/11 and the aerial bombings of cities or villages that result in the death of civilians are forms of
terrorism, as are the lynching of African Americans that occurred throughout America through the first half of twentieth century, the massacre of
civilians that occurred in 1981 in El Mozote, a village in El Salvador, and
the assassination of doctors who provide abortions.

If our consideration of terrorism is to be truthful and fair, along with suicide and car bombs, we must include land mines, drones, and strategic bombing (which by military definition means bombing off the battlefield, behind enemy lines, often in areas where civilians live). In the same vein, nuclear armaments are by definition terrorist weapons, especially because, even when uranium-tipped bullets are used, the radioactive materials stay in the environment long after a battle is waged, causing harm even to the unborn children of future generations.

Without acknowledging the broad range of suffering caused by terrorism, we cannot fully understand the current and serious threat we are facing in America today. This acknowledgment is also crucial if we are ever to break the cycle of violence that terror and terrorism fuel. We must see the problem clearly and acknowledge our own role before we can undertake any steps toward transformation. As Chinua Achebe has said, "You cannot solve any problems by blowing up innocent people."

Taken together, the essays in this chapter open up the boundaries of thought and imagination by inviting us to enlarge our picture of terrorism by including the purposeful creation of conditions that lead to destitution and starvation, for instance, or by reminding us that whether speaking of Christianity, Judaism, or Islam, religion does not cause terrorism. The essays in this chapter also explore unconscious elements that prevent us from thinking clearly about terrorism, including the use of terms such as "War on Terror" that truncate our ability to reflect on the nature of the crisis. To underscore the gravity of this issue, we have reprinted an address by Jan Egeland, former Undersecretary for Humanitarian Affairs and Emergency Relief Coordinator for the United Nations, on the prevalence of civilian casualties. In many conflicts civilian casualties are still not being counted or reported, and for this reason we have also included an excerpt from the biography of Marla Ruzicka, the young woman who gave her life to assess and redress civilian deaths in Iraq.

It is our hope that if terrorism is perceived as a threat to women, children, and men throughout the world, the worldwide movement against violence aimed at civilians that began to form after 9/11 can rise up again and turn the world away from a path of mutual, murderous violence.

Susan Griffin

. . .

CIVILIAN CASUALTIES: THE NEW FRONTLINE
Susan Griffin

These days I sense in myself a muted, nearly inexplicable unease. The cause is not just global warming and a frail economy, but a shadowy sense that right now, just under the skin of public awareness, something terrible is occurring. It is as if, in rare moments of silence, beneath the joys and vicissitudes of daily life, I can almost detect a muffled sound. Is this the sound of weeping, a cry of terror? Or a warning?

That we are currently engaged in more than one violent conflict and losing young men and women in battle every day is disturbing enough. But almost daily, another kind of casualty occurs, one that seems hidden from public scrutiny. As planes without pilots called drones fly over villages looking for Taliban fighters in Afghanistan and Pakistan, they drop bombs that kill far more civilians than terrorists. At the height of the war in Iraq, a war of words ensued over how many civilian deaths occurred since the war began in Iraq. Was it 650,000 as a study by Johns Hopkins estimated, or only 10,000 as the Bush administration once claimed? At least the subject of civilian casualties was in the news. Yet the horrific dimensions of these events do not seem to register in public consciousness. Since the Hopkins study received far less attention than the plight of a young family of four lost in the snow that week, the accidental juxtaposition of these events awakens another question in me, one that is filled with doubt, irony, and hope all at once. Why is the great feeling of care that was inspired by a single family not aroused equally toward the countless families who have been injured or have died because of the war in Iraq? This question takes on an especially urgent dimension since at this moment in history, as civilians, we are all in great danger.

A terrible shift has taken place during our century, a momentous change not only in international events but also in military tactics practiced all over the world. Though there has never been a time in recorded history when civilians did not die in warfare, over the last five decades civilians have become the primary target of warfare. The fact that at the present time more civilians are dying in battle than soldiers is at the front line of an accelerating advance, one that moves in a terrible direction. While at the beginning of the century civilians represented 10 percent of casualties and soldiers 90 percent, now those numbers are reversed. This means that today 90 percent of those injured in warfare are unarmed, untrained, vulnerable, in large part women and children. How is it that we came to this state of affairs? Somehow, we have come to think that the occurrence of massive civilian casualties in warfare is a permanent fixture of the world we inhabit, as if our drift into wholesale slaughter were a natural process, an inevitable and natural disaster.

The belief that this aspect of contemporary life cannot be changed must in some unconscious way be predicated on the fact that by the time many of us alive today were born, the deaths of thousands of civilians from the bombardment of cities had already taken place. Born in the midst of World War II, I admired the pilots who conducted bombing raids—young men, risking their lives, who were heroes to us. Though I saw photographs of burned and ruined cities, I encountered no images of the people who were wounded or killed during those raids. When I was young, it never occurred to me to question the morality of this tactic; I imagined that bombs had always existed.

But massive aerial attacks on civilians had two beginnings in modern times. If the first was the bombardment of civilians during World War I. A subtle turning point had occurred earlier, in 1907 at the Hague Convention, where in fact it was confirmed by the participating nations that to attack civilians would be against international law. Yet it was at the same conference that the ground for attacking civilians would be laid. If before that meeting it had been declared illegal for airplanes to drop weapons as a way to attack armies on the ground, now this conference agreed that airplanes would need to be able to defend themselves against attacks from the ground.

Throughout military history, arguments for various offensive weapons have been based on the need for defense. Because the adoption of any weapon will ensure it will soon be manufactured by other nations (who believe they will need it for defense, too), this argument induces a strangely somnolent drift toward mutual destruction. But there is another pattern that belongs to this history, one that on the surface would seem to support the argument. Once a weapon exists, there will be military commanders who will want to use it not just defensively, but offensively.

Although the international agreement reached at the Hague Convention of 1907 prohibited an attack on civilians by bombardments, the distinctions drawn between targets soon blurred. Early in World War I, the Deputy Chief of the Imperial German Navy Staff's request to use bombs to cow the British population into submission was denied, but the Kaiser did give the German Navy permission to attack "docks and military establishments in the Lower Thames and English coast." So on January 19, 1915, two zeppelins dropped eight explosives and two incendiary devices on Great Yarmouth. They were supposed to target a small naval base and the docks. But given the mist, snow squalls, and crude navigational equipment, it was a great achievement even to find Yarmouth at all. Two bombs fell in a densely populated area known as St. Peter's Plain and another damaged the fish wharf. Though many houses and shops burned, and a 72-year-old woman coming home from shopping, a shoemaker working in his own shop, a 14-year-old boy, and a 26-year-old war widow were all killed, little or no damage was done to any military site. Then, in May 1916, after London was accidentally bombed, the Kaiser sanctioned raids against larger cities. By the end of the war, 5,806 bombs had been dropped, killing 557 people and injuring 1,358.

Another series of mistakes led the British air force to drop bombs on German civilians. Their targets were munitions factories, usually located just outside metropolitan areas (a strategy described as a pacifist maneuver, a way to end the war by destroying the means to make weapons). Yet fearing attack from the ground, thus often flying where visibility was impeded and for this reason unable to find their targets, the pilots would release their bombs over populated areas.

After it became increasingly clear that it was not factories but civilians who were being wounded, maimed, and killed by their bombs, the British High Command held a secret meeting in which they acknowledged the strategy had failed. But, committed to a course of action that had cost a great deal of money, time, and many soldiers' lives, instead of changing the tactic, the command devised a new rationale for what was called strategic bombing. Secretly stated among themselves, the purpose would be to strike *terror* into the civilian population.

Their new aim was to undermine the will to fight. Perhaps in the sterile world of abstract thought this plan is logical, but experience should have led them to doubt the efficacy of the idea. Though the zeppelin attacks inspired panic, they only strengthened the patriotic feeling that Britain's enemy was monstrous. It was only after soldiers returned with reports of carnage on the battlefield that British citizens turned against war.

The second precedent for the large number of civilian casualties in warfare today occurred before World War I, as part of Europe's colonization of America, Asia, and Africa. In fact, the first violations of the Hague Convention's prohibition against the bombardment of civilians occurred in 1911, when the Italians dropped bombs on Tripoli. More than a decade before the savage bombing of Guernica that shocked the world prior to

World War II, Spain had dropped bombs on civilians in Morocco. Other European powers dropped bombs in Asia, Africa, and the Middle East, both before and after World War I. In this period, no one argued that it was morally right to attack civilians; rather, in a hazy and convoluted argument shaped by racist assumptions, it was declared that the air raids were planned to bring civilization to backward peoples.

On a subtle level of consciousness, colonial violence must have lowered the threshold of tolerance for violence against all civilians. Before World War II, British Major General Trenchard argued most vociferously for the creation of a strategic bombing force. He had commanded the squadrons of planes that dropped bombs behind enemy lines in World War I. Between the wars, he ordered squadrons to attack a tribal settlement in Iraq, and well before that, in the first years of the twentieth century, as the military governor of Nigeria, he had ordered British soldiers to set Zulu villages on fire. It was, in fact, common during the nineteenth century for European colonists and American forces to attack native villages.

One can see a tug of war occurring throughout this period between a seemingly inexorable march toward mass destruction and the awareness that these acts violated human rights. Gandhi himself was so disturbed by the burning of Zulu villages that he questioned his allegiance to the British Empire and began to conceptualize *Satyagraha,* the movement that was to free India from colonial rule. Within England, not only did Gandhi have allies, but loud and powerful protests arose against the bombing of villagers in Iraq. In the long run, attacks on civilians were to escalate, but in the short run, these protests were effective. At the start of World War II, British forces were committed to avoiding civilian deaths.

For a short period after bombing civilians in Guernica, then Poland, and finally in Rotterdam, because of the strength of international protests, Hitler declared that he would not wage a war against women and children, and ordered his air force to aim attacks only at military and industrial sites. Thus, in the first months of the war with Great Britain, both sides tried to keep their bombs from falling on civilians.

However, after the Luftwaffe accidentally dropped bombs over London, Churchill ordered raids against Berlin. In retaliation, a series of fierce attacks, now called *blitzkriegs,* were turned against Great Britain, which continued from the fall of 1940 until the spring of 1941. In 1940 alone, from August to November, London endured 200 bombing raids every night except one. By the end of the war, 43,000 civilians had been killed and 139,000 injured. Yet in contrast to the relatively minor attacks of World War I, very few British citizens panicked: the stated aim to weaken the will of the civilian population had failed again.

Still this failure did not stop Britain from using the same tactic, now called *morale bombing,* against Germany. On May 30, 1942, in Operation Millennium, 2,000 tons of high-explosive bombs and incendiaries were dropped over the medieval city of Cologne, burning the city to the ground. In this attack, 45,000 were left without homes. Only 382 civilians died; but as the raids continued, their ferocity grew, until finally in Operation Gomorrah targeted against Hamburg, an intense rain of bombs created a firestorm that left 42,600 dead. This was the precedent for the famous firestorm in Dresden, which killed somewhere between 25,000 and 35,000 civilians.

Despite their own suffering from German aerial attacks, British attacks on German civilians did not take place without protest. Many citizens protested what was being called "obliteration bombing." Prominent among them, the writer Vera Brittain led a campaign, publishing a statement signed by other prominent citizens and a series of pamphlets titled "Massacre by Bombing," which detailed the atrocities and argued against the government's justification for them.

But the attacks continued, becoming even more deadly under the command of the American military in the Pacific theater. Firestorms were deliberately created in Kobe, Japan, killing 8,800; in Tokyo, successive raids killed 73,000 civilians. What followed this was less an exception than a continuation of a pattern already well established: the atomic bombs dropped on Hiroshima and Nagasaki in 1945 together killed 135,000 civilians at once, and radiation poisoning, whose effects continue through genetic damage even today, killed countless others, many born well after the war.

It has often been suggested, albeit with a wistfully resigned tone, that the challenge of nuclear weapons is that they exist at all, as if the weapons themselves had initiated the problem. But before these weapons were invented, the use of explosive bombs and the brutality of colonial expeditions had seeded a strategy that made their invention possible. Though nuclear weapons present a grave danger in themselves, they were spawned by the policy of murdering civilians in the course of war.

Throughout the cold war, nuclear weapons were never used, but civilians continued to be the targets of warfare. During the Vietnam War, the city of Hanoi was bombed, and in both the South and North, Vietnamese civilians suffered from the use of napalm and Agent Orange. In the recent wars in the former Yugoslavia, women were targeted and gang raped by the thousands. In the shelling of Lebanon, the city of Beirut, where close to one million civilians live, was a target.

Is it any wonder that terrorists, insurgents, and armies of all kinds both official and unofficial would have adopted the same tactic? Not just weapons of mass destruction pose a risk to us all today, but also the mentality of massacre, the policy of targeting civilians. Suicide bombers are sent to places where ordinary people, not engaged in any military activity, eat, drink, celebrate, or worship. Civilians engaged in medical care or social work are taken as hostages, as are journalists. But are these awful acts, which appear to us so senseless and brutal, so different from the atrocities that the United States along with most European nations have committed against civilians?

In fact, the history of terrorist tactics is inextricable from the history of bombing civilians. In the impassioned pamphlet she published in 1944, Vera Brittain presciently warned that through attacks on civilians, Europe was creating "the psychological foundations for a Third World War."

Yet the human capacity to erase a dangerous reality from the mind is formidable. That most people panicked far less during the horrific blitzes of World War II than they had during the far milder attacks of World War I may seem strange. But on another level it makes a terrible sense. Many Londoners stopped going to the air raid shelters when the sirens sounded, and others resorted to magical thinking to explain why they had not died. Returning to Germany in 1945, just after the war, Alfred Doblin wrote that people walked "down the street and past the terrible ruins as if nothing had happened and . . . the town had always been like that." According to W. G. Sebald, reconstruction efforts in Germany adopted the same denial by creating "a new, faceless reality, pointing the population exclusively toward the future and enjoining on it silence about the past."

Ultimately, to adjust to the outrageous and unacceptable is a sign of profound hopelessness. Helpless to change a circumstance, we tend to mute the force of it in our minds. Yet this comes at a cost: as often happens with victims of trauma, with collective denial we lose the ability to respond at all, to protest or speak out.

Is it by conscious intent that civilian deaths are kept at a distance? The pilots who fly bombers today are thousands of miles away, looking only at coordinates. Even the suicide bombers, who must use their own bodies and mingle with their victims, manage to create a mental distance by shrouding themselves in fantasies conjured by ideologies masquerading as religious doctrines. The advantage of their own death is that they never have to wake to the reality of the mangled bodies of the innocents they have harmed.

Sadly, it is a similar distance that keeps us all from waking up to the accelerating dimensions of this terrifying aspect of contemporary battle. The fear of being attacked together with a sense of powerlessness disables our empathy for those who are being maimed and killed now. But the tide can be turned. Once we acknowledge the mutual danger we are in, the sleeping power of civilians all over the world can rise to stop these attacks, which are aimed in the end against all of us.

. . .

In still another photograph, the air marshal himself is looking at pictures. He is studying portraits, taken from the air, of cities that have been bombed. He looks at these images through a small aperture in a wooden box called a stereopticon, a device which adds a third dimension to what he sees. Through this instrument, a two-dimensional, gray landscape suddenly reveals *gaping craters, heaps of rubble, burned out buildings with the walls still standing, acres and acres of roofless buildings.*

On the opposing page, the air marshal leafs through his famous *Blue Book,* a huge document he has prepared to impress the leaders of the Allied effort with the efficacy of strategic bombing. It contains maps of several German sites, which he has marked, according to *Life* for *emasculation.*

I am, of course, stopped by this last word. The author has placed it in quotations. . . . What is meant by this word? Is it the implicit unmanning of the vanquished by conquering armies? Or is it that emasculation which occurs when one man's women and children are harmed by another man? Or both of these. And of course there is the obvious meaning, the loss of a part of the body, the sexual body by which a man is defined. But even this literal reading moves to a larger implication, the loss of identity itself. That stripping away of every extraneous layer, of every role we play in life, which one suffers when faced with unimaginable terror.

(Susan Griffin, from *A Chorus of Stones: The Private Life of War*)

. . .

STATEMENT OF THE UNDER-SECRETARY-GENERAL AT THE OPEN MEETING OF THE SECURITY COUNCIL ON THE PROTECTION OF CIVILIANS IN ARMED CONFLICT, JUNE 28, 2006

Jan Egeland

Madam President, Members of the Council, there are signs of progress in our work to better protect civilians caught in conflict. . . . Our collective efforts are having an impact: more systematic engagement by the Security Council in more crisis areas; more comprehensive peacekeeping; enhanced humanitarian response; and more mediation and effective judicial recourse offered in more places have contributed to stronger protection and the reduction of conflict related civilian deaths. Where there is concerted, coherent and systematic international action, and strong positive political engagement from the parties to conflicts, we can—and we will—make significant progress.

The recent adoption of Security Council Resolution 1674 [2006] on the protection of civilians in armed conflict, is fundamental to this progress. . . . We as the UN, and you specifically as the Security Council, now have the responsibility to protect, as reaffirmed in Resolution 1674. There are too many times when we still do not come to the defence of civilian populations in need. When our response is weak, we appear to wash our hands of our humanitarian responsibilities to protect lives. The world is, indeed, a safer place for most of us, but it is still a death trap for too many defenceless civilians—men, women and children.

In Iraq, Sudan, Uganda, Somalia, Afghanistan and the Democratic Republic of the Congo, civilians continue to bear the full brunt of armed conflict and terror. Despite all our efforts, women are still raped and violated as a matter of course, children are still forcibly recruited, and defenceless civilians continue to be killed in violation of the most basic principles enshrined in centuries of international law-making. . . .

Madam President, in the time that we will take today to debate how we best protect civilians, dozens will have died from the direct, blunt and brutal violence of conflict in only the six crisis situations I have just mentioned. . . .

Madam President, a key question is how we can we make the recently adopted Security Council Resolution 1674 on the protection of civilians offer a real platform for action. Protection has been placed as a central responsibility of peacekeeping mandates. This commitment acknowledges that it is by how well the United Nations protects that our missions will be judged.

You have created a range of protection tools at your disposal. These must be used more effectively. The Council's Presidential Statement of June 2005 rightly expressed grave concern over the limited progress to ensure the effective protection of civilians in many situations of armed conflict. It stressed the urgent need to provide better physical protection and underscored that the establishment of a secure environment for all vulnerable populations should be a key objective of peacekeeping operations.

States have the primary responsibility for the protection of their own people. But in the case of armed conflict within their own territory, they all too often lack the capacity and the will to do so. The humanitarian community helps create an environment where the will and the capacity can be re-established or re-created. The Centre for Humanitarian Dialogue has shown that humanitarian presence can have some beneficial effects, deterring violence. However, let us be honest. Humanitarian presence has limitations. In many situations, like in today's eastern Chad, security is so precarious that the civilians, and often humanitarian staff, need physical protection, which today is virtually non-existent. This is where your role as the Security Council in defining and facilitating the role and capacity of peacekeepers is so crucial.

Firstly, peace-keeping missions must be equipped with better, more comprehensive mandates and the means to fulfill them. . . . Our people on the ground are too often ill-equipped to fulfill their duty to protect. Realistic, well-designed mandates for missions and practical support for their implementation are fundamental to the effectiveness of their efforts. . . .

Secondly, new creative approaches to peacekeeping are required, and the composition of missions [must be] amended. Instead of being adapted to allow a flexible response to emerging threats, new tasks are often simply added on to old ones. In Côte d'Ivoire, new threats for civilians have emerged, with groups like the Jeunes Patriotes using street violence and criminality to advance their agenda. Soldiers are not trained to meet these challenges. . . . Peacekeepers must be given tools, guidance and support if they are to respond to these threats and provide better protection.

Humanitarian access is the first stepping stone to the protection of civilians. The Security Council must make every effort to ensure that access is granted and respected. By not responding more forcefully in cases where this access has been unreasonably denied, we risk placing humanitarian personnel in jeopardy, further exposing them to possible attack. Humanitarian workers remain at considerable risk to violence. In Afghanistan alone, 24 humanitarian colleagues have been killed since the beginning of the year [2006]. . . . On the West Bank and in the Gaza Strip, restrictions on access for humanitarian goods and supplies, coupled with limitations on the movement of UN and humanitarian personnel, continue to pose severe problems for humanitarian agencies operating in the occupied Palestinian territory.

One of the most important tools at our disposal is conflict mediation and the timely and effective use of good offices. A number of violent crises highlight the grave cost in human lives of inadequate timely mediation. It also underscores that conflict can only ever be resolved at the political level. International protection, whether by peacekeepers or humanitarians, can only ever be an interim response—a band-aid. Without political solutions, tragically, civilians continue to suffer, and the humanitarians are left to deal with intractable conflict and open-ended displacement.

We must activate, strengthen, and resource the Secretary General's good offices more often and earlier, seize every opportunity for mediation and speak out when political solutions are needed. . . .

Targeted sanctions and embargoes are also yet to be used optimally, despite our efforts to develop guidance for their effective use. Targeted sanctions should be employed at the earliest opportunity where violations against civilians prevail, to signal our concern and serve as a first step to protect. . . . Why are we not using sanctions strategically in other crises? And where embargoes are in place, but are violated, why is stronger action not being taken . . . ?

Protection is a collective responsibility. . . . Better methods of analysis are also needed to ensure that local populations are included as a crucial element in our decision-making process. The perceptions of the local population are critical to understanding where risks lie.

Joint planning is also essential. . . . In general, integration is most effective where it is formulated around a common objective, such as protection. . . .

Madam President, these actions will have limited impact if we fail to address the need to uphold and respect the universal values as enshrined in the tenets and rules of international humanitarian, human rights and refugee law. The new Human Rights Council is a welcomed addition to the international architecture to safeguard the rule of law. But if we are unable to fulfil our responsibilities or enforce the legal frameworks that we have created, and impunity prevails unchallenged, we will consistently fail to protect civilians caught in conflict.

Such protection must be provided consistently and without prejudice. We grapple, in particular, with how to meet the specific protection and assistance needs of indigenous groups and ethnic minorities who are amongst those at greatest risk. . . . We cannot stand by as passive witnesses to the loss of life and the loss of cultures.

Madam President, in conclusion, I sincerely believe that progress to ensure better protection for civilians has been made—just not enough. The numbers of innocent civilians who continue to be killed and live with the constant threat of violence is still unacceptable. We must work together at all levels and using every tool at our disposal to provide adequate protection for those living in the midst of conflict around the world.

There is much at stake. In these dangerous and polarised times, it could not be more important to reaffirm the rule of law, which lies at the heart of the protection agenda. Where we fail, countries emerging from crisis are at serious risk of spiralling back into conflict. . . . Together with my humanitarian colleagues, I stand ready to continue to work with you and Member States towards the creation of a real culture of protection and a safer world for all.

· · ·

U.S. NUCLEAR TERRORISM
Daniel Ellsberg

Long after the ending of the Cold War, the chance that some nuclear weapons will kill masses of innocent humans somewhere, before very long, may well be higher than it was before the fall of the Berlin Wall.

One phase of the Nuclear Age, the period of superpower arms race and confrontation, has indeed come to a close (though the possibility of all-out, omnicidal exchange of alert forces triggered by a false alarm remains, inexcusably, well above zero). But another dangerous phase now looms, the era of nuclear proliferation and with it, an increased likelihood of regional nuclear wars, accidents, and nuclear terrorism. And the latter prospect is posed not just by "rogue" states or sub-state terrorists but by the United States, which has led by example for sixty years of making nuclear first-use threats that amount to terrorism and may well be the first or among the first to carry out such threats.

Averting catastrophe—not only the spread of weapons but their lethal use—will require major shifts in attitude and policy in every one of the nuclear weapon states, declared and undeclared. But such change is undoubtedly most needed, and must come first, in the United States and Russia.

With each month and year that nuclear weapons states maintain large nuclear arsenals, postpone ratification of the Comprehensive Test Ban Treaty, and sustain nuclear policies that suggest that such weapons convey major-power status and are useful for political and military purposes, other nations can only conclude that acquiring and in some circumstances using nuclear weapons may well be in their national interest.

In the United States alone, a whole set of policies persist that have long tended to *encourage* proliferation.

Perhaps most dangerously, such potential proliferators are led by past and present American doctrine and behavior to consider—among the possible, acceptable and valuable uses of nuclear weapons—the employment of nuclear first-use threats: i.e., the "option" of threatening to initiate nuclear attacks, and if necessary of carrying out such threats. Precisely that example was set by repeated statements by President George W. Bush and Secretary of State Condoleezza Rice, echoed by leading members of Congress, that "all options are on the table" in their determination to prevent Iranian nuclear weapons capability. Such threats legitimize the prospect of first-use by any nuclear weapons state, and they have the perverse effect of challenging states without nuclear weapons, including Iran, to acquire them: to be able to deter or preempt nuclear attack, or to threaten first-use on their own.

Years after the former members of the Warsaw Pact, including Russia, began asking to be admitted to NATO, and after China has acquired most-favored-nation status, the United States still refuses to adopt a policy of "no-first-use." This means that the United States refuses to make a commitment to never under any circumstance initiate a nuclear attack. This is also true of Britain, France and now Russia, which abandoned its no-first-use doctrine in late 1993, citing the United States-NATO example and reasoning in doing so.

This is not only a matter of words, as some suppose. Despite sensible moves on both sides beginning in late 1991 to remove tactical nuclear weapons from the surface navy and from ground units—responding to realistic fears in both leaderships of "loose nukes" in the Soviet Union—both states have continued to deploy sizeable numbers of tactical weapons on air bases and still larger numbers in reserve storage. Since virtually all of these weapons are vulnerable to nuclear attack, they cannot be used for deterrence; they are weapons *only* for first-use or for use against non-nuclear opponents.

So long as these continue to be components of the nuclear arsenals of both the United States and Russia, even after their own overarching confrontation has ended, there is simply no logical argument for denying either the legitimacy or reasonableness of other countries acquiring nuclear arsenals sized and shaped to the same ends. Accordingly when in May 1990, a nuclear conflict between India and Pakistan over Kashmir was plausibly feared by U.S. officials, the United States was not in a position to invoke an internationally-accepted norm against Pakistan's tacit first-use threats, since Pakistan was so clearly imitating U.S. and NATO behavior.

U.S. Nuclear Weapons Use

Later in 1990, after Saddam Hussein attacked Kuwait, not one of the four nuclear states militarily arrayed against Iraq in the Gulf War—the United States, Britain, France and Israel—refrained from tacit threats to initiate nuclear attacks under some circumstances. Under public questioning, high U.S. and other Allied officials pointedly refused to rule out the possible first-use of nuclear weapons against Iraq: in particular, if the Iraqis used chemical weapons extensively, which was regarded as highly possible. Thus, nuclear weapons *were used* as a threat against a non-nuclear opponent during the Gulf War.

By the same token, contrary to the belief of most Americans that U.S. nuclear weapons have never been used in the fifty years since Hiroshima and Nagasaki, American presidents have employed nuclear threats over a dozen times, generally in secret from the U.S. public, in crises and limited wars in Indochina, East Asia, Berlin, Cuba and the Middle East.[1] The Soviet Union, Israel, and Pakistan have used nuclear weapons in the same way.

In each of these cases, nuclear weapons were *used* in the exact sense in which a gun is used when it is pointed at someone's head in a confrontation, whether or not the trigger is pulled. . . .

In this regard, the Pentagon concluded the tactic was successfully used in the Gulf War . . . But this success, if true, came at a high price. The message that the United States and its allies regarded such threats both as legitimate and as successful was not lost on potential proliferators, who could imagine themselves either as receiving or as imitating such threats themselves in the future.

Yet another spur to proliferation was the accompanying thought, among Third World observers, that Iraq might have been spared both these nuclear threats and the heavy conventional bombing it received if Saddam Hussein's efforts to acquire a nuclear weapon had already been successful. That inference became inescapable after 2003, with the dramatic difference in the U.S. responses to a supposed nuclear weapons program in Iraq and an actual successful one in North Korea. . . .

Nuclear Insanity

"Insane" is not too strong a word for arguments that occupy planners in the Pentagon and otherwise-serious arms control analysts in favor of maintaining thousands of thermonuclear warheads in the U.S. arsenal—hence thousands in Russia—in a world where neither any longer has a superpower adversary. . . .

Few Americans are aware of the elementary fact that every thermonuclear fusion weapon, or H-bomb—which comprise all of our strategic arsenal, still over 6,000 warheads—requires a Nagasaki-type fission warhead, or A-bomb, to set it off. . . .

The earliest thermonuclear blasts released 1,000 times the explosive power of the A-bomb detonator that triggered it, which was in turn 2,000 times more powerful than the largest "blockbuster" of World War II. The latter destroyed a city block with ten tons of TNT. The second fusion explosion, in February 1954, had a yield equivalent to 15 million tons of TNT, over seven times greater than the tonnage of all the bombs dropped by the United States in World War II, including the A-bombs on Hiroshima and Nagasaki. That single bomb—the first test of a droppable H-bomb—had greater explosive power than that of all the shells and bombs together in all the wars of human history.

It is in that unearthly light that bomb designer Herbert York, the first director of Livermore Nuclear Weapons Laboratory and later President Carter's test ban negotiator, gave an unfamiliar but plausible answer to the Cold War question: How many survivable, deliverable nuclear warheads would it take to deter an adversary rational enough to be deterred at all? York's answer was: "Somewhere in the range of 1, 10, or 100"; and, he conjectured, "I think it is closer to 1 than it is to 100."

Meanwhile, the United States arsenal—10,000 warheads, nearly 6,000 operational—is *one hundred times* the maximum suggested by York. The Russian stockpile—16,000 warheads, over 7,000 operational—is even larger. Even after reductions currently agreed under the current Strategic Offensive Reductions Treaty by 2012, the operational warheads alone—1,700–2,200 "operationally deployable" warheads, for each (apart from the much larger number of inactive/reserve weapons "on the shelf")—will be ten to twenty times the York levels.[2] And they will still be larger in 2013 and beyond than the arsenals that either deployed in 1968, when they signed the Non-Proliferation Treaty.

By their behavior, the two nuclear superpowers have been saying to every non-nuclear-weapon state over the forty years since then: "You don't need a single nuclear weapon ever. We need thousands indefinitely. And we feel free to use them, by threatening to use them, whenever we choose, to gain a stronger hand in diplomatic 'negotiations.' "

Without an effective international norm against both acquisition and threat/use of nuclear weapons, there cannot be an adequate basis for consensual, coordinated international action to prevent such acquisition or use, including intrusive inspection "any time any place," with comprehensive sanctions against violators of the norm. And such norms have to be universal: one set of rules for everyone.

It is urgent for the nuclear-weapon states to acknowledge the reality that they have been denying and the non-nuclear-weapon states have been proclaiming for almost forty years: that effective non-proliferation is inescapably linked to nuclear disarmament and to immediate changes in threat-policy.

It is all or none. Eventually—indeed, very shortly—either all nations forego the right to possess and threaten others with nuclear weapons or every nation will claim that right, and actual possession and use will be very widespread.

No First Use

Few Americans in or out of government are aware of the extent to which the United States and NATO first-use doctrine has always isolated the United States and its Western allies morally and politically from world opinion. . . .

UN Resolution 36/100, the Declaration on the Prevention of Nuclear Catastrophe, was adopted on December 9, 1981. It declares in its Preamble:

> Any doctrine allowing the first use of nuclear weapons and any actions pushing the world toward a catastrophe are incompatible with human moral standards and the lofty ideals of the UN.

The body of the UN Resolution 36/100 declares:

> States and statesmen that resort first to nuclear weapons will be committing the gravest crime against humanity. There will never be any justification or pardon for statesmen who take the decision to be the first to use nuclear weapons.

Eighty-two nations voted in favor of this declaration. Forty-one (under heavy pressure from the U.S.) abstained; 19 opposed it, including the United States and most NATO member nations.

That the dissenters were allies of the United States is no coincidence. The first-use doctrine underlies the basic strategic concept of NATO, devised and promoted by the United States from the early fifties to the present. NATO plans and preparations not only "allow" first use of nuclear weapons, if necessary to defeat an overwhelming attack; they promise it. . . .

This remains true despite the fact that the possibility of an overwhelming conventional attack against NATO no longer exists. Only China, of the five declared nuclear-weapon states, has made the simple, unqualified commitment that it would never be the first to use a nuclear weapon, and that it would not use nuclear weapons against a non-nuclear-weapon state.

With an era of widespread proliferation threatening, it should be unmistakably clear that accepting UN Resolution 36/100 as a universal principle would be in the best interests of the United States and the rest of the world. The United States and its allies would join, at last, in a moral judgment that is already asserted by the majority of governments of the world. . . .

The destruction of the World Trade Center buildings with their inhabitants on September 11, 2001, was rightly recognized as a terrorist action, and condemned as mass murder, by most of the world.

But in contrast . . . most Americans have . . . [never] recognized as terrorist in precisely the same sense the firestorms caused deliberately by RAF firebombing of Hamburg and Dresden or U.S. firebombing of Tokyo and the atomic bombings of Hiroshima and Nagasaki. These deliberate massacres of civilians, though not prosecuted after World War II as was the Japanese slaughter at Nanking, were by any prior or reasonable criteria war crimes, wartime terrorism, crimes against humanity. . . .

Just like the bombs that destroyed Hiroshima and Nagasaki—which would be considered, in terms of scale, "tactical" nuclear weapons today—any attack by a single tactical nuclear weapon near a densely populated area would kill tens to hundreds of thousands of noncombatants, as those did.

Virtually any threat of first-use of a nuclear weapon is a terrorist threat. (Exceptions might be tactical anti-submarine weapons underwater, or weapons in space, or air-bursts against military targets in a desert: but even these would be highly likely to lead to less discriminating exchanges.) Any nation making such threats—that means the United States and its allies, including Israel, along with Russia, Pakistan and India—is a terrorist nation. . . .

To reject terrorism—as we should, as moral beings—is to reject the possession of nuclear weapons. If a large fraction of the thousands of thermonuclear warheads on alert in the U.S. or Russia were launched, the hundreds of millions of deaths caused (half or more killed by fallout in "neutral" countries or their own allies) would transcend the conventional concept of genocide. The slaughter of innocents would be multi-genocide: or omnicide, if it resulted in global nuclear winter.

The elimination of nuclear weapons, of nuclear terrorism, will have to be accomplished by multilateral collaboration. But it must be accomplished. To recover fundamental moral bearings, as well as to preserve life and civilization, the United States, Russia, Britain, France, China, Israel, India, Pakistan and North Korea must cease to be terrorist states.

The challenge especially to citizens of these states, in company with others around the world, is to bring their national policies into line—overcoming the resistance of their present national leaderships—with fundamental morality, and thus with the global goal, the species-task, defined by the then UN Secretary-General Boutros Boutros-Ghali in his inaugural address to the NPT Review and Extension Conference in May 1995:

> The most safe, sure and swift way to deal with the threat of nuclear arms is to do away with them in every regard. This should be our vision of the future. No more testing. No more production. No more sales or transfer. Reduction and destruction of all nuclear weapons and the means to make them should be humanity's great cause.

1. See Daniel Ellsberg, "Call to Mutiny," available at www.ellsberg.net/archive/call-to-mutiny. For a more recent list of threats, see Robert S. Norris and Hans M. Kristensen, "U.S. Nuclear Threats: Then and Now," *Bulletin of the Atomic Scientists,* September/October 2006, 69–71.

2. All estimates, except for Israel, from Cirincione, op cit., Table 5.5, 98.

. . .

For me, the only way to see a war is through the eyes of the victims. And I think part of the problem is that we almost always see war through the eyes of the killers. We may understand that these people are demented, and we may understand that they do things they shouldn't do, but I think the subtext of that is that we identify with the power they possess. In fact, most people in a war zone are completely helpless and powerless—the vast majority of people. Part of the distortion of the war in Iraq is that we only see it through the eyes of the occupiers. We don't understand the terror that an Iraqi family feels when a patrol of Humvees goes in at 50 miles an hour racing through their village and an IED [improvised explosive device] goes off and they lay down suppressing fire and obliterate both sides of the street. . . . But the problem is that the voices of the victims who have something real and important to say about the war are almost never heard during wartime.

(Chris Hedges, from "The Truth of War")

. . .

AFTERNOON

Yannis Ritsos (translated by Edmund Keeley)

The afternoon is all fallen plaster, black stones, dry thorns.
The afternoon has a difficult color made up of old
    footsteps halted in mid-stride,
of old jars buried in the courtyard, covered by fatigue
    and straw.

Two killed, five killed, twelve—so very many.
Each hour has its killing. Behind the windows
stand those who are missing, and the jug full of water
    they didn't drink.

And that star that fell at the edge of evening
is like the severed ear that doesn't hear the crickets,
doesn't hear our excuses—doesn't condescend
to hear our songs—alone, alone,
alone, cut off totally, indifferent to condemnation or
    vindication.

. . .

A WORLD FREE OF NUCLEAR WEAPONS

George P. Shultz, William J. Perry, Henry A. Kissinger, and Sam Nunn

Nuclear weapons today present tremendous dangers, but also an historic opportunity. U.S. leadership will be required to take the world to the next stage—to a solid consensus for reversing reliance on nuclear weapons globally as a vital contribution to preventing their proliferation into potentially dangerous hands, and ultimately ending them as a threat to the world.

Nuclear weapons were essential to maintaining international security during the Cold War because they were a means of deterrence. The end of the Cold War made the doctrine of mutual Soviet-American deterrence obsolete. Deterrence continues to be a relevant consideration for many states with regard to threats from other states. But reliance on nuclear weapons for this purpose is becoming increasingly hazardous and decreasingly effective.

North Korea's recent nuclear test and Iran's refusal to stop its program to enrich uranium—potentially to weapons grade—highlight the fact that the world is now on the precipice of a new and dangerous nuclear era. Most alarmingly, the likelihood that non-state terrorists will get their hands on nuclear weaponry is increasing. In today's war waged on world order by terrorists, nuclear weapons are the ultimate means of mass devastation. And non-state terrorist groups with nuclear weapons are conceptually outside the bounds of a deterrent strategy and present difficult new security challenges.

Apart from the terrorist threat, unless urgent new actions are taken, the U.S. soon will be compelled to enter a new nuclear era that will be more precarious, psychologically disorienting, and economically even more costly than was Cold War deterrence. It is far from certain that we can successfully replicate the old Soviet-American "mutually assured destruction" with an increasing number of potential nuclear enemies worldwide without dramatically increasing the risk that nuclear weapons will be used. New nuclear states do not have the benefit of years of step-by-step safeguards put in effect during the Cold War to prevent nuclear accidents, misjudgments or unauthorized launches. The United States and the Soviet Union learned from mistakes that were less than fatal. Both countries were diligent to ensure that no nuclear weapon was used during the Cold War by design or by accident. Will new nuclear nations and the world be as fortunate in the next 50 years as we were during the Cold War?

Leaders addressed this issue in earlier times. In his "Atoms for Peace" address to the United Nations in 1953, Dwight D. Eisenhower pledged America's "determination to help solve the fearful atomic dilemma—to devote its entire heart and mind to find the way by which the miraculous inventiveness of man shall not be dedicated to his death, but consecrated to his life." John F. Kennedy, seeking to break the logjam on nuclear disarmament, said, "The world was not meant to be a prison in which man awaits his execution."

Rajiv Gandhi, addressing the U.N. General Assembly on June 9, 1988, appealed, "Nuclear war will not mean the death of a hundred million people. Or even a thousand million. It will mean the extinction of four thousand million: the end of life as we know it on our planet earth. We come to the United Nations to seek your support. We seek your support to put a stop to this madness."

Ronald Reagan called for the abolishment of "all nuclear weapons," which he considered to be "totally irrational, totally inhumane, good for nothing but killing, possibly destructive of life on earth and civilization." Mikhail Gorbachev shared this vision, which had also been expressed by previous American presidents.

Although Reagan and Mr. Gorbachev failed at Reykjavik to achieve the goal of an agreement to get rid of all nuclear weapons, they did succeed in turning the arms race on its head. They initiated steps leading to significant reductions in deployed long- and intermediate-range nuclear forces, including the elimination of an entire class of threatening missiles.

What will it take to rekindle the vision shared by Reagan and Mr. Gorbachev? Can a world-wide consensus be forged that defines a series of practical steps leading to major reductions in the nuclear danger? There is an urgent need to address the challenge posed by these two questions.

The Non-Proliferation Treaty (NPT) envisioned the end of all nuclear weapons. It provides (a) that states that did not possess nuclear weapons as of 1967 agree not to obtain them, and (b) that states that do possess them agree to divest themselves of these weapons over time. Every president of both parties since Richard Nixon has reaffirmed these treaty obligations, but non-nuclear weapon states have grown increasingly skeptical of the sincerity of the nuclear powers.

Strong non-proliferation efforts are under way. The Cooperative Threat Reduction program, the Global Threat Reduction Initiative, the Proliferation Security Initiative and the Additional Protocols are innovative approaches that provide powerful new tools for detecting activities that violate the NPT and endanger world security. They deserve full implementation. The negotiations on proliferation of nuclear weapons by North Korea and Iran, involving all the permanent members of the Security Council plus Germany and Japan, are crucially important. They must be energetically pursued.

But by themselves, none of these steps are adequate to the danger. Reagan and General Secretary Gorbachev aspired to accomplish more at their meeting in Reykjavik 20 years ago—the elimination of nuclear weapons altogether. Their vision shocked experts in the doctrine of nuclear deterrence, but galvanized the hopes of people around the world. The leaders of the two countries with the largest arsenals of nuclear weapons discussed the abolition of their most powerful weapons.

What should be done? Can the promise of the NPT and the possibilities envisioned at Reykjavik be brought to fruition? We believe that a major effort should be launched by the United States to produce a positive answer through concrete stages.

First and foremost is intensive work with leaders of the countries in possession of nuclear weapons to turn the goal of a world without nuclear weapons into a joint enterprise. Such a joint enterprise, by involving changes in the disposition of the states possessing nuclear weapons, would lend additional weight to efforts already under way to avoid the emergence of a nuclear-armed North Korea and Iran.

The program on which agreements should be sought would constitute a series of agreed and urgent steps that would lay the groundwork for a world free of the nuclear threat. Steps would include:

· Changing the Cold War posture of deployed nuclear weapons to increase warning time and thereby reduce the danger of an accidental or unauthorized use of a nuclear weapon.

· Continuing to reduce substantially the size of nuclear forces in all states that possess them.

· Eliminating short-range nuclear weapons designed to be forward-deployed.

- Initiating a bipartisan process with the Senate, including understandings to increase confidence and provide for periodic review, to achieve ratification of the Comprehensive Test Ban Treaty, taking advantage of recent technical advances, and working to secure ratification by other key states.

- Providing the highest possible standards of security for all stocks of weapons, weapons-usable plutonium, and highly enriched uranium everywhere in the world.

- Getting control of the uranium enrichment process, combined with the guarantee that uranium for nuclear power reactors could be obtained at a reasonable price, first from the Nuclear Suppliers Group and then from the International Atomic Energy Agency (IAEA) or other controlled international reserves. It will also be necessary to deal with proliferation issues presented by spent fuel from reactors producing electricity.

- Halting the production of fissile material for weapons globally; phasing out the use of highly enriched uranium in civil commerce and removing weapons-usable uranium from research facilities around the world and rendering the materials safe.

- Redoubling our efforts to resolve regional confrontations and conflicts that give rise to new nuclear powers.

Achieving the goal of a world free of nuclear weapons will also require effective measures to impede or counter any nuclear-related conduct that is potentially threatening to the security of any state or peoples.

Reassertion of the vision of a world free of nuclear weapons and practical measures toward achieving that goal would be, and would be perceived as, a bold initiative consistent with America's moral heritage. The effort could have a profoundly positive impact on the security of future generations. Without the bold vision, the actions will not be perceived as fair or urgent. Without the actions, the vision will not be perceived as realistic or possible.

We endorse setting the goal of a world free of nuclear weapons and working energetically on the actions required to achieve that goal, beginning with the measures outlined above.

· · ·

THE FIRST CAR BOMB
Mike Davis
FROM: *Buda's Wagon: A Brief History of the Car Bomb*

On a warm September day in 1920, a few months after the arrest of his comrades Nicola Sacco and Bartolomeo Vanzetti ("the best friends I have in America"), a vengeful Italian immigrant anarchist named Mario Buda parked his horse-drawn wagon near the corner of Wall and Broad streets, next to the new federal Assay Office and directly across from J.P. Morgan and Company. The Morgan partners, including the great Thomas Lamont and Dwight Morrow (Charles Lindbergh's future father-in-law), were discussing weighty financial matters in a lower-floor conference room. Perhaps Buda tipped his cap in the direction of the unsuspecting robber barons before he nonchalantly climbed down and disappeared unnoticed into the lunchtime crowd. A few blocks way, a startled letter-carrier found strange, crudely printed leaflets warning: "Free the Political Prisoners or it Will Be Sure Death for All of You!" They were signed: "American Anarchist Fighters."

Buda, aka "Mike Boda," was a veteran supporter of Luigi Galleani, anarchist theorist, and editor of *Cronaca Sovversiva* ("Subversive Chronicle") which the Department of Justice in 1918 had condemned as "the most dangerous newspaper in this country." ... The *Cronaca Sovversiva* reading circles that met in the shadows of Paterson silk factories and Youngstown steel mills—not unlike certain contemporary Quran study groups in gritty neighborhoods of Brooklyn and south London—were lightning rods for immigrant alienation; an alienation that grew into rage in the face of wartime anti-foreign hysteria, which resulted in the so-called Palmer Raids in 1919 against radicals of all denominations. ...

As Buda, who had appointed himself the avenging angel of the imprisoned and deported anarchists, made his escape from Wall Street, the bells of nearby Trinity Church began to toll noon. Before they had stopped, the wagon packed with high explosive ... and iron slugs erupted in a huge ball of fire, leaving a large crater in Wall Street. Windows exploded in the faces of office workers, pedestrians were mowed down by metal shrapnel or scythed by shards of glass, building awnings and parked cars caught fire, and a suffocating cloud of smoke and debris enshrouded Wall Street. ...

Buda's Wall Street bomb ... was ... an invention ... far ahead of the imagination of its time. The truly radical potential of the "infernal machine" would be fully realized only after the barbarism of strategic bombing had become commonplace, and after air forces routinely pursued insurgents into the labyrinths of poor cities. Buda's wagon, in essence, was the prototype car bomb: the first modern use of an inconspicuous vehicle, anonymous in almost any urban setting, to transport large quantities of high explosive into precise range of a high-value target.

Despite some improvisations (mostly failed) in the 1920s and 1930s, the car bomb was not fully conceptualized as a weapon of urban warfare until January 12, 1947, when rightwing Zionist guerrillas, the Stern Gang, drove a truckload of explosives into a British police station in Haifa, Palestine, killing 4 and injuring 140. The Stern Gang, soon joined by the paramilitaries of the Irgun from whom they had split back in 1940, would subsequently use truck and car bombs to kill Palestinians as well: a creative atrocity that was immediately reciprocated by British deserters fighting on the Arab side. (Fifty years later, *jihadis* training in Al Qaeda camps in Afghanistan would study Menachem Begin's *Revolt*, a memoir of the Irgun, as a classic handbook of successful terrorism.)[1]

Vehicle bombs thereafter were employed sporadically; producing notable massacres in Saigon (1952), Algiers and Oran (1962), Palermo (1963), and again in Saigon (1964–66). But the gates of hell were not truly opened until four undergraduates, protesting campus collaboration with the Vietnam War, exploded the first ammonium nitrate-fuel oil (ANFO) car bomb in front of the University of Wisconsin's Army Mathematics Research Center in August 1970. Two years later ("Bloody Friday," July 21, 1972) the Provisional IRA devastated the business center of Belfast with a series of such devices. These new-generation bombs, requiring only ordinary industrial ingredients and synthetic fertilizer, were cheap to fabricate and astonishingly powerful: they elevated urban terrorism from the artisan to the industrial level and made possible sustained blitzes against entire city centers as well as causing the complete destruction of ferro-concrete skyscrapers and residential blocks.

The car bomb, in other words, suddenly became a semi-strategic weapon that under certain circumstances was comparable to airpower in its ability to knock out critical urban nodes and headquarters as well as terrorize populations of entire cities.

1. Lawrence Wright, *The Looming Tower: Al Qaeda and the Road to 9/11* (New York, 2006), 303.

• • •

RADIATION AND CHILDREN: THE IGNORED VICTIMS
Cindy Folkers and Mary Olson

Hundreds of U.S. industrial sites that generate nuclear electricity and manufacture nuclear weapons regularly release radiation into our air, water, and soil via the burial of wastes. These same industries are now lobbying for permission from government to release radioactive materials for re-use in consumer products. There is no safe radiation dose. Whether the release is accidental or allowed is irrelevant. This dramatic surge in the release and distribution of radiation makes it ever more clear that we do not need a nuclear accident to cause disease.

Unfortunately, even when nuclear activities are performed within legal, "allowable limits," our children are not protected. This is for a simple reason: U.S. radiation protection standards assume that the individual exposed to the harmful radiation released is an adult male. A child exposed to the same release of radiation would often experience a larger dose. The "protection" standards ignore this fact.

Since no industrial scale nuclear operation is possible without the routine release of radioactive materials, regulators have established "allowable" levels of radiation exposure. . . . Radiation exposures are increasing due to planned and accidental releases of *man-made* radioactivity. . . . Natural uranium is radioactive, but putting uranium fuel in a reactor results in wastes that are millions of times "hotter" after only a few years of use. These materials are much more potent in contaminating human and environmental systems. Increasing radiation exposure increases risk to our health whether the radiation is natural, more biologically available due to human interference, or human-made.

Radiation—invisible, odorless, tasteless—tears at the very fabric of what makes us human: our genetic material. Children and the unborn are especially susceptible because of their rapid cell division during physical growth. DNA is most vulnerable to radiation impact while cells divide. In addition to cancer and birth defects, evidence exists that radiation is permanently mutating the gene pool and contributing to its gradual weakening, resulting in "developmental deficiencies in the fetus, hereditary disease, accelerated aging, and such nonspecific effects as loss of immune competence" [*The New Scientist*].

The work of Dr. Alice Stewart, a British epidemiologist, established in the 1950s that children born to women who received even one abdominal x-ray during pregnancy were four times more likely to suffer childhood cancer as a "post-birth defect." Childhood disease clusters have been found in many communities with nuclear facilities. This list includes increases in childhood leukemia near reprocessing facilities in La Hague, France, and at Sellafield in the British Isles and the Krummel nuclear reactor in Germany. Childhood leukemia cases near Sellafield are associated with occupational exposure to the father before *conception* of the child. Increases in childhood leukemia also occurred Europe-wide after the passage of the Chernobyl radiation cloud. Increases in other childhood cancers have been found near nuclear operations in the Navaho Nation (uranium mining), Brookhaven, New York (nuclear weapons), and nuclear power stations in Oyster Creek, NJ, and Clinton, Illinois. Increases in Down Syndrome are found near Yankee Rowe power station in Massachusetts. Heart defects of various types have been associated with ionizing radiation exposure as well.

The process of setting radiation standards and determining whether a particular release of radioactive water or other material meets those standards requires many assumptions. The first of these is about the individual receiving the radiation dose. Most regulators assume that this individual is the "Standard Man," a fictional individual whose physical characteristics have been defined by officials who set radiation standards. A standard height, weight, age, and other parameters are used in equations to project the radiation dose that this hypothetical individual is likely to receive from a given release of radioactivity. Women, fetuses, infants, children, elders, and those with compromised immune systems are not Standard Men. Due to many differences including smaller body size, as well as difference in habits (for instance, playing outside on the ground), a child may get a radiation dose many times larger than the official dose based on the Standard Man, as calculated by state and federal radiation "protection" agencies. This larger dose carries with it a greater risk of health consequences. National Council on Radiation Protection (NCRP) states that a child receives 10–50% more of a dose from gamma ground radiation than an adult because their organs are closer to the ground. . . . This is an external dose scenario. Internal dose scenarios with ingested or inhaled radionuclides often amount to more biological damage to children. For example, Strontium-90 (Sr-90) deposition in the bones can cause bone and blood cancers.

Exposure to radiation increases the risk of damage to tissues, cells, DNA, and other vital molecules—potentially causing programmed cell death (apoptosis), genetic mutations, cancers, leukemias, birth defects, and reproductive, immune, cardiovascular, and endocrine system disorders. The varying impacts on health of each of the hundreds of different radionuclides to which people may be exposed are simply not known. Since scientists do not truly know the specific impacts a given radionuclide may have on the organs and tissues of a specific person, the translation of the *amount* of radioactivity to which that person has been exposed (in curies or fractions of a curie) into a radiation *dose* (in rems or millirems) is basically speculation. . . .

No one can say for sure how many rems or millirems any one individual has (or has not) received; therefore, standards that use this unit cannot be enforced. . . . When accidents occur it should be assumed that children will be exposed . . . Prevention is the only cure.

. . .

CASIDA OF THE LAMENT
Federico García Lorca (translated by Susan Griffin)

I have shut the balcony
so I will not hear those cries,
but behind these grey walls
there is nothing but crying.

So few angels are singing,
so few dogs even bark,
a thousand violins fit
in the palm of my hand.

But the crying is an immense dog,
the crying is an immense angel,
the crying is an immense violin,
and as tears quiet the wind,
there is nothing to hear but crying.

. . .

AN INJURED CHILD

Jennifer Abrahamson

FROM: *Sweet Relief: Maria Ruzicka's Fight for Civilian Victims of War*

On April 4, Zahra Kathem and her family were fleeing the firestorm in Baghdad when a bomb struck their taxi. As the car burst into flames, her mother threw three-year-old Zahra and her three-month-old sister, Hawra, out the open window. The baby miraculously escaped with no more than a few superficial nicks and burns. Her mother, father, and five other siblings burned to death moments after the strike. Two weeks later, Zahra was close to death. She had little hope of surviving.

In the wave of looting that swept across Baghdad, many hospitals had been gutted, and medical supplies were impossible to find. Dr. Bilal al-Radaeei inspected the second- and third-degree burns that had charred Zahra's face, back, arms, and legs.

"Cold, cold," Zahra wailed, trembling uncontrollably. "Cover me, Mommy. Where are you, Daddy? I'm cold."

Zahra's grandmother, the girl's closest surviving relative, sat at her bedside imploring, "Please help my little girl Zahra. Please do not let her die. Please make her better for me."

Earlier, Marla had been inspired by the military's swift response to another crisis. Journalists had stumbled upon a twelve-year-old boy named Ali at Baghdad's al-Kindi Hospital during the bombing raids. A couple of weeks before, a U.S. bomb had flattened Ali's home in southeastern Baghdad. One of his forearms had been burned off, and the other was a bloody pulp. His torso was scorched black. Ali's immediate family, eight relatives in all, had died in the attack. Doctors predicted he had only weeks to live before septicemia, a lethal infection that commonly strikes burn victims, consumed him. Aided by horrifying photographs of the injured boy, several foreign correspondents rallied U.S. forces to evacuate Ali to a facility that could better treat him. He was saved and fitted with prosthetic arms. Ali effectively became a poster boy of sorts, showing that the United States cared about ordinary Iraqis it had harmed.

Daily, Marla attended every meeting between the Marines and the aid community at the Palestine, soaking up information and making connections. Ali was a hot topic of discussion during one meeting, and Marla approached the head of the Marines' health unit.

"I'm really happy to hear about Ali, that's such great work!" she told him brightly before sobering her tone. "But you know, he's only one child. I'm going to the hospitals every day, and there are so many injured civilians. If I find more people who need to be evacuated so they can survive, will you help them, too?"

"Absolutely, just come here to the hotel and give us the information. We'll do whatever we can," he promised.

On April 18, Good Friday, Jon told Marla about Zahra. Unfortunately, the Marines she'd met at the Palestine, with whom she'd already established a good rapport, were being replaced by the army the next day. Jon said that Zahra might only have twenty-four hours to live.

The next day at the Palestine . . . Marla pushed her way through the crowd to one of the soldiers.

"Hi, I'm Marla! I've got a serious situation and I need your help!" she screamed above the grinding roar of two large generators that coughed up clouds of exhaust. The soldier stared at Marla blankly. She didn't give him a moment to think.

"I work with Iraqis who were harmed in the bombing. I know the Marines, and they promised me they'd medevac injured people like that little boy Ali who they took to Kuwait. Well, there's a little girl in the burn hospital who was hit by a bomb and she's doing really bad. The doctors say she'll die really soon if she doesn't get better care!" Marla shouted over the generators.

"Sorry, I'd like to help, but I don't know what I can do."

"Okay, but who *can* help me? I mean, she's seriously going to *die!*" Marla pushed on.

"Well, the only thing I can suggest is that you go to the hospital and talk to the army unit guarding it. Maybe they can do something."

"Thank you *sooo* much, you rock!"

Now she just had to figure out how to get there. Bob Arnott, an MSNBC journalist and medical doctor, had expressed interest in covering Zahra's story. He was bound to have a driver. She bolted up to his room and told him it was time to go, but he wasn't ready. Growing frantic, she insisted that Zahra's life depended on leaving immediately, and he relented.

Rushing back downstairs, Bob led the way to his driver's taxi. After breaking free of a traffic jam, they began careening through the city's streets. They hunkered down at the sound of gunshots in the streets. . . . After forty-five minutes . . . they finally rounded a corner and screeched to a halt in front of al-Karameh Hospital. A U.S. Army Bradley tank was parked out front, protecting the facility from looters.

She dashed out of the car, rushing toward the tank. Two young African-American soldiers gripped their weapons, looking tense and uneasy. Marla repeated her story to the stunned men, begging them to let her pass. They unlocked the gate and let her and Bob through.

When Marla first laid eyes on Zahra, she was horrified. The little girl was enclosed in what appeared to be a wooden cage. Dr. al-Radaeei leaned over her small body, careful not to touch her. He removed the crude, homemade structure that balanced over her head and torso on a rickety bed frame. The cage prevented the sheets from coming into direct contact with her raw, singed skin. Gently peeling back the blanket so Marla and Bob could see the girl's injuries, Dr. al-Radaeei sucked in his breath to keep steady. All Marla could distinguish were swaths of loose bandages clinging to charred flesh. Despite the doctor's controlled hand, the blanket lightly rubbed against Zahra's body. She opened what was barely recognizable as a mouth and let out a harrowing scream that echoed through the bare hospital ward. . . .

If Zahra didn't die from the burns that covered 90 percent of her body, Dr. al-Radaeei explained, she would inevitably perish soon from a septicemia infection. Trying to stay composed, his sorrowful eyes betrayed an overwhelming sense of helplessness. Like many professionals in Iraq who study abroad, he had been trained in England and was used to having the supplies he needed to treat his patients. Although American soldiers guarding the front entrance meant that al-Karameh Hospital was spared the rampant looting, the war prevented the doctor from restocking basic yet vital supplies like oxygen, drugs, and clean water.

"We could help her ourselves, but the war, the war," Dr. al-Radaeei said, his voice trailing off as he replaced the cage.

There was no more time to waste. Leaving Bob behind, Marla ran out the front exit and toward the hulking tank.

"Hi, I'm Marla! Look, we have to get a helicopter here immediately to save that girl's life in there!"

"I'm not sure I can do that, ma'am," one of the soldiers said.

"That girl inside was severely burned when her family's car was hit by an American bomb. We've examined her, and I can verify that it's true. If she doesn't get better care *now*, she's not going to make it, and we can help her!"

The private signaled to his partner, realizing how serous she was, but there wasn't much they could do without the superiors' clearance. At the very least, they had to confirm Marla's story themselves, so they started inside. Marla jogged after the soldiers, keeping pace with their long strides.

Marla introduced the soldiers to Dr. al-Radaeei, who led the way to the burn unit. The soldiers slowly took in the scene before them and began inspecting Zahra and the other patients, meticulously recording their names and other personal information into a small notebook.

"We don't have any more time to lose, let's get her out of here!" Marla finally blurted.

After they collected the information, one of the soldiers told the doctor they would do their best to help Zahra, then turned to leave. Marla scurried after them.

"I'm coming up there too!" she hollered at the soldiers as they scaled the tank.

The soldier who seemed to be in charge of the situation returned. Offering his hand, he hauled Marla up onto the tank, her blue dress fluttering behind her. Gunshots rang out somewhere nearby, but she didn't flinch.

"Listen, we are wasting time here and we are playing with that little girl's life. Don't you want to save her? You can do it. Help me get her out of here!" she instructed him, her hand placed firmly on her hips.

The soldier pondered for a moment and then turned to say something to his partner that she couldn't hear. He then spoke into the radio mouthpiece embedded into his helmet, removed it from his head, and placed it on Marla's.

"Go ahead, Miss Marla. Go ahead. Tell him what you told me."

A voice crackled over the helmet's radio. It was the soldier's commanding officer.

"Hi, this is Marla! There's a three-year-old girl here at Karameh Hospital who was hit by an American bomb and she's badly burned. She's going to die unless we evacuate her to a better hospital. Over," she said, waiting for a response.

"Okay, do you have the hospital paperwork detailing the cause of her injuries? Over," the voice replied.

"Yeah, we've got it all here, and I've looked at the girl myself along with a doctor. Over."

"Good copy. Hold tight, Marla. We'll be there soon. Over."

The soldier plucked the helmet from her head and spoke tersely into his mouthpiece once again. Scampering down the side of the tank, Marla rushed back into the hospital to deliver the good news to Dr. al-Radaeei.

When she told him about Zahra's impending evacuation, he asked, "But what about the others, Miss Marla? I can only do so much to treat them here."

She didn't think the army would agree to evacuate the patients who weren't injured by U.S. firepower. The doctor was happy for Zahra, but distraught for the other patients. A couple of nurses draped the other patients' cages with blankets, so they wouldn't witness Zahra's evacuation, and they began preparing the girl for her departure.

Within minutes, the distant thump of a U.S. Army medevac helicopter turned into an ear-splitting howl. A bank robbery was under way close by, and the helicopter disappeared to find a safer place to touch down. Several minutes later, an armored Humvee thundered down the street and stopped next to the tank. Four army medics jumped out. With Marla in tow, the soldiers ran over. Marla begged them to evacuate the other burn victims as well as Zahra. After quick deliberation, they decided they had room for three patients. Dr. al-Radaeei made the painful decision, then Bob, the army medics, the doctors and the nurses all lifted Zahra and the other two patients into an ambulance.

"Allahu Akbar! Allahu Akbar!" God is great, God is great, a relative of one of the patients cried as the Humvee disappeared down the street toward the helicopter, the ambulance wailing behind. Bob jumped into his taxi and trailed after them to film the spectacle.

Marla collapsed against the hospital wall, her hands shaking. It occurred to her that she'd forgotten to ask where the army was taking Zahra. She walked over to the soldier who helped evacuate her. He didn't know where the patients were going, he said, but was sure that they would be well cared for.

"You have to go and tell your mother what you've done," Marla said to the soldier.

"I thought of my own two daughters back home. I was just doin' my job, ma'am," he responded in a southern drawl.

. . .

Before we can understand how we can prevent and suppress genocide, we have to *understand why we have allowed* and, at times, even abetted it. We have been bystanders not because we lacked information. The intelligence intercepts, the cables, the press, the interviews, all show that saying "we didn't know" is nonsense.

Now, having said that, it is of course worth asking, what is knowledge? There is a difference between knowledge of facts and deep, visceral knowledge—the kind . . . that makes you cry, the kind that makes you—if only for an instant—imagine your daughter being forced into round the clock service in a Serb rape camp, or your little boy being reduced to pleading to a machete wielding Rwandan extremist, "Please don't kill me. I'll never be Tutsi again," or to imagine you yourself so desperate to feed your children that, in order to earn the favor of a Khmer Rouge overlord, you informed on two of your neighbors for carrying out an illicit love affair—a confession that would result in the certain death of the young lovebirds, but which would mean your child would not starve to death.

(Samantha Power, from "Remarks at the Stockholm International Forum on Genocide Prevention")

· · ·

BEYOND THE *WAR ON TERROR:* UNDERSTANDING REFLEXIVE THOUGHT
George Lakoff

There are two all-too-real aspects of mind that the public is not aware of and that the media rarely discuss. The first is metaphorical thought—the way we think, not just talk, using metaphor. The second is reflexive thought: almost all of our thought is unconscious and beyond our control, like a reflex. Reflective thought, thought we are aware of and can reflect on, is relatively rare by comparison—the tip of the iceberg. Because our naïve view of reason has not caught up with how we really reason, our political life is being manipulated. Take the *war on terror.*

The very idea of a *war on terror* is metaphorical. Literal wars involve one army fighting another army. When one army defeats the other, there can be a peace treaty and an end to the war. Terror is an emotion, a state of mind. It is not an army or a country. Because extreme fear can be provoked at any time, terror cannot be ended. There can be no peace treaty with terror. The relentless use of the military force just exacerbates it.

War on terror means war without end. It was used by the Bush adminis-tration as a ploy to get virtually unlimited war powers—and further do-mestic influence—for the president.

Naïve reason, not recognizing metaphorical thought, leads one to see the *war on terror* as a literal war. Colin Powell initially argued within the administration against the *war on terror* metaphor on the grounds that 9/11 should be viewed as a crime committed by international criminals. Terrorism is best dealt with on the whole not with planes and tanks and search-and-destroy missions, but with infiltration, cultural and linguistic knowledge, and tracking of communications, bank accounts, social net-works, etc.—police work, as was done by British police in their success-ful anti-terrorist activities.

The discrepancy between the old and new views of the mind allowed *war on terror* to be taken literally. The Congress, the citizenry and the press did not rise up and shout, "Wait a minute! That's metaphorical think-ing. You don't go to a war based on an inappropriate metaphor." Instead they accepted this metaphor as literal and appropriate. The Bush admin-istration, having created a war metaphor that was taken literally, then created a literal war in Iraq. And when Saddam's army was defeated and an occupation began, Bush kept the war metaphor—and his war powers. Neither the press nor the citizenry would say, think, or speak of the truth of an *occupation* for years. A *war president* has war powers; an occupa-tion president might not.

How did the *war on terror* get established as *the* [way] to characterize our Middle East involvement? Neuroscience tells us that ideas are phy-sically instantiated as part of our brains and that changes occur at the synapses. We learn by changes at the synapses, under two conditions—trauma (where there is especially strong neural firing) and repetition (where neural firing recurs). As the saying goes among neuroscientists, *Neurons that fire together wire together*. The event called 9/11 was a national trauma, and *war on terror* was introduced under conditions of trauma, and then repeated over and over for years. The result was that the metaphorical idea became physically instantiated in the brains of most Americans.

Neuroscience also tells us that you can't simply erase such changes. You can add structure that might bypass the *war on terror* idea, or per-haps inhibit its activation, or have it activated along with a further un-derstanding of the idea—perhaps a cynical one that delegitimizes it. But you can't just get rid of it.

Moreover, when an expression like *war on terror* becomes a fixed part of your brain, you tend to use it, not reflectively, but reflexively, like a reflex, like the automatic movement of muscles you use when you ride a bicycle. You don't—and can't—control every muscle, one by one, as you ride the bike. You just ride and your brain and body take over, unconsciously controlling your movement. The same with *war on terror*. [Whenever you hear it], the metaphor takes over. When the synapses are established, the neurons just fire.

The event we call 9/11 has been used as the "salient exemplar"—the canonical example—of a terrorist attack. The effect of using salient exemplars is to raise the probability of occurrence of such an example. People all over the U.S.—from Davenport, Iowa, to Cheyenne, Wyoming—have become afraid of terrorist attacks when there is virtually zero probability of such an attack.

You cannot stop all of this rationally. Reading articles like this will not eliminate *war on terror* from your brain. The best you can do is neurally inhibit it with some more powerful mode of thought and speech. That is not easy. Since the fall of Saddam Hussein, the American military adventure in Iraq became an occupation. Occupations have mostly been unpopular—both with the inhabitants of the country occupied and with the country of the occupiers. Most Americans don't want to think of their solders as appropriately unpopular occupiers.

The establishment of the *war on terror* metaphor was the result of a concerted effort; inhibiting it will also take an organized concerted effort—and a reframing that accords with the truth. But the truth is hard for the American public to take. The American armed forces create terror elsewhere. In Iraq, the war the U.S. began led to, by some estimates, over 600,000 deaths of Iraqi civilians, and even more maimings. The U.S. brought terror to Iraqis, the people they were supposed to help. In addition, U.S. policy has brought terror to wounded American veterans, who have been systematically mistreated in Veterans' Hospitals, and to the families of American soldiers who have died.

War brings terror. Terror begets terror.

The neocons claimed that war shows our strength and resolve. It is the opposite. War shows our weakness. Our diplomatic weakness. Our international political weakness. And especially our moral weakness. Effective action on the international stage without war shows real strength.

Cognitive scientists have a major role to play here. The job of cognitive science is to make reflexive thought reflective. That should also be a major job of the media. Revealing the truth includes revealing the truth about the mind and how the mind can be manipulated.

. . .

THE AMERICAN PSYCHE AFTER SEPTEMBER 11
Nathan Schwartz-Salant

The devastation of September 11, 2001—the loss of nearly 3,000 lives, the fall of the Twin Towers, and the clouds of acrid smoke that shadowed much of the city—was an outer manifestation of terror that seeped deeply into the body and psyche and lives on inwardly as trauma, ever ready to release feelings of despair, anxiety and helplessness. Studies printed by the *New York Times* on September 8, 2003—"9/11 Still Strains New York Psyche"—show little change in the level of fear and anxiety that manifested in the weeks and months after the attack on the World Trade Center. The same situation persisted five years after 9/11. According to the *New York Times,* September 7, 2006—"9/11 Polls Find Lingering Fears in New York City"—forty percent of New Yorkers, and twenty-four percent of people nationally still felt nervous or edgy five years after 9/11, and over twenty percent of New Yorkers believed a terrorist attack would occur in the next two months.

Soon after 9/11 we were all told that there was no danger from the polluted atmosphere, but seventy percent of first responders at Ground Zero suffer lung problems, thousands of which have been debilitating.[1] Five years later, we also learned that air samples were known to actually contain 2.1–3.3 percent of asbestos, well above the 1 percent trigger that defines asbestos material.[2] While perhaps an attempt to soothe anxiety at the time, distortions such as this only promote deeper levels of anxiety and contribute to an enduring lack of safety. Just a few days ago, an ambulance siren triggered memories of the same sounds five years ago. "Wasn't that a long siren?" a patient asked. I also wondered the same thing, as I sat in my office in New York City, with an unusual degree of anxiety on the anniversary of 9/11.

Dissociation is a psychic capacity, possessed by some people more than others, that essentially pushes traumatic experiences aside, as though they were happening to someone else. When dissociation works it blocks re-experiencing the emotions, perceptions and bodily sensations of trauma. The following dream (of a woman who was five miles away from Ground Zero at the time of the attack), illustrates dissociation

functioning in her psyche eight months after September 11. The dream
is a good image of the American Psyche, both then and today.

> I am in the World Trade Center, on a high floor and there is an attack. A
> plane strikes one tower and I see it bursting into flame and falling. I rush to
> get down the stairs, but each staircase leads to a floor. People on each floor
> do not see what is happening. They act like everything is okay. I continue to
> find stairs, each floor at a time, with the same scene: people ignoring the
> disaster. I find two children and take them down. We finally get out. I see the
> other tower crashing.

In her conscious life, the dreamer had an awareness of the real danger that existed, and that shows in the dream. However, she also disso-
ciated from much of her experience, as indicated by the people in the
dream acting as if everything were okay. Awakening, she wondered if it
isn't better to deny that it could happen again. But remembering the
history of her own abuse she had an opposite reaction: "No, because
it's a lie; I've been lied to all my life. The only way to be prepared is with
the truth."

One hopes that consciousness will survive in the face of terror, and
prove powerful enough to desire truth, but this is surely opposed by the
belief that a "battle for civilization" is occurring, an ultimate battle between good and evil, in which facts can mean very little, and dissociation from truth is courted. As one former White House aide said, a
"judicious study of discernible reality (is) not the way the world really
works anymore."

When a person is emotionally contained in a family or group after a
traumatic experience and can share that experience, the trauma will
often rapidly diminish. This has been found to be the case recently with
children in the war zones of Lebanon and Israel. However, if safety does
not exist, the trauma will imbed and live on deeply within the psyche.
Thus, though the idea that fighting terrorists everywhere is the way to
provide safety in the United States is powerful rhetoric, this aggressive
approach has not provided safety.

How is the healing capacity of psyche to resurrect amidst powerful
rhetoric that creates its own myth of a Manichean struggle between good
and evil? The people creating it exploit the psyche's suggestibility at times
of terror.

Healing requires that the psyche be able to weave awareness, emotions and body states, such as occurred on 9/11, into stories that give a
larger moral and symbolic character to the traumatic events. Cultures

have always had names for the dangerous structures that are awakened through trauma, personified by figures such as the Devil, the dark Goddess Cybele, the ancient Iranian Goddess Az, or the Indian Goddess Kali, "the Destroyer." But the psyche's natural tendency to enfold experience in myth and story[3] can also falter in trauma, and especially when safety is absent. In this condition, dreams often present a repetition or distortion of traumatic experience. When a healing, inner response, a positive archetypal image and a story fail to consolidate, individuals gain no sense of meaning in their lives.

In his deeply moving essay "September 11 at the Movies," Daniel Mendelsohn, reviewing the films *United 93* and *World Trade Center*, draws a compelling contrast between the ways that Greek tragedians dealt with historical trauma, and the failure, so far, of any similar attempts in our culture. Rather than a catharsis, all we have is a documentary-like replay of events.

> If *United 93* brings to mind any genre, it is not Greek tragedy with its artfully wrought moral conundrums. But something much tinier ... phony "realism."

By contrast, Mendelsohn writes, in Aeschylus' play *Persians:* (He) focused his imaginative sympathy not on the exulting Greeks, but on the sorrowing Persians ... He asked his fellow Athenians to think radically, to imagine something outside of their own experience, to situate the feelings they were having ... in a vaster frame ... The sense of these larger, moral themes hovering over the play's spectacle is, in the end, what gives the play a resonance that transcends the particulars of history.[4]

The archetypal structures of the psyche tend to weave stories from historical events, thus yielding a capacity for meaning. As the alchemists would say, art furthers the work of nature. Yet we have had no such art to meet the devastation of 9/11 but instead only our hypervigilance, an ineffective and often paranoid response to trauma.

For those who realize the wisdom of Jung's remark that "the fate of the world hangs by a thin thread, and that thread is the human psyche," contacting, or enlivening a positive, inner, archetypal potential, and thus an inner story with a subtle sense of a growing core of meaning becomes essential. Achieving this requires that individuals confront official postures of absolute certainty and invincibility, attitudes that not only crush discourse and debate, but the inner life as well. Not knowing is the starting point.

Perhaps the end of the dominance of the heroic approach of asserting power over an enemy was foreshadowed by the events of September 11, 2001. For the archetypal level, events that traumatize an individual and a culture are also capable of creating a common ground of human experience, a sense of kinship.

Back in the '60s the poet Allen Ginsberg was part of a picketing demonstration against Madame Nhu, the "Dragon Lady" of Viet Nam. The sign he carried read, "Madame Nhu and Ho Chi Minh are in the same boat of meat." After September 11, for a while, we were in the same "boat of meat" as the rest of the traumatized and suffering human race. George Bush and Osama bin Laden were in the same boat of meat. We are all in that boat, and to truly know and feel that mystery means to sacrifice identifying with the separating, aggressive impulse that would forever find outer enemies to attack. That sense of kinship was the gift of the dark side of God, the dark numinosum as many felt it on September 11.

That gift was quickly squandered. Instead of taking time to reflect and to suffer, America sprang forward. The spirit of attack and retribution dominated, and manifested over a year later in images of a President declaring victory from the flight deck of an aircraft carrier, or in response to attacks, using the adolescent slogan: "Bring 'em on!" The possibility to collectively feel in the "same boat of meat," the chance for communion with a suffering world, was lost.

Before the tragic events on September 11 I had just started teaching a class on Samuel Beckett's work. This was fortuitous; Beckett has been a great source of comfort for me and for others. Beckett hit his stride, finally writing what felt true to him, after a dark vision in which he experienced, as he said, "how totally stupid I am." And, "I realized that everything I'd written had been a lie . . . all about what I knew, when the only thing I could write about truthfully was what I didn't know, didn't feel. . . ."[5] Beckett wrote his greatest works from this dark and terrifying honesty. In the face of terror a person needs the courage to feel stupid and just "go on." As Beckett's character says at the end of *The Unnamable,* "I don't know, I'll never know, in the silence you don't know, you must go on, I can't go on, I'll go on." But a new consciousness can come out of this, a new sense of meaning above and beyond any Manichean myth of good against evil.

If we have the courage to consciously suffer the trauma of terrorism and September 11, using it as a mirror that reflects a strange face which we soon see as our own—the face of our own terrorism, the way we terrorize parts of our own soul that we hate and fear, and ways we subtly, if not overtly, terrorize others we also love—then we are on the path of discovering the creative, life-giving side of psyche. Rather than dissociate from our fears and anxieties or rush to crush them, if we have the courage to acknowledge our own madness and our own ignorance, then we may gain a new orientation. If we can accept that our great American Democratic ideals, once a beacon for the entire world, have a terrible shadow side, we may also begin to regain a sense of kinship with others. We may also gain strength to fight such terror, not with blind slogans but with a new intelligence. And in this way we may encounter a positive face of the archetypal world and its wisdom that may lead us through the terrifying times in which we live.

1. "Lung Problems Rife among 9/11 Responders," Associated Press Release, September 6, 2006.

2. "Buildings Rise from Rubble While Health Crumbles," *New York Times,* September 11, 2006.

3. Claude Lévi-Strauss, *Structural Anthropology,* trans. C. Jacobson and B. Grundfest Schoepf (New York: Basic Books, 1963), 202.

4. Daniel Mendelsohn, "September 11 at the Movies," *New York Review of Books* 53, no. 14 (Sept. 21, 2006), 44f.

5. James Knowlson, *Damned to Fame* (New York: Simon & Schuster, 1996), 319.

. . .

ON RELIGION AND TERRORISM
Huston Smith

Religion, of course, is often cited as a cause of violent conflict. It bears importantly on terrorism, but I don't think we see clearly how it figures. The relationship is complicated. First, in conflict situations religion provides both sides with their respective identities. In the Islamic world, that identity is openly religious for Islam is by definition a religion. On our side, the separation of church and state makes the matter more complicated. It debars us from characterizing ourselves as a religious nation, but Paul Tillich has been useful here. He dug below the usual trappings of religion, doctrines, creeds, rituals to define it as "ultimate concern": Religion is what concerns us ultimately. By this existential definition, we are a religious nation, our religion being, *de facto* if not *de jure*, the American way of life. Religion enters at this basic level by providing both parties with their respective identities.

These different identities provide, as philosophers say, the necessary condition for conflict, but not the sufficient condition. A fight requires at least two people, but being two doesn't require that they fight. They could just as well use their twoness to be friends. This simple point, too often overlooked by the media, gives the lie to the charge that religion causes conflicts when in fact its typical role is to provide belligerents with their respective identities. Instead, violent conflict is caused by those four feelings—anger, hatred, humiliation and despair, which together are linked to human nature, or more precisely its egocentric propensities. We humans are richly endowed with capacities for virtue, but self-centeredness is the shadow side of our character. It may be needed for biological, Darwinian survival, but nevertheless, it is the underlying cause of all our woes. Christians attribute this flaw in our nature to the fall, Jews to sin, Muslims to *ghaflah* (forgetfulness of who we essentially are), Hindus to *avidya* (ignorance of who we really are), Buddhists to *tanha* or grasping. But by whatsoever name, this tendency to put ourselves first, before others, is the root cause of all conflict. When we group together in families, communities and nation states, self-interest compounds rapidly, for here it is reinforced by a virtue—fellow feeling. If we don't put our group's interest ahead of other groups, we will be letting our companions down.

· · ·

THE SPIRITUAL SOURCE OF ISLAM
Tariq Ramadan
FROM: *In the Footsteps of the Prophet: Lessons from the Life of Muhammad*

Life in the desert was to fashion the man and his outlook on creation and the elements of the universe. When Muhammad came to the desert, he was able to learn from the Bedouins' rich oral tradition and their renown as speakers to develop his own mastery of the spoken language. Later on, the Last Prophet was to stand out through the strength of his words, his eloquence, and above all his ability to convey deep and universal teachings through short, pithy phrases (*jawami al-kalim*). The desert is often the locus of the prophesies because it naturally offers to the human gaze the horizons of the infinite. For nomads, forever on the move, finitude in space is allied to a sense of freedom blended, here again, with the experience of fleetingness, vulnerability, and humility. Nomads learn to move on, to become strangers, and to apprehend, at the heart of the linear infinity of space, the cyclical finitude of time. Such is the experience of the believer's life, which the Prophet was later to describe to young Abdullah ibn Umar in terms reminiscent of this dimension: "Be in this world as if you were a stranger or a wayfarer."

In the first years of the Prophet's life he developed a specific relationship with nature that remained constant throughout his mission. This universe is pregnant with signs that recall the presence of the Creator, and the desert, more than anything else, opens the human to observation, meditation, and initiation into meaning. Thus, many verses of the Quran mention the book of creations and its teachings. The desert, apparently devoid of life, repeatedly shows and proves to the watchful consciousness the reality of the miracle of the return to life:

> And among His Signs is this: you see the earth humble [because of drought]; but when We send down rain to it, it is stirred to life and yields increase. Truly, He who gives it life can surely give life to the dead, for he has power over all things.

This relationship with nature was so present in the Prophet's life from his earliest childhood that one can easily come to the conclusion that living close to nature, observing, understanding, and respecting it, is an imperative of deep faith.

Many years later, when the Prophet was in Medina, facing conflicts and wars, a Revelation into the heart of night turned his gaze toward another horizon of meaning: "In the creation of the heavens and the earth, and the alteration of night and day, there are indeed signs for all those endowed with insight." It has been reported that the Prophet wept all night long when this verse was revealed to him. At dawn, when Bilal, the muezzin, coming to call for prayer, asked about the cause of those tears, Muhammad explained to him the meaning of his sadness and added: "Woe to anyone who hears that verse and does not meditate upon it!"

Another verse conveys the same teaching, referring to multiple signs:

> In the creation of the heavens and the earth; in the alteration of night and day; in the sailing of the ships through the ocean for the profit of humankind; in the rain that God sends down from the skies, and the life which He then gives to the earth after it had been lifeless; in the beasts of all kind that He scatters through the earth; in the change of the winds, and the clouds that run their appointed courses between the sky and the earth; [here] indeed are signs for people who are wise.

The first years of Muhammad's life undoubtedly fashioned his outlook, preparing him to understand the signs in the universe. The spiritual teaching that can be drawn from them is essential, both for the Prophet's education and for our own education throughout history: being close to nature, respecting what it is, and observing and meditating on what it shows us, offers us, or takes (back) from us requirements of faith that, in its quest, attempts to feed, deepen, and renew itself. Nature is the primary guide and intimate companion of faith. Thus, God decided to expose His Prophet, from his earliest childhood, to the natural lessons of creation, conceived as a school where the mind gradually apprehends signs and meaning. Far removed from the formalism of soulless religious rituals, this sort of education, in and through its closeness to nature, fosters a relationship to the divine based on contemplation and depth that will later make it possible, in a second phase of spiritual education, to understand the meaning, form, and objectives of religious ritual. Cut off from nature in our own towns and cities, we nowadays seem to have forgotten the meaning of this message to such an extent that we dangerously invert the order of requirements and believe that learning about the techniques and forms of religion (prayers, pilgrimages, etc.) is sufficient to grasp and understand their meaning and objectives. This delusion has serious consequences since it leads to draining religious teaching of its spiritual substance which actually ought to be its heart.

· · ·

TERRORISM: THEIRS AND OURS
Eqbal Ahmad

Until the 1930s and early 1940s, the Jewish underground in Palestine was described as "terrorist." Then something happened: around 1942, as news of the Holocaust was spreading, a certain liberal sympathy with the Jewish people began to emerge in the Western world. By 1944, the terrorists of Palestine, who were Zionists, suddenly began being described as "freedom fighters." . . .

From 1969 to 1990, the Palestine Liberation Organization (PLO) occupied center stage as a terrorist organization. Yasir Arafat has been repeatedly described as the "chief of terrorism" by the great sage of American journalism, William Safire of *The New York Times*. On September 29, 1998, I was rather amused to notice a picture of Yasir Arafat and Israeli prime minister Benjamin Netanyahu standing on either side of

President Bill Clinton. Clinton was looking toward Arafat, who looked meek as a mouse. Just a few years earlier, Arafat would appear in photos with a very menacing look, a gun holstered to his belt. That's Yasir Arafat. You remember those pictures, and you'll remember the next one.

In 1985, President Ronald Reagan received a group of ferocious-looking, turban-wearing men who looked like they came from another century. I had been writing about the very same moment for *The New Yorker*. After receiving them in the White House, Reagan spoke to the press, referring to them as "freedom fighters." These were the Afghan mujahideen. They were at the time, guns in hand, battling the "Evil Empire." For Reagan, they were the moral equivalent of our Founding Fathers.

In August 1998, another American President ordered missile strikes to kill Osama bin Laden and his men in Afghanistan-based camps. Mr. bin Laden, at whom fifteen American missiles were fired to hit in Afghanistan, was only a few years earlier the moral equivalent of George Washington and Thomas Jefferson. I'll return to the subject of bin Laden later. . . .

What is terrorism? Our first job should be to define the damn thing, name it, give it a description other than "moral equivalent of founding fathers" or "a moral outrage to Western civilization." This is what *Webster's Collegiate Dictionary* says: "Terror is an intense, overpowering fear." Terrorism is "the use of terrorizing methods of government or resisting a government." This simple definition has one great virtue: it's fair. It focuses on the use of violence that is used illegally, extra-constitutionally, to coerce. And this definition is correct because it treats terror for what it is, whether a government or private group commits it.

Have you noticed something? Motivation is omitted. We're not just talking about whether the cause is just or unjust. We're talking about consensus, consent, absence of consent, legality, absence of legality, constitutionality, absence of constitutionality. Why do we keep motives out? Because motives make no difference. In the course of my work I have identified five types of terrorism: state terrorism, religious terrorism (Catholics killing Protestants, Sunnis killing Shiites, Shiites killing Sunnis), criminal terrorism, political terrorism, and oppositional terrorism. Sometimes these five can converge and overlap. Oppositional protest terrorism can become pathological criminal terrorism. State terror can take the form of private terror. For example, we're all familiar with the death squads in Latin America or in Pakistan where the government has employed private people to kills its opponents. . . . It's privatized. In Afghanistan, Central America, and Southeast Asia, the CIA employed in its covert operations drug pushers. . . .

Of the five types of terror, the official approach is to focus on only one form—political terrorism—which claims the least in terms of loss of human lives and property. The form that exacts the highest loss is state terrorism. The second highest loss is created by religious terrorism, although religious terror has, relatively speaking, declined. If you are looking historically, however, religious terrorism has caused massive loss. The next highest loss is caused by criminal terrorism. A Rand Corporation study by Brian Jenkins examining a ten-year period (1978 to 1988) showed fifty percent of terrorism was committed without any political cause. No politics. Simply crime and pathology. So the focus is on only one, the political terrorist, the PLO, the bin Laden, whoever you want to take.

Why do they do it? What makes terrorists tick?

I would like to knock out some quick answers. First, the need to be heard. Remember, we are dealing with a minority group, the political, private terrorist. Normally, and there are exceptions, there is an effort to be heard, to get their grievances recognized and addressed by people. The Palestinians, for example, the superterrorists of our time, were dispossessed in 1948. From 1948 to 1968 they went to every court in the world. They knocked on every door. They had been completely deprived of their land, their country, and nobody was listening. In desperation, they invented a new form of terror: the airplane hijacking. Between 1968 and 1975 they pulled the world up by its ears. That kind of terror is a violent way of expressing long-felt grievances. It makes the world hear. . . .

Secondly, terrorism is an expression of anger, of feeling helpless, angry, alone. You feel like you have to hit back. Wrong has been done to you, so you do it. During the hijacking of the TWA jet in Beirut, Judy Brown of Belmar, New Jersey, said that she kept hearing them yell, "New Jersey, New Jersey." What did they have in mind? She thought that they were going after her. Later on it turned out that the terrorists were referring to the U.S. battleship *New Jersey,* which had heavily shelled the Lebanese civilian population in 1983.

Another factor is a sense of betrayal, which is connected to that tribal ethic of revenge. It comes into the picture in the case of people like bin Laden. Here is a man who was an ally of the United States, who saw America as a friend; then he sees his country being occupied by the United States and feels betrayal. . . .

Sometimes it's the fact that you have experienced violence at other people's hands. Victims of violent abuse often become violent people. The only time when Jews produced terrorists in organized fashion was during and after the Holocaust. . . . The experience of victimhood itself produces a violent reaction.

In modern times, with modern technology and means of communications, the targets have been globalized. Therefore, globalization of violence is an aspect of what we call globalization of the economy and culture in the world as a whole. We can't expect everything else to be globalized and violence not to be. . . .

Let's turn back for a moment to Osama bin Laden. *Jihad,* which has been translated a thousand times as "holy war," is not quite that. *Jihad* in Arabic means "to struggle." It could be struggle by violence or struggle by non-violent means. There are two forms, the small *jihad* and the big *jihad*. The small *jihad* involves external violence. The big *jihad* involves a struggle within oneself. Those are the concepts. The reason I mention it is that in Islamic history, *jihad* as an international violent phenomenon had for all practical purposes disappeared in the last four hundred years. It was revived suddenly with American help in the 1980s. When the Soviet Union intervened in Afghanistan, which borders Pakistan, Zia ul-Haq saw an opportunity and launched a *jihad* there against godless communism. The U.S. saw a God-sent opportunity to mobilize one billion Muslims against what Reagan called the Evil Empire. . . . CIA agents started going all over the Muslim world recruiting people to fight in the great *jihad*. . . . Bin Laden went around recruiting people for the *jihad* against communism.

I first met Osama bin Laden in 1986. He was recommended to me by an American official who may have been an agent. I was talking to the American and asked him who were the Arabs there that would be very interesting to talk with . . . in Afghanistan and Pakistan. The American official told me, "You must meet Osama." I went to see Osama. There he was, rich, bringing in recruits from Algeria, from Sudan, from Egypt, just like Sheikh Abdul Rahman, an Egyptian cleric who was among those convicted for the 1993 World Trade Center bombing. At that moment, Osama bin Laden was a U.S. ally. He remained an ally. He turned at a particular moment. In 1990 the U.S. went into Saudi Arabia with military forces. Saudi Arabia is the holy place of Muslims, home of Mecca and Medina. There had never been foreign troops there. In 1990, during the build-up to the Gulf War, they went in the name of helping Saudi Arabia defend itself. Osama bin Laden remained quiet. Saddam was defeated, but the American foreign troops stayed on in the land of the kaba (the sacred site of Islam in Mecca). Bin Laden wrote letter after letter saying, Why are you here? Get out! You came to help but you have stayed on. Finally he started a *jihad* against the other occupiers. His mission is to get American troops out of Saudi Arabia. His earlier mission was to get Russian troops out of Afghanistan.

A second point to be made about him is that he comes from a tribal people. Being a millionaire doesn't matter. His code of ethics is tribal. The tribal code of ethics consists of two words: loyalty and revenge. You are my friend. You keep your word. I am loyal to you. You break your word, I go on my path of revenge. For him, America has broken its word. The loyal friend has betrayed him. . . . These are the chickens of the Afghanistan war coming home to roost.

What is my recommendation to America?

First, avoid extremes of double standards. If you're going to practice double standards, you will be paid with double standards. Don't use it. Don't condone Israeli terror, Pakistani terror, Nicaraguan terror, El Salvadoran terror, on the one hand, and then complain about Afghan terror or Palestinian terror. It doesn't work. Try to be even-handed. A superpower cannot promote terror in one place and reasonably expect to discourage terrorism in another place. It won't work in this shrunken world.

Do not condone the terror of your allies. Condemn them. Fight them. Punish them. Avoid covert operations and low-intensity warfare. These are breeding grounds for terrorism and drugs. . . .

Also, focus on causes and help ameliorate them. Try to look at causes and solve problems. Avoid military solutions. Terrorism is a political problem. Seek political solutions. Diplomacy works. Take the example of President Clinton's attack on bin Laden. Did they know what they were attacking? They say they know, but they don't know. At another point, they were trying to kill Qadaffi. Instead, they killed his young daughter. The poor child hadn't done anything. . . .

Four of the missiles intended for Afghanistan fell in Pakistan. One was slightly damaged, two were totally damaged, one was totally intact. For ten years the American government has kept an embargo on Pakistan because Pakistan was trying, stupidly, to build nuclear weapons and missiles. So the U.S. has a technology embargo on my country. One of the missiles was intact. What do you think the Pakistani official told the *Washington Post*? He said it was a gift from Allah. Pakistan wanted U.S. technology. Now they have the technology, and Pakistan's scientists are examining this missile very carefully. It fell into the wrong hands. Look for political solutions. Military solutions cause more problems than they solve.

Finally, please help reinforce and strengthen the framework of international law . . . Enforce the United Nations. Enforce the International Court of Justice.

. . .

SOLIDARITY AGAINST ALL FORMS OF TERRORISM
Vandana Shiva

18th September I joined the millions to observe two minutes silence at 10:30 a.m. for those who lost their lives in the assault on the World Trade Center and the Pentagon. But I also thought of the millions who are victims of other terrorist actions and other forms of violence. And I renewed my commitment to resist violence in all its forms.

At 10:30 a.m. on 18th September, I was with Laxmi Raibari Suranam in Jhodia Sahi village in Kashipur district in Orissa. Laxmi's husband Ghabi Jhodia was among the 20 tribals who have recently died of starvation.

In the same village Subarna Jhodia had also died. Later we met Singari in Bilamal village who has lost her husband Sadha, elder son Surat, younger son Paila, and daughter-in-law Sulami. The deliberate denial of food to the hungry is at the core of the World Bank Structural Adjustment programs. Dismantling the Public Distribution System (PDS) was a World Bank conditionality. . . .

While observing two minutes of silence in the midst of tribal families who are victims of starvation, I could not help but think of economic policies that push people into poverty and starvation as a form of terrorism.

Starvation deaths in Maharashtra, Rajasthan, and Orissa are a symptom of the breakdown of our food systems. Kashipur was gifted with abundance of nature. Starvation does not belong here. It is the result of waves of violence against nature and the tribal communities. It is a result of a brutal state ever present to snatch the resources of the tribals for industry and private corporations, but totally absent in providing welfare and security to the dispossessed tribals.

Starvation deaths in Kashipur and other regions are a result of the ecological plunder of the resources of the region, the dismantling of the food security system under economic reform policies, and the impact of climate change which caused two years of crop failure due to drought and this year's crop failure due to excessive and unseasonal rain.

Twenty years ago, the pulp and paper industry raped the forests of Kashipur. Today the herbs stand naked, and the paper mills are bringing eucalyptus in from neighboring Andhra Pradesh.

The terrorism of the pulp industry has already left the region devastated. Now the giant mining companies—Hydro of Norway, Alcan of Canada, Indico, Balco/Sterlite of India—have unleashed a new wave of terror. They are eyeing the bauxite in the majestic hills of Kashipur. Bauxite is used for aluminium—aluminium that will go to make Coca Cola cans and fighter planes.

Imagine each mountain to be a World Trade Center built by nature over millennia. Think of how many tragedies bigger than what the world experienced on September 11th are taking place to provide raw material for insatiable industry and markets. We stopped the ecological terrorism of the mining industry in my home—the Doon Valley—in 1983. The Supreme Court closed the mines, and ruled that commerce that threatens life must be stopped. But our ecological victories of the 1980s were undone with the environmental deregulation [that accompanied] globalization policies.

Mining has been "liberalized" and corporations are rushing to find minerals wherever they can. The aluminium companies want the homelands of the Kashipur tribals.

But tribals of Kashipur refuse to leave their homes. They are defending the land and earth—through a non-violent resistance movement—the movement for the Protection of Nature and People. As Mukta Jhodia, an elderly woman leader of the movement said at a rally on the 18th in Kashipur, "The earth is our mother. We are born of her. We are her children. The mining companies cannot force us to leave our land. This land was given to us by God and creation, not by the government. The government has no right to snatch our land from us."

This forced apportion of resources from people too is a form of terrorism—corporate terrorism.

I had gone to offer solidarity to victims of this corporate terrorism which was not only threatening to rob 200 villages of their survival base but had already [taken many] lives when they were [fired on] ... on 16th December 2000 by the police.

Abhilash was one of the victims killed in the police firing. His wife Subarna Jhodia was expecting a baby when he was shot. When I went to meet her in her village Maikanch, she was sitting on the doorstep of her hut with the baby girl who was born after the father was brutally killed. I asked her what she had named her child, she asked me to give her daughter a name. I named her Shakti—to embody power in peaceful form —to carry in her the 'Shakti' her father and his tribal colleagues have displayed over a decade of resistance against the terrorism of mining companies and a police state and one combined shakti to fight all forms of terrorism.

Fifty million tribals who have been flooded out of their homes by dams over the past four decades were also victims of terrorism—they have faced the terror of technology and destructive development.

For the 30,000 people who died in the Orissa Supercyclone, and the millions who will die when flood, drought, and cyclones become more severe because of climate change and fossil fuel pollution, President Bush is an ecological terrorist because he refused to sign the Kyoto protocol.

And the WTO was named the World Terrorist Organisation by citizens in Seattle because its rules are denying millions the right to life and livelihood.

The tragedy of September 11 provides us with an opportunity to stop all forms of terrorism—militaristic, technological, economic, and political. Terrorism will not be stopped by militarized minds which create insecurity and fear and hence breed terrorism. The present "war against terrorism" will create a vicious cycle of violence. . . . It is wrong to define the post-September 11th world as a war between "civilization and barbarianism" or "democracy and terrorism." It is a war between two forms of terrorism which are mirror images of each other. They share the dominant culture of violence. . . . And their victims are innocent people everywhere.

The tribals in Jhodia Sahi had lit a lamp for me at the village shrine—a small stone. These tribal shrines are insignificant when one measures them in physical terms against the twin towers of the World Trade Center. But they are spiritually deeply significant because they embody a generous cosmology of peace—peace with the earth, peace between people, and peace within people. This is the culture of peace we need to reclaim, and spread.

The whole world repeatedly watched the destruction of the World Trade Center towers, but the destruction of millions of sacred shrines, homes, and farms by forces of injustice, greed, and globalization go unnoticed.

As we remember the victims of Black Tuesday, let us also strengthen our solidarity with the millions of invisible victims of other forms of terrorism and violence which are threatening the very possibility of our future on this planet. We can turn this tragic brutal historical moment into [a force for] building cultures of peace.

. . .

LYNCHED FOR NO OFFENSE
Ida B. Wells-Barnett

Perhaps the most characteristic feature of this record of lynch law for the year 1893 is the remarkable fact that five human beings were lynched and that the matter was considered of so little importance that the powerful press bureaus of the country did not consider the matter of enough importance to ascertain the causes for which they were hanged. It tells the world, with perhaps greater emphasis than any other feature of the record, that Lynch Law has become so common in the United States that the finding of the dead body of a Negro, suspended between heaven and earth to the limb of a tree, is of so slight importance that neither the civil authorities nor press agencies consider the matter worth investigating. July 21, in Shelby County, Tenn., a colored man by the name of Charles Martin was lynched. July 30, at Paris, Mo., a colored man named William Steen shared the same fate. December 28, Mack Segars was announced to have been lynched at Brantley, Alabama. August 31, at Yarborough, Texas, and on September 19, at Houston, a colored man was found lynched, but so little attention was paid to the matter that not only was no record made as to why these last two men were lynched, but even their names were not given. The dispatches simply stated that an unknown Negro was found lynched in each case.

. . .

FATWA ISSUED ON JULY 28, 2005
The Fiqh Council of North America

The Fiqh Council of North America wishes to reaffirm Islam's absolute condemnation of terrorism and religious extremism.

Islam strictly condemns religious extremism and the use of violence against innocent lives. There is no justification in Islam for extremism or terrorism. Targeting civilians' life and property through suicide bombings or any other method of attack is *haram*—or forbidden—and those who commit these barbaric acts are criminals, not "martyrs."

The Qur'an, Islam's revealed text, states: "Whoever kills a person unless it be for murder or spreading mischief in the land, it is as though he has killed all mankind. And whoever saves a life, it is as though he had saved all mankind" (Qur'an, 5:32).

Prophet Muhammad said there is no excuse for committing unjust acts: "Do not be people without minds of your own, saying that if others treat you well you will treat them well, and that if they do wrong you will do wrong to them. Instead, accustom yourselves to do good if people do good and not to do wrong (even) if they do evil" (Al-Tirmidhi).

God mandates moderation in faith and in all aspects of life when He states in the Qur'an: "We made you to be a community of the middle way, so that (with the example of your lives) you might bear witness to the truth before all mankind" (Qur'an, 2:143).

In another verse, God explains our duties as human beings when he says: "Let there arise from among you a band of people who invite to righteousness, and enjoin good and forbid evil" (Qur'an, 3:104).

Islam teaches us to act in a caring manner to all of God's creation. The Prophet Muhammad, who is described in the Qur'an as "a mercy to the worlds," said: "All creation is the family of God, and the person most beloved by God (is the one) who is kind and caring toward His family."

In the light of the teachings of the Qur'an and Sunnah we clearly and strongly state:

1. All acts of terrorism targeting civilians are haram (forbidden) in Islam.
2. It is haram for a Muslim to cooperate with any individual or group that is involved in any act of terrorism or violence.
3. It is the civic and religious duty of Muslims to cooperate with law enforcement authorities to protect the lives of all civilians.

We issue this fatwa following the guidance of our scripture, the Qur'an, and the teachings of our Prophet Muhammad—peace be upon him. We urge all people to resolve all conflicts in just and peaceful manners.

We pray for the defeat of extremism and terrorism. We pray for the safety and security of our country, the United States, and its people. We pray for the safety and security of all inhabitants of our planet. We pray that interfaith harmony and cooperation prevail both in the United States and all around the globe.

. . .

INVOCATION FOR THE NATIONAL DAY OF PRAYER AND REMEMBRANCE FOR 9/11

Nathan D. Baxter

When ancient Israel had suffered the excruciating pain and tragedy of militant aggression and destruction, God said to them through the prophet Jeremiah: "a voice is heard in Ramah, lamenting and bitter weeping, Rachel is weeping for her children; and she refuses to be comforted, because they are no more."

Today we gather to be reassured that God hears the "lamenting and bitter weeping" of Mother America, because so many of her children are no more. Let us now seek that assurance in prayer, for the healing of our grief-stricken hearts, for the souls and sacred memory of those who have died. Let us also pray for Divine wisdom as our leaders consider the necessary actions for national security, that despite our grief we may not become the evil that we deplore. Let us pray,

God of Abraham and Mohammed and Father of our Lord, Jesus Christ: we are today a people of heavy and distraught hearts. The evil hand of hate and cowardly aggression, which has devastated the innocent in many other lands, has visited America this week and too many of her children are no more. But we know you are not the God of hate and cowardice, but of courage and justice. So we gather this day asking that you provide us healing as a nation. Heal our grief. Soothe our suffering hearts. Save us from blind vengeance, random prejudice, and crippling fear.

Guide our leaders, especially George, our President. Let the deep faith that he and they share guide them in the momentous decisions they must make for our national security.

We thank you for the courage of flight crews and passengers in the face of certain death; the brave volunteers, police, and emergency workers who labor tirelessly, even as we pray. We thank you for the outpouring generosity by businesses, unions, agencies, spiritual communities, and individual citizens. Your Spirit is at work. Grant us wisdom, grant us courage, grant us peace for the facing of this hour. Amen.

(Delivered at Washington Cathedral on the National Day
of Remembrance after 9/11 in 2001.)

. . .

I HAVE COME TO THIS EARTH
Hafiz (translated by Susan Griffin)

I have come to this earth hoping
to see our weapons
arrested midair,
even if we are possessed with rage
because we know finally
there is only one body to wound, and
this is His body,
Christ, the Beloved.

I have come to this earth to see
all of us move through
this miraculous life together
as we become greater souls
made of ecstasy and light
part of Him, dancing with
Him.

I have come into this world to hear
every song that has been sung
since we all began
in the womb of heaven,
songs that fly, or swim
or gallop, songs
from hills, trees, women, children, rivers, rocks, flutes
songs made of gold, gems, flame,
every song the heart can cry
with such high feeling
once we know we are all part of
God and that everything else
except drinking in this Sun
will leave us thirsty.

I have come into the world
for this: to find among us
women and men so loving
they would rather die than
utter even one cruel word,

so honest they live in union
with Him, His promise,
our hope.

I have come into this world to see
our weapons laid down
even at the highest point of rage
because we know now
there is only one body we can wound.

CHAPTER 2

An Unbearable Heartache

Trauma, Violence, and Memory

And now I have this unbearable heartache and a wounded soul.
—Russian girl, after surviving a terrorist attack on her school

Healing the effects of terror and terrorism, an essential step in the process of transformation, must begin with an understanding of trauma. Trauma is the inevitable result of violence. Even the threat of violence produces measurable and enduring damage to both the body and the mind. The effects of trauma lodge in the flesh so that despite every attempt to forget, the body remembers. With even the slightest trigger—an unexpected burst of light through a window at night, a loud sound, a shadow falling suddenly across the road—those who have suffered from violence can be sent into a state of panic or anxiety. Over time, the accumulated effects of too much adrenaline—rapid heart beats and muscle tension—have been known to take a devastating toll on survivors, contributing to a wide range of serious health problems, from heart conditions to diabetes.

And in the meantime, even when survivors try to move beyond the past, unbearable memories remain. Whether buried or revealed, memories of trauma can cause violent or self-destructive responses, fearful and destructive relationships with others, and an inhibition if not paralysis of the ability to reflect, imagine, learn, and grow. Many survivors never heal from the psychological effects of what they have suffered, and when healing does take place, it takes a long time, infinitely longer than it took to inflict the original wound.

Often a survivor will report a sense of feeling broken. A woman may feel as if the rug had been pulled out from under her life, or a man may experience a collapse at the core of himself. In all cases, though the survivors were not responsible for the trauma they suffered, the experience undermines their self-esteem, eating away at a once healthy sense of self. The damage does not stay isolated but affects families and friendships, too. Trauma suffered in one generation will often be handed to the next, causing myriad psychological and physical problems, whether the younger generation has been made aware of this inheritance or not.

Traumas that occur in warfare become lodged in collective memory and thus erode whole cultures and civilizations. One can, for instance, trace a terrible line of bitterness that leads from the World War I to World War II, and from the latter to the more recent conflict in the former Yugoslavia. In warfare, those who find themselves having perpetrated violence against unarmed civilians often suffer severe psychological wounds when they realize they have committed acts that they would have found unconscionable before. As reporter Conn Hallinan has written, even to witness a traumatic event can cause Post Traumatic Stress Disorder. According to the testimony of a soldier who served in Iraq,[1] after his brigade fired mistakenly into a house where a wedding was being celebrated, he glimpsed a six-year-old girl lying dead on the floor inside, and that shattered him. Though he did not deny what he saw, he tried to "stuff it" into the back of his mind. Yet whether or not he pays heed to them, as memories like this accumulate in a soldier's mind, he often feels that life has lost its meaning.

In the lives of victims, the children of victims and soldiers, trauma can also lead to more violence. Evidence suggests that soldiers who have suffered trauma in warfare also pass this violence along to others, abusing, raping, beating, and even in a few cases murdering wives, children, and girlfriends. Ironically, the traumatic effects of being raped are very similar to the effects of being exposed to combat.

If we are to end the cycle of violence created by trauma, it is crucial to grasp, not only intellectually but emotionally, what trauma is like. For this reason, we include several stories about this experience here. As an old alchemical saying tells us, the blood of the wound can heal the wound. But this will happen only when we summon the collective courage to see the consequences of the choices we make.

Susan Griffin with Karin Lofthus Carrington

1. See Iraq Veterans against the War, and Aaron Glantz, *Winter Soldier, Iraq and Afghanistan: Eyewitness Accounts of the Occupations* (Chicago: Haymarket Books, 2008), 28 passim.

. . .

THE AFTERMATH OF VIOLENCE: TRAUMA
AND RECOVERY

Judith Herman

FROM: *Trauma and Recovery: The Aftermath of Violence—From Domestic Abuse to Political Terror*

In 1922 a young American psychiatrist, Abram Kardiner, returned to New York from a year-long pilgrimage to Vienna, where he had been analyzed by Freud. He was inspired by the dream of making a great discovery. . . . Kardiner set up a private practice of psychoanalysis, at a time when there were perhaps ten psychoanalysts in New York. He also went to work in the psychiatric clinic of the Veterans Bureau, where he saw numerous men with combat neurosis. He was troubled by the severity of their distress and by his inability to cure them. . . .

Kardiner subsequently acknowledged that the "ceaseless nightmare" of his own early childhood—poverty, hunger, neglect, domestic violence, and his mother's untimely death—had influenced the direction of his intellectual pursuits and allowed him to identify with the traumatized soldiers.[1] Kardiner struggled for a long time to develop a theory of war trauma within the intellectual framework of psychoanalysis, but he eventually abandoned the task as impossible and went on to a distinguished career, first in psychoanalysis and then, like his predecessor Rivers, in anthropology. . . .

Kardiner went on to develop the clinical outlines of the traumatic syndrome as it is understood today. His theoretical formulation strongly resembled Janet's late nineteenth-century formulations of hysteria. Indeed, Kardiner recognized that war neuroses represented a form of hysteria, but he also realized that the term had once again become so pejorative that its very use discredited patients: "When the word 'hysterical' . . . is used, its social meaning is that the subject is a predatory individual, trying to get something for nothing. The victim of such a neurosis is, therefore, without sympathy in court, and . . . without sympathy from his physicians, who often take . . . 'hysterical' to mean that the individual is suffering from some persistent form of wickedness, perversity, or weakness of will."[2]

With the advent of the Second World War came a revival of medical interest in combat neurosis. In the hopes of finding a rapid, efficacious treatment, military psychiatrists tried to remove the stigma from the stress reactions of combat. It was recognized for the first time that *any* man could break down under fire and that psychiatric casualties could be predicted in direct proportion to the severity of combat exposure. Indeed, considerable effort was devoted to determining the exact level of exposure guaranteed to produce a psychological collapse. A year after the war ended, two American psychiatrists, J. W. Appel and G. W. Beebe, concluded that 200–240 days in combat would suffice to break even the strongest soldier: "There is no such thing as 'getting used to combat.' . . . Each moment of combat imposes a strain so great that men will break down in direct relation to the intensity and duration of their exposure. Thus psychiatric casualties are as inevitable as gunshot and shrapnel wounds in warfare."[3] . . .

The treatment strategies that evolved during the Second World War were designed to minimize the separation between the afflicted soldier and his comrades. Opinion favored a brief intervention as close as possible to the battle lines, with the goal of rapidly returning the soldier to his fighting unit.[4] In their quest for a quick and effective method of treatment, military psychiatrists once again discovered the mediating role of altered states of consciousness in psychological trauma. They found that artificially induced altered states could be used to gain access to traumatic memories. . . . Kardiner and Spiegel used sodium amytal, a technique they called "narcosynthesis." As in the earlier work on hysteria, the focus of the "talking cure" for combat neurosis was on the recovery and cathartic reliving of traumatic memories, with all their attendant emotions of terror, rage, and grief.

The psychiatrists who pioneered these techniques understood that unburdening traumatic memories was not in itself sufficient to effect a lasting cure. . . . The effect of combat, they argued, "is not like the writing on a slate that can be erased, leaving the slate as it was before. Combat leaves a lasting impression on men's minds, changing them as radically as any crucial experience through which they live."[5] . . .

Systematic, large-scale investigation of the long-term psychological effects of combat was not undertaken until after the Vietnam War. This time, the motivation for study came not from the military or the medical establishment, but from the organized efforts of soldiers disaffected from war.

In 1970, while the Vietnam War was at its height, two psychiatrists, Robert Jay Lifton and Chaim Shatan, met with representatives of a new organization called Vietnam Veterans Against the War. For veterans to organize against their own war while it was still ongoing was virtually unprecedented. This small group of soldiers, many of whom had distinguished themselves for bravery, returned their medals and offered public testimony of their war crimes. Their presence contributed moral credibility to a growing antiwar movement. "They raised questions," Lifton wrote, "about everyone's version of the socialized warrior and the war system, and exposed their country's counterfeit claim of a just war."[6]

The antiwar veterans organized what they called "rap groups." In these intimate meetings of their peers, Vietnam veterans retold and relived the traumatic experiences of war. They invited sympathetic psychiatrists to offer them professional assistance. . . .

The purpose of the rap groups was twofold: to give solace to individual veterans who had suffered psychological trauma, and to raise awareness about the effects of war. The testimony that came out of these groups focused public attention on the lasting psychological injuries of combat. These veterans refused to be forgotten. Moreover, they refused to be stigmatized. . . .

By the mid-1970s, hundreds of informal rap groups had been organized. By the end of the decade, the political pressure from veterans' organizations resulted in a legal mandate for a psychological treatment program, called Operation Outreach, within the Veterans' Administration. Over a hundred outreach centers were organized, staffed by veterans and based upon a self-help, peer-counseling model of care. The insistent organizing of veterans also provided the impetus for systematic psychiatric research. In the years following the Vietnam War, the Veterans' Administration commissioned comprehensive studies tracing the impact of wartime experiences on the lives of returning veterans. A five-volume study on the legacies of Vietnam delineated the syndrome of post-traumatic stress disorder and demonstrated beyond any reasonable doubt its direct relationship to combat exposure.[7]

The moral legitimacy of the antiwar movement and the national experience of defeat in a discredited war had made it possible to recognize psychological trauma as a lasting and inevitable legacy of war. In 1980, for the first time, the characteristic syndrome of psychological trauma became a "real" diagnosis. In that year the American Psychiatric Association included in its official manual of mental disorders a new category, called "post-traumatic stress disorder."[8] The clinical features of this disorder were congruent with the traumatic neurosis that Kardiner had outlined forty years before. Thus the syndrome of psychological trauma, periodically forgotten and periodically rediscovered throughout the past century, finally attained formal recognition within the diagnostic canon.

The Combat Neurosis of the Sex War

The late nineteenth-century studies of hysteria foundered on the question of sexual trauma. At the time of these investigations there was no awareness that violence is a routine part of women's sexual and domestic lives. Freud glimpsed this truth and retreated in horror. For most of the twentieth century, it was the study of combat veterans that led to the development of a body of knowledge about traumatic disorders. Not until the women's liberation movement of the 1970s was it recognized that the most common post-traumatic disorders are those not of men in war but of women in civilian life.

The real conditions of women's lives were hidden in the sphere of the personal, in private life. The cherished value of privacy created a powerful barrier to consciousness and rendered women's reality practically invisible. To speak about experiences in sexual or domestic life was to invite public humiliation, ridicule, and disbelief. Women were silenced by fear and shame, and the silence of women gave license to every form of sexual and domestic exploitation.

Women did not have a name for the tyranny of private life. It was difficult to recognize that a well-established democracy in the public sphere could coexist with conditions of primitive autocracy or advanced dictatorship in the home. Thus, it was no accident that in the first manifesto of the resurgent American feminist movement, Betty Friedan called the woman question the "problem without a name."[9] It was also no accident that the initial method of the movement was called "consciousness-raising."[10] . . .

Though the methods of consciousness-raising were analogous to those of psychotherapy, their purpose was to effect social rather than individual change. A feminist understanding of sexual assault empowered victims to breach the barriers of privacy, to support one another, and to take collective action. Consciousness-raising was also an empirical method of inquiry. Kathie Sarachild, one of the originators of consciousness-raising, described it as a challenge to the prevailing intellectual orthodoxy: "The decision to emphasize our own feelings and experiences as women and to test all generalizations and reading we did by our own experience was actually the scientific method of research. We were in effect repeating the 17th-century challenge of science to scholasticism: 'study nature, not books,' and put all theories to the test of living practice and action."[11]

The process that began with consciousness-raising led by stages to increased levels of public awareness.... Beginning in the mid-1970s, the American women's movement also generated an explosion of research on the previously ignored subject of sexual assault. In 1975, in response to feminist pressure, a center for research on rape was created within the National Institute of Mental Health. For the first time the doors were opened to women as the agents rather than the objects of inquiry. In contrast to the usual research norms, most of the "principal investigators" funded by the center were women. Feminist investigators labored close to their subjects. They repudiated emotional detachment as a measure of the value of scientific investigation and frankly honored their emotional connection with their informants. As in the heroic age of hysteria, long and intimate personal interviews became once again a source of knowledge.

The results of these investigations confirmed the reality of women's experiences that Freud had dismissed as fantasies a century before. Sexual assaults against women and children were shown to be pervasive and endemic in our culture. The most sophisticated epidemiological survey was conducted in the early 1980s by Diana Russell, a sociologist and human rights activist. Over 900 women, chosen by random sampling techniques, were interviewed in depth about their experiences of domestic violence and sexual exploitation. The results were horrifying. One woman in four had been raped. One woman in three had been sexually abused in childhood.[12]

In addition to documenting pervasive sexual violence, the feminist movement offered a new language for understanding the impact of sexual assault. Entering the public discussion of rape for the first time, women found it necessary to establish the obvious: that rape is an atrocity. Feminists redefined rape as a crime of violence rather than a sexual act.[13] This simplistic formulation was advanced to counter the view that rape fulfilled women's deepest desires, a view then prevailing in every form of literature, from popular pornography to academic texts.

Feminists also redefined rape as a method of political control, enforcing the subordination of women through terror. The author Susan Brownmiller, whose landmark treatise on rape established the subject as a matter for public debate, called attention to rape as a means of maintaining male power: "Man's discovery that his genitalia could serve as a weapon to generate fear must rank as one of the most important discoveries of prehistoric times, along with the use of fire and the first crude stone axe. From prehistoric times to the present, I believe, rape has played a critical function. It is nothing more or less than a conscious process of intimidation by which *all* men keep *all* women in a state of fear."[14] . . .

Rape was the feminist movement's initial paradigm for violence against women in the sphere of personal life. As understanding deepened, the investigation of sexual exploitation progressed to encompass relationships of increasing complexity, in which violence and intimacy commingled. The initial focus on street rape, committed by strangers, led step by step to the exploration of acquaintance rape, date rape, and rape in marriage. The initial focus on rape as a form of violence against women led to the exploration of domestic battery and other forms of private coercion. And the initial focus on the rape of adults led inevitably to a rediscovery of the sexual abuse of children. . . .

Only after 1980, when the efforts of combat veterans had legitimized the concept of post-traumatic stress disorder, did it become clear that the psychological syndrome seen in survivors of rape, domestic battery, and incest was essentially the same as the syndrome seen in survivors of war. The implications of this insight are as horrifying in the present as they were a century ago: the subordinate condition of woman is maintained and enforced by the hidden violence of men. There is war between the sexes. Rape victims, battered women, and sexually abused children are its casualties. Hysteria is the combat neurosis of the sex war.

Fifty years ago, Virginia Woolf wrote that "the public and private worlds are inseparably connected . . . the tyrannies and servilities of one are the tyrannies and servilities of the other."[15] It is now apparent also that the traumas of one are the traumas of the other. The hysteria of women and the combat neurosis of men are one. Recognizing the commonality of affliction may even make it possible at times to transcend the immense gulf that separates the public sphere of war and politics—the world of men—and the private sphere of domestic life—the world of women.

Will these insights be lost once again? At the moment, the study of psychological trauma seems to be firmly established as a legitimate field of inquiry. With the creative energy that accompanies the return of repressed ideas, the field has expanded dramatically. Twenty years ago, the literature consisted of a few out-of-print volumes moldering in neglected corners of the library. Now each month brings forth the publication of new books, new research findings, new discussions in the public media.

But history teaches us that this knowledge could also disappear. Without the context of a political movement, it has never been possible to advance the study of psychological trauma. The fate of this field of knowledge depends upon the fate of the same political movement that has inspired and sustained it over the last century. In the late nineteenth century the goal of that movement was the establishment of secular democracy. In the early twentieth century its goal was the abolition of war. In the late twentieth century its goal was the liberation of women. All of these goals remain. All are, in the end, inseparably connected.

1. A. Kardiner, *My Analysis with Freud* (New York: Norton, 1977), 141.

2. A. Kardiner and H. Spiegel, *War, Stress, and Neurotic Illness* (rev. ed. *The Traumatic Neuroses of War*) (New York: Hoeber, 1947), 406.

3. J. W. Appel and G. W. Beebe, "Preventive Psychiatry: An Epidemiological Approach," *Journal of the American Medical Association* 131 (1946), 1468–71, quote on 1470.

4. R. R. Grinker and J. Spiegel, *Men Under Stress* (Philadelphia: Blakeston, 1945); Kardiner and Spiegel, *War, Stress.*

5. Grinker and Spiegel, *Men Under Stress,* 371.

6. R. J. Lifton, *Home from the War: Vietnam Veterans: Neither Victims nor Executioners* (New York: Simon & Schuster, 1973), 31.

7. A. Egendorf et al., *Legacies of Vietnam,* vols. 1–5 (Washington, DC: U.S. Government Printing Office, 1981).

8. American Psychological Association, *Diagnostic and Statistical Manual of Mental Disorders,* 3rd ed. (DSM-III) (Washington, DC: American Psychological Association, 1980).

9. B. Friedan, *The Feminine Mystique* (New York: Dell, 1963).

10. K. Amatniek (Sarachild), "Consciousness-Raising," in *New York Redstockings: Notes from the Second Year, 1968* (self-published). For a history of the origins of the feminist movement in this period see S. Evans, *Personal Politics* (New York: Vintage, 1980).

11. K. Sarachild, "Consciousness-Raising: A Radical Weapon," in *Feminist Revolution,* ed. K. Sarachild (New York: Random House, 1978), 145. (Orig. ed. *New York Redstockings,* 1975).

12. D. E. H. Russell, *Sexual Exploitation: Rape, Child Sexual Abuse, and Sexual Harrassment* (Beverly Hills, CA: Sage, 1984).

13. S. Brownmiller, *Against Our Will: Men, Women, and Rape* (New York: Simon & Schuster, 1975).

14. Ibid., 14–15.

15. V. Woolf, *Three Guineas* [1938] (New York: Harcourt, Brace, Jovanovich, 1966), 147.

. . .

The first time I came into contact with groups of campesinos displaced by the war, I felt that much of their behavior showed aspects of paranoid delirium. They were constantly alert and hyper-vigilant, and they mistrusted anyone they didn't know. They were suspicious of everyone who approached them, scrutinizing gestures and words, looking for possible danger. And yet, when I learned about what had happened to them and the real dangers still preying on them, as well as their defenselessness and impotence against any type of attack, I quickly began to understand that their hyper-mistrust and vigilance were not signs of persecution delirium born of their anxiety, but rather the most realistic response to their life situation. . . .

(Ignacio Martín-Baró, from *Writings for a Liberation Psychology*)

. . .

GHOSTS AND ECHOES: REFLECTIONS AFTER 9/11
Robin Morgan

It's the details—fragile, individual—that melt numbness into grief. An anklet with "Joyleen" engraved on it—found on an ankle. Just that: an ankle. A pair of hands—one brown, one white—clasped together. Just that. No wrists. A burly welder who drove from Ohio to help, saying softly, "We're working in a cemetery. I'm standing in—not on, *in*—a graveyard." Each lamppost, storefront, scaffolding, mailbox, is plastered with homemade photocopied posters, a racial/ethnic rainbow of faces and names: death the great leveler, not only of the financial CEOs—their images usually formal, white, male, older, with suit-and-tie—but the mailroom workers, receptionists, waiters. You pass enough of the MISSING posters, and the faces, names, descriptions become familiar. The Albanian window-cleaner guy with the bushy eyebrows. The teenage Mexican dishwasher who had an American flag tattoo. The janitor's assistant who'd emigrated from Ethiopia. The Italian American grandfather who was a doughnut-cart tender. The 23-year-old Chinese American junior pastry chef at the Windows on the World restaurant who'd gone in early that day so she could prep a business breakfast for 500. The firefighter who'd posed jauntily wearing his green shamrock necktie. The dapper African American midlevel manager with a small gold ring in his ear who handled "minority affairs" for one of the companies. The middle-aged secretary laughing up at the camera from her wheelchair. The maintenance worker with a Polish name, holding his newborn baby. Most of the faces are smiling. Most of the shots are family photos. Many are recent wedding pictures. . . .

The sirens have lessened. But the drums have started. Funeral drums. War drums. . . . The Justice Department is seeking increased authority for wider surveillance, broader detention powers, wiretapping of persons (not, as previously, just phone numbers), and stringent press restrictions on military reporting.

And the petitioners have begun. For justice but not vengeance. For a reasoned response but against escalating retaliatory violence. For vigilance about civil liberties. For the rights of innocent Muslim Americans. For "bombing" Afghanistan with food and medical parcels, *not* firepower. There will be the expectable peace marches, vigils, rallies. . . . One member of the House of Representatives—Barbara Lee, Democrat of California, and African American woman—lodged the sole vote in both houses of Congress against giving Bush broadened powers for a war response, saying she didn't believe that a massive military campaign would stop terrorism. . . .

Those of us who have access to the media have been trying to get a different voice out. But ours are complex messages with long-term solutions— and this is a moment when people yearn for simplicity and short-term, facile answers. . . .

Meanwhile, we cry and cry and cry. I don't even know who my tears are for anymore, because I keep seeing ghosts, I keep hearing echoes. The world's sympathy moves me deeply. Yet I hear echoes dying into silence: the world is averting its attention from Rwanda's screams. . . .

Ground Zero is a huge mass grave. And I think: Bosnia. Uganda.

And I see ghosts. Hiroshima. Nagasaki. Dresden. Vietnam.

I watch the mask-covered mouths and noses on the street turn into the faces of Tokyo citizens who wear such masks every day against toxic pollution. I watch the scared eyes become the fearful eyes of women forced to wear the *hijab* or *chodor* or *burka* against their will. . . .

I stare at the MISSING posters' photos and think of the Mothers of the Disappeared, circling the plazas [in Argentina]. And I see the ghosts of other faces. In photographs on the walls of Holocaust museums. In newspaper clippings from Haiti. In chronicles from Cambodia. . . .

I worry for the people who've lost their homes near the site, though I see how superbly social-service agencies are trying to meet their immediate and longer-term needs. But I see ghosts: the perpetually homeless who sleep on city streets, whose needs are never addressed. . . .

I watch normally unflappable New Yorkers flinch at loud noises, parents panic when their kids are late from school. And I see my Israeli feminist friends like Yvonne, who've lived with this dread for decades and still (even yesterday) stubbornly continue to issue petitions insisting on peace. . . .

I watch sophisticates sob openly in the street, people who've lost workplaces, who don't know where their next paycheck will come from, who fear a contaminated water or food supply, who are afraid for their sons in the army, who are unnerved by security checkpoints, who are wounded, who are mourning, who feel terrified, humiliated, outraged. And I see my friends like Zuhira in the refugee camps of Gaza or West Bank, Palestinian women who have lived in precisely that same emotional condition—for four generations.

Last weekend, many Manhattanites left town to visit concerned families, try to normalize, get away for a break. As they streamed out of the city, I saw ghosts of other travelers: hundreds of thousands of Afghan refugees streaming toward their country's borders in what is to them habitual terror, trying to escape a drought-sucked country so war-devastated there's nothing left to bomb, a country with 50,000 disabled orphans and two million widows whose sole livelihood is begging; where the life expectancy of men is 42 and women 40; where women hunch in secret whispering lessons to girl children forbidden to go to school, women who risk death by beheading—for teaching a child to read.

The ghosts reach out their hands. *Now you know*, they weep, gesturing at the carefree, insulated, indifferent, golden innocence that was my country's safety, arrogance, and pride. *Why should it take such horror to make you see?* The echoes sigh, *Oh please do you finally see?*

This is calamity. And opportunity. The United States—what so many of you call America—could choose now to begin to understand the world. And join it. Or not.

For now my window still displays no flag, my lapel sports no red-white-and-blue ribbon. Instead, I weep for a city and a world. Instead, I cling to a different loyalty, affirming my un-flag, my un-anthem, my un-prayer—the defiant un-pledge of a madwoman who also had mere words as her only tools in a time of ignorance and carnage, Virginia Woolf: "As a woman I have no country. As a woman I want no country. As a woman my country is the whole world."

If this is treason, may I be worthy of it.

In mourning—and absurd, tenacious hope.

. . .

BE AHEAD OF ALL PARTING

Rainer Maria Rilke (translated by Anita Barrows and Joanna Macy)

Be ahead of all parting, as if it had already happened,
like winter, which even now is passing.
For beneath the winter is a winter so endless
that to survive it at all is a triumph of the heart.

Be forever dead in Eurydice, and climb back singing.
Climb praising as you return to connection.
Here among the disappearing, in the realm of the transient,
be a ringing glass that shatters as it rings.

Be. And, at the same time, know what it is *not* to be.
That emptiness inside you allows you to vibrate
in resonance with your world. Use it for once.

To all that has run its course, and to the vast unsayable
numbers of beings abounding in Nature,
add yourself gladly, and cancel the cost.

. . .

THE DEEPER WOUND
Deepak Chopra

As fate would have it, I was leaving New York on a jet flight that took off 45 minutes before the unthinkable happened. By the time we landed in Detroit, chaos had broken out. When I grasped the fact that American security had broken down so tragically, I couldn't respond at first. My wife and son were also in the air on separate flights, one to Los Angeles, one to San Diego. My body went absolutely rigid with fear. All I could think about was their safety, and it took me several hours before I found out that their flights had been diverted and both were safe.

Strangely, when the good news came, my body still felt that a truck had hit it. Of its own accord it seemed to feel a far greater trauma that reached out to the thousands who would not survive and the tens of thousands who would survive only to live through months and years of hell.

And I asked myself, Why didn't I feel this way last week? Why didn't my body go stiff during the bombing of Iraq or Bosnia?

Around the world my horror and worry are experienced every day. Mothers weep over horrendous loss, civilians are bombed mercilessly, refugees are ripped from any sense of home or homeland. Why did I not feel their anguish enough to call a halt to it?

As we hear the calls for tightened American security and a fierce military response to terrorism, it is obvious that none of us had any answers.

However, we feel compelled to ask some questions. Everything has a cause, so we have to ask, what was the root cause of this evil? We must find out not superficially but at the deepest level. There is no doubt that such evil is alive all around the world and is even celebrated. Does this evil grow from the suffering and anguish felt by people we don't know and therefore ignore?

Have they lived in this condition for a long time?

One assumes that whoever did this attack feels implacable hatred for America. Why were we selected to be the focus of suffering around the world?

All this hatred and anguish seems to have religion as its basis. Isn't something terribly wrong when jihads and wars develop in the name of God? Isn't God invoked with hatred in Ireland, Sri Lanka, India, Pakistan, Israel, Palestine, and even among the intolerant sects of America?

Can any military response make the slightest difference in the underlying cause? Is there not a deep wound at the heart of humanity?

If there is a deep wound, doesn't it affect everyone?

When generations of suffering respond with bombs, suicidal attacks, and biological warfare, who first developed these weapons? Who sells them? Who gave birth to the satanic technologies now being turned against us?

If all of us are wounded, will revenge work? Will punishment in any form toward anyone solve the wound or aggravate it? Will an eye for an eye, a tooth for a tooth, and limb for a limb, leave us all blind, toothless and crippled?

Tribal warfare has been going on for two thousand years and has now been magnified globally. Can tribal warfare be brought to an end? Is patriotism and nationalism even relevant anymore, or is this another form of tribalism?

What are you and I as persons going to do about what is happening? Can we afford to let the deeper wound fester any longer?

Everyone is calling this an attack on America, but is it not a rift in our collective soul? Isn't this an attack on civilization from without that is also from within?

When we have secured our safety once more and cared for the wounded, after the period of shock and mourning is over, it will be time for soul searching. I only hope that these questions are confronted with the deepest spiritual intent. None of us will feel safe again behind the shield of military might and stockpiled arsenals. There can be no safety until the root cause is faced. In this moment of shock I don't think any one of us has the answers. It is imperative that we pray and offer solace and help to each other. But if you and I are having a single thought of violence or hatred against anyone in the world at this moment, we are contributing to the wounding of the world.

. . .

At first Rwanda's seeming normalcy made the pain and loss wrought by the genocide almost impossible to grasp. The restaurants were open, the banks in operation, and bustling markets offered everything from women's shoes to black-market foreign currency. It took me some weeks to realize that the legacy of Rwanda's genocide lived on in people's inner lives. Survivors, whether Tutsi or Hutu, went through the motions of everyday existence but not its emotions; they skated across their feelings, frightened of experiencing them too deeply. One of my translators, Françoise—whose family had been killed in the genocide—answered me this way, when I asked her how the slaughter had affected Rwandan society. "Look right in front of you," she replied. "We have all lost something. We even have an expression for it: *bapfuye buhagazi*. It means the walking dead. This is the land of the walking dead."

(Elizabeth Neuffer, from *The Key to My Neighbor's House: Seeking Justice in Bosnia and Rwanda*)

. . .

JUST ONE STORY
Jodie Evans (as told to Susan Griffin)

Until the moment the soldiers began to fire on her family, the neighborhood where Anwar's parents lived had been mostly peaceful. Middle class if not prosperous, the even concrete facades opened through gates to quiet courtyards. The street was beautiful then, lined with trees, ending at the Tigris, the ancient river that flows through Baghdad, where just overhead, the bridge leading to the Green Zone appeared. That was where the soldiers usually stationed themselves, perhaps to watch the traffic going over the bridge. They would offer cigarettes and water to residents who passed by. Until that night they paid no particular attention to the respectably serene street in back of them.

Anwar lives on this street now with her parents, but that night she was only visiting them. If visiting grandparents is a cross-cultural phenomenon, for Iraqis, the extended family is even more important than for Americans. (So much so that at times one man's salary provides income for older generations as well as his wife and children.)

At 9:30 that night, after saying goodbye, Anwar, her three children, and her husband all piled into their car. Anwar's husband was driving; Anwar, who was pregnant then, sat in the front seat, and her three children sat in back. Her son, of whom the family was so proud because he was just finishing medical school, sat on one side, her older daughter who was just finishing high school, on the other, and her younger daughter, just eight years old, in the middle. They saw two Humvees in the middle of the street, an uncommon sight for this neighborhood, but the two vehicles were facing each other. It was very dark. There had been a failure of electricity, though this was not uncommon in post-invasion Iraq. Perhaps the soldiers never saw them getting into their car. When their own car started up they were surprised to see soldiers spread out in the street. Suddenly bullets were being fired at them.

While Anwar slid out of her seat and down to the floor, her husband waved his hand out the window, calling out frantically, "Stop, cease fire. We have children here. We are a family." But the soldiers just kept on firing until her husband was wounded. Shot first in his stomach and then in his head. Bleeding profusely, he lay over her. Trying to save her life and the life of her unborn child, Anwar escaped from the car. But by the time the shooting stopped, two of Anwar's children, her son and older daughter, were dead. At first it appeared that her eight-year-old had been killed, too. (An American female soldier must have thought so when she took the child's gold earrings from her ears.) But though the child was badly wounded, she lived. She was shot in the head, stomach, neck, and arms and still has extensive shrapnel and fragments of bullets in her body, yet despite these wounds, she was not taken to the hospital until two days after the shooting.

When Anwar accompanied her daughter to the examination room, a doctor revealed that if her husband had been taken to the hospital immediately, instead of three hours later, he might have lived, too. As it was, he bled to death.

Without any way to support herself, Anwar moved into her parents' home. She was never able to receive any significant financial compensation from the United States.

Anwar told her story to a delegation of American women, including several from Code Pink, and Marla Ruzicka from CIVIC, while they were visiting Iraq. When later this delegation tried to bring Anwar to the United States to join an Iraqi delegation of women who were telling their stories, she was refused a visa on the grounds that she did not have enough family in Iraq to make her want to return.

(This story, told by Jodie Evans to Susan Griffin, was taken from transcripts of an interview that occurred in Iraq in February 2004.)

. . .

UNFOLDING
Nelly Sachs (translated by Anita Barrows)

And it unfolds, like linen cloths
in which birth and death are swaddled—
the word-womb, pupa emerging
from green and red and white darkness—
and folds itself back into the suffering of love,
as mothers do. For sorrow is where light is hidden.

Thus, while it works like summer or like winter,
what is longed for hovers above, transforms itself, full of longing.

. . .

THE HIDDEN DAMAGE OF NUCLEAR WEAPONS
Terry Tempest Williams

FROM: *Refuge: An Unnatural History of Family and Place*

A little over a year after Mother's death, Dad and I were having dinner together. He had just returned from St. George, where the Tempest Company was completing the gas lines that would service southern Utah. He spoke of his love for the country, the sandstoned landscape, bare-boned and beautiful. He had just finished hiking the Kolob trail in Zion National Park. We got caught up in reminiscing, recalling with fondness our walk up Angel's Landing on his fiftieth birthday and the years our family had vacationed there.

Over dessert, I shared a recurring dream of mine. I told my father that for years, as long as I could remember, I saw this flash of light in the night in the desert—that this image had so permeated my being that I could not venture south without seeing it again, on the horizon, illuminating buttes and mesas.

"You did see it," he said.

"See what?

"The bomb. The cloud. We were driving home from Riverside, California. You were sitting on Diane's lap. She was pregnant. In fact, I remember the day, September 7, 1957. We had just gotten out of the Service. We were driving north, past Las Vegas. It was an hour or so before dawn, when this explosion went off. We not only heard it, but felt it. I thought the oil tanker in front of us had blown up. We pulled over and suddenly, rising from the desert floor, we saw it, clearly, this golden-stemmed cloud, the mushroom. The sky seemed to vibrate with an eerie pink glow. Within a few minutes a light ash was raining on the car."

I stared at my father.

"I thought you knew that," he said. "It was a common occurrence in the fifties."

It was at this moment that I realized the deceit I had been living under. Children growing up in the American Southwest, drinking contaminated milk from contaminated cows, even from the contaminated breasts of their mothers, my mother—members, years later, of the Clan of One-Breasted Women.

. . .

Belgrade, April 18, 1999

It is Sunday, but who cares? We have been living the same day ever since the war started. In Belgrade there are efforts at normality—the traditional marathon was held in heavy rain; there was a big wedding on TV—but personally I'm done with anything that resembles human life. I'd rather be a cockroach, at this point, much safer.

Last night three factories in Pančevo were hit again, including the chemical factory, where there was an acid leak. Some people are being evacuated. We in Belgrade had a good wind, we were lucky once more. In Batajnica, near the airport, a three-year-old girl was killed by falling glass after an explosion. Her father said she'd been difficult in the night. First she wanted to go to the bathroom, then she didn't, then she did. And then he let her go in and she never came out.

(Jasmina Tešanović, from *The Diary of a Political Idiot: Normal Life in Belgrade*)

. . .

UNDER BOMBARDMENT IN BEIRUT
Mahmoud Darwish
FROM: *Memory for Forgetfulness*

I no longer wonder when the steely howling of the sea will stop. I live on the eighth floor of a building that might tempt any sniper, to say nothing of a fleet now transforming the sea into one of the fountainheads of hell. The north face of the building, made of glass, used to give tenants a pleasing view over the wrinkled roof of the sea. But now it offers no shield against stark slaughter. Why did I choose to live here? What a stupid question! I've lived here for the past ten years without complaining about the scandal of glass.

But how to reach the kitchen?

I want the aroma of coffee. I want nothing more than the aroma of coffee. And I want nothing more from the passing days than the aroma of coffee. The aroma of coffee so I can hold myself together, stand on my feet, and be transformed from something that crawls, into a human being. The aroma of coffee so I can stand my share of this dawn up on its feet. So that we can go together, this day and I, down into the street in search of another place.

How can I diffuse the aroma of coffee into my cells, while shells from the sea rain down on the sea-facing kitchen, spreading the stink of gunpowder and the taste of nothingness? I measure the period between two shells. One second. One second: shorter than the time between breathing in and breathing out, between two heartbeats. One second is not long enough for me to stand before the stove by the glass facade that overlooks the sea. One second is not long enough to open the water bottle or pour the water into the coffee pot. One second is not long enough to light a match. But one second is long enough for me to burn.

I switch off the radio, no longer wondering if the wall of this narrow hallway will actually protect me from the rain of rockets. What matters is that a wall be there to veil air fusing into metal, seeking human flesh, making a direct hit, choking it, or scattering shrapnel. In such cases a mere dark curtain is enough to provide an imaginary shield of safety. For death is to see death.

I want the aroma of coffee. I need five minutes. I want a five-minute truce for the sake of coffee. I have no personal wish other than to make a cup of coffee. With this madness I define my task and my aim. All my senses are on their mark, ready at the call to propel my thirst in the direction of the one and only goal: coffee.

Coffee, for an addict like me, is the key to the day.

And coffee, for one who knows it as I do, means making it with your own hands and not having it come to you on a tray, because the bringer of the tray is also the bearer of talk, and the first coffee, the virgin of the silent morning, is spoiled by the first words. Dawn, my dawn, is antithetical to chatter. The aroma of coffee can absorb sounds and will go rancid, even if these sounds are nothing more than a gentle "Good morning!"

Coffee is the morning silence, early and unhurried, the only silence in which you can be at peace with self and things, creative, standing alone with some water that you reach for in lazy solitude and pour into a small copper pot with a mysterious shine—yellow turning to brown—that you place over a low fire.

Oh, that it were a wood fire!

Stand back from the fire a little and observe a street that has been rising to search for its bread ever since the ape disentangled himself from the trees and walked on two feet. A street borne along on carts loaded with fruits and vegetables, and vendors' cries notable for faint praise that turns produce into a mere attribute of price. Stand back a little and breathe air sent by the cool night. Then return to your low fire—*If only it were a wood fire!*—and watch with love and patience the contact between the two elements, fire colored green and blue and water roiling and breathing out tiny white granules that turn into a fine film and grow. Slowly they expand, then quickly swell into bubbles that grow bigger and bigger, and break. Swelling and breaking, they're thirsty and ready to swallow two spoonfuls of coarse sugar, which no sooner penetrates than the bubbles calm down to a quiet hiss, only to sizzle again in a cry for a substance that is none other than the coffee itself—a flashy rooster of aroma and Eastern masculinity.

Remove the pot from the low fire to carry on the dialogue of a hand, free of the smell of tobacco and ink, with its first creation, which as of this moment will determine the flavor of your day and the arc of your fortune: whether you're to work or avoid contact with anyone for the day. What emerges from this first motion and its rhythm, from what shakes it out of a world of sleep rising from the previous day, and from whatever mystery it will uncover in you, will form the identity of your new day.

Because coffee, the first cup of coffee, is the mirror of the hand. And the hand that makes the coffee reveals the person that stirs it. Therefore, coffee is the public reading of the open book of the soul. And it is the enchantress that reveals whatever secrets the day will bring.

The dawn made of lead is still advancing from the direction of the sea, riding on sounds I haven't heard before. The sea has been entirely packed into stray shells. It is changing its marine nature and turning into metal. Does death have all these names? We said we'd leave. Why then does this red-black-gray rain keep pouring over those leaving or staying, be they people, trees, or stones? We said we'd leave. "By sea?" they asked. "By sea," we answered. Why then are they arming the foam and waves with this heavy artillery? Is it to hasten our steps to the sea? But first they must break the siege of the sea. They must clear the last path for the last thread of our blood. But that they won't do, so we won't be leaving. I'll go ahead then and make the coffee.

The neighborhood birds are awake at six in the morning. They've kept the tradition of neutral song ever since they found themselves alone with the first glimmer of light. For whom do they sing in the crush of these rockets? They sing to heal their nature of a night that has passed. They sing for themselves, not for us. Did we realize that before? The birds clear their own space in the smoke of the burning city, and the zigzagging arrows of sound wrap themselves around the shells and point to an earth safe under the sky. It is for the killer to kill, the fighter to fight, and the bird to sing. As for me, I halt my quest for figurative language. I bring my search for meaning to a complete stop because the essence of war is to degrade symbols and bring human relations, space, time, and the elements back to a state of nature, making us rejoice over water gushing on the road from a broken pipe.

Water under these conditions comes to us like a miracle. Who says water has no color, flavor, or smell? Water does have a color that reveals itself in the unfolding of thirst. Water has the color of bird sounds, that of sparrows in particular—birds that pay no heed to this war approaching from the sea, so long as their space is safe. And water has the flavor of water, and a fragrance that is the scent of the afternoon breeze blown from a field with full ears of wheat waving in a luminous expanse strewn like the flickering spots of light left by the wings of a small sparrow fluttering low. Not everything that flies is an airplane. (Perhaps one of the worst Arabic words is *Ta:'irah*—airplane—which is the feminine form of *Ta:'ir*—bird.) The birds carry on with their song, insistent in the midst of the naval artillery's roar. Who said water has no flavor, color, or smell, and that this jet is the feminine form of this bird?

But suddenly the birds are quiet. They stop their chatter and routine soaring in the dawn air when the storm of flying metal starts to blow. Are they quiet because of its steely roar, or from the incongruity of name and form? Two wings of steel and silver versus two made of feathers. A nose of wiring and steel against a beak made of song. A cargo of rockets against a grain of wheat and a straw. Their skies no longer safe, the birds stop singing and pay heed to the war.

. . .

I JUST MISSED THE BUS AND I'LL BE LATE FOR WORK
Ariel Dorfman (translated by Ariel Dorfman and Edith Grossman)

I'd have to piss through my eyes to cry for you
salivate, sweat, sigh through my eyes,
I'd have to waterfall
I'd have to wine
I'd have to die like crushed grapes
through my eyes,
cough up vultures spit green silence
and shed a dried-up skin
no good to animals
no good for a trophy
I'd have to cry these wounds
this war
to mourn for us.

. . .

INTERRUPTED SUBJECTS

Helene Shulman Lorenz

From dry flowers you make a memorial wreath, and from dry bones,
a vision of resurrected bones.

—Yehuda Amichai

A heart-breaking scene appears in a documentary released in 2002. First there is a close-up of shovels, more than one, digging in a remote area of barren countryside. There is a hole in the earth as deep as a grave. Hands reach in and pick up small objects. Are they bones, pieces of clothing or paper, part of a shoe? Each small object is placed in a plastic bag. Then the camera pulls out, and we see the whole surround. Dozens of people encircle the dig, many weeping or holding worn photographs to their breasts, straining to see the shovels.

In the last year, I have seen this sequence in three different documentaries dealing with histories of terror.[1] The first was *The Pinochet Case* by Patricio Guzmán about the many disappeared activists in Chile during the dictatorship of the 70s and 80s and the attempt to bring Pinochet to trial in Spain in 1998. The second was *Amandla* by Lee Hirsch about the fifty-year anti-apartheid struggle in South Africa, and the role of music in keeping alive spirit and memory. The third was *Discovering Dominga* by Pat Flynn, the journey of a Guatemalan woman adopted by a missionary family and raised in Iowa after a massacre in her village.

Why is this scene so powerful that it was presented in three different films? Why the need to return again and again to these uninhabited areas of the country to dig? Large numbers of people in each country accuse those who engage in such activities of being obsessed with the past. Many have received death threats or have been killed for raising issues about the history of human rights abuses. Why unearth mass graves when energy should be invested in moving into a better future? In fact, a war of memory is occurring in many countries where past oppression led to suffering, death, torture, or disappearance of thousands of community leaders.

I have been on the side of both forgetting and remembering at different moments in my life. Being born in the right historical moment to be part of the 1960s, and later solidarity movements with Latin America and Africa, I was on the side of sweeping away the cobwebs of the past. In our idealism (that today seems naive), we believed we could change everything for a better future. We didn't understand then that what seemed like progress and even victory could produce a backlash, and later a crushing defeat. It would take years before we could acknowledge our own complicity and blindness in maintaining some of the values we had hoped to transform.

It wasn't until midlife that I began to think about the legacies of the past, and about the memories of the adults who surrounded me when I was a child. Then I was flooded with dreams about all the bits and pieces I'd managed to forget about my own childhood: mysterious numbers tattooed on the forearms of cousins, disturbing photographs of piles of shoes and suitcases, states of suffering that caused migraines and backaches but could find no words, whispered conversations about events in Jewish communities in Germany and Poland so terrible they could not be spoken aloud. Visceral connections to images of Auschwitz and Bergen-Belsen undoubtedly underlay every later impression of state of siege, torture center, prison camp, shantytown, or favela I have ever encountered. I saw state terror firsthand while I was in Chile during the dictatorship and in El Salvador and Nicaragua during civil wars, but it linked somatically with a childhood fear of Nazi storm troopers. Though I was not imprisoned or tortured personally, I have lived all my life as part of communities that were traumatized by such experiences.

I began to understand that there are unforgettable events that survive, not in memory, but in disconnected images, slices of life that cannot be digested at the time they occur, which live on in families year after year like a metaphorical unburied corpse, rotting, haunting, demanding some work like a proper burial that we no longer know how to perform. These images are not properly symbols connected with the grammar of language, but more like metonymy, a kind of debris lying around nearby the events. We cannot reclaim the surrounding narratives that would express the memories or logic of these events, because such narratives never existed. Instead we have gaps in memory that are the fullest expression of what was experienced at the time. State terror always enforces a culture of silence and forgetting.

Unless we return to collect and honor whatever remaining debris surrounds the historic events that affect us and raise them up for public scrutiny, witness, and ritual, we will continue to be haunted by dis-ease and partial amnesia. It may be that after ten or twenty years, such images begin to form a kind of abscess, an infection that causes unbearable pain in the social body, a symptom that can no longer be ignored. I have changed camps now and am obsessed with the question of how we remember and memorialize the past and how that shapes our capacity (or failure) to confront suffering in the present. This transformation in my own sensibility has caused a fascination with theories of trauma, memory, and dissociation. I am beginning to understand that my sense of personal identity, as well as the histories we have learned in school, may be "interrupted subjects" based on gaps in memory.

Much of the early work on trauma theory imagined trauma as the problem of individuals whose unique experiences of abuse caused identities to fragment. Healing modalities that approach such personal trauma create protected spaces for personal remembering with the help of dialogue, imagination, and creativity, hopefully leading to mourning and, later, revitalization. According to psychoanalyst Peter Shabad, suffering turns into trauma in the first place when this type of environment is absent, when suffering is unwitnessed and unacknowledged. "It suggests that being alone and not being able to convey one's experience immediately are intrinsic to the transformation of suffering into trauma."[2] A child who experiences suffering without an empathetic witness gradually enters a state of derealization, a world of doubt, fantasy, and obsession over the actuality of experience. Symptoms, addictions, or illness may become the only markers of the historical event, and these cannot be given up, because without them there would be no recognition at all of what happened.

Only recently, as a result of too many experiences with survivors of trauma that is social and historical as well as personal, healers have begun to explore the possibility that there are also dimensions of collective trauma. Dealing with threatened Native American and White communities being destroyed by pollution, Kai Erikson defines it this way:

> By *collective trauma* . . . I mean a blow to the basic tissues of social life that damages the bonds attaching people together and impairs the prevailing sense of communality. The collective trauma works its way slowly and even insidiously into the awareness of those who suffer from it, so it does not have the quality of suddenness normally associated with "trauma." But it is a form of shock all the same, a gradual realization that the community no longer exists as an effective support and that an important part of the self has disappeared. . . . "I" continue to exist, though damaged and maybe even permanently changed. "You" continue to exist, though distant and hard to relate to. But "we" no longer exist as a connected pair or as linked cells to a larger communal body."[3]

Collective trauma damages not only the individuals who are its victims, witnesses, or bystanders, but also community and culture. When the organic memory of a neighborhood is undermined, the fabric of meaningful life connections, guiding symbols, daily rituals, and orienting narratives begins to fray. People then have the sense of living in a state of alienation and isolation from others, a way of life being widely reported in American cities. In such states of anonymity, few feel responsible for public policy, violence, or hunger that is always someone else's affair. Reflecting on a civil war over memory and memorial sites going on in Argentina during the last decade, Elizabeth Jelin and Susana G. Kaufman find the need for dialogue and reminiscence crucial for livable communities:

> Societal forgetting is also a collective intersubjective affair. It implies a societal cleft, a rupture between individual memory and public and/or collective practices (that may become ritualized and repetitious), or a faulty line in the intergenerational process of transmission. . . . Interpretations and explanations of the past cannot be automatically conveyed from one generation to the next, from one period to another, from those who experienced events to others who did not. . . . An active transmission of memory requires fostering a process of identification that can produce a broadening of the "we," the active subjects of reminiscing. Yet it requires leaving open the door for processes of reinterpretation, both on the part of the young and of those who were alive at the time and "did not know what was happening." . . . Memory is, in fact, part of the symbolic and political struggle of each time, of each present.[4]

When organic memory is destroyed by terror, survivors may be in a state of despair while surrounded by others who are in a process of denial and cannot bear witness to their experiences. In such scenarios, potential healing processes of ritual, mourning, and working through trauma are frozen in time. According to Idelber Avelar, the historical trauma continues to remain "lodged within the ego as a foreign body . . . unnamable except through partial synonyms." The trauma becomes, then, a kind of "*allegorical crypt* . . . an intrapsychic tomb," which leads to melancholia, where bits and pieces of the past become an exterior tomb that must be obsessively revisited again and again. Practices of counter-memory and counter-memorial then stage the act of recollection as "an interruptive machine."[5]

It is important to note that it is also possible to literalize the need to create an "interruptive machine" in public environments bent on denying histories of suffering. The despair produced by the catastrophe of an unacknowledged oppression can be publicly reenacted through fratricidal wars or terrorist bombing. The "symbolic tomb" of erased suffering can be represented on every television set in the world by blowing up buildings. Remembering our histories is tricky territory. We are in a downward spiral of such events according to United Nations statistics on civil wars, and it is crucial to find ways to return to the repressed without explosives.

While we can hope for a future in which there could be an honest public accounting of a genocidal past that many have colluded to disown—combined with a successful process of memorial, restoration, reparation, and rededication—at present we have only hints of what such a process could be. In order to think about what type of theory can help in the recognition and healing of memory and trauma in broken communities, we need to imagine an interruptive, non-normative ethics that is willing to go outside the defense of the status quo to support and nurture a process of social mourning. That is, we would need to stop doing rapid recovery and business as usual, and begin to imagine entering into disturbing contexts where a new type of meditative listening and witnessing can be processed in community.

The sensibility I have been describing has emerged in the last decades in a number of fields as what I will call an *ethics of interruption*. In the ethics of interruption, the point of the work is to produce a process that will cause participants to return to a traumatic subject where there has been a frozen or incomplete possibility of imaginative understanding and mourning. The return is staged within a community setting where the rules have changed: what was not heard must now be heard, what was "normal" will be seen as a cover-up, what was dead is to be resurrected in imagination and returned to life. Such work is not a regular mourning process, which requires a period of grieving and then a return to daily activities. In this way, it is different from many individual scenarios of therapy, where, in the long run, the point is to get on with life. Within the ethics of interruption, mourning is nonredemptive in the sense that it will need to be done in ritual space over and over again because there is no possible closure about what has been lost within the current climate where so many are invested in forgetting.

Community-based projects of interruption have developed around the world in recent years through practices of liberation psychologies and liberation arts.[6] These have involved creating spaces for public witness that begin at the moment where memory became amnesia, where narratives froze and deadened, breaking the silences about the past. In these spaces, differences and antagonisms can be revived, symbolized, reimagined, worked through, and sometimes forgiven by community members dedicated to building a more peaceful future. These processes can lead to new forms of individual or community art, film, music, storytelling, altar-building, performance, and ritual, facilitating the retrieval of previously unbearable memories and the honoring of an unmourned past. Often they open out toward participatory research and political action.

While none of this activity is a final healing of wounds, an ethics of interruption seems to be a necessary stage that many have arrived at in a historical epoch where too much suffering remains invisible and unheard in national and transnational dialogues. Liberation in this context signifies an interruption of amnesia and the freedom to hope for a transformation of apathy to exploration, silence to symbolization, and fatalism to regeneration. To dig for unmarked graves is an act of faith in the potential of ritual and imagination to heal communities, a vision of resurrection through relatedness here and now.

1. Patricio Guzmán, *The Pinochet Case* (*Le cas Pinochet*) [2001], dir. Patricio Guzmán (First Run/Icarus Films, 2002); Lee Hirsch, *Amandla! A Revolution in Four-Part Harmony* [2002], dir. Lee Hirsch (Artisan Home Entertainment, 2003); Patricia Flynn and Mary Jo McConahay, *Discovering Dominga: A Survivor's Story* [2003], dir. Patricia Flynn (Berkeley Media, 2002).

2. Peter Shabad, "The Most Intimate of Creations: Symptoms as Memorials to One's Lonely Suffering," in *Symbolic Loss: The Ambiguity of Mourning and Memory at Century's End*, ed. Peter Homans (Charlottesville: University Press of Virginia, 2000), 200.

3. Kai Erikson, *A New Species of Trouble: The Human Experience of Modern Disasters* (New York: W.W. Norton, 1994), 233.

4. Elizabeth Jelin and Susana G. Kaufman, "Layers of Memories: Twenty Years after in Argentina," in *The Politics of War Memory and Commemoration*, ed. T. G. Ashplant, Graham Dawson, and Michael Roper (London/New York: Routledge, 2000), 106.

5. Idelber Avelar, *The Untimely Present: Postdictatorial Latin American Fiction and the Task of Mourning* (Durham, NC: Duke University Press, 1999), 8–10.

6. Mary Watkins and Helene Shulman, *Toward Psychologies of Liberation* (New York: Palgrave Macmillan, 2008).

. . .

A piece of paper held in the hand can evoke homelessness. When the Allied Forces liberated the concentrations camps, they handed out small cards to those of us who were still living. Not everyone got one. There was so much chaos. But I did. "Not a Pass" was printed on one side and on the other, "Keep this card at all times to assist your safe return home." Even today, whenever I see this card, I feel homeless. . . . The card was given from care and concern for us. But the contrast between reality and those words, which suggested we might get home soon, was too great. There were no homes to go back to any longer.

(Lenke Rothman, from "Not a Pass"
[translated by Susan Griffin])

. . .

PEACE

Spojmai Zariab (translated by Susan Griffin)

Countless wars, small and large, have disrupted the twentieth century even if, for me, no war is small. The two world wars plunged the whole planet into fire and blood, but throughout the century many other wars have inflamed and bloodied all kinds of countries. Afghanistan, Algeria, Israel, Palestine, Iran and Iraq, Yugoslavia, Cambodia, Laos, Vietnam, Central America, Africa—Oh, how long this list is!

And in all these countries, for how many disasters have we become impotent witnesses? War crimes, forced exile, hostages, rape, torture have been currency, leaving effects which in many cases last forever. In most of these countries, for a long time peace has been reduced to the state of an impossible dream. Why? What should the world and its inhabitants do that they are not doing now? What should we stop doing? These are sad questions, and the answers are even more so, but aren't the questions really the answers after all?

The child asks his mother, "Mama, what is it? Peace?"

An iron bird buzzes, and before the child's question even reaches the ears of his mother, a loud ringing follows, and then an explosion tears through the air. Consequently, the mother, shocked by the buzz of the metal bird, does not hear the question.

Almost crying now, the child repeats, "Mama, what is it, peace?"

The mother is unable to hide her trembling, and while she searches for an answer, some explanation, she shoots an anxious look out the window. Destroyed houses in the midst of burning, dead trees, charred, fill her view. A jumble of words crashes through her head. She endeavors in vain to call up and forge an explanation that the spirit of her child, who has grown up in war, can understand.

He is always there waiting for an answer, his eyes riveted on the dried-up lips of his mother. She, all the time racking her brain, thinks of the appearance of the town, which has changed so much. She realizes that most of the houses look like prisons, the gardens like cemeteries. The iron bird is always buzzing in the sky. The kid, trembling at each passage, grasping the hem of his terrorized mother's dress, huddles against her and, in the rare moment of silence, repeats with insistence, "Mama, what is peace?" pleading again and again in a desperate search for an answer.

During a brief silence between the sounds of the mechanical bird, memories from a long time ago come back to her. A quiet village in a halo of greenery. She wants with all her heart to preserve the image in her mind and better yet to install it exactly so, perfectly intact, in her son's overwhelmed little head. But the spectacle that surrounds her—burned grass, trees without branches or leaves, blackening smoke which, rising to the sky and turning as if it wants to flee the earth—chases the image of the quiet green village from her and prevents her thus from articulating her answer.

She has the impression then that even memories cannot be saved: the jolt of each engine's buzz pulverizes them, blowing them into little pieces, preventing her from assembling them, from sitting for even an instant to review them tranquilly, eyes shut.

The kid is not resigned. He waits for an answer. Suddenly she has an idea. She composes herself to approach the cabinet. Like small starving animals, her feverish fingers leaf among the books. She looks for the dictionary. Thanks to it, she will be able to give her child the meaning he wants, the explanation for which she searches. But there it is: the dictionary is nothing more than a fragment now, among books burnt to a crisp.

The word *peace* has been consumed.

And a burning odor spreads into the room, into the village, through the whole continent. Her hands are shaking. The child who knows nothing of peace, who has never even tasted it, still waits for an answer. Perhaps he is still waiting now. And you, you don't have it either, do you? An answer?

. . .

SHANTIDEVA'S PRAYER
Buddhist Traditional Prayer (translated by the Dalai Lama)

May I become at all times, both now and forever
A protector of those without protection
A guide for those who have lost their way
A ship for those with oceans to cross
A bridge for those with rivers to cross
A sanctuary for those in danger
A lamp for those without light
A place of refuge for those who lack shelter
And a servant to all in need

For as long as space endures,
And for as long as living beings remain,
Until then may I, too, abide
To dispel the misery of the world.

. . .

WE ARE FIELDS BEFORE EACH OTHER
St. Thomas Aquinas

How is it they live for eons in such harmony—
the billions of stars—

when most men can barely go a minute
without declaring war in their mind against someone they know.

There are wars where no one marches with a flag,
though that does not keep casualties
from mounting.

Our hearts irrigate this earth.
We are fields before
each other.

How can we live in harmony?
First we need to
know

we are all madly in love
with the same
God.

CHAPTER 3

Denial, Dogma, and the Heroic Myth

Whoever goes out in search of knowledge is on the path of
God until they return.
—Muhammad

Remember what you have seen, because everything forgotten
returns to the circling winds.
—Navajo chant

We have put the subjects—denial, dogma, and the heroic myth—together
in this chapter because they are interconnected, both historically and
psychologically. Jointly these habits and assumptions shape and limit
consciousness, encouraging violence and often arguing that force is the
best or even the only possible response to conflict. Denial, a basic human
response that protects both body and mind from shocks too strong to
absorb, can be very powerful, as Joan Didion so beautifully describes,
overwhelming both reason and evidence. To deal with trauma, those
who have suffered trauma may construct an unrealistic sense of strength,
If at times this response is temporary, at other times this defense can lead
to the development of a false self, an inflexible personality that is brittle
and thus, paradoxically, fragile. Finally, the tendency to denial in the face
of fear is often exploited by those in power who deliberately give false
promises of invincibility.

Denial should not confused with bravery. In fact, though denial in the
form of shock allows the body to survive pain and loss temporarily, in
the long run denial undermines the ability to cope with unexpected tragedy and hardship, if not the crucial ability to respond appropriately to
real danger.

When denial is not just an individual response but a public position, whole societies can conspire in collective self-deception. The underside of this deception is an unexamined terror, one that may be expressed with irrational, sometimes cruel or unjust actions, such as the torture of detainees at the U.S. detention camps at Guantánamo, where for example one prisoner was chained by his hands and feet to the floor for over eighteen hours in a fetal position, denied food or water and left to defecate and urinate on himself.

Despite the costs, whether consciously or unconsciously, many societies and cultures propagate a false idea of heroism through images and stories of mythic heroes, who, like Rambo, are never afraid and cannot be defeated. These exaggerated notions of heroism are often passed on to our children, giving them a seductive and dangerously unrealistic idea of warfare. Though this mythology has been used by many leaders throughout history in the service of ambition or even greed, to claim that heroic myths cause organized violence would be far too simple. No single cause suffices to explain any act of terrorism. Poverty and lack of education must both be considered. But as Suba Chandra, deputy director at the Institute of Peace and Conflict Studies in New Delhi has pointed out, the men who committed so many murders in Mumbai were "not poor and illiterate." And if resentments over patterns of injustice, what Chandra calls "grievance real and imagined," should also be added to the causes of terrorism, before they become lethal, these grievances must be shaped by ideologies that name and blame an enemy.

Denial and the heroic myth work together as essential ingredients of dogmatisms that simultaneously proffer rigid, unrealistic views along with the motivation and *modus operandi* for violence. Under the spell of dogma, men and women often find themselves committing acts of violence that otherwise they would consider immoral and criminal.

Dogma comes in many forms. It is easy to see the fanaticism in certain fundamentalist religions, but secular governments can be equally dogmatic, holding onto ideas and views of reality despite all evidence to the contrary. The rigidity of dogma betrays the denial of a profound aspect of human vulnerability: uncertainty. While the assertion of an exclusive claim on truth may be aimed toward the dominance of consciousness alone, such a posture can also lead to violence. Because unbelievers pose a threat to certainty, those who do not agree with fundamentalist precepts are often perceived as enemies.

Not just the capacity for independent thought but also the authentic self become the first casualties of such ideologies. Rigid systems of thought require adherents to relinquish the human capacity to think and perceive independently. In the service of dogma, even individual emotional intelligence must be sacrificed to authority, including compassion, an intuitive sense of right and wrong, or even, as in the case of suicide bombers, the will to live.

This process must also include the psychological process of projection. Doubts and fears that arise will be projected onto nonbelievers, critics, and perceived enemies. These habits of mind, which create a continuing cycle of destruction, must be transformed if the problem of terrorism is to be met in any lasting way.

This chapter also includes a portrait of a different kind of courage, the courage to step out of a cycle of violence, and it ends with prayers that urge the acceptance of vulnerability as a fact of life.

Susan Griffin

· · ·

HOW TO CURE A FANATIC
Amos Oz
FROM: *How to Cure a Fanatic*

So, how do you cure a fanatic? To chase a bunch of fanatics through the mountains of Afghanistan is one thing. To struggle against fanaticism is another one. I'm afraid I don't have any particular ideas on how to catch the fanatic in the mountains, but I do have one or two thoughts about the nature of fanaticism and the way, if not to cure it, then at least to contain it. The attack on America on September 11 was not simply about poverty versus wealth. Poverty versus wealth is one of the world's most horrible problems, but we will misdiagnose such terrorist attacks if we simply think that this was an attack by the poor on the rich. It is not just about the "haves" and the "have-nots." If the case were as simple as that, you would rather expect the attack from Africa, the poorest, perhaps to be launched against Saudi Arabia and the Gulf, the oil-producing states, the richest. No, this is a battle between fanatics, who believe that the end, any end, justifies the means, and the rest of us, who believe that life is an end, not a means. It is a struggle between those who think that justice, whatever they would mean by the word, is more important than life, on the one hand, and those of us who think that life takes priority over many other values, convictions, or faiths. The present crisis in the world, in the

Middle East, in Israel/Palestine, is not about the values of Islam. It is not about the mentality of the Arabs, as some racists claim, not at all. It is about the ancient struggle between fanaticism and pragmatism. Between fanaticism and pluralism. Between fanaticism and tolerance. September 11 was not even about the question of whether America was good or bad, whether capitalism is ugly, or whether globalization should stop or not. This was about the typical fanatic claim: If I think something is bad, I kill it along with its neighbors.

Fanaticism is older that Islam, older than Christianity, older than Judaism, older than any state or government, or political system, older than any ideology or faith in the world. Fanaticism is unfortunately an ever-present component of human nature, an evil gene, if you like. People who blow up abortion clinics in America, people who burn mosques and synagogues in Europe, differ from bin Laden only in the scale but not in the nature of their crimes.

My own childhood in Jerusalem rendered me an expert in comparative fanaticism. Jerusalem of my childhood, back in the 1940s, was full of self-proclaimed prophets, redeemers, and messiahs. Even today, every other Jerusalemite has his or her personal formula for instant salvation. Everyone says they came to Jerusalem, and I'm quoting a famous line from an old song, they came to Jerusalem to build it and to be built by it. In fact, some of them—Jews, Christians and Muslims, socialists, anarchists, world reformers—actually came to Jerusalem not so much to build it, not so much to be built by it, but rather to get crucified, or to crucify others, or both. There is an established mental disorder, a recognized mental illness known as the "Jerusalem syndrome": people come to Jerusalem, they inhale the wonderful lucid mountain air, and then they suddenly get up and set fire to a mosque or a church or a synagogue.

I confess, as a child in Jerusalem, I was myself a brainwashed little fanatic all the way. Self-righteous, chauvinistic, deaf and blind to any view that differed from the powerful Jewish Zionist narrative of the time. I was a stone-throwing kid, a Jewish Intifada kid. In fact, the first words I ever learned to say in English, except for "yes" and "no," were the words "British, go home!" which was what we kids used to shout as we were throwing stones at the British patrols in Jerusalem. . . .

I have called myself an expert on comparative fanaticism. This is no joke. If you ever hear of a school or university starting a department of comparative fanaticism, I am hereby applying for a teaching post. . . . Fanaticism is almost everywhere, and its quieter, more civilized forms are present all around us and perhaps inside of us as well. . . . I'm not saying, of course, that anyone who raises his or her voice against any-thing is a fanatic. I'm certainly not suggesting that anyone who has a strong opinion is a fanatic. I'm saying that the seed of fanaticism always lies in uncompromising self-righteousness, the plague of many centu-ries. Of course, there are degrees of evil. . . . Yet all fanatics have a spe-cial attraction, a special taste for kitsch. Very often the fanatic can only count up to one, two is too big a figure for him or her. At the same time, you will find that very often fanatics are hopelessly sentimental: they often prefer feeling to thinking and have a particular fascination with their own death. They despise this world and feel eager to trade it for "heaven." Their heaven, however, is usually conceived of as the everlast-ing happiness that occurs in the conclusion of bad movies.

Let me digress into a story. . . . A dear friend and colleague of mine, the wonderful Israeli novelist Sammy Michael, had once the experience that some of us writers have from time to time, of a very long intercity car drive with a chauffeur who was giving him the usual lecture on how ur-gent it is for us Jews to kill all the Arabs. And Sammy listened to him, and rather than screaming, "What a terrible man you are. Are you a Nazi, are you a fascist?" he decided to deal with it differently. He asked the chauf-feur, "And who do you think should kill the Arabs?" The chauffeur said, "What do you mean? Us! The Israeli Jews! We must! There is no choice, just look at what they are doing to us every day!" "But who exactly do you think should carry out the job? The police? Or the army? Or maybe the fire brigade? Or the medical teams? Who should do the job?" The chauffeur scratched his head and said, "I think it should be fairly divided between every one of us, every one of us should kill some of them." Sammy Michael, still playing the game, said, "OK, suppose you are allo-cated a certain residential block of your hometown of Haifa and you knock on every door, or ring the doorbell asking, 'Excuse me, sir, or excuse me, madam, do you happen to be an Arab?' and if the answer is yes, you shoot them. Then you finish your block and you are about to go home, but just as you turn to go home," Sammy continued, "you hear some-where on the fourth floor in your block a baby crying. Would you go back and shoot this baby? Yes or no?" There was a moment of quiet and then the chauffeur said to Sammy Michael, "You know, you are a very cruel man." Now, this is a significant story because there is something in the nature of the fanatic that essentially is very sentimental and at the same time lacks imagination. And this sometimes gives me hope, albeit a very limited hope, that injecting some imagination into people may help cause the fanatic to feel uneasy. This . . . is not a quick cure, but it may help.

Conformity and uniformity, the urge to belong and the desire to make everyone else belong, may be the most widespread if not the most dangerous forms of fanaticism. . . . I have to add that very often the cult of personality, the idealization of political or religious leaders, the worship of glamorous individuals, may be another widespread form of fanaticism. The twentieth century seems to have excelled at both. Totalitarian regimes, deadly ideological aggressive chauvinism, violent forms of religious fundamentalism, on the one hand, and the universal idolization of a Madonna or a Maradona, on the other. . . .

The essence of fanaticism lies in the desire to force other people to change. The common inclination to improve your neighbor, mend your spouse, engineer your child, or straighten up your brother, rather than let them be. The fanatic is a most unselfish creature. The fanatic is a great altruist. Often the fanatic is more interested in you than in himself. He wants to save your soul, he wants to redeem you, he wants to liberate you from sin, from error, from smoking, from your faith or from your faithlessness, he wants to improve your eating habits, or to cure you of your drinking or voting habits. The fanatic cares a great deal for you; he is always falling on your neck because he truly loves you or else he is at your throat in case you prove to be unredeemable. . . . One way or another, the fanatic is more interested in you than in himself, for the very simple reason that the fanatic has very little self or no self at all.

Mr. bin Laden and his ilk do not just hate the West. It's not that simple. Rather, I think they want to save your souls; they want to liberate you, us, from our awful values, from materialism, from pluralism, from democracy, from freedom of speech, from women's liberation. . . . All these, the Islamic fundamentalists maintain, are very, very bad for your health. Bin Laden's immediate target may have been New York, or Madrid, but his goal was to turn moderate, pragmatic Muslims into "true" believers, into his kind of Muslim. Islam, in bin Laden's view, was weakened by "American values," and to defend Islam, you must not just hit the West and hit it hard, you must eventually convert the West. Peace will prevail only when the world is converted not to Islam, but to the most fundamentalist and fierce and rigid form of Islam. It will be good for you. Bin Laden essentially loves you; by his way of thinking September 11 was a labor of love. He did it for your own good, he wants to change you, he wants to redeem you.

Very often, these things begin in the family. Fanaticism begins at home. It begins precisely with the very common urge to change a beloved relative for his or her own good. It begins with the urge to sacrifice oneself for the sake of a dearly loved neighbor; it begins with the urge to tell a child of yours, "You must become like me not like your mother," or "You must become like me not like your father," or "Please, become something very different from both your parents." Or, among married couples, "You have to change, you have to see things my way or else this marriage is not going to work." Very often it begins with the urge to live your life through someone else's life. To give yourself up in order to facilitate the next person's fulfillment or the next generation's well-being. Self-sacrifice very often involves inflicting dreadful feelings of guilt upon the beneficiary, thus manipulating, even controlling, him or her.

Let us turn now to the gloomy role of fanatics and fanaticism in the conflict between Israel and Palestine, Israel and much of the Arab world. The Israeli-Palestinian clash is essentially not a civil war between two segments of the same population, of the same culture. It is not an internal but an international conflict. Which is fortunate, as international conflicts are easier to resolve than internal ones—religious wars, class wars, value wars. I said easier, I did not say easy. Essentially the battle between Israeli Jews and Palestinian Arabs is not a religious war, although the fanatics on both sides are trying very hard to turn it into one. It is essentially no more than a territorial conflict over the painful question, "Whose land?" It is a painful conflict between right and right, between two very powerful, very convincing claims over the same small country. Not a religious war, not a war of cultures, not a disagreement between two traditions, but simply a real-estate dispute over whose house this is. And I believe that this can be resolved.

In a small way, in a cautious way, I do believe that imagination may serve as a partial and limited immunity to fanaticism. I believe that a person who can imagine what his or her ideas imply when it comes to the crying baby on the fourth floor, such a person may become a less complete fanatic, which is a slight improvement. I wish I could tell you at this point that literature is the answer because literature contains an antidote to fanaticism by injecting imagination into its readers. I wish I could simply prescribe: Read literature and you will be cured of your fanaticism. Unfortunately, it's not that simple. Unfortunately, many poems, many stories and dramas throughout history have been used to inflate hatred and nationalistic self-righteousness. Yet, there are certain works of literature that, I believe, can help up to a point. They cannot work miracles, but they can help. Shakespeare can help a great deal. Every extremism, every uncompromising crusade, every form of fanaticism in Shakespeare ends up either in a tragedy or in a comedy. The fanatic is never happier or more satisfied in the end; either he is dead or he becomes a joke. . . .

And if you promise to take what I'm about to say with a big pinch of salt, I can tell you that, in principle at least, I think I have invented the remedy for fanaticism. A sense of humor is a great cure. I have never once in my life seen a fanatic with a sense of humor, nor have I ever seen a person with a sense of humor become a fanatic, unless he or she has lost that sense of humor. Fanatics are often sarcastic. Some of them have a very pointed sense of sarcasm, but no humor. Humor contains the ability to laugh at ourselves. Humor is relativism, humor is the ability to see yourself as others may see you, humor is the capacity to realize that no matter how righteous you are and how terribly wronged you have been, there is a certain side to life that is always a big funny. . . .

Many years ago, when I was still a child, my very wise grandmother explained to me in very simple words the difference between Jew and Christian—not between Jew and Muslim, but between Jew and Christian: "You see," she said, "Christians believe that the Messiah was here once and he will certainly return one day. The Jews maintain that Messiah is yet to come. Over this," said my grandmother, "over this, there has been so much anger, persecution, bloodshed, hatred. . . . Why?" she said. "Why can't everyone simply wait and see? If the Messiah comes, saying 'Hello, it's nice to see you again,' the Jews will have to concede. If, on the other hand, the Messiah comes, saying, 'How do you do, it is very nice meeting you,' the entire Christian world will have to apologize to the Jews. Between now and then," said my grandmother, "just live and let live." . . .

I began by saying that fanaticism often begins at home. Let me conclude by saying that the antidote can also be found at home, virtually at your fingertips. No man is an island, said John Donne, but I humbly dare to add: No man and no woman is an island, but every one of us is a peninsula, half attached to the mainland, half facing the ocean—one half connected to the family and friends and culture and tradition and country and nation and sex and language and many other things, and the other half wanting to be left alone to face the ocean. I think we ought to be allowed to remain peninsulas. Every social and political system that turns each of us into a Donnean island and the rest of humankind into an enemy or a rival is a monster. But at the same time every social and political and ideological system that wants to turn each of us into no more than a molecule of the mainland is also a monstrosity. The condition of a peninsula is the proper human condition. That's what we are and that's what we deserve to remain. So, in a sense, in every house, in every family, in every human cognition, in every human connection, we actually have a relationship between a number of peninsulas, and we'd better remember this before we try to shape each other and turn each other around and make the next person turn our way while he or she actually needs to face the ocean for a while. And this is true of the social groups and of cultures and of civilizations and of nations and, yes, of Israelis and Palestinians. Not one of them is an island, and not one of them can completely merge with the other. These two peninsulas should be related and at the same time they should be left on their own. I know it is an unusual message in these days of violence and anger and revenge and fundamentalism and fanaticism and racism, all of which are loose in the Middle East and elsewhere. A sense of humor, the ability to imagine the other, the capacity to recognize the peninsular quality of every one of us may be at least a partial defense against the fanatic gene that we all contain.

· · ·

The anthropological data have demonstrated that the instinctivistic interpretation of human destructiveness is not tenable. While we find in all cultures that men defend themselves against vital threats by fighting (or by fleeing), destructiveness and cruelty are minimal in so many societies that these great differences could not be explained if we were dealing with an "innate" passion. Furthermore, the fact that the least-civilized societies like the hunter-gatherers and early agriculturalists show less destructiveness than the more-developed ones speaks against the idea that destructiveness is part of human "nature." Finally, the fact that destructiveness is not an isolated factor, but as we have seen, part of a syndrome, speaks against the instinctivistic thesis.

(Erich Fromm, from *The Anatomy of Human Destructiveness*)

· · ·

A RITUAL TO READ TO EACH OTHER
William Stafford

If you don't know the kind of person I am
and I don't know the kind of person you are
a pattern that others made may prevail in the world
and following the wrong god home we may miss our star.

For there is many a small betrayal in the mind,
a shrug that lets the fragile sequence break
sending with shouts the horrible errors of childhood
storming out to play through the broken dyke.

And as elephants parade holding each elephant's tail,
but if one wanders the circus won't find the park,
I call it cruel and maybe the root of all cruelty
to know what occurs but not recognize the fact.

And so I appeal to a voice, to something shadowy,
a remote important region in all who talk:
though we could fool each other, we should consider—
lest the parade of our mutual life get lost in the dark.

For it is important that awake people be awake,
or a breaking line may discourage them back to sleep;
the signals we give—yes or no, or maybe—
should be clear: the darkness around us is deep.

· · ·

TERROR COMES FULL CIRCLE
Martha Harrell

Before Tuesday, September 11, I'd had several spiritual awakenings, years as a Jungian analyst—even a personal vision of unity—yet I was still secretly afraid in the face of conflict that I'd go blank, pull back, and cover my fear. But the World Trade Center tragedy shattered my habit of splitting off and hiding behind cerebral intelligence. Perhaps some of you have also been jolted hard enough to turn to the intelligence of the heart. I hope so. The weapons unleashed by split consciousness are more likely to doom us than those loosed by splitting the atom. How am I so certain? Let me explain.

On that fateful morning, I was waiting for my first analysand, a suave New Yorker who always arrives precisely on time. That day, he rang the bell early, rushed in with the whites of his eyes showing, and said, "Do you have a television? Somebody said the World Trade Center is on fire!" When I turned it on, we saw the north tower burning. Then right in front of our eyes a plane flew into the middle of the south tower. We said in unison, "Oh my God, how could two planes go off course at the same time?"

I watched a plane curve into the tower and embed itself into the middle of the building. Yet something made me sure it had gone off course accidentally. We sat down in my office and carried on an analytic session in complete denial. When the session was over, we turned on the television set to see how quickly firemen had put out the fires. What we saw instead was implosion. As we watched the towers crumble one after the other, I also watched my denial implode into numbness. My insides were ice—yet I felt different: part of me watched myself go into shutdown mode.

The horror downtown had birthed a new presence alongside my numb state. Before then, I would shut down without realizing it and create an ego-willed reaction that hid my split-off condition. This time I was *aware* that I had no feeling at all.

I spent the next five days barely functioning. By Saturday night, after walking miles past thousands of victims' pictures, then circling the smoldering fire at ground zero, I came home and slept. At midnight I woke up trembling—awakened by the sight of Hiroshima's victims through the eyes of a bewildered five-year-old. The towers' fall shook loose the cataclysmic memory that had shut down part of my psyche years earlier.

My father was second in command under General MacArthur in post-war Japan. My mother, ten-month-old sister and I were the first family to arrive in occupied Japan. We lived in General Yamamoto's home—confiscated after the war. Setsiko, whose father had been killed at Hiroshima, cared for my sister and me. Obsessed with her father's death, she secretly took my sister and me many times from Tokyo to Hiroshima. Holding my hand and carrying my sister, she walked around looking for her father. For the first time in over fifty years, I remembered her pointing out to us—over and over—the disfigured victims of the nuclear blast.

The five-year-old me, overwhelmed by such suffering, buried my feelings in the rubble of that massive implosion. I then erected a personality on top of the rubble, unaware of the foundation it had been built on. I always knew I was afraid deep down inside, but I bulled ahead every day with my will-driven heroic ego.

When I awoke that Sunday, after reliving my walks through another ground zero, I felt like a different person. I felt all my weight for the first time. Fear went away. It might reappear in another crisis, but never the same way. I felt supported by a wordless yet very potent context of wholeness.

In reliving this childhood trauma, I now realize that Setsiko must have been grief stricken, obsessively walking the streets with us in tow looking for her father. Or perhaps she was drawn like I was to the slaughter of innocents. Before 9/11 I'd always hated her, the evil witch who'd punished me for what our country had done to her family. I laid many of my psychological ills at her feet.

Working through this trauma, holding on to a place I call the "continuity of consciousness," Setsiko became human. I understood she was not just trying to destroy me. Crazed with grief, she haunted the streets of Hiroshima to find some connection to her father. Understanding her pain, I could feel and come to grips with my own.

If Setsiko and I were to meet today, I hope there'd be a resonance between us that would lift us out of enmity into unity. We could retire our hero armor and live in the same world of vulnerability. We might make room for tenderness and love. Consciousness, free from conditioned reactions, has an evolved wisdom that can lead us toward unity instead of a quagmire of conflicting positions.

In today's world, there is no longer a place for the heroic consciousness of World War II, when we seemed to be the good guys fighting a clear enemy. Today, the lines are not clear, there is ambiguity, an enemy who is barely visible.

Subject and object can no longer be separate. We are called to free ourselves from the oscillating opposites of attack and counterattack. Since they endlessly wrestle on the same plane, opposites don't allow us to evolve beyond a standoff. We must develop an innate capacity to tolerate two-ness or duality. By holding contradictory feelings and impulses within ourselves, we might then expand to contain the ambiguity of the world.

Evil is a false oneness. Those who perpetrate evil reject anything that is not a part of *their* oneness, anything that would crack the belief that they are the one. Good and evil are forever split in this belief system. It becomes an endless "us against them" mind-set. To work for good, we must tremble in the face of this reality. When we see the lopsided, short-cut of evil arising, we must stop it, firmly, but without hate. Because we understand that it is born from the incapacity to tolerate diversity in the world around us.

David Bohm, professor of physics at the University of London, is leading science down the same path each individual psyche has to walk. He offers a radical departure from once prevailing views of reality. He speaks of coherence in large systems and a vast interconnectedness in the universe. Eventually this crystallizes into what he calls the "implicate order": an underlying order, not directly knowable, but constituting the ground of all being. This order fills the universe and travels in waves throughout all existence. Matter is the organization and solidification of these waves into information. It is somewhat stable; it is particle, but it is also wave, always related to the implicate. Bohm calls the unfolding and enfolding movement of the whole, "holomovement," an invisible movement, which produces all forms in the universe. These forms he calls the "explicate order"—what we experience as rocks, trees, feelings, human consciousness.

To Bohm, instead of starting with parts and showing how they work together—the Cartesian order—we can choose to start with the whole. His concept of "unbroken wholeness" postulates that at the most fundamental level all things, including space, time, and matter, are forms of "that which is."

Jung speaks of this paradox another way. He said both poles of a polarity exist in a complementary, rather than a conflictual relationship. He recognized the basic fact that life on our planet presents itself in opposites, which are paradoxically both true at the same time. For those interested in resolving conflict, isn't it good news that the opposing sides of a conflict are made out of the same stuff? Conflicts are two that have dropped out of the one; in their essence, therefore, they must be compatible.

Jung also recognized that the male-female polarity is the fundamental model for all other polarities—heat and cold, day and night, life and death, joy and sorrow. When we base our underlying assumption on coupling, rather than conflict and competition, we experience life more fully. For many ancients, creation begins when the primordial couple differentiates into mother and father. The complexity, the synergistic nature of the process is built right into the system from the beginning. The paradox is that these two fall out of a state of oneness and differentiate into twoness, which is but a prelude to their eventual union. The notion that separation is a necessary prelude to union offers a rationale for massive amounts of patience from diplomats mediating conflict!

The cosmic principles that fertilize and balance each other are the creative principles that sustain life. When anyone takes a one-sided position, he or she creates a false whole that becomes sterile and can't support life. Those so possessed do horrific things, like crashing a planeload of people into a building and cremating thousands more. Or bombing a country of broken people into annihilation to take revenge on the monstrous rulers who enslaved them . . . starting another cycle of war's dualistic delusion.

Centuries ago, the sages imagined an alternative: saying the aim of existence is self-knowledge. Such a search is necessary for the development of an individual, and this development cannot take place without a relationship between opposites. In their realization that male and female are complementary rather than contradictory entities, the alchemists anticipated the discoveries of Jung. Like his predecessors, he was concerned about the bisexual nature of the human being and the fact that the individual tends to be unaware of or repress its bisexual nature. Jung's alchemical psychology, with its anima and animus, aims to bring this shattered reality back to our consciousness in order to remind us that we are ultimately one and not two. The Jungian term for such a process is individuation. In the course of individuation, a person acquires self-knowledge and becomes aware of his androgynous nature. With such awareness, one can heal perpetually recurring splits of personality. Individuation is thus the modern term for the desire to find what the alchemists call the "Aurea Apprehensio," or the Golden Awareness. This is the presence I began to experience as a result of my shattering after 9/11.

On September 11, our denial of being a player in a dueling world imploded. We as a country and me as an individual had long hidden in a one-sided heroic consciousness. Because of our indifference to any suffering but our own, we were inevitably set up to fall. Now we have been drawn into the tectonic shifts of these cosmic forces—maybe pushing us toward a new way of being. If coupling is unity's verb, isn't relationship unity's noun? And how can opposites live in relationship?

This is perhaps the biggest question before us, what vessel is up to the task of holding without shattering? Certainly not the mind, where causality reigns. Only the heart is strong enough, vast enough, and fluid enough to contain a state referred to in the new physics as quantum coherence—the chaotic state of creative flux. The heart can support a realignment of psyche right down to the cellular matrix. In our heart, we can bring into relationship the thoughts that fly under the radar of our consciousness. We can learn to clear away those dark thoughts that wind themselves through our hearts and, like the imprint of a long forgotten riverbed, will always direct the river's flow in times of stress into outdated patterns.

The challenge is getting there. Science is telling us that within nature is a mysterious unity, yet our very separateness is what creates our ability to live and perceive. What a strange tangle life is. A type of exploration outside the ego's ability is the only way to see the situation in which it sits. If there is no Archimedean point to give us our bearings, ego consciousness remains too small to apprehend wholeness.

An intelligence of the heart brings these paradoxical elements together in a living matrix, an unbroken whole. We can stand in the middle of that mystery and not shatter.

The heart lights up when we become aware of both the darkness in our disowned thoughts and the warmth of hope. Here we look past the lesser abyss of disappointment and abandonment (the personal), embrace the greater abyss of emptiness (the impersonal), and don't shatter into a million pieces. Here we participate in our own as well as the healing of the world. Here we don't have to be perfect; we just have to begin the journey.

Many roads lead to the Rome of unity inside us. Most have three elements: symbol and image of ancient myths in a variety of sacred texts; the shared experience of living communities; and the direct experience of divine unity in daily contemplative practices such as prayer and meditation. Each path offers its devotees a methodology to enter this continuity of consciousness, a shimmering state of Golden Awareness and unity—such as the one that softened the capsule of denial around my childhood visits to the killing field of Hiroshima. Only if our heart can welcome paradox—the parallel glories of opposites—can we know that joy's defiance of sorrow is real.

. . .

HE WOULD NEED SOME SHOES
Joan Didion

It was deep into the summer, some months after the night when I needed to be alone so that he could come back, before I recognized that through the winter and spring there had been occasions on which I was incapable of thinking rationally. I was thinking as small children think, as if my thoughts or wishes had the power to reverse the narrative, change the outcome. In my case this disordered thinking had been covert, noticed I think by no one else, hidden even from me, but it had also been, in retrospect, both urgent and constant. In retrospect here had been signs, warning flags I should have noticed. There had been for example the matter of the obituaries. I could not read them. This continued from December 31, when the first obituaries appeared, until February 29, the night of the 2004 Academy Awards, when I saw a photograph of John in the Academy's "In Memoriam" montage. When I saw the photograph I realized for the first time why the obituaries had so disturbed me.

I had allowed other people to think he was dead.

I had allowed him to be buried alive.

Another such flag: there had come a point (late February, early March, after Quintana had left the hospital but before the funeral that had waited on her recovery) when it had occurred to me that I was supposed to give John's clothes away. Many people had mentioned the necessity for giving the clothes away, usually in the well-intentioned but (as it turns out) misguided form of offering to help me do this. I had resisted. I had no idea why. I myself remembered, after my father died, helping my mother separate his clothes into stacks for Goodwill and "better" stacks for the charity thrift shop where my sister-in-law Gloria volunteered. After my mother died Gloria and I and Quintana and Gloria and Jim's daughters had done the same with her clothes. It was part of what people did after death, part of the ritual, some kind of duty.

I began. I cleared a shelf on which John had stacked sweatshirts, T-shirts, the clothes he wore when we walked in Central Park in the early morning. We walked every morning. We did not always walk together because we liked different routes but we would keep each other's route in mind and intersect before we left the park. The clothes on this shelf were as familiar to me as my own. I closed my mind to this. I set aside certain things (a faded sweatshirt I particularly remembered him wearing, a Canyon Ranch T-shirt I had brought him from Arizona), but I put most of what was on this shelf into bags and took the bags across the street to St. James' Episcopal Church. Emboldened, I opened a closet and filled more bags: New Balance sneakers, all-weather shoes, Brooks Brothers shorts, bag after bag of socks. I took the bags to St. James'. One day a few weeks later I gathered up more bags and took them to John's office, where he had kept his clothes. I was not yet prepared to address the suits and shirts and jackets but I thought I could handle what remained of the shoes, a start.

I stopped at the door to the room.

I could not give away the rest of his shoes.

I stood there for a moment, then realized why: he would need shoes if he was to return.

The recognition of this thought by no means eradicated the thought.

I have still not tried to determine (say, by giving away the shoes) if the thought has lost its power.

. . .

Is it not for us to confess that in our civilized attitude towards death we are once more living psychologically beyond our means, and must reform and give truth its due? Would it not be better to give death the place in actuality and in our thoughts which properly belongs to it, and to yield a little more prominence to that unconscious attitude towards death which we have hitherto so carefully suppressed? This hardly seems indeed a greater achievement, but rather a backward step . . . but it has the merit of taking somewhat more into account the true state of affairs.

(Sigmund Freud, from "Thoughts for the Times on War and Death")

. . .

OUR CULTURE'S DIVIDED SOUL
Howard Teich

We live in a culture that divides us from each other and within our selves. The two primary modes of thinking that constitute human consciousness, one intuitive, sensual, and emotional, the other analytical, focused, and goal oriented, are complementary. Both modes, which have been called respectively, lunar and solar, work best in tandem, through an internal collaboration that creates balance in thought, perception, and emotion. Yet, in our divided culture, solar consciousness has become so dominant and the lunar so diminished, that we have lost this balance. We think without feeling and yet underneath our logical postures, we are driven by passions that we never examine.

This destructive habit of mind we have inherited shares a history with both terrorism and the war on terror. The events of September 11, 2001, set in motion the latest phase of an epic conflict that began thousands of years ago with the development of three religions: Judaism, Christianity, and Islam. All three of these religions grew out of cultures that originally worshipped a variety of gods and goddesses. But the move toward monotheism, a defining characteristic of all these traditions today, necessitated the repression of many deities, along with the various values they represented; a diverse pantheon of deities, both solar and lunar, was replaced by a single solar god with one set of values.

At first glance this theological history may appear irrelevant to American actions. While Osama bin Laden and his followers are describing the war on terrorism as a war against infidels and calling their own acts of violence a "holy war," we deny that we are conducting a religious war. We pride ourselves on the separation of church and state.

However, though it is undeniable, on a conscious level, that the stated motivations of our efforts against terrorism are secular, concealed within this rhetoric, less secular motivations can be detected, even in the official language of the government. In remarks made after the bombing of the World Trade Center, President Bush used the words "evil" and "crusade" to describe, respectively, terrorist acts and our response. Although the Bush government had been at pains to distinguish between the Islamic religion and terrorism, the use of the word "evil" has continued to work at cross purposes to this policy, unconsciously expressing a covertly religious judgment.

"Evil" has powerful religious connotations. When Bush referred to bin Laden as "the evil one" he was invoking a centuries-old tradition of religious dualism, which divides the world into good and evil, those who serve God and those who serve Satan. It is not irrelevant here that Bush is a proclaimed born-again Christian. His language tells us that just as he demonizes our opponents he also identifies America with a monotheistic God.

Many organized religions have been plagued by the tendency to believe that other religions are evil, an attitude exaggerated in fundamentalist sects. Ideas of good and evil are often used to deny internal conflict. When we characterize the other as "evil," most often the other is an unconscious symbol for an aspect of ourselves that we deny. The same process can and does occur in political discourse within and between nations. If a quality such as aggressiveness is denied as a trait of our nation, this quality will be projected onto the behavior of other groups or nations.

Though what bin Laden encouraged and possibly planned himself was destructive and immoral, the use of the word evil to describe him prevents us from seeing or acknowledging our own aggressive behavior. The denial that accompanies projection undermines our capacity for self-reflection and understanding. We were shocked and horrified by bin Laden's attack on innocent civilians, and yet within a few weeks we began bombing raids ourselves that led to many innocent civilian deaths. Instead of acknowledging the ethical consequences of our actions, we describe these deaths as "collateral damage."

The religiosity of our rhetoric, which paradoxically allows us to deny our own ethical violations, has other implications too. The monotheistic tradition we share contributes to violence in many ways. With the assertion that there is only one god came the corollary beliefs that there is only one religion, one truth, and one perspective that are valid. Such beliefs will of necessity give rise to seemingly insolvable conflicts.

A culture's unresolved issues are often formed in the early period of its evolution. All three religions in the current conflict claim the same mythological father: Abraham, and ironically, they share many sacred texts and stories. Yet, though sharing a mythological past could create a bond between these religions, while both Judaism and Islam claim the agreement between Abraham and God as the foundation for their religious beliefs, both religions also claim exclusive possession of a covenant with God. In the Judeo-Christian tradition, Abraham's first son, Ishmael, represents the alienated stranger, often a symbol for heresy.

He is the outsider who has no place in the tradition. To the Muslims, on the other hand, Isaac is an oppressive foreigner who must be rejected.

Regardless of competing claims, all three religions share in Abraham a figure, who, as we shall see, represents a set of desires and designs that in preceding cultures have been connected to gods and goddesses associated with the sun, and in turn with the solar aspect of human consciousness.

In the pantheons that once existed in religions throughout the world, a range of solar deities can almost always be found whose attributes reflect a particular set of human characteristics allied with power—strength, protectiveness, and power—with the ability to assert control, and correspondingly, the clarity of mind that comes from analytical thought.

But in these pantheons, these deities were matched and balanced by another group associated with the moon, consisting of both gods and goddesses, whose attributes reflect the lunar side of consciousness. This aspect of the human psyche contains the attributes that enable cooperation and relationship, including emotional and sensual awareness and empathy.

You can find remnants of both lunar and solar deities in the story of Abraham. Abraham stands at the beginning of Judaic and hence also Christian history. According to the Old Testament Bible, commanded by Yahweh, this prophet was given a special destiny: he was to become the father of Israel, and as part of this divine bequest, his descendants were to possess the land of Canaan (or Israel) as their own. But according to the same tale, Abraham is also the father of another people. As the story goes, because Abraham's wife Sarah was not able to bear him children, she told him to sleep with her Egyptian maidservant Hagar so they would build a family through her. Thus, Abraham fathered the child Ishmael with Hagar.

Yet years later, according to the same myth, claimed as a story of origin by both the nation of Israel and Islam, the Lord appeared to Abraham declaring a covenant between Abraham and his descendants and promising too that he would bless Sarah, now ninety, with a son. Following Isaac's birth, Sarah, who was jealous of Hagar's son Ishmael, asked Abraham to banish him.

As with any myth, this story has more than one level of meaning. Along with the birth of an intimate connection to one jealous god, the narrative also depicts the cultural and psychological transformations that were necessary in order to fulfill the aspirations toward Empire held by both cultures. A shift from the tribal and hence more lunar consciousness of the old way of life to the more solar individual consciousness that exists within a competitive social order was occurring.

Abraham's covenant elevates both individual rights and private property above the collective good. Moreover, it was also crucial to this shift, as a single god was claimed as the only god, that the human personality be distanced from nature. Now a god with human features was placed above all of natural existence, including the sun and the moon. The descendants of Abraham were hence alienated from the earth. As inheritors of this new cosmology, we no longer see ourselves as part of a whole but instead strive to achieve mastery over nature and each other.

Though this way of thinking is deeply ingrained in our shared cultural consciousness, centuries before the story of Abraham was told, the peoples of this area, including the Hebrews, worshipped a range of gods and goddesses who represented diverse aspects of nature. Indeed, Abraham's new god Yahweh evolved from just one god in the larger pantheon, a deity known as El, who was a sun god. Though according to the bible Abraham's god was no longer called a sun god, his ascendance was a precursor to the adoption of a set of exclusively solar values, which when separated from lunar values became exaggerated and disconnected from the larger web of existence.

Solar values are not in themselves destructive. But whether in service to a private life or a society, solar values require balance from lunar values. To fulfill any goal, the ability to connect with others or a larger web of existence is crucial. Moreover, the rejected lunar aspect of consciousness does not disappear but is repressed, only to reappear as a negative projection onto other peoples. In a historical context between nations and peoples, demonization is often reciprocal. While Islam is often demonized from a Judeo-Christian perspective, Westerners, Jews, and Christians have been demonized for decades by extreme Muslim sects.

The story of Islam, like that of Judaism, began after Sarah gave birth to Isaac, when instead of supporting and loving both Isaac and Ishmael, Abraham and Sarah banished Ishmael to the wilderness. Muhammad took the same story as the cornerstone of the Muslim religion. According to myth, Islam was founded in the seventh century C.E. when Muhammad, who was then a wealthy merchant, had the first of a series of visions that eventually became the Qu'ran.

Muhammad's new religion was to move in two directions at once, both to bolster communal values and to assert a monotheism that worked to support the values of private property. Muhammad's tribe worshiped among other gods al-Lah (which means "the God"), who many historians believe was the same god who was earlier called El and later Yahweh. But most significant here is that, as with the Hebrew god "El," Allah was also a solar god who came to dominate the other gods and goddesses in Muhammad's teachings. Worshipping one god brought a focal point not only to Muhammad's tribe, the Quraysh, but also a focus, which would settle violent quarrels between various tribes and help to unify them. And as with the Hebrews, economic change provided a motive for this unification.

Now while Islam claimed the Muslim religion as the only authentic revelation of God, a drive to accumulate new territories and to improve the tribes' economic condition began. Eventually, as with Judaism and later Christianity, both goals were pursued through military incursions that imposed Muslim beliefs by violence and domination.

With the advent of monotheism and private property, among both Hebrews and Muslims individualism as we know it arose. Now each person was imagined as having an individual fate, a concept crucial to the modern ego. The psychological transformation from group to individual consciousness constituted a significant shift. Before this time, each fate was understood only as part of a larger story, the history of a tribe or a people and belonging to a larger web of connections.

Thus, with the shift from polytheism to monotheism, the lunar vision of reality, a way of knowing bound to community and the earthly experience of life, one that valued relatedness and sensual knowledge, was sacrificed. This vision of the universe as an organic and sacred whole was replaced by fragmentation; now humanity was opposed to nature, intellect to emotion, spirit to matter; tribe was set against tribe, whole peoples set in conflict.

Over the next thousand years as the solar side of the psyche became more and more dominant, the lunar side became a secondary phenomenon, habitually projected by these three religions, Judaism, Islam, and Christianity, onto those described as "other," who were often demonized. Today, our image of terrorists evokes this shadow land of lunar consciousness.

Yet to say that Western culture projects the lunar onto Ishmael is not to imply that terrorists from the Middle East are lunar. Despite the fact that we project the lunar onto them, terrorist organizations are as solar-dominated, if not more so, as the American and European governments that battle them. In 1998, in a clear example of solar thinking, Osama bin Laden declared that his *jihad* was a "holy war" against the United States because the "crimes and sins committed by the Americans are a clear declaration of war on God, his messenger and Muslims."

The word *jihad,* which means "striving," appears frequently in the Qu'ran in the phrase "striving in the path of God." In one interpretation of the phrase it signifies an internal struggle for enlightenment, an interpretation that would signify the more lunar process of reflection. But the same phrase has been used both in the past and recently by fundamentalists to mean armed struggle for the advancement of Muslim power. It was appropriated by bin Laden, who erased reflective consciousness from the meaning of *jihad*.

The same process of excising lunar consciousness has occurred in the West. To banish Ishmael is to banish our sense of collective identity and relationship to the whole of existence.

The rejection of lunar values in Western traditions however is not confined to the story of Abraham. Though Christianity began with a revival of lunar values, lunar consciousness was soon diminished in this religion, too. Despite the fact that Christ is known as the Prince of Peace, Christianity also sacrificed the clear lunar teachings of Christ for another set of values. A predisposition to war gained early ascendancy within Christianity during the reign of the Roman emperor Constantine after his conversion in 312 C.E. Because he attributed a major military victory to the power of Christ, he committed himself to the Christian faith. As the official religion of an empire, rather than advocating peace, Christianity adapted itself to the ambitions of empire, a task made easier by the dualism between spirit and matter, emotion and intellect, solar and lunar values. Our culture has been deeply imprinted with these histories. But we do not have to repeat them. If we reclaim our lunar resources not only can we avoid self-destruction, but we will be better able to address the very real threat that terrorists pose today.

From an exclusive solar perspective we are not able to distinguish between defense and aggression, nor can we explore the full range of diplomatic solutions. Through the prominence of military values and the idealization of the warrior, which takes place during warfare, violence increases solar aggression. To resolve this conflict in other than militaristic ways will require all of us to cultivate the lunar values of compassion and relationship as part of our response to terrorism.

Yet as radical as this shift may seem, all lunar modes of consciousness, including the emotional understanding and empathy needed for diplomacy, belong to a primal way of knowing and being that developed thousands of years ago as survival skills, long before language and other cognitive abilities had fully evolved.

This knowledge still exists in us, even if only on a cellular level. Lacking access to the lunar we are like plants without roots into the earth that shrivel up. It is not just our current crisis that hangs in the balance. We need to reclaim the full dimensionality of being if we are ever to have lasting peace, both inner and outer, and live harmoniously with the earth that sustains us.

• • •

The first thing we have to do with heroism is to lay bare its underside, show what gives human heroics its specific nature and impetus. Here we introduce directly one of the great rediscoveries of modern thought: that of all things that move man, one of the principal ones is his terror of death. After Darwin the problem of death as an evolutionary one came to the fore, and many thinkers immediately saw that it was a major psychological problem for man. They also very quickly saw what real heroism was about, as Shaler wrote just at the turn of the century: heroism is first and foremost a reflex of the terror of death. We admire most the courage to face death; we give such valor our highest and most constant adoration; it moves us deeply in our hearts because we have doubts about how brave we ourselves would be. When we see a man bravely facing his own extinction we rehearse the greatest victory we can imagine. And so the hero has been the center of human honor and acclaim since probably the beginning of specifically human evolution. But even before that our primate ancestors deferred to others who were extrapowerful and courageous and ignored those who were cowardly. Man has elevated animal courage into a cult.

(Ernest Becker, from *The Denial of Death*)

• • •

THE VERBAL WEAPON OF MASS DESTRUCTION
Robert H. Ressler

In his 2002 State of the Union message, the President of the United States identified three nations of the world as members of an "axis of evil." The way that phrase entered the public realm is revealing. A presidential speechwriter revealed in a memoir that the famous phrase "axis of evil" was originally proposed to President Bush as "axis of hatred," before more senior officials in the administration changed the phrase to "axis of evil" to make it sound more "theological."[1]

After the speech, the word *evil* was used abundantly by the Bush administration, some thought extravagantly and demagogically, in the period leading up to and following the invasion of Iraq in 2003. An added irony was hard to avoid. Iraq is the modern name for a part of ancient Mesopotamia, and the Tigris and Euphrates rivers that flow through it are said to have watered the Garden of Eden. Was the word *evil* chosen for its power to evoke in the minds of a predominantly Christian electorate, especially his fundamentalist Christian political base, an image of the threat of evil in paradise?

Norman Mailer wrote that this President used the word "as if it were a button he could push to increase his power."[2] The word *evil* has been used as an instrument of power for ages in the persecution of heretics, the repression of dissent, propaganda for war, and the demonization of enemies. The word certainly has magic in it. Like the shaman, who could point a bone at someone in the tribe and thereby cause their death in a matter of days, calling an enemy "evil" today can unleash upon them all the indiscriminate violence and lethality in the modern military or terrorist arsenal.

The word *evil* directs a blinding moral spotlight on its target, obliterating shades of gray, casting the wider context into darkness, throwing the complexities of history, the likelihood of unintended consequences, and the suffering of innocents into the shadows. The spotlight of evil also helps make the one who points it invisible to the moral scrutiny of others. Evil represents, after all, the metaphysical force that would presume to defeat the will of God. The one who points the word appears to do so on God's behalf.

The word's power is embedded in our consciousness. Most of us first heard it as children, when we had scant appreciation for its full semantic, philosophical, or political weight and no appreciation for the history of its use, but only a sense of its meaning as an opposite to good. More likely than not, this first exposure to the phrase "good and evil" occurred in connection with the "tree of the knowledge of good and evil," a phrase that appears in English translations of the story of Adam and Eve in the Bible, the account of our beginnings made sacred by time and religious teaching. This is how evil gets its reputation as a primordial force as fundamental as a force of nature or, depending on one's religious philosophy, as fundamental as God.

In fact, evil has been variously defined in different ages, by different cultures, and by different philosophers, theologians, and church officials. It entered the Western mind through a process of assimilation from other cultures in the ancient Near East and was installed as a cornerstone of Christian religious doctrine through a political process. In short, it is a human construct as variable in different minds and different cultures as the concept of the divine itself.[3] But centuries of Christian sermons and religious art and literature, as well as a flood of popular derivatives that have saturated mass culture, all have taught us to envision evil's menacing presence as a fundamentally corrupting force present from the time of our beginnings in the Garden of Eden.

Yet the biblical story of our creation has been misunderstood. Careful attention to the original text and to the culture that produced the Eden story has led me, along with many scholars, to some different conclusions. Astonishing as it may seem, the word *evil* does not appear in the original name of the tree of knowledge. The word *evil*—indeed the concept of evil—never appeared *anywhere* in the original story of the Garden of Eden.

Regarding Evil: The Cross the Tree Has Borne

The devil can cite scripture for his purpose.

—William Shakespeare

The single most crucial source of misunderstanding concerning the meaning of the Eden story is found in the terrifying word *evil*, the word that has haunted the story for centuries and blinded us to its original meaning.

The word *evil* is a translation of the Hebrew word *ra*, which occurs more than 600 times in the Hebrew Bible with a wide range of different meanings in different contexts and eras of usage. In the King James Version, the translators used more than twenty English words for *ra*, including *bad, wickedness, mischief, ill, naught,* and *sore.* In the vast majority of instances, over 400 times, they translated *ra* as *evil.* In the Eden story, where it occurs four times, it is translated as *evil* in each instance. In the more recently produced and widely used Revised Standard Version, quoted below, the same holds true:

And out of the ground the Lord God made to grow
every tree that is pleasant to the sight and good for food,
the tree of life also in the midst of the garden,
and the tree of the knowledge of good and evil. (Genesis 2:9)

Evil is the word given for *ra* in most other English translations of the Eden story as well, particularly those intended for Christian use. But a more faithful sense of its meaning in the Eden story would simply be *bad*. The difference is not just a matter of style or degree, but of kind, and it's crucial.

The concept of evil has a long and varied history in later biblical and post-biblical writings, both Jewish and Christian, as well as in other cultures of the ancient Near East. But the use of the word *evil* in translations of the Eden story is misplaced and anachronistic. It refers to a Christian doctrinal interpretation that was not formulated until long after the birth of Jesus, as much as a thousand years after the Eden story was written, and was then applied retroactively to the Hebrew name of the tree in the center of the garden.

But it wasn't unusual for Christian translators throughout history and even in modern times to take liberties with the Hebrew text. David Rosenberg, former editor-in-chief of the Jewish Publication Society, wrote in 1990:

> Modern biblical scholarship arose in European universities, yet in religion departments from Geneva to Oxford, Jews were prohibited. The professors of Bible were of Christian belief or education. German scholars who developed the Documentary theories known as Higher Biblical Criticism were charmed by their Christian superiority into primitive misunderstandings of the Hebrew.[4]

Whether through ignorance of early Hebrew usage, or through religious and cultural cooptation of the text, *evil* was inserted into the Eden narrative where it didn't belong. Its appearance in English translations of the Eden narrative usually reflects the translator's retroactive application of Christian theology to the story without regard for the original Hebrew meaning or the Israelite culture at the time of its writing. When an English word for *ra* is considered for a nonsectarian or a Jewish translation, on the other hand, it is usually rendered as *bad*, not *evil*. This is so in Speiser's 1964 translation for the nonsectarian *Anchor Bible*.[5] The same holds true in the 1985 translation by the Jewish Publication Society,[6] as well as in more recent translations by David Rosenberg, Mary Phil Korsak, and Richard Elliott Friedman.[7]

So how then should we understand the meaning of *ra* when it appears in the Eden story? Social anthropologist Donald Taylor explains that in the early Hebrew of the period, "*Ra* meant primarily worthlessness or uselessness, and by extension it came to mean bad, ugly or even sad. . . . It meant simply bad as opposed to good."[8]

As the *Theological Lexicon of the Old Testament* states, the adjective *ra* "can be neutral, with no ethical accent . . . it need not state anything more than the fact that something seems inappropriate."[9] It goes on to give various non-metaphysical and non-ethical usages of *ra*, where, for example: land is [*ra*] infertile, water is [*ra*] unhealthy, and animals or fruits have defects and are [*ra*] inferior.

Evil had nothing to do with the tree of knowledge in the biblical story of Eden. And the doctrines of the Fall and Original Sin are nowhere to be found in the Hebrew Scriptures. The idea of a God-opposing metaphysical principle called *evil*, its application to the name of the tree, and its personification in a shape-shifting figure called Satan, who was said to appear in the story as the serpent, all are the additions of later theologians. The work of the artists and writers they influenced has permeated the culture and imagination of the Western world. But all these were imposed on the original story a thousand years or more after it was written.[10]

These additions, deeply embedded in every convolution of Western consciousness, have contributed not only to the modern distortion and misunderstanding of the story's original meaning, but to the concept of evil, which as it divides creation into holy and unholy, naming some as friends and others as enemies of the divine, sows the seeds of conflict and violence.

1. See Hendrik Hertzberg, "Axis Praxis," *The New Yorker*, 13 January 2003, 27; and David Frum, *The Right Man: The Surprise Presidency of George W. Bush* (New York: Random House, 2003), 238 ff.

2. Norman Mailer, "Only in America," *New York Review of Books*, 27 March 2003, 50.

3. See Elaine Pagels, *Adam, Eve, and the Serpent* (New York: Random House, 1988); Elaine Pagels, *The Origin of Satan* (New York: Random House, 1995); and David Parkin (Ed.), *The Anthropology of Evil* (New York: Basil Blackwell, 1985).

4. Harold Bloom and David Rosenberg, *The Book of J* (New York: Grove Weidenfeld, 1990), 327–328.

5. E. A. Speiser, *The Anchor Bible, Genesis: Introduction, Translation, and Notes* (New York: Doubleday, 1964).

6. Nahum M. Sarna, *Genesis: The Traditional Hebrew Text with New JPS Translation/Commentary by Nahum M. Sarna* (Philadelphia: The Jewish Publication Society, 1989).

7. Bloom and Rosenberg, *The Book of J*; Mary Phil Korsak, *At the Start: Genesis Made New* (New York: Doubleday, 1993); Richard Elliott Friedman, *The Hidden Book in the Bible* (San Francisco: HarperSanFrancisco, 1998).

8. Donald Taylor, "Theological Thoughts about Evil," in Parkin, *The Anthropology of Evil*, 27.

9. H. J. Stoebe, "*ra*: to be bad," in Ernst Jenni and Claus Westermann (Eds.) (Trans. Mark E. Biddle), *Theological Lexicon of the Old Testament, Vol. 3* (Peabody, MA: Hendrickson, 1997), 1250.

10. If not good and evil, what might the Eden story have been about? My research has persuaded me that it was women's understanding of their fertility and infertility, not good and evil that was central to the original Eden story. Eve's eating the fruit of "the tree of knowing, good and bad" symbolized women gaining an understanding of the difference between so-called "good knowing" (fertile sex acts) and so-called "bad knowing" (infertile sex acts). This understanding came from realizing that the vaginal deposit of male semen was essential for conception. Sharing this discovery of biological paternity with men then led to a sexual revolution, the institution of the monogamous patriarchal family, and a population increase. A growing population required people to relinquish foraging and light horticulture and begin to adopt grain agriculture. In my view, it was these events in prehistory and their adverse consequences for women, men, our relationships, and the environment, which were portrayed and lamented so poetically in the original story of Adam and Eve.

. . .

SPEECH OPPOSING THE POST–9/11 USE OF FORCE
PACT, SEPTEMBER 14, 2001
Barbara Lee

Mr. Speaker,

I rise today with a heavy heart, one that is filled with sorrow for the families and loved ones who were killed and injured in New York, Virginia, and Pennsylvania. Only the most foolish or the most callous would not understand the grief that has gripped the American people and millions around the world. This unspeakable attack on the United States has forced me to rely on my moral compass, my conscience, and my God for direction.

September 11 changed the world. Our deepest fears now haunt us. Yet I am convinced that military action will not prevent further acts of international terrorism against the United States.

I know that this use-of-force resolution will pass although we all know that the President can wage war even without this resolution. However difficult this vote may be, some of us must urge the use of restraint. There must be some of us who say, let's step back for a moment and think through the implications of our actions today—let us more fully understand their consequences. We are not dealing with a conventional war. We cannot respond in a conventional manner. I do not want to see this spiral out of control. This crisis involves issues of national security, foreign policy, public safety, intelligence gathering, economics, and murder. Our response must be equally multifaceted.

We must not rush to judgment. Far too many innocent people have already died. Our country is in mourning. If we rush to launch a counterattack, we run too great a risk that women, children, and other noncombatants will be caught in the crossfire.

Nor can we let our justified anger over these outrageous acts by vicious murderers inflame prejudice against all Arab Americans, Muslims, Southeast Asians, and any other people because of their race, religion, or ethnicity.

Finally, we must be careful not to embark on an open-ended war with neither an exit strategy nor a focused target. We cannot repeat past mistakes.

In 1964, Congress gave President Lyndon Johnson the power to "take all necessary measures" to repel attacks and prevent further aggression. In so doing, the House abandoned its own constitutional responsibilities and launched our country into years of undeclared war in Vietnam.

At that time, Senator Wayne Morse, one of two lonely votes against the Tonkin Gulf Resolution, declared, "I believe that history will record that we have made a grave mistake in subverting and circumventing the Constitution of the United States . . . I believe that within the next century, future generations will look with dismay and great disappointment upon a Congress which is now about to make such a historic mistake."

Senator Morse was correct, and I fear we make the same mistake today. And I fear the consequences. I have agonized over this vote. But I came to grips with it in the very painful yet beautiful memorial service today at the National Cathedral. As a member of the clergy so eloquently said, "As we act, let us not become the evil that we deplore."

· · ·

AGAINST CERTAINTY
Jane Hirshfield

There is something out in the dark that wants to correct us.
Each time I think "this," it answers "that."
Answers hard, in the heart-grammar's strictness.

If I then say "that," it too is taken away.

Between certainty and the real, an ancient enmity.
When the cat waits in the path-hedge,
no cell of her body is not waiting.
This is how she is able so completely to disappear.

I would like to enter the silence portion as she does.

To live amid the great vanishing as a cat must live,
one shadow fully at ease inside another.

. . .

ANOTHER KIND OF HEROISM

Susan Dominus

In some ways, the first 20 minutes were the hardest, because she couldn't judge how much worse it might get, or how quickly. Uli Derickson had been preparing to serve drinks to the passengers in first class not long after takeoff when two men barreled down the aisle of the plane, screaming in Arabic and waving around grenades. One put the muzzle of a gun to her head. "What do you want?" she shouted. "I am German. Maybe I can help you." Today, perhaps, there would be no conversation, only a paralyzed silence; but in 1985, hijackers had a history of at least making overtures toward negotiation. These men, Lebanese Shiite Muslims, wanted the release of more than 700 prisoners held by Israel. The flight crew could not help them with that. All the crew could do was take them, as they demanded, from Athens, the departure point of T.W.A. Flight 847, to Beirut and Algiers—rather than to Rome, as planned.

Heroism can happen by chance rather than by choice. The terrorists spoke almost no English, but one spoke German, which meant that Derickson was suddenly responsible for the flight's safety. She was the only crew member able to communicate with the captors. Derickson was 40, a useful age for a woman dealing with two frenzied men in their 20s—young enough to be pleasing yet nearly old enough to be their mother. Though she cried and shook uncontrollably during those first 20 minutes, when the terrorists pistol-whipped the pilot and co-pilot, they told her she wouldn't be hurt. Their assurance didn't exactly soothe her, but it did give her something she could use.

She worked on accepting her responsibility, her mortality. She started strategizing.

Derickson enjoyed a comfortable married life in New Jersey, but she wasn't soft. As a child, she had faced a different form of terror while fleeing with her mother across the border from East to West Germany, sleeping in haystacks by day, fearful of land mines and soldiers and border guards. Now she was an adult, staring down two wild-eyed, scared young men. "No matter how difficult it was, I always looked upon them as human beings," she later told *The Los Angeles Times*. "If you don't, you might as well give up."

When the plane made its initial landing in Beirut, she made her first move. She pleaded with the terrorists, Let the women go. The terrorists refused. The older women, then, and the children, she insisted. Amazing what can happen if you ask: they relented. Derickson rounded up the selected hostages and coaxed them down the emergency slide, even as they resisted, too terrified to move. Then it was on to Algiers.

With the terrorists, she later wrote, she realized that communication was her strongest tool. So she talked to them. She talked to them about the Koran. She offered them tea, she commented on the American sneakers one wore, even made them smile. She told them about her 7-year-old son. They looked at her with apparent concern, told her she should be home, surrounded by family.

And she talked to the passengers, reminding them calmly but urgently to do as the hijackers demanded, to stay silent, to keep their heads down. She advocated for the most desperate, the ones who needed the bathroom, or some water, or some more room for a pregnant wife.

The plane landed in Algiers for refueling. The ground crew had no intention of fueling the plane without pay; the terrorists became agitated, threatening violence. Derickson, like a soccer mom on board some minivan from hell, reached into her purse, pulled out her Shell credit card and told them to charge it. They did. . . .

Sitting beside the hijackers . . . Derickson started to sing softly to calm herself down, maybe, or to calm them down: Brahms's Lullaby, a German version of patty-cake. As she sang, the two men relaxed. At times she felt she was gaining control of the situation. The hijacker who spoke German told her his partner would like to marry her. She summoned the kind of smooth but firm demurral used by effective administrators and parents. "This is not the time and place to talk about this," she replied. Then, when they weren't watching, she put her head in her hands and cried.

As the plane neared Beirut, the hijackers began beating a second passenger. Derickson physically grabbed one of the hijackers as he pulled out his gun. "Stop it!" she said, looking straight into his eyes. "Stop it right now." Her singing, her talking, her jokes—it all now hung between them, a fragile filament of human connection she felt they wouldn't deny. Catching some of the blows, she thrust herself between the passenger and the hijackers. They backed away, and she escorted the beaten man to his seat.

Derickson couldn't ultimately save the first passenger, whom the terrorists shot dead after they landed in Beirut. (Before they did, they moved Derickson out of their lines of sight, perhaps to spare her or perhaps to spare themselves her judgment.) From there, the plane went back to Algiers, where the hijackers, after 32 hours of terror, finally released Derickson, who insisted that she take with her the flight attendants and 10 of the remaining women on board.

Later that day, almost all of the passengers were released, with the exception of some 30 hostages who were flown back to Beirut and, over the next two weeks, shuttled from prison to prison and gradually released. (One hijacker has never been captured; the other, apprehended two years later, was imprisoned in Germany.)

. . .

ON VULNERABILITY AND THE SUKKAH OF SHALOM
Rabbi Arthur Waskow

In 2001, just a few weeks after the 9/11 attacks, the Jewish community celebrated the harvest festival of Sukkot. Many did so by building a *sukkah*—a fragile hut with a leafy roof, the most vulnerable of houses. Vulnerable in time, since it lasts for only a week each year. Vulnerable in space, since its roof must be not only leafy but leaky enough to let in the starlight and gusts of wind and rain.

In our evening prayers throughout the year, just as we prepare to lie down in vulnerable sleep, we plead with God, "Spread over us Your sukkah of shalom—of peace and safety."

Why does the prayer plead for a sukkah of shalom rather than a temple or fortress or palace of shalom, which would surely be more safe and more secure?

Precisely because the sukkah is so vulnerable.

For much of our lives we try to achieve peace and safety by building with steel and concrete and toughness:

Pyramids

Air raid shelters

Pentagons

World Trade Centers

But the sukkah reminds us: We are in truth all vulnerable. If as the prophet Dylan sang, "A hard rain's gonna fall," it will fall on all of us. And on 9/11/01, the ancient truth came home: We all live in a sukkah. Even the widest oceans, the mightiest buildings, the wealthiest balance sheets, the most powerful weapons did not shield us.

There are only wispy walls and leaky roofs between us. The planet is in fact one interwoven web of life. The command to love my neighbor as I do myself is not an admonition to be nice: it is a statement of truth like the law of gravity. However much and in whatever way I love my neighbor, that will turn out to be the way I love myself. If I pour contempt upon my neighbor, hatred will recoil upon me.

Only a world where all communities feel vulnerable, and therefore connected to all other communities, can prevent such acts of rage and mass murder.

The sukkah not only invites our bodies to become physically vulnerable, but also invites our minds to become vulnerable to new ideas. To live in the sukkah for a week, as Jewish tradition teaches, would be to leave behind not only the rigid walls and towers of our cities, but also our rigidified ideas, our assumptions, our habits, our accustomed lives.

Indeed, the tradition teaches that Sukkot is the festival on which we open ourselves to what is foreign to us. We pray especially that prosperity and peace pervade all nations, not only the Jewish people. Sukkot is the festival when we invite holy guests into the sukkah—"guests" precisely because they are our higher selves, our unaccustomed selves.

By leaving our houses, we create the time and space to reflect upon our lives. To "reflect" is to look in the mirror at our "reflections." Indeed, for a moment in 2001 many Americans did pause to ask themselves the question, "Why did those attackers hate us? Did we do anything to bring such hate upon us?"

But the government of the United States moved at once to change that question into, "Why did those attackers dare to hate us?" And it immediately gave the answer, "Because we are free and they hate freedom."

Can we imagine a president addressing Congress to say:

For forty days your government will take no action except to gather evidence of who perpetrated this mass murder. We urge all Americans to gather in *sukkot*—in all the places where we might explore the open weave of half-walled space between us and the rest of the world, between humanity and the rest of the planetary web of life. We urge us all to reflect.

We invite not only those who from a distance have studied Islam but those Americans and others who themselves are Muslims, to talk with the rest of us in these *sukkot* (the plural of Sukkah).

We invite those who have lived in the despairing slums and rain-ravaged huts of the world, who have studied alongside the humiliated, angry citizens of the future in the crippled nations that make up half the world, to talk with the rest of us in these sukkot. To reflect with us.

We can imagine it, but in 2001 we could not expect it from the government of the United States. For we have built a culture that has as little space for the sukkah of reflection, of hospitality to new, uncomfortable ideas, as it does for the sukkah of vulnerability and physical discomfort.

So we got what was most to be expected: Not a call to reflect. Not a call to pursue the criminals through new forms of international and transnational law. Not a call to understand and address the underlying grievances that turned a few to terrorism and many more to rage against American power.

Instead, from the government of the United States a call to war. Not merely a war, but a "Crusade"—the word that beyond all others was most likely to arouse suspicion, fear, and rage in the Muslim world. War and Crusade—the archetypal reverse of self-reflection. The opposite of looking inward. The impulse not only to look outward but to smash whatever is out there.

And in the year and a half that followed the 9/11 attacks, the U.S. government launched not just one war but two. In each, all it cared about was smashing a repressive government that did not obey American dictates (repressive governments that did obey were not attacked) and establishing its control over resources or strategic territory that it wanted.

Our leaders responded to our vulnerability by trying harder to make ourselves invulnerable. But in a vulnerable world, this takes more and more ferocity, more and more coercion, more and more violence—at home as well as abroad.

What would it mean to recognize that we all live in vulnerable sukkot? Here are a few examples:

Could we teach all our children the Torah, the Prophets, the Song of Songs, the Talmud, the New Testament, the Quran, the Upanishads, the teachings of the Buddha and of King and Gandhi, as treasuries of wisdom—and sometimes of great danger—that are as crucial to the world as Plato and Darwin and Einstein?

Could we learn to see the dangers in "our own" as well as in "the other" teachings, and learn to strengthen those elements in all traditions that call for nonviolence, not bloody Crusades and jihads and holy wars for holy lands?

Instead of only mouthing wishes, could we insist on doing deeds: Strengthening the International Criminal Court and expanding its jurisdiction to cases of international terrorism? Creating peace between a secure Israel and a viable Palestine? Sharing abundance between the Starving World and the Obese World? Sharing disarmament between nations with suicide bombers and those with thousands of "weapons of mass destruction"? Learning to breathe easy instead of choking the planet with gases of mass desolation?

Not every demand of the poor and disempowered is legitimate simply because it is an expression of pain. But can we open the ears of our hearts to ask: Have we ourselves had a hand in creating the pain? Can we act to lighten it?

Can we create for ourselves a sukkah in time, a sukkah of reflection and renewal, as well as recognizing the sukkah of vulnerable space in which we actually live?

Could we in every year use the days that surround 9/11 to gather for reflection, for self-examination? Could we gather in a mood of Awe rather than fear, to mourn what tears the world apart and learn what weaves the world together?

The choice we face is broader than politics, deeper than charity. It is whether we see the world chiefly as property to be controlled, defined by walls and fences that must be built ever higher, ever thicker, ever tougher; or made up chiefly of an open weave of compassion and connection, open sukkah next to open sukkah.

Whatever we build where the tall Twin Towers stood, America and the World will be living in a leafy, leaky, shaky sukkah. Hope comes from raising that simple truth to visibility. We must spread over all of us the sukkah of shalom.

PART TWO

Paths to Transformation

You desire to know the art of living, my friend? It is contained in one phrase: make use of suffering.

—Henri-Frédéric Amiel

The damage that the infliction of terror causes cannot be overestimated.
Like toxic radiation, such damage has widespread consequences, psychological and spiritual wounds that are often passed from one generation to the next. In some lives, this damage can never be entirely erased.
But the same human genius that devised weapons of mass destruction by
probing the nature of the molecule and atom has also probed the nature
of consciousness, finding compelling ways to understand and heal the
human spirit.

Each of the chapters that follow explore various aspects of the understanding of the experience of terror, terrorism, and healing, insights
with the potential to act as catalysts to the transformations, both personal and social, that the violence we face requires. Along with ecologists, philosophers, and witnesses, we have included a number of articles and essays from psychologists and from a range of spiritual leaders
who offer wisdom from diverse, older traditions. Such knowledge is
often considered irrelevant to problems that have been defined as political. But just as the personal is political, so, too, violent acts committed
in the public realm are not only suffered personally but committed by
human beings. So the great knowledge of the human soul that humanity
has accrued over thousands of years can be brought to bear on the crises
we face now.

We do not offer a definitive solution here but rather take the reader
through a series of steps that are crucial if we are to change the current

climate that fosters terrorism into an atmosphere of trust and cooperation. We chart this process beginning with a chapter on the necessity of
accepting mortality and suffering as part of the human condition, followed by a chapter on the critical need for truth telling and justice, and
then a chapter on the reclamation of authenticity in our lives, and how the
soul can be distorted by social constructs of gender. We follow this with a
chapter that renders conceptual understandings of interdependence and
explores the emotional experience and riches of compassion. The last
chapter in our book, "Paths to Transformation," offers some current
strategies toward change. You will find no definitive or complete answers
here. Instead, we end this volume with examples of work that is already
being done to further the transformation of terror, to make it clear that
this vision is not just an ideal but a practical and realistic possibility.

Susan Griffin with Karin Lofthus Carrington

CHAPTER 4

In a Dark Time

The Wisdom in Grief, Fear, and Despair

There is no change in consciousness without pain.
—Carl Jung

Held back, unvoiced grief bruises the heart,
not reaching the river, a raindrop is swallowed by dust.
—Mirza Ghalib

The poet Theodore Roethke's words, "In a dark time the eye begins to see," serve as potent reminder for our time. Assaulted by ads and images that tell us we can look young forever or be happy all the time, we have been taught to look away from tragedy and suffering. Yet something valuable is lost in the bargain. As our constant good cheer becomes more superficial and brittle, we forgo the rich knowledge that comes from the dark side. Yet if terror inspires blind and unthinking reactions, as with any threat, this crisis also affords the opportunity to see more deeply. The dangers we face require us to understand the world and ourselves with greater depth and clarity. The best defense is to know your enemy, even when that enemy is inside you. Paradoxically, if we are to make the world a safer place, we will need to face the unpredictability of existence and our mutual vulnerability in the face of violence. As Carl Jung has also written, the failure to face dark emotions, including fear, anger, grief, and despair can be dangerous.

Whether in private or public life, the resistance to dark emotions reflects the unconscious fear that such feelings will last forever. Yet it is not facing these emotions but avoiding them that can cause a paralysis of will and imagination. But when we navigate grief, anger, or despair with awareness, these strong emotions have the power to transform both consciousness and the real dangers we face, making us stronger and more resilient. As Miriam Greenspan writes, "The heart heals itself when we know how to listen to it." Invited into consciousness, sorrow, trauma, and despair yield compassion, and along with an even deeper love for life, a fierce capacity for survival.

Because facing painful emotions gives us a greater understanding of ourselves and the world, many religions include among their teachings stories of journeys into the dark. From Jonah and the whale to Christ's crucifixion to Persephone's descent and Innana's journey into the underworld, such parables show how crucial dark emotions are to the evolution of the soul.

Those who fail to know the dark side of themselves often imagine that the emotions or qualities they deny belong to others. Not only individual men and women but whole cultures and nations avoid self-knowledge through projection. Anti-Semitism, racism, and demonization of all kinds act as systematic modes of projection; such ideologies not only encourage hatred, they limit self-awareness.

More subtle forms of prejudice eschew nuance and ambiguity while painting a portrait of other cultures or nations as evil. When in 2002, then President Bush spoke of three nations as "an axis of evil," his rhetoric mirrored the language of terrorists who have characterized the United States, a complex and diverse society, as decadent and aggressive. In any kind of relationship, whether private or public, such characterizations are alienating and narrow the possibilities for productive communication.

Even when no communication is possible, since the best defense is to "know your enemy," it is dangerous to distort images of those who pose a danger to us. And since so often the cartoon figures we make of others are projections containing unacknowledged aspects of ourselves, we also run the danger of diminishing crucial elements of self-knowledge, too.

Though the dark may contain aspects of ourselves that we do not want to recognize, to be effective we must know the whole story. If we are to defend human rights internationally, we must acknowledge that we as a nation have violated human rights more than once, not just at Abu Ghraib and Guantánamo, but in many other instances. For this reason, we have included in this chapter an account of the imprisonment of Japanese American citizens during World War II. Whether speaking of individuals, nations, or the world, we cannot achieve our better angels without remembering our worst fears or facing the demons inside us all.

Yet though this region of knowledge may be frightening, along with the subtlety of our own emotions and the ability to perceive nuance in others, we inherit a rich repository of wisdom that can be used to transform the conditions that have led to terrorism.

Susan Griffin with Karin Lofthus Carrington

. . .

HEALING THROUGH THE DARK EMOTIONS
IN AN AGE OF GLOBAL THREAT
Miriam Greenspan

Our world, a place of great beauty and wonder, is also a place of poised weapons of mass destruction, global terrorism, perennial violence, ecological devastation, and a baffling, overwhelming collection of ongoing sorrows. In this global context, the dark emotions of grief, fear, and despair are likely to be unwelcome guests in our consciousness. We all suffer these emotions, or the ailments that stem from denying or numbing ourselves to them. One by one by one, we in the psychotherapy profession see the common suffering of our age: the depressed and suicidal, chronically anxious, psychically numb, attention-deficient, relationally impaired, multiply addicted, spiritually wounded women, men, and children who come to us for help and healing. In increasing numbers, at younger and younger ages, Americans are finding it impossible to sleep without Ambien, to work without Prozac, to live without alcohol, nicotine, or heroin, to exist without our endless array of technotoys. Mood-altering drugs, once a type of medication largely confined to the closed halls of psychiatric inpatient units, are now household words. Who hasn't heard of Prozac? (Or isn't on it?) Words like "serotonin-deficiency" are now in the common lexicon, expressing our culture's reductive view of chronic despair.

One by one by one psychiatry diagnoses and treats these problems as though we are all little narcissistic bubble-selves floating around in space, with no relation to the social universe or earth we inhabit. Not one of the approximately 360 diagnoses of the *DSM IV*—the psychiatric bible of pathology—for instance, makes any connection between our emotional disturbances and the state of the world. What conventional psychiatry does instead is to reduce human suffering to a plethora of categories of pathology, and document the escalation of these "mental disorders" in our time. We know that some 20 million people in the United States are diagnosed with depression each year, 100 million worldwide; and that there has been a serious rise in depression in this country over the past century. A worldwide trend is clear: each successive generation is more depressed than the one before. In addition, about 50 million people in the United States suffer from crippling phobias and severe anxiety disorders. Children are being increasingly diagnosed with mental disorders once reserved entirely for adults, as well as with increasing disorders of learning, attention, and attachment.

Our inability, individually and collectively, to mindfully tolerate the core triad of dark emotions—grief, fear, and despair—is a crucial source of what ails us. These are the emotions we most avoid and that we most need to attend to in our time. Aborted or suppressed grief easily devolves into depression, anxiety, and addiction. Benumbed fear often turns into xenophobia, psychosomatic ailments, and acts of violence. Overwhelming despair can lead to severe psychic numbing or express itself through destructive acts to oneself and others, including suicide and homicide. The inability to tolerate the dark emotions is a major cause of addictions such as alcohol, drugs, technology, work, and sex, which afflict our civilization. In short, unattended grief, fear, and despair are at the root of the characteristic psychological disturbances of our time. Sadly, these destructive patterns play themselves out on the world stage as much as in the individual psyche. Our children, growing into a world in which the psychology of the "normal man" has traumatically endangered the earth and the future, are carrying the burden of dark emotions that even adults can barely name or tolerate.

In this dawning of the twenty-first century, psychology's view of human nature and behavior, if it is to have any relevance to what truly ails us, will have to contend with human suffering in a social context that is becoming more and more destructive and a planet that is in the process of being seriously damaged. In this emotional ecology of our age, we need to ask the hard questions that have no immediate, simple, or easy answers, including How are "personal" dark emotions related to a worldwide context of collective violence, environmental destruction, and global terror? How can we psychologically face the challenge of global crisis? How do we address the need for healing of the human family and the earth, as well as the individual?

What my life and work as a psychotherapist for the past thirty years have taught me, repeatedly, is that the dark emotions have a wisdom as critical to human survival and development as what we call "reason." While we think of sorrow, fear, and despair as "negative" emotions, it's not the emotions that hurt us but our fear of them, and our inability to bear them mindfully. There are no "negative" emotions, only human emotions; but there are negative attitudes toward emotions we don't like, and negative consequences of emotions we can't bear.

I call grief, fear, and despair "dark" not because they are unwholesome or pathological but because they are shunned, silenced, and devalued in our culture. In patriarchy, we associate emotions with irrationality and weakness, women and children. We reflexively avoid them if they are painful. I call this pervasive fear *devaluation,* and avoidance *emotion-phobia.* Psychiatric dictums contribute to emotion-phobia when they tell us that despair is a "mental disorder" if it lasts more than two weeks; or that grief becomes pathological if it lasts more than two months. In an emotion-phobic social context, it is hard to see the value of the dark emotions, much less experience their innate alchemy—a movement toward healing, harmony, and transformation that happens when we know how to open to them, honor their wisdom and power, and use their energies wisely.

I was impelled to write *Healing Through the Dark Emotions: The Wisdom of Grief, Fear, and Despair* not by my work as a psychotherapist but by my life as a mother. Esther, my third child, was born with a neuromotor and developmental disorder for which medical science has no name. In 1989, she took a fall from her crib, and I was warned by her orthopedist that she was at risk of being paralyzed. I spent a long dark night staring into the face of my terror for this child's fragile life—and found that this fear, fully experienced in my body, had a trajectory that culminated in a state of unexpected, exuberant joy. In this moment, the book came to me, inspired and complete with chapter headings. But it had been germinating for a long time before this. I date its beginnings to 1981, the year my first child was born and died. This grief was my spiritual initiation, my most harsh and extraordinary teacher. It was a tornado that uprooted and threw me into a devastated landscape that somehow opened into a magical world where spirit was alive, even after death. It led me by the hand, like a child, and showed me that great suffering can open the gate to a world charged with the sacred.

What I learned was that the heart heals itself when we know how to listen to it. Grief, fear, and despair are primary human emotions, as fundamental to human existence as love, awe, joy, and hope. When we attend, befriend, and mindfully surrender to them, the dark emotions transmute to spiritual strengths. Each emotion has its own wisdom and alchemy. Grief arises because we are not alone, and what connects us to others and to the world also breaks our hearts. It is a great teacher of empathy, compassion, and gratitude. When we grieve fully for what we've lost, we discover, as though for the first time, what we really have—and we are grateful. This is grief's alchemy.

Fear is a messenger that alerts us to protect life, extending beyond our instinct for self-preservation to our concern for the survival of others. Though fear is strongly stigmatized in our culture, especially for men, it is a very powerful, energizing emotion—an alarm that we ignore at our own peril. It is the adrenaline surge of "fight or flight" that moves us to act. The trick in the alchemy of fear is mindfully allowing this emotion to move us to the right action, rather than prematurely trying to "kill" it through aggression or violence (e.g., "preemptive" war). The more we open to fear, the more we learn the art of living mindfully with vulnerability, which is the secret of joy.

Is there a use for despair? The darkest of the dark emotions, despair impels us to create meaning from unbearable pain, to radically change the ways we think and behave if we are to avert destruction. Despair is a call to transformation. In the Age of Prozac, the feel-good allure of the serotonin-boosters, like the soma of Aldous Huxley's *Brave New World,* appears to make despair obsolete. Feeling this bad in a feel-good culture is transgressive; it goes against the grain of social denial and psychiatric pathologization. Why not medicate what we can't tolerate? The answer is that despair, like grief and fear, carries vital information that we miss when we chemically obliterate it. In my view, depression is unalchemized despair, despair that has become chronically stuck in the body. Our low tolerance for despair actually complicates and extends it. Arising as a response to something in ourselves or in the world that we cannot bear to accept, despair asks us to confront our illusions, our failures to live up to our own expectations, or to create a humane world. We need to rewrite our culture's story about depression to make it a story that honors despair's insistent call for transformation of self and world; and that recognizes the alchemy through which the Dark Night of the Soul delivers us to a more resilient and trustworthy faith in life.

Each of the dark emotions has a purpose and a gift, a sacred, redemptive power that we discover when we come to it with mindful openness. These gifts can only be found if we know the art of attending, befriending, and consciously surrendering to emotions that are challenging and unpleasant. Attending is a heightened awareness of emotions as in-the-body energies. Befriending extends this process—deepening and lengthening our emotional attention spans and developing what psychologists call "affect tolerance." Surrender is not about giving up our will, wallowing in our pain, or becoming victims of our feelings. It is the art of acceptance, of mindfully allowing the energy of the dark emotions to flow through the body to its end point. In surrendering, we let the dark emotions be. What follows is often unexpected and magical.

In a culture of speed and distraction, we are generally so alienated from the natural flow of emotions in the body and so entrenched in emotion-phobia that we don't experience the alchemy of the dark emotions. We have deeply internalized a set of patriarchal norms, beliefs, and attitudes that can be summarized as the "contain and manage" model of coping with emotions we don't like. We learn in our families, in our schools, and in the culture as a whole that control is the best or only way to handle intense, difficult feelings. In keeping with patriarchy's ethos of hierarchy, suppression, and fragmented consciousness, with its fear of nature and the feminine, we try to keep those nasty feelings down before they overtake our reason. The "contain and manage" model, however useful it may be in certain contexts, is not a transformational approach to emotions. What's needed is a more feminine ethos of "connection and flow" in which mindfulness, not control, is the key. When we know how to ride the energy of the dark emotions on the surfboard of awareness, emotional flow becomes alchemical.

Healing in a Brokenhearted World

Mass terrorism, political uncertainty, economic decline, ethnic, religious, national, tribal, and internecine wars have made the dark emotions pervasive and overwhelming in our time. In addition, the loss of connection to nature in Western postindustrial society, the destruction of our ecological underpinnings, and the devastating effects of patriarchy are the largely overlooked global contexts that trigger and complicate our grief, fear, and despair. In this age of global threat, the dark emotions are inevitable responses. Affective markers of our collective fate, they carry information our conscious minds would often rather deny or avoid. They are the repository of this information, the conduit of our moral responsiveness to the world, and the unrecognized vehicles of an urgently needed worldwide social and spiritual transformation. The emotions we most dread offer essential information that humans need in order to survive and evolve, and to live in balance with nature. If ever we needed the wisdom of the dark emotions, we need it now.

Huge mushroom clouds of unalchemized dark emotions afflict us in this century, transmitted transpersonally to all of us, in some form. Some carry these emotions in their bodies unawares, putting them at risk for a host of mind/body ailments. Others are largely bystanders to the dark emotions—detached from and numb to themselves, others, and the world. This too brings with it a host of problems, including interpersonal impasses, violence both perpetrated and tolerated, and moral failures to respond empathically and to protect those who are harmed. One way of describing patriarchy, in emotional terms, is that it is an emotional bystander culture. This way of dissociating from our emotions is literally killing us. We are called to make a shift to a meaning system in which emotions are viewed as powerful ways of knowing that guide us to develop empathy, compassion, nurturance, and care of others—a shift in which these qualities are no longer privatized or devalued but elevated to their true importance for the world. Such a shift would break through the dead dichotomies of patriarchy so that we could see and feel the ways that reason *needs* emotion, mind *is* body, inner and outer are profoundly connected, self and world interpenetrate one another. Perhaps then emotions—devalued, trivialized, and privatized in patriarchy—would not lose their potential for healing and transformation.

We can use the energy of our most dreaded emotions to heal ourselves and our world. This is their message: because we all feel sorrow, fear, and despair, because these emotions are universal, we are, in fact, *intervulnerable*. Only in recognizing the profound ways that we are interconnected in our suffering do we stand a chance of healing ourselves in a way that extends beyond balms for individual pain. We each have something to contribute to global healing—a particular gift or vision, skill or song. Healing has a lot to do with finding this gift and using it for the sake of the world, finding our song and singing it. When we do this, we break out of the isolating prison of ego. We build our courage. We become fuller, and grow in compassion. We are made more whole. A healed life is always a work in progress; not a life devoid of all traces of suffering but a life lived fully, deeply, authentically, and compassionately engaged with the world.

"There is nothing so whole as a broken heart," said Rabbi Mendel of Kotzk, a Hasidic sage. The world breaks our hearts open, and the openness makes us whole. Engaged with a brokenhearted world, we cannot and should not expect to be "cured" of grief, fear, and despair. Rather, we learn how to become more comfortable with our shared human vulnerability. We learn the art and power of no protection—a spiritual power, not an egoic conquest won through armoring ourselves against pain, or against an enemy. To learn this alchemy, we must be willing to accept suffering and vulnerability as a normal part of life. Because we are vulnerable, life hurts. We are not here to be free of pain. We are here to have our hearts broken by life, and to transform that pain into love.

. . .

It's said that Americans are inured to images of violence, but I don't think this has been caused by an inundation of images of *true* violence. We've been numbed by counterfeit images of violence, and by our own insensitivity, our own inability to react. We've made of violence an abstraction. If we truly perceived the pain of a particular image—and let's refer to a photographic image now, rather than a poetic one—such pain as is apparent in a photograph of a maimed victim of a Salvadoran death squad would be too excruciating, if truly perceived, to contemplate or regard.

In situations of extremity, rather than our becoming numb to pain, the pain worsens, and lessens our ability to endure. Each death seems more difficult than the last, and each inflicts its wound on the survivor, who remains tender from the wound when the next is inflicted, when the next loss is suffered.

To write out of such extremity is to incise, with language, that same wound, to open it again, and, with utterance, to inscribe the consciousness. This inscription restructures the consciousness of the poet.

What has happened in America has less to do with violence itself than with the way such images of violence are read and with the desire to abstract the violence, as a means of anesthetization. As Americans, we cling, however precariously, to the myth of our staunch individualism. We are inclined to view ourselves as apart from others. Perhaps we do this because we are haunted by the past, by the occulted memory of the founding genocide. If it were true that we imagined ourselves as connected to others, as part of a larger human body, it would no longer be true that we would suffer the lack of feeling in ourselves which we now describe as the condition of being inured to images of violence.

(Carolyn Forché, from "An Interview by David Montenegro")

. . .

IN A DARK TIME
Theodore Roethke

In a dark time, the eye begins to see,
I meet my shadow in the deepening shade;
I hear my echo in the echoing wood—
A lord of nature weeping to a tree.
I live between the heron and the wren,
Beasts of the hill and serpents of the den.

What's madness but nobility of soul
At odds with circumstance? The day's on fire!
I know the purity of pure despair,
My shadow pinned against a sweating wall.
That place among the rocks—is it a cave,
Or winding path? The edge is what I have.

A steady storm of correspondences!
A night flowing with birds, a ragged moon,
And in broad day the midnight come again!
A man goes far to find out what he is—
Death of the self in a long, tearless night,
All natural shapes blazing unnatural light.

Dark, dark my light, and darker my desire.
My soul, like some heat-maddened summer fly,
Keeps buzzing at the sill. Which I is *I*?
A fallen man, I climb out of my fear.
The mind enters itself, and God the mind,
And one is One, free in the tearing wind.

· · ·

THOUGHTS IN THE PRESENCE OF FEAR
Wendell Berry

I. The time will soon come when we will not be able to remember the horrors of September 11 without remembering also the unquestioning technological and economic optimism that ended on that day.

II. This optimism rested on the proposition that we were living in a "new world order" and a "new economy" that would "grow" on and on, bringing a prosperity of which every new increment would be "unprecedented."

III. The dominant politicians, corporate officers, and investors who believed this proposition did not acknowledge that the prosperity was limited to a tiny percentage of the world's people, and to an ever smaller number of people even in the United States; and that it was founded upon the oppressive labor of poor people all over the world; and that its ecological costs increasingly threatened all life, including the lives of the supposedly prosperous.

IV. The "developed" nations had given to the "free market" the status of a god, and were sacrificing to it their farmers, farmlands, and rural communities, their forests, wetlands, and prairies, their ecosystems and watersheds. They had accepted universal pollution and global warming as normal costs of doing business.

V. There was, as a consequence, a growing worldwide effort on behalf of economic decentralization, economic justice, and ecological responsibility. We must recognize that the events of September 11 make this effort more necessary than ever. We citizens of the industrial countries must continue the labor of self-criticism and self-correction. We must recognize our mistakes.

VI. The paramount doctrine of the economic and technological euphoria of recent decades has been that everything depends on innovation. It was understood as desirable, and even necessary, that we should go on and on from one technological innovation to the next, which would cause the economy to "grow" and make everything better and better. This of course implied at every point a hatred of the past, of all things inherited and free. All things superseded in our progress of innovations, whatever their value might have been, were discounted as of no value at all.

VII. We did not anticipate anything like what has now happened. We did not foresee that all our sequence of innovations might be at once overridden by a greater one: the invention of a new kind of war that would turn our previous innovations against us, discovering and exploiting the debits and the dangers that we had ignored. We never considered the possibility that we might be trapped in the webwork of communication and transport that was supposed to make us free.

VIII. Nor did we foresee that the weaponry and the war science that we marketed and taught to the world would become available, not just to recognized national governments which possess so uncannily the power to legitimate large-scale violence, but also to "rogue nations," dissident or fanatical groups, and individuals—whose violence, though never worse than that of nations, is judged by the nations to be illegitimate.

IX. We had accepted uncritically the belief that technology is only good; that it cannot serve evil as well as good; that it cannot serve our enemies as well as ourselves; that it cannot be used to destroy what is good, including our homelands and our lives.

X. We had accepted too the corollary belief that an economy (either as a money economy or as a life-support system) that is global in extent, technologically complex, and centralized is invulnerable to terrorism, sabotage, or war, and that it is protectable by "national defense."

XI. We now have a clear, inescapable choice that we must make. We can continue to promote a global economic system of unlimited "free trade" among corporations, held together by long and highly vulnerable lines of communication and supply, but *now* recognizing that such a system will have to be protected by a hugely expensive police force that will be worldwide, whether maintained by one nation or several or all, and that such a police force will be effective precisely to the extent that it oversways the freedom and privacy of the citizens of every nation.

XII. Or we can promote a decentralized world economy which would have the aim of assuring to every nation and region a *local* self-sufficiency in life-supporting goods. This would not eliminate international trade, but it would tend toward a trade in surpluses after local needs had been met.

XIII. One of the gravest dangers to us now, second only to further terrorist attacks against our people, is that we will attempt to go on as before with the corporate program of global "free trade," whatever the cost in freedom and civil rights, without self-questioning or self-criticism or public debate.

XIV. This is why the substitution of rhetoric for thought, always a temptation in a national crisis, must be resisted by officials and citizens alike. It is hard for ordinary citizens to know what is actually happening in Washington in a time of such great trouble; for all we know, serious and difficult thought may be taking place there. But the talk that we are hearing from politicians, bureaucrats, and commentators has so far tended to reduce the complex problems now facing us to issues of unity, security, normality, and retaliation.

XV. National self-righteousness, like personal self-righteousness, is a mistake. It is misleading. It is a sign of weakness. Any war that we may make now against terrorism will come as a new installment in a history of war in which we have fully participated. We are not innocent of making war against civilian populations. The modern doctrine of such warfare was set forth and enacted by General William Tecumseh Sherman, who held that a civilian population could be declared guilty and rightly subjected to military punishment. We have never repudiated that doctrine.

XVI. It is a mistake also—as events since September 11 have shown—to suppose that a government can promote and participate in a global economy and at the same time act exclusively in its own interest by abrogating its international treaties and standing apart from international cooperation on moral issues.

XVII. And surely, in our country, under our Constitution, it is a fundamental error to suppose that any crisis or emergency can justify any form of political oppression. Since September 11, far too many public voices have presumed to "speak for us" in saying that Americans will gladly accept a reduction of freedom in exchange for greater "security." Some would, maybe. But some others would accept a reduction in security (and in global trade) far more willingly than they would accept any abridgement of our Constitutional rights.

XVIII. In a time such as this, when we have been seriously and most cruelly hurt by those who hate us, and when we must consider ourselves to be gravely threatened by those same people, it is hard to speak of the ways of peace and to remember that Christ enjoined us to love our enemies, but this is no less necessary for being difficult.

XIX. Even now we dare not forget that since the attack of Pearl Harbor—to which the present attack has been often and not usefully compared—we humans have suffered an almost uninterrupted sequence of wars, none of which has brought peace or made us more peaceable.

XX. The aim and result of war necessarily are not peace but victory, and any victory won by violence necessarily justifies the violence that won it and leads to further violence. If we are serious about innovation, must we not conclude that we need something new to replace our perpetual "war to end war"?

XXI. What leads to peace is not violence but peaceableness, which is not passivity, but an alert, informed, practiced, and active state of being. We should recognize that while we have extravagantly subsidized the means of war, we have almost totally neglected the ways of peaceableness. We have, for example, several national military academies, but not one peace academy. We have ignored the teachings and the examples of Christ, Gandhi, Martin Luther King, and other peaceable leaders. And here we have an inescapable duty to notice also that war is profitable, whereas the means of peaceableness, being cheap or free, make no money.

XXII. The key to peaceableness is continuous practice. It is wrong to suppose that we can exploit and impoverish the poorer countries, while arming them and instructing them in the newest means of war, and then reasonably expect them to be peaceable.

XXIII. We must not again allow public emotion or the public media to caricature our enemies. If our enemies are now to be some nations of Islam, then we should undertake to *know* those enemies. Our schools should begin to teach the histories, cultures, arts, and languages of the Islamic nations. And our leaders should have the humility and the wisdom to ask the reasons some of those people have for hating us.

XXIV. Starting with the economies of food and farming, we should promote at home and encourage abroad the ideal of local self-sufficiency. We should recognize that this is the surest, the safest, and the cheapest way for the world to live. We should not countenance the loss or destruction of any local capacity to produce necessary goods.

XXV. We should reconsider and renew and extend our efforts to protect the natural foundations of the human economy: soil, water, and air. We should protect every intact ecosystem and watershed that we have left, and begin restoration of those that have been damaged.

XXVI. The complexity of our present trouble suggests as never before that we need to change our present concept of education. Education is not properly an industry, and its proper use is not to serve industries, either by job-training or by industry-subsidized research. Its proper use is to enable citizens to live lives that are economically, politically, socially, and culturally responsible. This cannot be done by gathering or "accessing" what we now call "information"—which is to say facts without context and therefore without priority. A proper education enables young people to put their lives in order, which means knowing what things are more important than other things; it means putting first things first.

XXVII. The first thing we must begin to teach our children (and learn ourselves) is that we cannot spend and consume endlessly. We have got to learn to save and conserve. We do need a "new economy," but one that is founded on thrift and care, on saving and conserving, not on excess and waste. An economy based on waste is inherently and hopelessly violent, and war is its inevitable by-product. We need a peaceable economy.

. . .

In a murderous time,
    the heart breaks and breaks
        and lives by breaking.
it is necessary to go
    through dark and deeper dark
        and not to turn.
           (Stanley Kunitz, from "The Testing-Tree")

. . .

SEEING RED: IN A DARK NIGHT OF THE AMERICAN SOUL

Aaron Kipnis

The United States often casts its moral spotlight on the human rights violations of other nations. But little self-reflection is evident concerning abuses toward an increasingly broad swath of our own citizenry. With close to 7 million Americans under criminal justice supervision today, our incarceration rate is the highest in the world. The rapid-cell-growth of this American Gulag is historically unprecedented in a free nation.

Ideals of equality, liberty, and justice are deeply etched into America's psyche. The brighter a light, however, the more distinct shadow it casts. For many living in the eclipse zones, a dark night of the American soul permeates the borderlands of the American dream. America's minorities are visibly overrepresented in the prison industrial complex's archipelago of despair. Widespread neglect and abuse of prisoners has created a pervasive clinical fallacy about rehabilitation. The nihilistic mantra of policy makers fueling our incarceration jihad is: Nothing Works.

The seeming irrationality of a society spending more to incarcerate than to educate the "criminal class" serves an unbroken continuum of ruthless labor commodification, from Colonial era enslavement to private prisons' portfolios on twenty-first century stock exchanges. Psychologically, when a dominant culture uses its full power to disenfranchise a minority, a scapegoat complex is active in the national psyche. The trauma in the heart of American justice today opens vents into deeper strata of the cultural unconscious. Our degree of injustice, oppression, and violence has some people "seeing red"—a condition of blind instinctual activation in which both heroic and horrific acts can occur.

American violence is a pervasive social phenomenon that far exceeds the rates of other industrial democracies. Like the blind reporting on elephants, most psychological schools merely investigate small slices of this complex phenomenon. Cognitive psychology reduces violence's etiology to faulty thinking; developmental and dynamic theory see recapitulations of familial history; sociology examines hierarchical impacts on groups; ecological and social psychologies point to environmental degradation; humanism finds negative self-regard; neuroscience spotlights organic deficits; behaviorism prescribes retraining; psychiatry cites brain chemistry; religion laments moral decay; and criminal justice blames deviance. This paper considers some themes that depth psychology might contribute.

The Deep Psychology of Violence

Jung cautions that it is more dangerous to deny the hidden recess of the cultural imagination than to face its shadows. Archetypal psychology suggests further that, as a person or nation, we risk possession by the complexes we fail to address. Cultural identity is as deeply defined by what we resist as by ideals we affirm, informing both the overt and covert forms of violence that dominant groups project against minorities. What then do we imagine is feeding our nation's disastrous attempt to literalize, isolate, and contain its shadow? Upon what imaginal foundations does America continue expansion of the world's largest penal system?

Violent acts readily confuse inner and outer life. Violence is iconoclastic. It shatters the rigid details of egoic life into disassociated fragments. Violence, like Eros, can draw us out of a diminished self into greater complexity. In nature, an ecology of violence fosters endless transformations. The cracked shell surrenders the chick, seedpods burst with new life, snakes grow through splits of skin, and wildfire ash feeds wild flowers.

Violence is rarely "senseless." It has a function. People employ violence as a tool to produce specific external and internal reactions in attempts to create homeostasis in unbalanced systems. Violence is readily provoked by tyranny and injustice—the American Revolution, for example.

Not unlike various drugs, violence has quasi-biological and psychological aspects. Some sociopaths, for example, actually become calmer when witnessing violent acts. Violence is energetic. It has force, direction, and flow. Violence has numinous, intoxicating, and archetypal dimensions. Perpetrators of violent acts frequently report feeling powerful, even godlike during their commission. Paradoxically, however, with all but the truly psychopathic, tremendous shame and grief can arise in the wake of violent acts. This unbearable weight can then provoke more violent behavior in a self-propagating cycle. Violent acts are often symptomatic of an addictive system. Like most addictions, when left untreated, frequency and intensity tend to increase.

History demonstrates that the more inhumane a culture becomes, the more violence it generates, internally or externally. Violent behavior is thus sometimes a completely normal response to an abnormal situation. With the highest rates of child poverty, abuse, and neglect in the industrial world, American children also have the highest violent death rates. Abuse inculcates shame. Shame induces pain. Pain can be masked by drugs, alcohol, sex, overwork, money, and other compulsions. Psychic pain can also be ameliorated by the cold, narcissistic deadness of sociopathy. But the psychic numbing of a libido wrapped up in a quasi-biological state of narcissistic stasis is often more disturbing than pain itself.

Some sociopaths become vampiric in a desperate quest to draw heat to a soul in ice. Violence then becomes the way such an emotionally numbed person feels fully alive. Violence is vivid. Violence, for a moment, can return vitality to an imaginal life desiccated by the vapid badlands of American consumer culture or pummeled into quiescence by brutality and indifference. Violence can produce a range of secondary gains that promote its repetition.

Reddening the Work

Violence "reddens" psyche. Perpetrators of violent acts speak of "seeing red; reaching a breaking, bursting, or flash point; exploding with rage."

Criminals get caught red handed (with blood on their hands). Red permeates the lexicon of emotional intensity. Passions are not mauve, taupe, or tangerine. They are crimson, scarlet, and incarnadine. Desire and hate smolder. Love sparks, becomes inflamed. Anger turns red hot.

Reddening reveals the flush of desire, fever, excitement, estrus, embarrassment, pride, frustration, or rage. Dionysian revelry paints the town red. The mid-life crisis abandons the beige sedan for a red sports car. Women don red "power" suits for executive suites and redden their lips in other pursuits. Sun, irritation, and spanking all redden the hide. Simply viewing red can speed respiration and raise blood pressure. Red is primary. It vibrates at the lower end of the visible spectrum. When recovering from color-blindness induced by brain injury, patients see red first.

Red tape infuriates. Red ink bankrupts. Red lining isolates. Red lights demand Stop! They signal ambulance, fire truck, police car; sex sold here; heavy equipment moving, out of gas, oil pressure low, live wire, system failure, melt down, radiation leak, explosion imminent. Red alert! Red flag! Red Zone! Code Red! The president's red phone is a "Hot Line" to a finger on a Red Button. The matador's red cape captivates the bull's red eye. Ole!

America was forged in a red-hot crucible of war. Thomas Jefferson's liberty tree is steeped in the blood of tyrants and patriots alike. America fought Red Coats, Redskins, Red Guard, and the Red Brigade. The English projected power under their Red Ensign. Hitler's Nazi banner was literally dipped in martyrs' blood. Japan's flag is emblazoned with the red solar disk of the Shinto war goddess, Amataratsu, the mythic ancestor of Japanese emperors. The blood of slaves upon whose backs a few built wealth here permeates the mortar of our nation's foundations. No attempts to whiten history have washed away their reddened imprints.

Reddening confers life and takes it. Violent death is red as birth. Seeing red signals a moment of great transformation. Reddening empowers a mother to lift a car off her child, a soldier to rush a machine gun, or a culture to throw off oppression, becoming "mad as Hell" (where a red Devil lives). In alchemy, reddening (rubedo) denotes the last stage of the "work" before base material turns into gold. The alchemist's object of desire, the Philosopher Stone, was also named "Red Lion" or "Great Red Water." The Hebraic God of the Old Testament's divine alchemy created Adam out of red earth.

Hawaiian goddess, Peli, embodies the paradox of red's destructive and generative power. An erupting volcano spews red molten rivers. Everything in her path inflames. Yet new soil and fertile ash follow her wake. As incandescent lava pours into the sea, the roiling birth of new earth begins. Hephestus inhabits the volcanoes of Europe's mythic landscapes. He works the magma as a forge to create wonders for the gods. Hephestus is Aphrodite's lover. She also mates with Aries, war god of the red planet—Mars. These archetypal personifications present two faces of the masculine soul, one reddened by generative power, the other by destruction. Beauty loves them both.

Tempering

Many indigenous cultures understand psychological reddening as a post-latency phenomenon calling for the focus of the entire adult population. Africans call this adolescent libido surge *Latima*. Tradition holds that if the wild red horse of Latima is not harnessed to the cart of community, uninitiated young men will run wild and set fire to the village. With more young men dying from gunshots in American cities than in global civil wars, this metaphor is not so distant from us.

America has lost the sacred technologies, which sustained social homeostasis for thousands of years. Instead of hosting the alchemical process by which adolescent soul fire is directed into the engine of culture, advocates for social order increasingly attempt to turn down the heat of youth, contain their passions, and even extinguish their sacred fire altogether.

As diagnostic criteria for attention "disorders" increasingly pathologize the reddening of adolescence, roughly one in ten American schoolboys are prescribed Latima-quenching chemicals. Archetypal forces, however, do not submit to neurological flattening. Latima will seek expression.

A person without fire has no will. They lack the power to actualize their dreams, protect others' boundaries, or even defend their own. Passion, creativity, and fire are intimately linked. When our talents are engaged we get "fired up." When suppressed, Latima smolders, like a coal fire burning underground for decades, until it finds a new vent to the surface and erupts.

The Criminalization of Despair

Facing violence turns us toward self-knowledge. But the province of Violence is not hospitable to tourists, nor does it readily issue exit visas. Like rapacious Hades reaching for lush Persephone, Violence abducts. Those previously held for ransom in its underworld enter our offices as trauma survivors and lost souls.

In eras past, lepers were confined apart from the rest of society. Today, we shutter troubled hearts and minds in penal colonies. The most shameful chapter in the annals of psychiatric history was clinicians' presence on the leading edge of the Holocaust. It began with rounding up mental patients for the community's good, then sterilization and eventually . . . extermination. As psychology is increasingly conscripted by the state to aid its social norming and containment efforts, every educator and clinician must now ask themselves: To whom do I owe my first allegiance—the state or the soul?

While the American Gulag impacts the lives of many, its primary targets are young men of color at the bottom of the socioeconomic hierarchy. The incarceration frenzy, with one in three young African American men in its thrall, defies rational explanation, sharing more features with historical genocides than social justice ideals. The severity and scale of U.S. imprisonment questions our status as a free or even civilized nation. Exile to the American Gulag is tantamount to a death sentence for many nonviolent offenders. One tool in the slow motion extermination of the underclass is the unrestrained rape of thousands of incarcerated young men. Their AIDS and hepatitis C transmission rates soar far beyond the greatest at-risk, free populations.

Dehumanization of any group can result when certain cultural markers are regarded as indicative of their moral inferiority. Through their silence our policy makers passively sanction medical neglect, sexual assault, chemical immobilization, torture, and even the murder of the American Gulag's inhabitants. This year, half a million inmates will be ejected from the bitter heart of this burgeoning prison industrial complex straight into our communities. What then?

Conclusion

What effect does repression of collective rage on such a megalithic scale have on our cultural soul? Does out of sight really ensure out of mind? Prisons contain dense psychological material—anger, despair, grief, revenge, and apocalyptic fantasy. The more a dream is deferred, the stronger the container needed to suppress it. The alchemical metaphor of psychological containment suggests value in holding volatile transformations well enough to allow base material to undergo transformation. The alchemist's goal is for material to become ennobled without exploding or converting into poison. As a psychological axiom, this alchemical principle explains one reason why our prison system keeps growing unabated. Modern penology builds excellent crucibles but seldom turns leaden lives golden.

Prison was first imagined as a place for solitude, reflection, and penance—a penitentiary—in which broken spirits could mend and impoverished imaginations could refresh. From this temenos prisoners would return renewed. Today, most return more humiliated than humbled and more broken than healed. Many emerge enraged. Just as the energy of uranium is enriched in nuclear reactors, violence becomes more virulent in the very crucibles designed to contain it.

Concerned citizens can turn this red tide through demanding justice reform with opportunities for education, rehabilitation, recovery, and social inclusion for all conscripted into the underworld of the American Gulag.

. . .

Even though our disturbed veterans may only be incomplete initiates, their presence all through the nation could serve to inoculate the body politic against the worst disease brought by the god of war: the headlong rush into action by the uninitiated. Is that why many older generals and veteran citizens speak out and hold the line against the march of folly?

"Veteran" from *vetus*, old, ripe, worn, belonging to the past. Time alone does not make veterans. A twenty-year-old German student writes: "all about us death hissed and howled. Such a night is enough to make an old man of one." Combat is instant aging. The veteran has survived an initiation; the fact of that survival, that chance or miracle, forces upon one the deepest questioning and the veteran's burden of carrying the dead into life. Of course a veteran is ripe and worn and burnished by the past.

(James Hillman, from *A Terrible Love of War*)

. . .

MORPHOLOGIES OF SILENCE
Joan Miura

The night before we leave our white house on Halcyon Road, my mother plays Beethoven on the piano. She cries silently as my father packs. His face grim; he is unapproachable. I am two. My sister is three and a half. We dare not make a sound.

Meanwhile, hundreds of miles north, my grandfather digs a long trench in his backyard. Then he and my grandmother circle room by room through their house. They scurry down hallways and through the screen door to the trench. Photographs, letters, beloved books, music, business and church records, pressed wedding flowers, scrolled art, sandalwood fans fall from their arms into the gaping trench.

No time for tears. Lit matches ignite a flamed gash. My grandparents stir the fire, watch every trace of their histories return to the gods. Sumi smoke brushes write birth and death, laughter and tears, victories, defeats on the darkening sky, and paint precious dreams on the withers of cloud horses riding the wind to memory. When the fire retires to the quarter from whence it came, my grandparents sweep excavated earth back into the trench, burying the ashes of their lives and restoring the ground to its own original face. This night before they leave their home, my grandparents fall to sleep exhausted on the floor, their bed frames and box springs gone. They have been ordered to donate all metal to the war effort.

Morning on Halcyon Road, we leave our home in a frenzy. My father's car, my mother's piano, our furniture, clothing, family keepsakes, and all our toys are abandoned to the landlord who promises to care for them. We arrive at the bus station into a surreal confusion of men, women, and children in best hats, coats, and suits amid bundles and bursting suitcases, shocked into silence by the severity of shouting soldiers. One soldier, rifle swaying from his shoulder, leans down to wind the white string of a numbered luggage tag around the top button of my coat. This number is now my name. All internees must wear luggage tags. They flutter as we move. We are ordered into buses. No questions allowed. Destination unknown. My mother is weeping. My father compresses fierce rage to stony silence.

Hours later our bus passes concertina wire, through sentry checkpoints, and shudders to a stop. We disembark weary into dust and stultifying heat, line up before soldiers and guns, and wait to be processed. We are inside the Tulare Fair Grounds. Surrounded by barbed wire, watch towers, and searchlights.

My sister and I whine with fatigue, for something to drink, for our abandoned stuffed toys, cool white sheets on soft beds, warm bath water and honeysuckle bubbles up to our necks, for the rustling of our father's evening newspaper, the reassuring thud of the refrigerator door, and the comforting clatter of pots, china, and silverware emanating from the kitchen. After a long wait, an armed guard escorts us to a horse stall. This is our new house. My parents stare speechless through unseeing eyes as they feel their future vanish in the exhalation of a single held breath.

I miss my grandparents. They're staying in a horse stall at Santa Anita Racetrack. My grandmother holds a bar of soap next to her nose so she will not faint from horse stench. My mother worries about them all the time. Sometimes she cries as she scrubs clothes on the laundry room washboards. If anyone sees her tears she tells them she is not crying, she is just too hot and sweating. Nobody is supposed to cry in Camp. Everyone has to *gaman*. Endure.

Five months later, we are all ordered to the train. Once again, coat buttons are wound with numbered luggage tags. The train stops only once in a desolate area. Everyone is ordered outside. Like circus animals off loaded from dark box cars into sunlight, we stretch sinuous in fresh air, sniff strange leaves, kick stones, and scan the horizon for memories of home. Guards surround us, guns at the ready. Here in desolation there is nowhere to hide or run unless you wish for a bullet in your back. We re-board and move onward in cinematic catatonia toward indeterminate incarceration.

A brash young girl with flashing eyes takes out her guitar. She chides her captive audience for their grim faces and pronounces that things are definitely not that bad. Life is bound to be better wherever we are going. You'll see. It will be a blast. She plays old standards and orders everyone to sing along. My father and others disapprove. They consider her behavior inappropriate. At last the train slows to a stop. We disembark. My mother gasps and can barely stand. My father is unable to speak. The bright-eyed singer puts down her guitar and bursts into tears.

It is September 1942, and we have arrived at Tule Lake Relocation Center. We share Barracks #77 with several families. There is one stove for heat in the center and almost no privacy. Dust blows constantly through floorboards and walls. There are no lavatory, bathing, or laundry facilities in the barracks. To reach these communal buildings, we must walk through wind, rain, and snow, sinking often to our ankles in dust and mud. I am afraid of the dark. My mother is distressed that nothing ever stays clean in the constant dust. She scrubs wordless, uncommonly subdued. My mother believes we will never be free again.

My father is released periodically for labor assignments outside Camp. In stark contrast to Tule Lake's barren dead lake bed, the soil immediately adjacent is rich and verdant. My father works this land which produces vegetables in abundance for the Camp's population. Soon he is appointed supervisor of these fields.

The skies above are a flyway for thousands of migratory ducks and geese. Hard prison labor and the bountiful fields outside Tule Lake sustain life for sanctuary birds and captive prisoners alike. Ducks and geese soar, while beneath them, in a vast wire cage, earthbound captives cast their eyes to the skies, and the sanctuary birds with their eloquence and beauty keep hope alive.

One of my father's tasks is to assign bird patrols to walk up and down the furrows and chase sanctuary ducks and geese away. My father and his patrol invent symbolic acts of rebellion in the process. In fields distant from the scrutiny of their guards, my father's bird patrol would dig a large hole. A man would sit in the hole and cover himself with two pieces of plywood, leaving an opening between the boards. His co-conspirators would then sprinkle the boards with soil, spread seeds on the soil and hurry to the perimeter of the field to watch. Ducks would sweep down from the sky, landing on the plywood for a tasty treat. Instantly, the man hidden in the hole would seize a duck by one foot, tie one end of a string around the duck's foot and the other end to a stake in the ground. Seeds were left for the ducks who spent the rest of the day struggling to get airborne. When work ended, the bird patrol would collect the ducks, execute a quick twist, and smuggle them under their jackets past the sentries into Camp. A feast of duck roasted in our barrack's single pot belly stove was a clandestine victory.

My father's scheme was nearly discovered one day as a guard squinted into the distance at some ducks behaving strangely. They appeared to jump straight up in the air then fell back to earth like winged yo-yos. My father told the guard it was a mating ritual and quickly distracted him with a bogus task, diverting him from walking out to the field to investigate. After that, my father and his patrol refined their technique. They used shorter strings.

A few months after our arrival, Tule Lake is designated as the National Segregation Center for the entire Internment System. A loyalty oath is administered in all Camps. Those who answered no to Questions

27 and 28 are considered disloyal and segregated at Tule Lake. All those answering yes are reassigned to the remaining Camps in the system. My parents answer yes to both questions. However, my mother is pregnant with her third child, and she is forbidden to travel. Our family must remain at Tule Lake. The population increases to 18,700, 3,700 more than the Camp's maximum capacity. Conditions are volatile and highly politicized. Tule Lake is placed under martial law.

My "Yes-Yes" parents experience a double oppression, shunned not only by the "No-No" prisoners, but by Camp administrators and guards as well. My father is harassed daily. Bones are hung over our mess hall table. Threatening notes are posted on our barrack's door. "No-Nos" with baseball bats hunt "Yes-Yes" for sport. My father had been a respected and popular leader. Now he is vilified and attacked. My entire family endures silent shunning, the collective's most damaging social censure. Some parents will not let their children play with me and my sister. They tell them we are bad.

To protect his wife and children as well as to conceal his pain, my father makes a decision to separate himself from us. He rarely joins our family for mess hall meals. Later he accepts an opportunity to work in the sugar beet and potato fields of Idaho. During one of his brief returns on furlough, my mother tells him she is hurt because he did not write to her during his long absence. In their shared barracks without privacy, he whispers word bullets through clenched teeth that he wrote no letters because his blistered chapped hands bled most of the time from freezing hours in the fields, that it hurt to move a pen to write, and that he was too exhausted to think. Furthermore, there was no news but grief to report from the fields of Idaho. Remorse shatters my mother's soul.

My mother is convinced my father does not love her or his children. Her spirit seeps slowly away. She tells my grandmother that all the life is going out of her in Camp. She can feel herself dying and confesses she has been afraid every single day of her imprisonment. My grandmother scolds her. "*Gaman,*" she says. Endure with dignity. "*Shikata ga nai.*" It can't be helped. It is into this atmosphere that my parents' third daughter is born. An armed sentry drives my mother alone in a jeep to the hospital.

My father is away in the fields of Idaho.

Months later, our family is reassigned to Topaz in Utah's high Sevier desert. My father is again in Idaho. My mother travels alone with three children. Our train steward will not serve us. He lounges, on strike with studied defiance, gazing with contempt through half-lidded indolent eyes at his cargo of women and children. My mother struggles in silence to feed her new baby cold milk which the steward refuses to warm. His hatred is palpable, and my mother can barely contain her tears.

Eventually we are released from Topaz. But we are not welcome back into our California community. Friends of my parents sleep in hallways because people shoot at them through their windows at night. Our landlord who promised to take care of our things while we were in Camp sold all four tires on my father's car, our family keepsakes, furniture, and appliances. Even our toys are gone. My father moves us to Colorado because it is safer there.

Two years pass before we return to California. My father has a job, but no one will rent us a house. A family friend lets us stay in the wooden shack on his farm. It takes time to begin again. But in our next house we will have a piano.

Over the following decades, on those rare occasions when my father did respond to a question on Camp, he would only retell the same two funny stories, including the one about catching ducks. Then he would throw his head back with uproarious laughter and immediately leave the room. And so it was that the family newsreel remained intact. My father had a fun time in Camp.

My mother's response, when asked about Camp, was distinguished also for decades by its sameness. "I don't remember; I don't want to remember, don't remind me," spoken rapidly as an uninterrupted mantra. "Camp is over," she would announce with severe finality.

This sacrilization of silence remained inviolate for about forty years until my mother realized how "over" Camp was not—how it shredded her soul, lived as a permanent ache in her heart, how she and her body could not stop remembering. My mother gradually came to share every memory she could retrieve, and the telling of her stories freed her spirit and mine as well.

My father, however, remained mostly silent on this period of his life until a few weeks before his death. Only then did he agree to be questioned by my sister about Camp. They talked for about forty-five minutes before he could go no further. My father, who was never seen crying, had wept the entire time.

Such grief conjoins in psychic trauma. Trauma which remains unhealed is passed on to our children who then struggle with feelings of inferiority, self-blame, denial, repression, and displaced hostility. Something huge between my father and my mother was extinguished during their incarceration. Their spirits together were like the sanctuary ducks at Tule Lake, originally wild, free, and joyous. Until, suddenly, they were seized and tied to the ground.

I also have not escaped. The trauma of my mother, my father, and my grandparents is lived out in my own life. To sanctify is to veil. To shroud is to repress the psychic armor against feeling and awareness. Silence kills without lifting a hand, and the war within continues. But, with conscious intentionality, it is possible to reprogram our patterns, and to reshape our lives.

Shattering silence is a beginning of the quest for an arrival to the place of the winds. The holder of hidden histories and secrets concealed within smoky filigrees of pain and yearning rising from that fiery trench in my grandparents' backyard. Morpheus, God of Dreams, carried by his cloud horse streaming story ribbons through fields of luggage tags. Fluttering remembrance into the transformative language of truth, forgiveness, and love.

And as night gives way to dawn, at the altar on my knees, I write as if I were dying, of the valor, the grace, the messiness of the lives of my father, my mother, my grandparents. We dance on the edge of the scream. Sing in the center of the shriek. Excavate the space between the sigh and the gasp. Caress the velvet-gloved hand of trauma. Morph silence into redemption and liberation.

• • •

OVERCOMING CRUELTY

Sharon Salzberg

FROM: *The Force of Kindness: Change Your Life with Love and Compassion*

The physiological root that empowers a natural sense of morality is the compassion that comes from empathy. Through the quality of empathy we understand that suffering hurts others in just the same way that it hurts us. This ability is what gives us an organic, straightforward sense of conscience. It reveals to us how likely it would be for someone to feel diminished if they were lied to, violated if they were stolen from, disempowered if they were excluded from decision, desperate if they were hungry.

In Buddhist teachings, the image used to reflect this quality of mind is that of a feather held near a flame, and the way it instantly curls away from the heat. In just that way, when our minds become imbued with an understanding of how suffering feels, and filled with a compassionate urge not to cause suffering in others, we naturally recoil from causing harm. This happens without self-consciousness or self-righteousness; it happens as a natural expression of the heart. We remember not to harm others because we actually understand how our actions could hurt them, as though it were our own bodies that could be injured, our own emotions set reeling, our own confidence broken. We see a piece of ourselves in them.

In contrast, if others are seen as objects rather than as feeling beings, it becomes quite easy to harm them, even in awful ways. Our lack of empathy reflects an inability to truly relate to other beings, to respect their boundaries or accept that their feelings, their needs, their hopes and dreams are viable, alive, and *theirs*. This is the misapprehension that allows a person to exploit and abuse others—and when it is extreme, this is what allows us to be unkind without care. More and more, we begin to view those we encounter mostly as likely competitors for the goodies we want, obstructions on our path to free enjoyment, potential challengers to our beliefs, and characters to be measured in light of the self-absorbed narrative we tell about our lives. From this vantage point, we can objectify anyone. And once someone appears to us primarily as an object, kindness has no place to root.

When we experience the world dualistically, there is a pervasive sense of us and them, or self and other. Inevitably, separation and distance are enhanced because of this duality. Instead of feeling intimacy with others, recognizing our shared wishes and vulnerabilities and our mutual dependence on one another, we resist; we put up "narrow, domestic walls," as poet Rabindranath Tagore termed them, and we cut ourselves off more and more. Sometimes those walls, that isolation, can come to feel like the most palpable, alive thing in our existence.

It's easy for us to feel separate from other people and from other forms of life, especially if we don't have a reliable connection to our own inner world. Without insight into our internal cycles of pleasure and pain, desires and fears, there is a strong sense of being removed, apart, or disconnected. When we do have an understanding of our inner lives, it provides an intuitive opening, even without words, to the ties that exist between ourselves and others.

The Buddha said that within this fathom-long body lives the entire universe. If we can understand our own experience and connect to it, we can connect to all life, to the whole universe. We know that when we experience anger, it has a certain flavor and tone. We experience the pain of that anger, and we sense that it's not different from the pain other beings experience when angry. The causes may be completely different, the manifestations may be poles apart, one's sensitivity to how much it hurts may be blunted or exquisite, but the painful nature of anger holds true.

When we feel seen for who we are and loved, there is a liberating joy in that. It is distinctive and special, and we can know from clearly seeing love's spirit how enlivening it could be for others, too. This is not to say we project our experience onto others and impose our views of what someone "must be" feeling, but rather that we can fathom, regardless of who is involved, states like the churning nature of mixed emotions, the hurt of being discounted, the relief of being cared about.

Without inner vision, it's easy to feel cut off and distant from others as though their experience is completely alien from our own. This is not only in terms of human beings—we might feel it even more so with other forms of life. If we live in this separated mode, if we constantly feel removed or alienated, we will develop a pervasive sense of self and other, with a very big "other" out there.

Upholding these divisions, the fundamental way we see the world is altered. Our commitments, our relationships, our sense of who belongs and who doesn't, who is "in" and who is "out," all change. We become more and more alone in a world we have created, a world where what we say or do to those who don't seem to matter doesn't seem to count. Once a person fully becomes an object in our eyes, fully becomes the "other," we can do absolutely anything to them, and the upholding of kindness dies.

I don't have to go through any litany here of the many different kinds of cruelty people are capable of. We are blasted by reports of horrifying behavior every day in the news. At times, we witness it tragically exhibited in our own families or communities. Sometimes those actions are just about beyond our comprehension. When I consider people diluting chemotherapy drugs, robbing senior citizens, discriminating against those of another race, or smacking kids, I inevitably think, "How in the world can they do that?" And then I pause and think again, about the times I slice through someone's eagerness to connect with me with my indifference, my disregard, because I am not paying attention. I think about times I hold onto petty grievances and don't see the totality of the person I am resenting. I think about the times when I just don't care enough about the person in front of me because I'm busy contemplating what I next will need from someone else.

We might not behave in a terrible fashion in any given moment because of our backgrounds or wisdom or circle of friends or sheer good luck, but we all know what it is like to look right through someone as though they weren't important. We all know what it is like to deny the vitality of someone's vulnerable, complex, mutable life once we have him or her nicely pigeonholed as the "other."

The Advaita Vedanta master, H. W. L. Poonja, once said in response to a question about bringing peace to the world, "As long as there are two, there will be war. " As long as there is that insidious sense of self and other creating "two," and we can objectify that "other" for our own ends, there will be war in our hearts, in our families, in our neighborhoods, and throughout the world.

A dedication to kindness offers us a chance to try to make a real difference despite the obstacles and unhappiness we might face. No matter what our belief system, actions, or status, we are joined together in this world through strands of relationship—interconnection. That suffering child, orphaned through a tsunami, that we see in Indonesia or Sri Lanka is part of our own lives, and we need to not forget that. There is nothing that just happens only "there" anymore—not a war, not an exploitation of the weak, not a disease, not a hope for change. We need to stop reinforcing the sense of dehumanization, of "us" and "them," of separation that leads to wanton cruelty in the first place.

And we must realize, if tomorrow is going to look any better than today, that the currency for compassion isn't what someone does, right or wrong—it is the very fact that that person exists. Commitment to the possibility of kindness cannot be discarded as foolish or irrelevant, even in troubling times when we often can't find answers. If we abandon the force as we confront cruelty, we won't learn anything to take into tomorrow—not from history, not from one another, not from life.

Even if we are encountering cruelty, we must try to understand its roots and determine not to be the same as those acting it out. We must determine not to simply keep perpetrating the forces of separation and disregard. If we don't make that effort, what will we really have accomplished?

We can all keep on trying, through the extension of lovingkindness to others, making the effort to pay attention to them in an inclusive way rather than splitting them off into the "other" and the "different" ones who can be hurt with impunity. This doesn't mean that we become complacent or passive about naming wrongdoing as wrong or about seeking change, sometimes very forcefully, with our whole heart.

It does mean that we learn to see the lives of others, really see them, as related to our own lives. It means that we open up to the possibility of caring for others not just because we like them or admire them or are indebted to them in some way, but because our lives are inextricably linked to one another's. We use the practice of lovingkindness meditation as a way to recover our innermost knowledge of that linkage, as we dissolve the barriers we have been upholding and genuinely awaken to how connected we all are.

WAYS TO OFFER LOVINGKINDNESS TO OTHERS

- Reflect on a time you have been objectified by someone. What were the consequences? Reflect on a time you have objectified someone else. What were the consequences?
- Take the time to pay attention to a stranger—someone you pass on the street or see in the subway. As you exercise, imagine where they are going and what their day will be like.
- Stay aware of the internal feelings generated when someone hurts you through their own unskillful actions. Remember that this is what others feel as well when they are hurt or harmed.
- Stay aware of the internal feeling generated when someone gives you a gift or is kind to you. Remember that this is what others feel as well.
- Pay full attention and really look at and listen to someone you usually ignore or find annoying.
- Practice lovingkindness mediation towards others as well as yourself.

· · ·

EULOGY FOR THE MARTYRED CHILDREN
Martin Luther King, Jr.

Now I say to you in conclusion, life is hard, at times as hard as crucible steel. It has its bleak and difficult moments. Like the ever-flowing waters of the river, life has its moments of drought and its moments of flood.

Like the ever-changing cycle of the seasons, life has the soothing warmth of its summers and the piercing chill of its winters. And if one will hold on, he will discover that God walks with him, and that God is able to lift you from the fatigue of despair to the buoyancy of hope, and transform dark and desolate valleys into sunlit paths of inner peace.

CHAPTER 5

Truth Telling and Justice

Injustice anywhere is a threat to justice everywhere. We are
caught in an inescapable network of mutuality, tied in a
single garment of destiny. . . .

—Martin Luther King, Jr., *Letter from Birmingham Jail*

The state of mutual respect and trust that constitutes lasting peace must
of necessity include the public recognition of any injustice committed in
the present or the past.

Justice is often confused with revenge. But if these are linked, as
when, for instance, the desire for revenge is satisfied by justice, there are
also distinct differences between them, significant to the healing of both
victims and society as a whole. If the desire for revenge is an under-
standable response to abuse, revenge by itself cannot liberate consciousness from the weight of trauma. Indeed, revenge is often the starting point for obsessive rounds of rage and violence. The momentary but
transitory sense of power that comes from committing a violent act is
addictive. Correspondingly, as opposed to justice, revenge is often di-
vorced from any meticulous attempt to discover the truth. At times, revenge will even be enacted on an innocent person or group. This may
occur through a simple mistake or, as often happens, when a group becomes the symbolic object of revenge because they share a general characteristic with the perpetrator. (In the period of the Troubles in Northern Ireland, for example, the death of a Catholic man or woman might
have been avenged on any Protestant.) Sometimes scapegoating reflects
the prejudices of society as, for example, when a man abused by his
mother takes his anger out on women in general. Or revenge may be
enacted against someone who shares no characteristics at all with the
original perpetrator but is simply a member of a group already designated

through prejudice as a target, such as women, African Americans, or Jews during the holocaust. In all these cases, revenge itself is an act of injustice.

By contrast, justice is inseparable from truth. In attempting to render a just verdict, any judicial body must hear and weigh evidence, mitigating the possibility of injustice. Truth telling is also important in itself. To reveal the truth is the passionate desire of those who have been victimized and it is critical to the process of healing. But private healing is deeply connected to a larger social process. It is not knowledge alone that heals. What is also needed is public acknowledgment from society.

Naming the perpetrator can be a very difficult and thus courageous act, yet if crimes that have been perpetrated are not to be repeated, they must be delineated, defined, and seen. Under apartheid in South Africa, for instance, countless crimes were enacted that were never officially recognized as such. Until very recently, rape, which has been a part of violent conflicts over centuries, was not even acknowledged as a war crime. Whenever the truth is not told and no justice is rendered, crimes against humanity are silently sanctioned. Moreover, as has been so beautifully demonstrated by the Truth and Reconciliation process in South Africa, truth telling is the first step toward evaluating and addressing the causes of violence, and toward the transformation of violent actions into peaceful transactions.

Finally, the rendering of justice preserves collective memory. To declare an act of violence a crime is a public sacrament, one that takes the burden of suffering and guilt into a larger circle so that we can all share the knowledge of horrific crimes. A society that turns a blind eye to injustice becomes an unwitting collaborator in a pattern of abuse, linking, even if unconsciously, authority with injustice, rendering an impunity to violence and quietly condoning the victory of the strong and unscrupulous over those who are vulnerable.

No lasting peace can be built on such a legacy.

Susan Griffin

. . .

UNIVERSAL DECLARATION OF HUMAN RIGHTS
*Adopted and proclaimed December 10, 1948, by the
General Assembly of the United Nations, resolution
217 A (III)*

Article 1.

All human beings are born free and equal in dignity and rights. They
are endowed with reason and conscience and should act towards one
another in a spirit of brotherhood.

Article 2.

Everyone is entitled to all the rights and freedoms set forth in this Declaration, without distinction of any kind, such as race, color, sex, language,
religion, political or other opinion, national or social origin, property,
birth or other status. Furthermore, no distinction shall be made on the
basis of the political, jurisdictional or international status of the country
or territory to which a person belongs, whether it be independent, trust,
non-self-governing or under any other limitation of sovereignty.

Article 3.

Everyone has the right to life, liberty and security of person.

Article 4.

No one shall be held in slavery or servitude; slavery and the slave trade
shall be prohibited in all their forms.

Article 5.

No one shall be subjected to torture or to cruel, inhuman or degrading
treatment or punishment.

Article 6.

Everyone has the right to recognition everywhere as a person before
the law.

Article 7.

All are equal before the law and are entitled without any discrimination to equal protection of the law. All are entitled to equal protection
against any discrimination in violation of this Declaration and against
any incitement to such discrimination.

Article 8.

Everyone has the right to an effective remedy by the competent national tribunals for acts violating the fundamental rights granted him by the constitution or by law.

Article 9.

No one shall be subjected to arbitrary arrest, detention or exile.

Article 10.

Everyone is entitled in full equality to a fair and public hearing by an independent and impartial tribunal, in the determination of his rights and obligations and of any criminal charge against him.

Article 11.

(1) Everyone charged with a penal offence has the right to be presumed innocent until proved guilty according to law in a public trial at which he has had all the guarantees necessary for his defence.

(2) No one shall be held guilty of any penal offence on account of any act or omission which did not constitute a penal offence, under national or international law, at the time when it was committed. Nor shall a heavier penalty be imposed than the one that was applicable at the time the penal offence was committed.

Article 12.

No one shall be subjected to arbitrary interference with his privacy, family, home or correspondence, nor to attacks upon his honour and reputation. Everyone has the right to the protection of the law against such interference or attacks.

Article 13.

(1) Everyone has the right to freedom of movement and residence within the borders of each state.

(2) Everyone has the right to leave any country, including his own, and to return to his country.

Article 14.

(1) Everyone has the right to seek and to enjoy in other countries asylum from persecution.

(2) This right may not be invoked in the case of prosecutions genuinely arising from non-political crimes or from acts contrary to the purposes and principles of the United Nations.

Article 15.

(1) Everyone has the right to a nationality.

(2) No one shall be arbitrarily deprived of his nationality nor denied the right to change his nationality.

Article 16.

(1) Men and women of full age, without any limitation due to race, nationality or religion, have the right to marry and to found a family. They are entitled to equal rights as to marriage, during marriage and at its dissolution.

(2) Marriage shall be entered into only with the free and full consent of the intending spouses.

(3) The family is the natural and fundamental group unit of society and is entitled to protection by society and the State.

Article 17.

(1) Everyone has the right to own property alone as well as in association with others.

(2) No one shall be arbitrarily deprived of his property.

Article 18.

Everyone has the right to freedom of thought, conscience and religion; this right includes freedom to change his religion or belief, and freedom, either alone or in community with others and in public or private, to manifest his religion or belief in teaching, practice, worship and observance.

Article 19.

Everyone has the right to freedom of opinion and expression; this right includes freedom to hold opinions without interference and to seek, receive and impart information and ideas through any media and regardless of frontiers.

Article 20.

(1) Everyone has the right to freedom of peaceful assembly and association.

(2) No one may be compelled to belong to an association.

Article 21.

(1) Everyone has the right to take part in the government of his country, directly or through freely chosen representatives.

(2) Everyone has the right of equal access to public service in his country.

(3) The will of the people shall be the basis of the authority of government; this will shall be expressed in periodic and genuine elections which shall be by universal and equal suffrage and shall be held by secret vote or by equivalent free voting procedures.

Article 22.

Everyone, as a member of society, has the right to social security and is entitled to realization, through national effort and international cooperation and in accordance with the organization and resources of each State, of the economic, social and cultural rights indispensable for his dignity and the free development of his personality.

Article 23.

(1) Everyone has the right to work, to free choice of employment, to just and favourable conditions of work and to protection against unemployment.

(2) Everyone, without any discrimination, has the right to equal pay for equal work.

(3) Everyone who works has the right to just and favorable remuneration ensuring for himself and his family an existence worthy of human dignity, and supplemented, if necessary, by other means of social protection.

(4) Everyone has the right to form and to join trade unions for the protection of his interests.

Article 24.

Everyone has the right to rest and leisure, including reasonable limitation of working hours and periodic holidays with pay.

Article 25.

(1) Everyone has the right to a standard of living adequate for the health and well-being of himself and of his family, including food, clothing, housing and medical care and necessary social services, and the

right to security in the event of unemployment, sickness, disability, widowhood, old age or other lack of livelihood in circumstances beyond his control.

(2) Motherhood and childhood are entitled to special care and assistance. All children, whether born in or out of wedlock, shall enjoy the same social protection.

Article 26.

(1) Everyone has the right to education. Education shall be free, at least in the elementary and fundamental stages. Elementary education shall be compulsory. Technical and professional education shall be made generally available and higher education shall be equally accessible to all on the basis of merit.

(2) Education shall be directed to the full development of the human personality and to the strengthening of respect for human rights and fundamental freedoms. It shall promote understanding, tolerance and friendship among all nations, racial or religious groups, and shall further the activities of the United Nations for the maintenance of peace.

(3) Parents have a prior right to choose the kind of education that shall be given to their children.

Article 27.

(1) Everyone has the right freely to participate in the cultural life of the community, to enjoy the arts and to share in scientific advancement and its benefits.

(2) Everyone has the right to the protection of the moral and material interests resulting from any scientific, literary or artistic production of which he is the author.

Article 28.

Everyone is entitled to a social and international order in which the rights and freedoms set forth in this Declaration can be fully realized.

Article 29.

(1) Everyone has duties to the community in which alone the free and full development of his personality is possible.

(2) In the exercise of his rights and freedoms, everyone shall be subject only to such limitations as are determined by law solely for the

purpose of securing due recognition and respect for the rights and free-doms of others and of meeting the just requirements of morality, public order and the general welfare in a democratic society.

(3) These rights and freedoms may in no case be exercised contrary to the purposes and principles of the United Nations.

Article 30.

Nothing in this Declaration may be interpreted as implying for any State, group or person any right to engage in any activity or to perform any act aimed at the destruction of any of the rights and freedoms set forth herein.

. . .

NAMING THE PERPETRATOR
Terri Jentz

Perhaps it seems obvious to say that there is an innate human need for justice. That when faced with wrongdoing, the individual, or society, can't rest until the malfeasance is addressed, put right, redressed. Per-haps it is logical to say, if there is not some kind of reckoning for perpe-trators (at the very least, identifying the wrongdoers and naming them in the public sphere), then they will be able to continue their crimes. That nothing encourages lawlessness more than the sight of wrongdoers get-ting away with their deeds. That lack of justice creates apathy in a society. That without justice, there can be no courage. No peace.

Why then are calls for justice so often unheard? Why then is the cul-ture of impunity so entrenched? Whenever the victims are the most vul-nerable within society, generally women and children, or groups margin-alized by race or class or ethnicity, a culture of impunity seems strikingly universal.

For the victims of violence, the blind eye of impunity has direct con-sequences. I wish I could say it's always beneficial for survivors to tell the truth in public about who committed the crime, but to do so would be glib. It isn't easy to name the perpetrator. If it brings great rewards, it carries great risks as well.

I have personal experience with the matter. In June of 1977, my col-lege roommate and I, high-spirited and ambitious twenty-year-old girls, were seven days into a cross-country journey across America by bicycle.

We were camped in the Oregon desert when, near midnight, a truck struck our small tent, and parked on my chest. As I gasped for thimblefuls of oxygen, I heard my roommate scream, then I heard several blows, and by then my acutely alert consciousness managed to make sense of the unimaginable—that we were being murdered by a lone psycho. Wondering all the time why his truck hadn't suffocated me, I heard him climb back into his truck, then he drove off of my body, liberating me to gulp for air. After a moment of reprieve, he was back, bludgeoning me with a weapon. Finally making a bid for my life, I opened my eyes to a meticulously dressed young cowboy standing over me, holding an axe over my heart, his face dissolved in darkness. Inexplicably, a solicitation from me worked magic. "Please leave us alone," I said, calmly, and just as calmly, he withdrew the axe, walked away and peeled off in his truck. Against considerable odds, my roommate and I had both survived. But this double attempted murder was never solved, and the identity of this headless torso of a young cowboy remained a mystery, seemingly more remote with each passing year.

At first, I denied the importance of knowing the identity of the man who had tried to end my life. It wasn't until fifteen years had passed that I awakened to the sure knowledge that the attack I had endured at the age of twenty had divided my life into a before and after. Though in my memory my assailant lacked a face, he had left visible scars, both physical and psychological. As the years wore on, I began to notice that my energies were mysteriously debilitated, my concentration dispersed; my will power, once strong and focused, flapped back and forth, easily deflected. An exquisitely sensitive responsiveness of my stress hormones made me susceptible to even the smallest frights. Once, around the age of thirty, I did the math: 70 percent of my energy, I wagered, went to worrying about the omnipresent threats to my life. It seemed to me that cataclysm could come from everything, everywhere, from myriad sources of danger: car accidents, disease, strangers in the night, earthquakes, and apocalyptic fires—a hundred fears in one converging threat could at any moment drag me into a familiar region of dread.

Finally I had a deep insight that truth seeking might restore something vital in my core, would resurrect my vitality, dampen my fears, and give me courage to control my destiny; that finding out who my attacker was, naming him, and nailing him to the deed, might aid me in recovering from a dislocation of body and mind that clinicians would call Post Traumatic Stress Disorder.

It worked. Against great odds, fifteen years after the crime had taken place, I conducted my own investigation, found my assailant, labeled him in the public arena as the number one suspect, and wrote a book, *Strange Piece of Paradise,* about my detective work and how solving the crime affected my own psyche. There was something profoundly fortifying in filling in an abstraction with a specific form, in attaching a face to a heretofore-faceless threat in my unconscious. It made me less phobic. I had lifted the generalized fear, which arose from my past, out of the deep psyche, brought it to the surface, attached to the threat of a specific man in the present day. I had told the truth about the man I called "Dirk Duran" to the world.

Duran had other victims, a string of women whom he had abused. There was the girl he was dating during the time he attacked me. (He had beaten her so viciously that he nearly killed her, the very day after the attack on me.) There was the woman he married and tortured for five years. There were women he tormented after his wife finally escaped from him. They were desperate to tell the truth about him to me. They were willing to reveal personal details, even of a shameful nature, because they recognized how important it was that their stories be told publicly.

When my narrative was finally between hard covers, I felt a tangible restoration of dignity, a diminishing of fear, and most of all, a resurgence of will. As a voice for these other abused women, who would not have had a voice otherwise, I had exercised my will in service to the larger social good.

Over time, as I realized it is not always possible to name the perpetrator who has assaulted you, my victory became even more meaningful and poignant to me. The book had been out a few months when I got a message from my friend, whom I'll call Maura, sobbing on the phone. "You were able to name your perpetrator publicly. I never can." Her childhood abuse hadn't been easy to prosecute, even though she herself was a lawyer. "Sometimes you can't just name your perpetrator. Whether to do it or not takes careful consideration. You can be isolated. Labeled insane . . ."

She reminded me of what I already knew: there can be great risks in naming the one who has abused you. Not only can you be ostracized, but also you can be shamed, blamed, traumatized all over again. You can even be killed.

In Pakistan, under the Zinna laws, if a woman names her rapist and he isn't convicted of rape (which is next to impossible under the rules stacked in his favor), she can wind up in jail for having sex outside of marriage.

Though the plight of Pakistani women may ring extreme to American ears, consider the situation of an American woman who wrote to tell me that she lost her job for naming her perpetrator. She'd known a man a short while when one day, for no apparent reason, he beat her and knifed her. She called the police and testified in court. When her boss found out, he fired her. He believed that since his employee was attacked by someone she knew, she must have done something to provoke him. Therefore she must be trouble, a risk to his business.

The producer of a popular American talk show, *Montel Williams,* told me that she gets calls all the time from people who want to confide in Montel the names of people who have committed crimes against them. They had been reluctant to tell the police—terrified of retaliation, and of having to appear as witnesses in a trial where they would have to lay eyes on their attacker again, associate themselves with him, perhaps have their pictures twinned with his in the same column of a newspaper. But still they wanted to bring what happened into the public eye, somehow.

I too had courted danger by naming my attacker. I had put myself in jeopardy by exposing a dangerous man who still was free (because at the time of his crime the statute of limitations on attempted murder was only three years in Oregon, he could never be indicted for the attack against me and my roommate). But I always rationalized my behavior to worried friends, telling them that I was risking minimal peril to interview people about his suspected involvement in my crime, while he was working nearby in the same little town. Actually there were days in my investigation when I was paralyzed by heart-stopping terror. Yet I was always compelled to continue my inquiry, however dangerous. It felt like a matter of my soul's life or death to do so. Everything was at stake.

No further harm came to me physically at the hands of "Dirk Duran." Yet there are occasions when his malevolence still haunts me psychologically. Recently I was reminded of the terror of him that I still hold in my subconscious. Duran's ex-wife, Ruby, called me out-of-the-blue one day. I hadn't heard from Ruby in eleven years, when she had candidly told me of her years of bondage to her sadistic husband. Why she was calling? Now that I had published her story, had her ex-husband retaliated against her? Would he retaliate against me for revealing the shocking atrocities he committed during their marriage? An irrational dread convulsed me once more. I tried to pinpoint exactly what I was feeling: it had been nearly ten years since I had first taken the risk to name this perpetrator in the public arena. In the mid-1990s, I had called a press conference in three Oregon cities, and had spoken his name into the microphone as my number one suspect in this crime that could never be prosecuted. He had never taken revenge on me then. Now my position was even more secure. I had authorial authority. I lived in another state. He had no resources to travel, and even if he did, he wouldn't have a clue where to find me. And yet, because he had had dominion over my life one long ago night, by naming him, and therefore enraging him, I felt irrationally vulnerable. A picture formed in my mind: that I was living alone, stark naked, in a house with all glass walls, and I knew his eyes were on me, watching my every move, invisibly powerful over me.

Then another woman called me out of the blue. My book had been making its way through the public for well over a year when a newspaper reporter e-mailed me that a woman was urgently trying to reach me regarding "Dirk Duran" in the days of the 1977 Oregon campground attack. I returned her call to a town thousands of miles from Oregon.

I was astonished when "Lucianne," as I'll call her, described how she fit into Duran's life. My book had chronicled a timeline of every girlfriend he had abused, but three years remained unaccounted for. Here was the missing girl.

She was a woman in her early 40s who'd learned about my book, although she hadn't read it, and admitted it was hard for her to muster the courage to contact me. Her pronounced Western drawl was unsteady, from drink or drugs, as she launched into the revelation that ever since she dated the handsome young cowboy as a teen, "that sociopathic man has had the most catastrophic effect of my life." She was scared of him to this day, although she'd left her hometown for good in the early '80s. Not long ago when she was visiting that Oregon town, she happened to see him, looking haggard and toothless, had spoken to him, then vomited afterwards.

Lucianne was clearly suffering emotional anguish as she talked to me. She cried and regained control, cried again, only to dissolve to ambiguous remarks about the "terrible things, *terrible things*," he had subjected her to. When I suggested that I was capable of hearing what she had to tell, no matter how awful, she responded, "It's some *bad* stuff, *Missy*."

She was reaching hard to name what he had done to her. But she couldn't quite do it. She circled. She repeated herself. She had a secret.

Something she couldn't yet utter. Something the existence of my book had inspired her to tell me, and me specifically.

She asked, "Do we have to look at something that dark and awful? Did what you did save you? Going into the dark like that?" Before I could answer she rambled on, never getting to the point, until I reassured her that we could continue our conversations later, if it was too hard for her to talk just now. Then she cut me off:

"No, Miss Jentz, I don't think I can read your book. I have to go. This has been a very bad day," and I noted, as I was losing her, how she drew out the word "baaaad." The line went dead.

Later in the day my cell phone rang. A gruff, rude voice identified himself as Lucianne's husband. He indicated that my conversation with his wife had destabilized her. "Miss Jentz. Don't call here any more!"

"Your wife called *me*," I corrected.

"*I know,* but *never call here again!*" He hung up.

If she had given me an opportunity to answer her question "Did what you did save you? Going into the dark like that?" I would have told her that it's true that since I dared to name my assailant in public, that some part of my psyche will always fear his malevolence. But I cannot imagine a life in which I had not tracked him down, named him, and nailed him to the deed. In this year, the thirtieth anniversary of the attack, I cannot conceive of having lived until today in a state of hazy helplessness. By publicly attributing specific crimes to a specific individual, I was able to reorder the moral chaos that had befogged body and mind, and I liberated myself to navigate the planet again as I had before the age of twenty—as a determined, buoyant girl with an inviolable sense of self.

The sudden presence of Lucianne in my life, clutching to her baneful secrets, is evidence of something important: that my story, now part of the public record, is a tale that will continue to pass from one individual to the next, on into a distant future, emboldening those who fear to tell the truth about their assailants.

Everyone who names her assailant does it also for someone else who couldn't do it for herself. All truth-tellers create a possibility for justice in the larger society. Who knows what smaller gestures behind closed doors have been inspired by one individual's bold, public act? Perhaps Lucianne has shuttered again, and will clamp down on her secrets for the rest of her lifetime. But I suspect otherwise. My guess is that she'll dare tell a few others in her circle what she suffered at the hands of a malevolent boy long ago.

I would like to have had the chance to tell Lucianne that her phone call to me was proof: yes, what I did was worth it. Out of my act of truth telling, something vital in her core, once crushed and suffocated to soul-death, is now taking in thimblefuls of fresh air.

. . .

THERE WAS NO FAREWELL

*Taha Muhammad Ali (translated by Peter Cole,
Yahya Hijazi, and Gabriel Levin)*

We did not weep
when we were leaving—
for we had neither
time nor tears,
and there was no farewell.
We did not know
at the moment of parting
that it was a parting,
so where would our weeping
have come from?
We did not stay
awake all night
(and did not doze)
the night of our leaving.
That night we had
neither night nor light,
and no moon rose.
That night we lost our star,
our lamp misled us;
we didn't receive our share
of sleeplessness—
so where
would wakefulness have come from?

. . .

FACING THE INFERNO: TRANSFORMING TERROR
INTO TENDERNESS
Morgan Farley

September 11, 2006—five years ago today. I grieve, and I am grateful.
The tragedy that robbed so many people of their lives gave me a second
chance at mine. It seems almost sacrilegious to say it, given the enormity
of our loss. But the truth is, 9/11 saved me. The shock brought down
defenses I had spent my life erecting, exposing an inner devastation I had
kept secret even from myself.

When the planes slammed into the towers and exploded inside them, it
felt like my body was being violated, the ten-year-old body I had abandoned on a cot in a locked attic so that I could have a normal life. But what
I had without that child self was only half a life, the life of a woman who
moved through the world leaving no footprints. Under my accomplished
veneer I felt unreal, disembodied, ghostly. In my ruthless drive to rise above
that trauma I had sacrificed more of myself than I could afford to lose.

Nothing less than 9/11 would have made me go back for the molested child. In almost fifty years, nothing ever had. But watching rescue
workers running into the burning towers, risking their lives to save the
lives of strangers, I knew I had to do it. I had escaped harm, I thought,
by leaving her behind. Now I saw how wrong I was. She was still back
there, a little girl all alone, trapped in another kind of rubble. And she
was my own, closer to me than my daughter, my sister. How could I live
with myself if I let her die? All my life I had fled from her. After 9/11 I
turned and ran the other way, into the inferno, to save her.

I was haunted by the ones who jumped. Their excruciating vulnerability, combined with wild acts of grace, showed me a way through.
I saw two women hold hands and step into the sky. I saw a man in
shirtsleeves, upright on a sill, balance for a second on the balls of his
feet and swan dive. He didn't fall, he flew. These were glimpses only—
the shocking footage was not shown again—but they proved to me that
it is possible to stay humanly connected, and inwardly free, in the face
of terror beyond imagining, terror far more grievous than my own.

What terrified me was my blasted heart. That is what I thrust away
in horror—the shattered child. I thought her pain would kill me. I
thought she was damaged beyond repair. I thought if I ever let her in I
would have to take care of her for the rest of my life. I thought her huge
need would exhaust and defeat me, devour me whole and ruin my chance
at happiness.

My terror took on the force of a mission: never to be that alone again, never to feel anguish like that again. From ten on, my life became a desperate effort to triumph over that catastrophic year as if it had never happened. But my heroic effort was misguided. It took me in the wrong direction, away from myself, away from love. 9/11 turned me around. The sight of those helpless bodies plunging from the towers broke my heart again and made me remember how vulnerable and hurt I really was.

In that stark hour I turned to writing because writing had always been my refuge and my way of contributing to our common life. I was a poet; the country would need its poets now, I thought. And writing was not only what I knew, it was the best of me, the part that had always been in the clear, soulful and eloquent. But my eloquence was no match for this subject, the raw chaos of ground zero. The new poems fell apart in my hands. I could not speak powerfully about ground zero at the World Trade Center because I had never had the courage to stand at ground zero in my own life, to look with clear-eyes into the smoking crater of my own heart. It was that burnt ground I had to write from now, the place that had always been too painful for words.

Full of dread, I wrote the first poem. I understood that it was now or never. The relief was tremendous, but brief. I had opened the flood gates. In the next six months, I wrote 160 poems about the disastrous year I was ten.

I approached the first poem gingerly, from the safe distance of my 56-year-old self. It told a poignant but stereotypical story of innocence and victimization, buttressed with insights hard won in my years of therapy. At this travesty of reality, the ten-year-old girl sprang up in me, outraged, and insisted on writing the rest of the poems herself. If anybody was going to tell that story, she was. It was hers—her secret, her fate.

She swept my literary ambitions out of the way so that she could speak in her own voice, use her own words. *She* would tell *me* exactly what happened and, more important, how it felt while it was happening. She would make me understand what she went through, and then I would have to love her. She had never given up on me. Even though I had proved to be just as untrustworthy as the other grownups in her life, she had never stopped loving me. To my surprise, she had never stopped loving any of us: the parents who knew something was happening, yet made no attempt to protect her; the man who both doted on and violated her; even his wife who, finding them in her bed one afternoon, quietly shut the door and walked away.

The child lived inside the fragile heart of the experience, carried in her bones its agonies and ambiguities. I had stood outside it all those years, judging and condemning, battling with despair. Now she had her chance to set me straight. She would do it by taking me back inside her body. She would slow down the ordeal. She would knit me into the felt truth of that time and thereby knit me back into my own skin.

All she asked was that I meet her with pen in hand each day. It was almost more than I could do. Nightmares, memories, and feelings flooded in, threatening to overwhelm me. I procrastinated, filling the mornings with other tasks. A clear voice appeared in my dreams: "Dance with the dazzling split ashes of yourself. Survive, survive!" I took a vow to write with her every morning without fail, reconciled myself to being merely the scribe and waited to see what she would tell me.

She was relentless. Abstract words like pedophile and molestation had no meaning for her. She took me places I had never allowed myself to go. She pushed me into the inferno where language disintegrated into gasps and grunts, cries and shivers. The truth was searing and fleshy. She made me smell it and taste it: the stained pillows he slid under my hips, the sweat darkening his thin hair, the cold creeping into me until I lay frozen on the cot. The strange unearthliness.

To claim her ordeal as mine meant reclaiming the ravaged ten-year-old body. This was the hardest thing of all. To enter that body was to fall—into a numb, paralyzed state in the attic and a state of near collapse at home. She tripped over the cracks in the sidewalk and bloodied her knees. She leaned on her father, as if she couldn't hold herself up, until he laughingly nicknamed her Leanerd. Her spine sagged into an S and would not straighten. She lost inches of height. She sobbed at night from the ache in her hips, unable to sleep. Rashes wept down her legs.

The more I let her speak, the more my body became her body. My back muscles had been in spasm for forty years, and now my right hip throbbed and angry rashes reappeared at my breasts and thighs. I remembered these ailments but not their intensity—the maddening itch, the ache so deep it kept me awake. They were a desperate language, the unheard child signaling for help the only way she could.

She held my body in that fire with the force of her urgency until the ice around my heart slowly melted. I put down the pen and stared into space for an hour, stunned by what she was telling me. I held my head in my hands and wept. That was the balm for her wounds, the rescue she had been waiting for—someone willing to feel and suffer with her at this depth, to weep for her and hold her close.

During that hard lonely winter of daily writing, our long enmity flowered into tenderness. In a dream I saw a winter tree with tiny blood-red leaves unfurling from its black branches. This unexpected tenderness was the healing we had almost despaired of—so small a thing, and yet everything. To admit to her that what happened had actually happened put solid ground under my feet at last. And then to reenter the labyrinth of that year together, to take each other's hand as we groped our way forward in the dark, was an inexpressible comfort. The worst of it, for each of us, had been our utter aloneness. Now that was over.

Our tender acceptance of each other made us braver, helped us to leave nothing unmet, even the unbearable things, and nothing unsaid. That long patience led us to the very center of the labyrinth where there was no monster after all, only love. By then we had seen into the secrets of each heart. We had said yes to life, and once that yes was truly said, there was nothing to forgive. Her impassioned and meticulous truth-telling had carried us into the paradox and mystery at the heart of our story. The inferno had turned into an open forge where our base metals were fused and refined, our unspeakable secrets hammered into poetry.

In the years since I wrote the poems, I have flourished. The ten-year-old girl has come back to life in me, and she is feisty and funny—not damaged at all but, by some mystery, whole. I thought I was saving her, but it is she who is saving me. She has given me back my vitality and spontaneity, my joy. Once subdued and soft-spoken, I am now lively and bold. Once intense and over-earnest, I am light-hearted and full of laughter. The rift between us is gone, as if tectonic plates deep in my being had merged. I am no longer divided against myself.

This is a different order of change from the changes I made in twenty years of therapy. My dream voice foretold it: "Come back from the beach of nothingness, needing no treatment, seeking no cure." I move fluidly now, letting my breasts sway and my hips swing. The telltale rashes have gone—for good, I think. The chronic back spasms have released their fierce grip on me, and I am free of pain for the first time in years. My spine will always be curved, but I think of it now as a tree on a wild coast, twisted by ferocious winds but beautiful in its bending. I honor it as my ally, for telling my secret when I was mute.

The inner freedom I feel is reflected in my life. One night the dream voice announced, "The heroine of mistiness wears red inside her blue." This statement set in motion a process that changed my whole appearance. I gave away the pale, loose attire I had chosen unconsciously as protective coloration, shed fifteen cushioning pounds, and splurged on a brand new wardrobe of shape-hugging clothes in scarlet and coral, apricot and emerald green. By some unlooked-for grace, I fell in love at almost sixty and gave my heart fearlessly. With my partner's blessing, I spent ten months on a remote island writing the book I had always wanted to write.

One Halloween, at a costume party for my whole community, I dressed as a femme fatale in a slinky red and black satin dress with a long red feather boa. Emboldened by false eyelashes and a French accent, I flirted outrageously. A friend laughingly named me Edith Pilaf, and before I knew it I had been persuaded to sing her famous song, "Non, Je Ne Regrette Rien." I started by translating the lyrics for the crowd. "No, I regret nossing, nossing at all," I purred. "I don' geeve a sheet about the past." Whoops and whistles greeted this line, and I launched into the song, belting it out like a torch singer. I had not sung my heart out since I was ten, but as Edith Pilaf I knew exactly how to do it. I could have been standing in the spotlight at the Moulin Rouge.

There must be many ways of facing the inferno. I am haunted still by the ones who jumped; the two women who held hands as they stepped off the ledge, the man who flung out his arms and flew. Surely they found not just an exit but an entrance into a place that held them as they fell. I listen for their lost voices. There is everything to say. And nothing. Thanks to them, I rock in the small boat of my deliverance. The ocean I rest on is deep and still. Its touch is tenderness itself.

. . .

HALF-LIFE OF A DESPOT

Ariel Dorfman

Is Gen. Augusto Pinochet, Chile's former dictator, really dead?

Though there can be no doubt that his body has been proven to indeed be mortal, I fear that his spirit may live on interminably in the Chile he misruled from 1973 to 1990 and then continued to terrorize as commander in chief of the army for eight more years. In order to truly exorcise him from our existence it would have been necessary that he stand trial, that he defend himself from the accusations of murder and torture, kidnapping and grand larceny, which have been brought against him in innumerable court cases in Santiago.

In order to cleanse his image from our land, we would have had to witness him looking into the face of each and every one of his victims, the mothers whose children he disappeared, the wives whose husbands he massacred, the sons who were persecuted and exiled. In order to be rid of his dire influence, we should have left the job of mourning him to his family and few close friends. Instead we must watch the sad spectacle of one-third of the country lamenting his departure, one-third of Chile still silent accomplices to his crimes, still justifying his crimes, still rejoicing that the general overthrew Salvador Allende, the constitutional president of Chile. . . .

Only a country still full of fear would dare to stoop so low, pay public homage to such a despot.

And yet, in spite of all these signs of General Pinochet's continuing dominance from beyond death, I feel that something has in fact changed quite categorically with his demise. What convinced me were the thousands upon thousands of Chileans who spontaneously poured into the streets here to celebrate the news of his extinction. I tend to be wary of any attempt to turn the death of anyone into an occasion for joy, but I realized that in this case it was not one man's death that was being welcomed but rather the birth of a new nation.

Dancing under the mountains of Santiago there was one word they repeated over and over and it was the word shadow. "La sombra de Pinochet se fue," one woman said, his shadow is gone, we have come out from under the general's shadow. As if the demons of a thousand plagues had been washed from this land, as if we were never again to be afraid, never again the helicopter in the night, never again the air polluted by sorrow and violence.

For those who were celebrating (most of them young), it was as if something had been definitely, gloriously shattered when Augusto Pinochet's bleak and unrepentant heart ceased beating. They had spent their lives, as I had spent mine, awaiting this moment, this day when the darkness receded, this December when our country would be purged, ready to start over again. This moment when we need to grow up and stop blaming General Pinochet for everything that goes wrong, everything that went wrong, this moment when he disappears from our horizon.

Has the general really died? Will he ever stop contaminating every schizophrenic mirror of our life? Will Chile ever cease to be a divided nation? Or is she right, that future mother, seven months pregnant, who jumped for joy in the center of Santiago, was she right when she shouted to the seven winds that from now on everything would be different, that her child would be born in a Chile from which Augusto Pinochet has forever vanished?

The battle for the soul of this country has just begun.

· · ·

It is not probable that this monomania in him took its instant rise at the precise time of his bodily dismemberment. Then, in darting at the monster, knife in hand, he had but given loose to a sudden, passionate, corporal animosity; and when he received the stroke that tore him, he probably but felt the agonizing bodily laceration, but nothing more. Yet, when by this collision forced to turn towards home, and for long months of days and weeks, Ahab and anguish lay stretched together in one hammock, rounding in mid winter that dreary, howling Patagonian Cape; then it was, that his torn body and gashed soul bled into one another; and so interfusing, made him mad.

(Herman Melville, from *Moby Dick*)

· · ·

The presence of what Ellsberg has called the process of "internal self-deception" is beyond doubt. . . . In the realm of politics, where secrecy and deliberate deception have always played a significant role, self-deception is the danger par excellence; the self-deceiver deceived loses all contact not only with his audience, but also the real world. . . .

(Hannah Arendt, from *Crises of the Republic*)

· · ·

I lay in bed that Tuesday morning and thought: This is the system that I have been working for, the system I have been part of, for a dozen years—fifteen, including the Marine Corps. It's a system that lies automatically, at every level from bottom to top—from sergeant to commander in chief—to conceal murder. . . .

And it was still going on. I thought: I'm not going to be part of it anymore. I'm not going to be part of this lying machine, this cover-up, this murder, anymore.

(Daniel Ellsberg, from *Secrets:
A Memoir of Vietnam and the Pentagon Papers*)

· · ·

THE TENACITY OF MEMORY (*LA TENACIDAD DE LA MEMORIA*)

Claudia Bernardi

To modify the past is not only to modify a single account: it is to annul its consequences, which tend to be infinite. (*Modificar el pasado no es modificar un solo hecho: es anular sus consecuencias, que tienden a ser infinitas.*)

—Jorge Luis Borges, "The Other Death," *El Aleph*

I. Empathy

A few years ago, I was standing at a bus stop in Buenos Aires, the crowded, cosmopolitan, densely populated capital of Argentina where I was born.

A man's intense look upon me, his gaze deep, dark, and tragic, alerted me although it did not feel as a threat but as a distant plea. I tried to ignore him. His insistent scrutiny made me turn around and face him directly.

He stepped toward me and with a voice that seemed more a lament than a question, asked me: "Are you Claudia Bernardi's sister?"

His question startled me.

I answered: "No! I *am* Claudia Bernardi."

He looked at me as if seeing a ghost. In a gesture that conjured sadness and relief, he took my hands, briefly contained himself trying not to cry, and pronounced softly: "Claudia . . . I thought you had 'disappeared.'"

Argentina is a country where if someone has not been seen for some time, years, or decades, one is assumed "disappeared." The man I met at the bus stop had not seen me because I left Argentina in 1979 during the military dictatorship, 1976–1983. Given the absence and the time of absence, he had assumed over the years that my name was in the list of 30,000 disappeared people, a litany of pain that defines our history.

"My disappearance" had become so tactile to him, that when he saw me standing at the bus stop, he could not conclude that his assumption had been wrong. He was looking at a woman that he had thought long dead. The resemblance to the absent one could only be attributed to kinship. The standing woman alive today in this busy city of Buenos Aires could only be "her sister."

We hugged, laughed and cried, promising one another to call and remain in touch.

We never did that.

I suspect that one cannot change the assumptions of the past easily or willingly. We remain hostages of our own memory encapsulated in a continent of sorrow.

As I remember now this episode, causing me an incalculable sadness and a fresh fear, I realize the magnitude of the damage caused by the military junta in Argentina. This random encounter with a lost friend at a bus stop catapulted the past into the present with the solid fact that "I" could have been one of the disappeared, eroding the distance between "them" and "I," thinning the frontier between what happened and what could have happened.

We have lost "innocence" in Argentina. The abuses committed during the military junta are the result of organized harm designed and inflicted upon a large proportion of civilians. This awareness, I believe, exceeds the consideration of politics. It becomes, or perhaps it should become, a consideration of ethics, of a transformed and wounded history, and of empathy.

A system of power, namely the self-imposed military junta, constructed a structure of repression based on torture and degradation.

That is the success of state terror.

The military dictatorship in Argentina produced the death of the country. . . .

To modify or annul the past is, indeed, impossible, for its infinite consequences manage to define the present. When talking about "reconstruction" we are not just facing the rebuilding of a country but a recollection and collection of the wreckage from Argentina's past.

Even those who are not personally related to the victims or to the perpetrators during this darkest period in our recent history have to face that we are partakers of this tragedy simply by having been alive during those years, by having witnessed, even if we did not fully comprehend what we were looking at, the collapse of democracy and the implanting of terror.

There is no amendment, no healing to genocide.

Victims of state terror or genocide who undergo torture and unimaginably denigrating treatment, who have endured demolishing techniques that cause the collapse of human dignity cannot heal, cannot become the person who existed before. It is precarious, even offensive to expect "healing."

Those who survive are amputated from the person they once were.

Their pain becomes our shame.

After a brutal accident, if someone loses a leg, it is not expected that another leg will grow back. The amputated person might walk again, dance and travel the world, but this person will always be in absence of a vital part. This truth, painful and monumental as it is, is necessary if we are to choreograph a new future.

II. Impotence

In the United States today, I see the installing of effective and fraudulent systems of repression similar to those designed and placed in action by the military dictatorship in Argentina. The wording has changed. "Terrorism/terrorist" replaced "subversion/subversive." The practice of abuses of civil rights is the same. Unlawful laws were created justifying persecution and prejudice. Perversely, this was advertised as defending democracy.

In Argentina, the profound fear inflicted upon a persecuted generation produced another success of state terror, perhaps the most damaging one: a sentiment of nihilism that impacts the next generation. The success of state terror is to craft a young generation incapable of exercising analysis or criticism. A tame, isolated mass of young people sedated by a sentiment of impotence.

In 1992, taking testimony from survivors of massacres in El Salvador, I sat in a precarious lodging to converse with people who miraculously had evaded a massacre or those whose relatives had perished. They would talk softly, almost apologetically, naming long lists of dead people in their families, identifying the exact number of cows, pigs, and chickens, and even how many plants of corn had been burned after the massacre.

They would finish their testimony with a question: "Why did this happen to us?"

III. Memory

Memory, personal and collective, becomes militancy in the postwar period. It is a way to reflect upon that which already has managed to change forever our way to interpret our past and consequently to vindicate people we have loved and who are looking at us from the other side of death, leaving us with a painful caress on our lips and a question: why are we still alive?

More than guilt it is perplexity.

This perplexity screams back to us that "I," too, could have been a disappeared.

The Foam of Time Impregnates the Soul

On a cold afternoon of 1984, I witnessed for the first time an exhumation at the cemetery of Avellaneda, in Buenos Aires. Shortly after the dictatorship ended and while the country transited toward a frail democracy, there was the need to gather proof of violations of human rights perpetrated by the military junta. Mass graves were identified and investigated. My sister Patricia who was, and still is, a member of the Argentine Forensic Anthropology Team, warned me of the spectacle that a mass grave could cause. I saw her descend to an open cavity of the earth. When she emerged, she was bringing two shattered craniums. The fractures were the evidences of how they had died, with a gunshot wound inflicted at very short distance, execution style. The average age of the two individuals whose craniums she was collecting was estimated at 24 years of age.

Memory Is Not a Privilege of a Few but the Militancy of Many

The practice of memory as a way to accomplish consciousness, an awareness that attempts to acknowledge the errors of the past in order to avoid worse calamities in the future, remains one of the most demanding and challenging episodes of culture.

In recent years, buildings that once functioned as clandestine centers of detention during the military dictatorship in Argentina have been reclaimed by the relatives of the disappeared, by survivors of imprisonment, by human rights Non Governmental Agencies, by poets, writers, and artists. The buildings are open to the public as centers of memory. Their open doors welcome a visitation that produces simultaneously empathy and nausea.

In 2002, I visited the "Pozo de Rosario"/"The Hole of Rosario" located inside the police department of a densely populated city of the Republic. It is estimated that more than 3,000 people were taken to this camp from which few survived.

The building occupying an entire block has two large iron-door apertures through which trucks filled with people, mostly young, would cross the frontier between outside and inside "el Pozo," between life and torment.

I walked inside the building until I faced the entrance of a particular catacomb, a space opening downward where the blindfolded prisoners were deposited for an unpredictable length of time and tortured regularly, mortified at all times, and, eventually, selected to be "transported": the euphemism that always meant execution.

The stairs were weak as if the weight of many men and women had caused a fragility that was dangerous. The space was uneven, peculiarly shaped rooms opened to nowhere. There were blind entrances and doors that led to narrow passages. It appeared that the place was staged to produce confusion. I sat in one of the main rooms looking around without fully comprehending what it could have been like to be a prisoner there, to hear the daily screams of the tortured inmates, to be the ones tortured to the point of agony.

I reclined my back on the wall and I wept.

When I helped myself to stand up, placing my hand on the wall behind me, I noticed a thumbprint in the location where my own thumb, by total coincidence, had landed. The thumbprint was almost unnoticeable until I discovered it, and then it became all that I could look at for a long time. Another handprint, soft, quiet, and elusive, had a scratch next to it, done with the indentation of a nail on plaster, reading: "I was here."

My hand over the disintegrating handprint of someone whose tragedy I cannot start imagining or measuring.

Places of Memory Construct Consciousness

The absent bodies of the disappeared hold an immense archive of information that can be preserved from degradation only through the collective act of memory. Their unknown bodies have become a private and public entity. Documents, photographs, literature, and art narrating histories of the *disappeared* allow a liaison between the vacant generation standing from this side of the abyss and the past which belongs to us all.

Memory is a tool to build consciousness.

As they march silently but not unnoticed, the disappeared whisper their testimonies to the realm of the living.

Art may be the only apt language to address genocide.

Art is a communal tool for listening.

We are listening.

IV. *Truth*

The first time that I participated in an exhumation was not in Argentina. It was in El Salvador, in a hamlet located in Morazán, where a massacre occurred in 1981. Rufina Amaya Márquez, the sole survivor of the massacre at El Mozote, saw her community being divided in groups, men, women, younger women, and children. Rufina saw her husband being decapitated and could identify the voices and screams of her own children before they were shot.

No one but Rufina survived at El Mozote. Over 1,000 people perished on December 11 of 1981. The exhumation in 1992 confirmed the allegation of mass murder against civilians by identifying the presence of human remains of 143 individuals, of whom 136 were children under the age of 12, with an average age of 6 years old.

As part of the investigation and exhumations performed by the Argentine Forensic Anthropology Team in the case of the massacre at El Mozote, I created archeological maps identifying the location of the found human remains, associated objects, and ballistic evidence.

Until then, I had never exhumed the remains of children. The bones were frail, resembling bones of a small bird. The young age of the victims and the multiple fractures inflicted upon them caused the bones to deteriorate as fine powder, tender sawdust nestled quietly, for more than a decade.

Memory, consciousness, the truth.

The last victim of genocide is truth.

Killing truth is not a one time act.

It transcends history.

The past cannot be modified. Its infinite consequences may, gently, embroider a possible future.

V. Art

Una red de mirada	A net of gazing eyes
mantiene unido al mundo	keeps the world united
no lo deja caerse . . .	it does not allow it to fall . . .

—Roberto Juarroz, "Poesía Vertical/Vertical Poetry"

I am an artist. My art is born from memory and loss.

I design and facilitate community-based art projects in countries where there have been armed conflicts, transiting into the postwar period.

My art lives in the intersection of art and war.

In 2005, in Perquin, a small community four kilometers north from El Mozote, I created the School of Art and Open Studio of Perquin, serving children, youth, adults, and the elderly. It is a community art project that uses the strategies of art to rebuild a region torn apart by the Salvadoran civil war, 1980–1992, and its legacy: social, institutional, and economic collapse in the postwar period.

The School of Art and Open Studio of Perquin welcomes all members of the community regardless of their political or religious affiliation. Public art projects are debated and designed in partnership, leading to the creation of public art interventions and murals that narrate, as open history books, the life and memories of the people of the region.

It is not easy to achieve collegiality among people who have been pulled apart by local politics, war, and poverty. Within the School of Art and Open Studio of Perquin we intend and so far we have succeeded in utilizing the skills of art to build and reconstruct community relationships. It would be imprudent to think that art can remedy tragedies. It would be untrue to suggest that art can amend conflicts, but art as "a net of gazing eyes" may prove to be a pivotal tool to exercise and reestablish trust.

"Art" and "Genocide" belong to fundamentally opposite paradigms. Genocide (*genos,* Grk: kind, race; *cidium,* Latin: destruction) is the purposeful and effective praxis of destruction, annihilation in its most successful form. Art generates from nothingness. Art exists through the conviction, skills, and determination of the maker. Art is remembrance, fatigue, loss, pain, and hope, finding in the proposition of beauty its vindication. Art may not mean, necessarily, an improvement, but art will assist in the recapitulation of the suffering endured, transformed and rebirthed as a communal creation.

Art adds to the effort in the difficult journey of recovering memory while rebuilding a community such as El Mozote where no one survived the massacre.

Don Florentin, who lives in the repopulated hamlet of El Mozote, told me:

> *Aqui nos han matado la tierra. Les agradecemos a los artistas por ayudarnos a que la tierra viva otra vez.*

> Here, they have killed us the land. We are thankful to the artists for helping make the earth be alive again.

We painted a mural at El Mozote in the church adjacent to the building where more than 136 children perished in 1981. The community shared meetings, diplomatic negotiations from which emerged the collegial idea for the theme of the mural. They would not depict the carnage of the massacre for that was not the message to be preserved in this unique history book. The mural would represent El Mozote as it once was: a prosperous community of civilians who planted and harvested coffee, maguey, and corn. The community had lived in harmony for generations. They had been poor, as most rural *campesinos* are, but they had not known what devastation meant until they were attacked and killed by the U.S.-trained Atlacatl Battalion.

The names of the victimized children and their ages, starting at three days old up to twelve years of age, were etched on ceramic tiles placed at the base of the mural. On December 9, 2006, commemorating the 25th anniversary of the massacre at El Mozote, the children alive today recited the names of the ones who had perished, bringing them from the anonymity of death into the realm of the present.

The sadness of the past will never be forgotten. No one can. No one will. No one wants to do that.

There is no amendment for genocide.

To count dead civilians in the aftermath of massacres confirms a moral, legal, political, and spiritual catastrophe.

VI. Epilogue

The soul of the world, ephemeral and resilient, is a tender tapestry in which each thread is a voice, a hand, a song, and a memory of someone who has the right to live in dignity. On this fabric, communally, we may deposit the breath of hope.

. . .

Fragile, tentative democracies time and again hurl themselves toward an abyss, struggling over this issue of truth. It's a mysteriously powerful, almost magical notion, because often everyone already knows the truth—everyone knows who the torturers were and what they did. . . . Why, then, this need to risk everything to render that knowledge explicit?

The participants at the . . . conference worried this question around the table several times—the distinctions here seemed particularly slippery and elusive—until Thomas Nagel, a professor of philosophy and law at New York University, almost stumbled upon the answer. "It's the difference," Nagel said haltingly, "between knowledge and acknowledgment. It's what happens and can only happen when it becomes officially sanctioned, when it is made part of the public cognitive scene." Yes, several of the panelists agreed. And that transformation, offered another participant, is sacramental. . . .

(Lawrence Weschler, from *A Miracle, a Universe: Settling Accounts with Torturers*)

· · ·

RAPE AS A WAR CRIME
Theodor Meron
FROM: "Rape as a Crime under International Humanitarian Law"

It is a pity that calamitous circumstances are needed to shock the public conscience into focusing on important, but neglected, areas of law, process and institutions. The more offensive the occurrence, the greater the pressure for rapid adjustment. Nazi atrocities, for example, led to the establishment of the Nuremberg Tribunal;[1] the evolution of the concepts of crimes against peace, crimes against humanity and the crime of genocide; the shaping of the fourth Geneva Convention;[2] and the birth of the human rights movement. The starvation of Somali children prompted the Security Council to apply chapter VII of the UN Charter to an essentially internal situation, bringing about a revolutionary change in our conception of the authority of the United Nations to enforce peace in such situations. There is nothing new in atrocities or starvation. What is new is the role of the media. Instant reporting from the field has resulted in rapid sensitization of public opinion, greatly reducing the time lapse between the perpetration of such tragedies and responses to them.

It took the repeated and massive atrocities in former Yugoslavia, especially in Bosnia-Hercegovina, to persuade the Security Council that the commission of those atrocities constitutes a threat to international peace, and that the creation of an ad hoc international criminal tribunal would contribute to the restoration of peace. . . . This editorial considers only one example of the egregious violations of human dignity in former Yugoslavia—rape.

That the practice of rape has been deliberate, massive and egregious, particularly in Bosnia-Hercegovina, is amply demonstrated in reports of the United Nations, the European Community, the Conference on Security and Co-operation in Europe and various nongovernmental organizations. The special rapporteur appointed by the UN Commission on Human Rights, Tadeusz Mazowiecki, highlighted the role of rape both as an attack on the individual victim and as a method of "ethnic-cleansing" "intended to humiliate, shame, degrade and terrify the entire ethnic group."[3] Indescribable abuse of thousands of women in the territory of former Yugoslavia was needed to shock the international community into rethinking the prohibition of rape as a crime under the laws of war.[4] Important as the decision to establish the tribunal is, institutional process must work in tandem with substantive development of international law. What, then, is the current status of rape as a crime under international humanitarian law?

Rape by soldiers has of course been prohibited by law of war for centuries, and violators have been subjected to capital punishment under international military codes. . . . Indeed, rape committed on an individual soldier's initiative has frequently been prosecuted in national courts. In many cases, however, rape has been given license, either as an encouragement for soldiers or as an instrument of policy.[5] Nazi and Japanese practices of forced prostitution and rape on a large scale are among the egregious examples of such policies.[6]

Under a broad construction, Article 46 of the Hague Regulations can be considered to cover rape,[7] but in practice it has seldom been so interpreted. Rape was neither mentioned in the Nuremberg Charter nor prosecuted in Nuremberg as a war crime under customary international law.[8] But it was prosecuted in Tokyo as a war crime.[9]

Another seed for future normative development was sown in Control Council Law No. 10,[10] adopted by the four occupying powers in Germany as a charter for war crimes trials by their own courts in Germany. It expanded the list of crimes against humanity found in the Nuremberg Charter to include rape. . . .

It is time for a change. Indeed, under the weight of the events in former Yugoslavia, the hesitation to recognize that rape can be a war crime[11] or a grave breach has already begun to dissipate. The International Committee of the Red Cross (ICRC) and various states aided this development by adopting a broad construction of existing law. The ICRC declared that the grave breach of "willfully causing great suffering or serious injury to body or health" (Article 147 of the fourth Geneva Convention) covers rape.[12] If so, surely rape—in certain circumstances—can also rise to the level of such other grave breaches as torture or inhuman treatment.[13] Moreover, the massive and systematic practice of rape and its use as a "national" instrument of "ethnic cleansing" qualify it to be defined and prosecuted as a crime against humanity. . . .

Confirmation of the principle stated in Control Council Law No. 10, that rape can constitute a crime against humanity, is, both morally and legally, of ground-breaking importance. Nevertheless, the possibility of prosecuting the far more frequent cases of rape that are regarded as the "lesser" crimes of war crimes or grave breaches should not be neglected. The references to war crimes and grave breaches in the proposed charters, together with the recognition that rape can be a war crime or a grave breach, provide a basis for such prosecutions.

Although, formally, the law stated by the Security Council under chapter VII is necessarily contextual and applicable only to former Yugoslavia, the tribunal's charter, like that of Nuremberg, is likely quickly to become a fundamental normative instrument of the general law of war. The approval by the Security Council (Res. 827), acting under chapter VII of the UN Charter, of the tribunal's charter recognizing rape as a punishable offense under international humanitarian law validates this important normative development and, it is hoped, may expedite the recognition of rape, in some circumstances, as torture or inhuman treatment in the international law of human rights as well.[14] Meaningful progress in combating rape can only be made by more vigorous enforcement of the law. The recognition of rape as a crime under international law punishable by the future war crimes tribunal for former Yugoslavia is a step in that direction.

1. See Agreement for the Prosecution and Punishment of the Major War Criminals of the European Axis, Aug. 8, 1945, 59 Stat. 1544, 82 UNTS 279 [London Agreement].

2. Convention Relative to the Protection of Civilian Persons in Time of War, Aug. 12, 1949, 6 UST 3516, 75 UNTS 287 [Geneva Convention No. IV].

3. Tadeusz Mazowiecki, Report on the situation of human rights in the territory of the former Yugoslavia, UN Doc. A/48/92-S/25341, Annex, at 20, 57 (1993).

4. There has already been considerable recognition that custodial rape, or rape in circumstances for which a government is liable under the law of state responsibility, violates the prohibitions of torture or inhuman treatment in international human rights. The reports of Peter Kooijmans, special rapporteur of the UN Commission on Human Rights, have greatly contributed to this development. See also European Commission of Human Rights, *Cyprus v. Turkey,* Applications Nos. 6780/74 and 6950/75 (1976); Andrew Byrnes, "The Committee against Torture," in *The United Nations and Human Rights: A Critical Appraisal,* ed. Philip Alston (New York: Oxford University Press, 1992), 509, 519, n.38.

5. Theodor Meron, *Henry's Wars and Shakespeare's Laws: Perspectives on the Law of War in the Middle Ages* (Oxford: Clarendon Press, 1993), chapter 6; see also Theodor Meron, "Common Rights of Mankind in Gentili, Grotius and Suáres," *American Journal of International Law* 85 (1991): 110, 115–16.

6. For another example, see Walter Kälin, Report on the Situation of Human Rights in Kuwait under Iraqi Occupation, UN Doc. E/CN.4/1992/26, at 47–48.

7. "Family honour and rights, the lives of persons, and private property, as well as religious convictions and practice must be respected." Convention Respecting the Laws and Customs of War on Land, with Annex of Regulations, Oct. 18, 1907, 36 Stat. 2277, 1 Bevans 631 [Hague Convention No. IV].

8. In some cases, enforced prostitution was prosecuted in national courts outside Germany. 15 United Nations War Crimes Commission, Law Reports of Trials of War Criminals 121 (1949). A Netherlands court in Batavia, for example, found some Japanese persons responsible for forced prostitution guilty of violating the laws and usages of war. Philip R. Piccigallo, *The Japanese on Trial: Allied War Crimes Operations in the East, 1945–1951* (Austin: University of Texas Press, 1979), 179–80.

9. Charter of the International Military Tribunal for the Far East, Jan. 19, 1946, TIAS No. 1589, 4 Bevans 20. The International Military Tribunal in Tokyo found some Japanese military and civilian officials guilty of war crimes, including rape, because they failed to carry out their duty to ensure that their subordinates complied with international law. See John Alan Appleman, *Military Tribunals and International Crimes* (Westport, CT: Greenwood, 1971), 259. The IMT considered rape a war crime; *The Tokyo Judgment: The International Military Tribunal for the Far East,* 2, eds. B. V. A. Rölling and C. F. Ruter (Amsterdam: APA-University Press, 1977), 965, 971–72, 988–89; 1 id. at 385; Gordon Ireland, "Uncommon Law in Martial Tokyo," in *Yearbook of World Affairs* 4 (1950), 54, 61, n.14. Regarding the case of Admiral Toyoda, who was charged with violating laws and customs of war by tolerating various abuses, including

rape (he was acquitted of all charges), see William H. Parks, "Command Responsibility for War Crimes," *Military Law Review,* Fall 1973, at 1, 69–73.

10. Control Council for Germany, Official Gazette, Jan. 31, 1946, at 50, reprinted in Naval War College, Documents on Prisoners of War 304 (International Law Studies vol. 60, ed. Howard S. Levie, 1979).

11. War crimes are crimes against the conventional or customary law of war that are committed by persons "belonging" to one party to the conflict against persons or property of the other side. The perpetrator, as the Nuremberg jurisprudence makes clear, need not necessarily be a soldier. Attacks committed by persons against other persons belonging to the same side are not considered war crimes.

12. ICRC, Aide-Mémoire (Dec. 3, 1992).

13. As early as 1958, the ICRC Commentary on the fourth Geneva Convention recognized that the grave breach of "inhuman treatment" (Art. 147) should be interpreted in the context of Article 27, which also prohibits rape. Commentary on the Geneva Conventions of 12 August 1949; Geneva Convention Relative to the Protection of Civilian Persons in Time of War 598 (ed. Oscar M. Uhler and Henri Coursier, 1958).

14. The pernicious phenomenon of rape continues unabated in war as in peace. See, e.g., Majority Staff of the Senate Judiciary Committee 102d Cong., 2d Sess.: Violence against Women: A Week in the Life of America (1992); Americas Watch, Untold Terror: Violence against Women in Peru's Armed Conflict (1992); Middle East Watch, Punishing the Victim: Rape and Mistreatment of Asian Maids in Kuwait (1992); Americas Watch, Criminal Injustice: Violence against Women in Brazil (1991). For efforts by the Committee on the Elimination of Discrimination to combat violence against women, see CEDAW General Recommendation No. 19: Violence against Women, in Compilation of General Comments and General Recommendations Adopted by Human Rights Treaty Bodies, UN Doc. HRI/GEN/1, 74 (1992).

. . .

Justice delivered by an international war crimes court had made them no richer and no more secure. . . . Yet their participation in the Akayesu case had left them strong in the knowledge that, as victims, they had a court in which to tell their story. Gone was the look of helplessness that some years before had etched their faces. Replacing it was a look of steely determination.

(Elizabeth Neuffer, from *The Key to My Neighbor's House: Seeking Justice in Bosnia and Rwanda*)

. . .

FACING INTO TRUTH

The Most Reverend Frank T. Griswold, XXV Presiding Bishop and Primate, the Episcopal Church, USA

The chief priests and the elders approach Jesus. They are outraged. Their power to control, dominate, and decree the very will of the Most High has been overridden by one who dares to speak, dares to teach with a different kind of power: the life-giving love and mercy of God. "By what authority are you doing these things, and who gave you this authority? How dare you challenge the order of things? How dare you call into question by your indiscriminate acts of healing, by your profligate welcome of tax collectors and prostitutes, the carefully constructed righteousness upon which the identity of our nation and our power as God's chosen depend?"

By what authority? By the authority of his own self-emptying and transparency to God: "though he was in the form of God, [he] did not regard equality with God as something to be exploited, but emptied himself taking the form of a slave, being born in human likeness, and being formed in human form he humbled himself and became obedient to the point of death—even death on a cross."

Jesus' self-emptying was a profound act of availability—availability to God's passionate desire for the well-being of human kind and the whole creation transformed, healed and made new through a dynamic of radical reordering, of shalom: the unrelenting peace of God which passes all understanding and knows no rest until all walls of division have been breached and broken down and we are overtaken by "a new heart and a new spirit" which renders us makers of peace and ministers of reconciliation.

How do we get there? How does shalom become the truth of who we are and have yet to become? Ezekiel gives us the answer: "Repent and turn from all your transgressions; otherwise iniquity will be your ruin." To repent is to turn: to turn from fondly held falsehood, the self-constructions of our egos, and to turn toward the searing and convicting and liberating truth that "in Christ God was reconciling the world to himself"—reconciling us to himself in order that we, made limbs and members of Christ's risen body through baptism, might be one with Christ in engaging God's work of reconciling all people to God and one another in Christ. This, the Prayer Book tells us, is God's project and therefore the mission of the Church.

As a nation, we are accustomed to waging war: wars on poverty, il- literacy, drugs, cancer, terrorism, and now we are faced with the possi- bility of war with Iraq. As the costs involved and the uncertainty of the outcome become clearer, the debate on war with Iraq becomes more intense and the question arises not simply should we or shouldn't we, but how are we as a nation called to be an agent of reconciliation in our troubled and broken world, rather than an instrument of retribution.

I take very seriously the notion that we are one nation under God— a God who cares equally for all the peoples of the world—a God who weeps as Israelis and Palestinians kill each other in seemingly unbreak- able cycles of violence; as children starve to death in the Sudan; as AIDS devastates whole villages in sub-Saharan Africa leaving only orphans; as the working poor in our own land are further deprived of the mini- mal means to lead lives of dignity.

We are called upon as persons of faith to wage something other than war. We are called to wage reconciliation: to engage actively in disman- tling and deconstructing all that holds back and blocks the free flowing of God's unrelenting compassion, a compassion which embraces all things, reorders all relationships and brings all people together in a fierce embrace of shalom. Shalom, that deep peace which is more than a human construction or the enforced containment of hostility we usually mean by peace—shalom: that deep and true peace that flows from the heart of God, a peace we have obscured and buried under the weight of what Ezekiel calls all our transgressions.

"Get yourselves a new heart and a new spirit," Ezekiel tells us. "Let the same mind be in you that was in Christ Jesus," proclaims Paul. Re- pent and give root room to God's imagination, God's way of seeing us and the world around us with eyes of everlasting and all embracing love.

To adopt God's point of view in place of our own means letting go of our fears, our suspicions, our mistrust, and our judgments of one an- other, the ways in which we see ourselves over against one another, our tendency to define ourselves at the expense of others. "I am better, more virtuous, more accomplished, more important because I am not like you." To adopt God's point of view means attending to the language we use, which can either draw us together or drive us apart. How we speak to one another determines in large measure how we respond to one another. This is true not only with respect to us personally within the community of faith and as a conference of bishops, but as nations as well. Even as we consider the threat posed by Iraqi weaponry, we must look at the rhetoric that has been used by the present administration: intemperate, extreme, dehumanizing, guaranteed to produce an equally strong response and avalanche of verbal threats from the other side.

We as Christians are not immune to such behavior. If we are to speak with any credibility to the world about reconciliation we must, through repentance, embody reconciliation in our own lives. We must become the very thing we preach.

Here I am put in mind of Francis of Assisi, that great exemplar of God's shalom who himself once made a pilgrimage of peace to the Muslim world and who said to his fellow friars, "Preach the gospel always and when necessary use words." That is, the word cannot simply linger on our lips; it must find a home in our life.

In this case the word is reconciliation: that active process initiated by God and revealed on the cross as Jesus stretches out his arms and draws all people and all things to himself. We share that ministry of reconciliation, and it is reconciliation that brings about, or rather reveals what already exists: shalom, God's peace.

Reconciliation does not mean passivity in the face of evil, or avoidance for the sake of some false peace. It means facing into truth, as difficult and as costly as it may be, but doing so knowing that even the enemies of truth have a place in the heart of God. Reconciliation requires entering into the reality of the other, their fears as well as their assertions, and not simply imposing our own. Reconciliation requires self-examination: what is it about me/us that provokes such strong reactions of hostility? Is there the potential of seeing myself/ourselves through the eyes of the others that calls us to change our ways? Reconciliation takes time, takes endurance, involves suffering: the crucifixion of one's own unyielding rightness in order to find another way, a new place in which both can stand in a changed relationship to one another. Reconciliation requires careful and measured speech: convicting accuracy rather than sweeping demonization. Reconciliation seeks the common good: it is about all things being drawn together in shalom's embrace. Reconciliation counts the cost of various forms of engagement and seeks always the way of suasion rather than that of bold assertion. Reconciliation is profoundly aware of "collateral damage" to those who are potential victims rather than beneficiaries of a proposed course of action.

As a church, as bishops, as persons of faith, as a nation we are called with Christ to the ongoing and costly work of reconciliation. Lest we lose heart, remember that on the cross it has already been achieved. With the authority of Christ, which is nothing less than God's unyielding desire for the full flourishing of all, let us press on knowing that God's power working in us can do infinitely more than we can ask or imagine.

Amen.

(This sermon was delivered at Trinity Cathedral, Cleveland, Ohio on 9/29/2002 to a convocation of bishops and their spouses.)

· · ·

ZOROASTRIAN PRAYER

In this house
May thy acceptance smite defiance
    Peace triumph over discord
    Generosity over greed
    Devotion over arrogance
Honest discussion dominate over falsehood
    May righteousness prevail
    Over evil of lies.

CHAPTER 6

Reclaiming Our Selves

Gender and Violence

Like Nietzsche and Wagner, Hitler regarded leadership as
sexual mastery of the "feminine" masses, as rape.

—Susan Sontag, "Fascinating Fascism"

Just as conventional ideas about masculinity and femininity keep us
from realizing and expressing our full potential as human beings, these
limitations contribute to many forms of violence, including terrorism.
If we are to meet the challenges posed by terror and terrorism, we must
address the way societies define and shape humanity according to gender. Indeed, the characteristics of masculinity that many cultures promote resemble the qualities required of a good soldier. The notion that
"real" men are naturally aggressive, if not at times pitiless, and are
always brave under fire fuels violence and war, as does the valoriza-
tion in our society of what we call "masculine" values, domination and
power, a tendency that works hand in hand with the marginalization
of virtues we have labeled "feminine," emotional intelligence and
empathy.

Hoping that women will exert a softening influence on violence, recently India sent an all-female brigade as a peace-keeping force to Libe-
ria. This is a creative and promising approach. Yet understanding gender as a social construction that can be changed can lead to even more
profound solutions. Organized violence has been caused not by masculinity alone but by larger systems of gender arising in conjunction with
the formation of empires, which required most men to become soldiers.
Correspondingly, the idea that femininity includes passivity and dependence enables the denial needed to continue violence. As the Israeli

professor of education, Nurit, who lost her own child to warfare has said, in the service of patriotism many women have sent their sons and daughters into battle. But just as an awareness of fear and feelings of compassion belong to every human psyche, both male and female, so do courage and strength. At the same time that she retains the ability to connect to others, in order to be whole, a woman must have the courage of her convictions and be able to act on them. For both men and women, the conventional definitions of gender divide us against ourselves, severing self-knowledge from action, connection from strength, empathy and caring from agency and power.

The system of gender is also a system of domination, one that is replicated in many ways throughout diverse societies, reflected in injustice and inequality but also expressed as violence against women or between gangs of young people. In wartime, when nations are threatened or under attack, cultures defined by the "masculine" value of dominance too quickly become psychologically militarized, increasing the likelihood of a violent response to conflict and provocation. At the same time, when what we call the feminine is banished from public life and consigned exclusively to private realms, we tend to derogate or ignore human capacities such as the ability to read and understand emotions, graciousness, and diplomacy—skills that are critical in finding peaceful, nonviolent solutions to conflicts.

In fact, men do not lack emotional knowledge or the ability to relate to others, and that is why it is common in military training to undermine the natural capacity all human beings possess to connect to others by separating recruits from community and family. By the same stroke, as they are trained to disassociate from their emotions and even their bodies, young soldiers are ridiculed for any perceived vulnerability.

The separation of the masculine from the feminine creates a vicious cycle in individual psyches as well as in the mentality of whole cultures. Not only is emotional knowledge and connection to the mother, the source from which we are all born, consigned to a forgotten realm, but, unconsciously, an awareness of death and loss is also repressed. In this way, a false idol is created, an invulnerable, unconquerable Rambo-like hero, a nation that cannot lose. In the worst cases, neither loss, wounding, nor death interfere with this fantasy but instead such tragedies only strengthen the repression of the feminine, leading to more and more disastrously unrealistic heroics. History has seen the sad consequences of this kind of hubris more than once.

For all these reasons, to reclaim our selves from the inauthentic roles dictated by gender is a crucial part of transforming terror.

Susan Griffin and Karin Lofthus Carrington

. . .

TERROR, DOMINATION, AND PARTNERSHIP
Riane Eisler

I learned about terror very early. It was on Crystal Night, the night of the first official terrorism against Jews in Germany and my native Austria. That night Gestapo storm troopers and Nazi youth gangs destroyed synagogues, burned and looted Jewish homes and shops, and arrested over 30,000 Jews. One of these Jews was my father.

I used to love to walk on the streets of Vienna holding my father's hand. But suddenly everything changed. I remember one day when I saw a crowd standing around on a bridge across the Danube, jeering and laughing. I was shocked when I saw what they were laughing at: two old bearded Jewish men forced to scrub the pavement on their knees.

Still, it was not until Crystal Night (so named for all the glass in Jewish homes, synagogues, and shops shattered all over Germany and Austria) that Jews were beaten to death, thrown from windows, shot on the spot, or shipped off to concentration camps. It was on that night that a gang of Nazis broke into our home and dragged my father away.

By a miracle, my mother obtained his release, and we were able to flee Vienna to France and from there to Cuba, where I grew up. I was seven years old when all this happened, but it profoundly affected my whole life.

These early experiences led me to ask questions—questions many of us have asked at some point in our lives. Why is there so much insensitivity and cruelty? Why is there so much hatred and violence?

As time went on, there were more questions. In Havana my parents and I lived in a poor industrial area that contrasted sharply with the suburbs where rich Cubans lived. That experience made me conscious of another form of injustice and suffering, and led to further questions: Why do some people have to go hungry? Why do others have infinitely more than they could ever use?

Then, after World War II ended I saw the newsreels of what the Nazis did to six million Jews, including my grandparents and most of my aunts, uncles, and cousins. Looking at the films of the liberated concentrations camps, at the piles of skeletal corpses and the hollow-eyed, equally skeletal survivors, I saw what would have happened to me and my parents had we not escaped. And so again I found myself asking questions: Does it really have to be this way? Is all this cruelty and violence inevitable, as we're often told, just "the way things are"? Or are there alternatives?

My Quest for Answers

When I went to college, I looked for answers to these questions in philosophy, psychology, sociology, and other disciplines. But I did not find any satisfactory answers. Indeed, I found that conventional studies of society were not of much use in my quest. So eventually, I embarked on my own cross-cultural and historical study.

My decision to embark on my multidisciplinary research came after another important event in my life. In the 1960s, like thousands of women all over the world, I woke up to the issue of women's rights. I had always felt an outsider as a Jew, an immigrant, and a foreigner. But suddenly I realized that I was even more of an outsider because I happened to have been born female.

I became aware that most of what I had been taught in my many years of schooling had been by, about, and for men. What I had simply taken for granted as "just the way things are" was that in the reams of books I had been assigned in my university classes the needs, problems, and situation of women were rarely even mentioned, and when they were, it was as a little sidebar rather than a matter of any real consequence.

At this point in my life, it became obvious to me that this curious failure to include no less than half of humanity from what is considered important about human society was an enormous methodological flaw. I understood one of the reasons that conventional social categories such as religious versus secular, right versus left, East versus West, capitalist versus communist, and industrial versus pre- or post-industrial had not been useful in answering my questions. I saw that these categories actually fragment our consciousness, as none of them recognizes the critical importance of how a culture constructs the primary human relations: the relations between women and men and between parents and children where people first learn what is considered normal or abnormal, moral or immoral, possible or impossible.

In my study, I drew from a much larger data base than conventional studies. This approach takes into account the *whole* of our lives: both the so-called public sphere of politics and economics and the private sphere of our family and other intimate relations. It also looks at the *whole* of our history, including the long span of time we call prehistory. And unlike most studies, which are often aptly called "the study of man," it includes the *whole* of humanity: both its female and male halves.

Two Social Possibilities: Domination and Partnership

Drawing from this larger data base, it was possible to see patterns or configurations that had not been discerned before. These configurations kept repeating themselves, regardless of a society's time period, location, level of technological development, and other differences.

Because there were no names to describe these configurations, I chose the name *domination model* for one and *partnership model* for the other.

The configuration of societies that orient closely to the domination model is of beliefs and institutions—from the family, education, and religion to politics and economics—that support rigid top-down rankings backed up by fear and force. The configuration of societies that orient more to the partnership model is of more peaceful and egalitarian societies where beliefs and institutions support relations based on mutual respect, mutual accountability, and mutual benefit.

And a key element of these two very different configurations is how a society structures the roles and relations between the female and male halves of humanity and between them and their daughters and sons.

Starting early on, what happens to people in cultures that orient either to the partnership or domination model is very different. In their formative family relations, they learn either respect for human rights or acceptance of human rights violations as normal, inevitable, even moral. These primary human relations also teach important lessons about violence. When children experience violence, or observe violence against their mothers, they learn it's acceptable to use force to impose one's will on others. And they learn this not only intellectually but emotionally through early traumatic experiences that they often carry into their adult years and unconsciously replicate in the families they in turn create.

If children grow up in families where females serve and males are served—and, as is the case in many world regions, where females get less food and healthcare—they also often learn to accept economic injustice in all spheres of life. They learn that one kind of person is put on this earth to be served and another kind is put on earth to serve. And this mental map can then easily be generalized to different races, religions, or ethnicities—in other words, to other differences.

We have long known from psychology that unless people become conscious of their formative experiences, and particularly of experiences that involve fear and abuse, they often grow up to accept abusive economic and government institutions. But today we also know that this unconscious learning takes place on a neural level. Findings from neuroscience show that the brain's neural pathways are largely laid *after* birth—and that early experiences are key to whether neural patterns of fight-or-flight that perpetuate both intimate and international violence become habitual.

What this tells us is that if we are serious about changing cultural traditions in which terror is used as a method of control, we have to start with our intimate relations. This too is one of the lessons of history.

Consider that Hitler's Germany (a technologically advanced, Western, rightist society), Stalin's USSR (a secular leftist society), Khomeini's Iran (an Eastern religious society), and Idi Amin's Uganda (a tribalist society) were some of the most brutally violent and repressive societies of the twentieth century. There are obvious differences between them. But they all share the core configuration of the domination model. They are all characterized by top-down rankings in the family and state or tribe maintained through physical, psychological, and economic control; the rigid ranking of the male half of humanity over the female half; and a high degree of culturally accepted abuse and violence, and thus terror—from child-and-wife-beating to chronic warfare.

Then consider cultures with the contrasting configuration of a democratic and egalitarian structure in both the family and the state or tribe; equal partnership between women and men; and a low degree of built-in violence because it's not needed to maintain rigid rankings of domination. These partnership-oriented cultures can be found in different places, times, and at different levels of technological development. They can be tribal, such as the Teduray of the Philippines, agrarian such as the Minagkabau of East Sumatra, or industrial/postindustrial, like Sweden, Norway, and Finland.

Gender, Childhood, and Terror

One of the most arresting aspects of these more partnership-oriented cultures is that here nurturance and nonviolence are not despised as unfit for "real men." As the status of women rises, so also does the status of stereotypically "feminine" traits and activities—whether they reside in women or men. This is why more men are today able to change fathering from a stereotypical punitive role (as in "wait till your father gets home") to one of feeding and diapering babies in ways stereotypically considered feminine.

Although old stereotypes of "masculinity" and "femininity" are still with us, more and more women and men are able to access their full human possibilities. This is a very important step toward a more partnership-oriented world—a world in which "real masculinity" is no longer associated with domination and violence and women can be assertive without being labeled "unfeminine."

Of course, there are biological differences between women and men. But even if it were true that men are more predisposed to learn violent behaviors—which has yet to be established—this is all the more reason that male socialization must stop teaching men to equate their masculine identity with destructive and inhuman behaviors. Moreover, women can also be violent, as we see in traditions of dominator parenting where not only men but also women have been taught, and continue to be taught, to terrorize their children.

One of the most important lessons from looking at cultures from the perspective of whether they orient more to the partnership or domination system is something that once articulated may seem obvious. This is that the way a culture structures the primary human relations—the relations between the female and male halves of humanity and between them and their daughters and sons—is foundational to its entire system of beliefs and values as well as to the construction of all its institutions, from the family, education, and religion, to politics and economics.

Indeed, when we look at terror from this perspective, we see that it is built into cultures and subcultures that orient closely to the domination model, starting in childhood. We also see that there is no realistic way to end traditions of terror—be they in intimate or in international relations—unless we accelerate the shift to partnership worldwide.

The Nordic nations show that this can be done. Nordic nations such as Sweden, Norway, and Finland are not utopias. But these nations are regularly at the top of the U.N. national quality of life charts. They are democratic cultures where there aren't huge gaps between haves and have-nots. They have laws prohibiting physical punishment of children and a strong men's movement disentangling "masculinity" from domination and violence. Here women play important leadership roles, constituting approximately 40 percent of legislatures. Accordingly, stereotypically feminine traits and activities such as nurturance, nonviolence, and caregiving are considered appropriate for men as well as women. And these traits and activities are supported by fiscal policies, such as funding for universal health care, elder care, child care allowances, paid parental leave, peace studies, and environmental protection.

In short, while these are not ideal nations, their beliefs and institutions support much greater respect for human rights in both families and the family of nations. As I detail in *The Chalice and the Blade, Sacred Pleasure,* and other books, there is also strong evidence that the original direction of civilization during prehistory was in a more partnership-oriented direction in societies where women were not subordinate, female deities were venerated, and there was more social and economic equality across the board.

What We Can—and Must—Do

Despite all the evidence that what's good for women and children is good for the whole of society, many people working for democracy and equality still view "women's rights" and "children's rights" as secondary. Yet, ironically, those trying to push us back to the "good old days" when most men and all women still "knew their place" in rigid rankings of domination recognize the importance of the gender and childhood relations for what kind of society we have.

Be it Hitler in Germany, Khomeini in Iran, the Taliban in Afghanistan, or the rightist-fundamentalist alliance in the United States, these people give top priority to "getting women back into their traditional place" in a "traditional family"—a code word for an authoritarian "male-headship" family where women are subordinate and children learn that it's extremely painful to question orders no matter how brutal or unjust.

It is not coincidental that the 9/11 terrorists came from cultures where women and children are terrorized into submission. Nor is it coincidental that the rightist-fundamentalist alliance in the United States first organized as a powerful political block around a "women's issue"— the defeat of the proposed Equal Rights Amendment to the U.S. Constitution. Or that the people from the "Christian Right" who make pushing women back to a subservient place in a punitive male-headed family often see nothing wrong with torture and other forms or terror, and like their Muslim fundamentalist counterparts, advocate "holy wars."

Of course, the fundamentalist agenda is not a religious one. Despite their dominator overlay of angry, vengeful Father Gods, there are many teachings of caring and nonviolence in religious scriptures. The fundamentalist agenda—be it Eastern or Western—is a dominator agenda: an integrated agenda to push us back to a world of authoritarian, coercive families and states, rigid male dominance, and the use of violence and terror to maintain top-down rule.

It is not easy to change religious traditions that teach us that the highest power is the power to dominate and destroy. In the domination system you have to have angry punitive gods, whether it is Zeus, Thor, or Yahweh. These deities always carry a weapon, be it a thunderbolt, a sword, or, as in Zeus's case, both—just in case we don't get his terrorizing message the first time around.

When we come upon dominator teachings such as that God will only save "true believers" or that God rewards terrorists who randomly kill women and children and commands that women be stoned to death, we must say, wait, this is only part of the story. Instead of focusing on control, coercion, and violence, we must build on the partnership values of empathy, nonviolence, and caring that are at the core of most religions—on the nurturing power of the Chalice rather than the lethal power of the Blade.

We must also change the conception of deity as exclusively male, as in Judeo-Christian and Muslim religion, or as more powerful than female deities as in Hindu tradition, where even though we are told Shiva has no power without the goddess Shakti, in the iconography she is usually portrayed as only half his size.

We must challenge destructive dominator archetypes of "masculinity" like the punitive father and the hero as killer. If we don't, our culture will continue to idealize terror—and with this, the very behaviors that in our age of nuclear and biological weapons could take us to an evolutionary dead end.

We must address the gender sickness that pollutes so much of our personal, social, economic, and spiritual lives. We must remind ourselves that the nations that have moved closest to the partnership model, Nordic nations like Sweden, Finland, and Norway, have the greatest gender equality, with their legislatures almost half female. If we are to speak of real democracy, it is clear that we must work to bring more women into governance worldwide.

We must also work together to change social and economic structures that support, indeed require, insensitivity and lack of caring. If we remember that these structures are not inevitable, that there is a viable partnership alternative, we can change the legal and cultural framework to instead support partnership social and economic structures. This is the theme of my latest book, *The Real Wealth of Nations: Creating a Caring Economics,* which describes key levers for fundamental social, economic, and political change.

We must bring a strong—still missing—moral voice to end violence against women and children. This is the goal of the Spiritual Alliance to Stop Intimate Violence (SAIV), an international initiative of the Center for Partnership Studies that I co-founded. We must show religious and political leaders, as well as the public at large, that intimate violence is training for using violence as a means of imposing one's will on others— that we can't break cycles of international violence without changing traditions of intimate violence.

In sum, we must construct the solid foundations on which a better society can be built—beginning with the fundamental relations between women and men and between parents and children. It won't be easy and it won't be quick, but if enough of us join together, we can leave behind traditions of terror and move to a more peaceful and equitable world.

. . .

What is significant, of course, is that everything and everyone is judged according to his power. Whoever can forcibly twist someone else's arm is considered to be powerful, that is, a man, an ideal man, the authority on everything. A man is a two-way element of emasculation: he emasculates those below him and is emasculated by those above him. But the one who really holds the absolute power, turns it into the charismatic *farreh,* rules by divine authority and becomes a walking god on earth [that] is the Shah.

All emasculated men move in degrees toward the status of women. Women are judged by the criteria of men. They are not women; they do not have an identity of their own. They are men emasculated to the ultimate degree. Even a poor worker, who belongs to the most oppressed class of society, becomes a bourgeois as soon as he sets foot in his own house. His orders rain upon his wife and daughter in the same fashion as the orders of the factory owner had fallen upon him. Repression and oppression multiply oppressors.

(Reza Baraheni, from *The Crowned Cannibals*)

. . .

THE MIND AS EROTIC WEAPON

Fatema Mernissi

FROM: *Scheherazade Goes West: Different Cultures, Different Harems*

Scheherazade is the Persian name of the young bride who tells the stories in *The Thousand and One Nights*. These stories, of "various ethnic origins, Indian, Persian, and Arabic,"[1] which are a symbol of Islam's genius as a pluralist religion and culture, unfold in a territory that stretches from Mali and Morocco on the Atlantic Coast of North Africa to India, Mongolia, and China. When you enter the tales, you are navigating in a Muslim universe that ignores the usual borders separating distant and divergent cultures. . . . However, the tales' cosmopolitan grace, their capacity to transcend cultural boundaries, does not extend to the relationship between the sexes. That is portrayed as an abysmal, unbridgeable frontier, a bloody war between men and women.

The Thousand and One Nights begins as a tragedy of betrayal and revenge, and ends as a fairy tale, thanks entirely to Scheherazade's intellectual capacity to read her husband's mind. When the stories begin, Shahrayar's younger brother, Shahzaman, is ruling happily over "The Land of Samarcand," only to return to the palace one day to find his wife in the arms of a "kitchen boy."[2] He kills the two of them and decides to leave his kingdom for a while, in the hopes of healing his wounds. He sets out to visit his older brother, Shahrayar.

Running away from the crime scene works for only a few days. One morning, the depressed Shahzaman looks out the window into his brother's harem garden and thinks he is hallucinating:

> When he agonized over his misfortune, gazing at the heavens and turning a distracted eye on the garden, the private gate of his brother's palace opened, and there emerged, like a dark-eyed deer, the lady, his brother's wife, with twenty slave girls, ten white and ten black. . . . They sat down, took off their clothes, and suddenly there were ten slave girls and ten black slaves dressed in the same clothes as the girls. Then the ten black slaves mounted the ten girls, while the lady called, "Mas'ud, Mas'ud," and a black slave jumped from the tree to the ground, rushed to her, and, raising her legs, went between her thighs and made love to her. Mas'ud was on top of the first lady, while the ten slaves were on top of the ten girls, and they carried on till noon.[3]

The wife's sexual betrayal of her husband, King Shahrayar, reflects and mirrors the political betrayal of the master by the slave. In Arabic the sentence "Mas'ud was on top of the first lady" (*wa mas'ud fawqa a-sit*)[4] seems to sum up the entire harem tragedy: the woman's fatal need to topple the hierarchy built by the husband who has locked her up, by siding and copulating with his male slave. . . .

But to get back to Scheherazade, she arrived at Shahrayar's palace years after the garden incident, by which time Shahrayar had killed not only his wife and her slave Mas'ud, but had also systematically beheaded hundreds of innocent virgins, marrying each one at night and killing them at dawn. "He continued to do this, until all the girls perished, their mothers mourned, and there arose a clamor among the fathers and mothers. . . ."[5] We see here once again how sex and politics mingle in the *Nights*. What started as a war between the sexes has turned into a tragic political upheaval, with bereaved fathers rebelling against the King. Now only one privileged father, the King's Vizier, who has carried out the death sentences, still had two virgin daughters: Scheherazade and her younger sister, Douniazad.

While the Vizier frantically tries to plot an escape for his daughters, Scheherazade insists on sacrificing herself and confronting the King in the hopes of stopping the killing. This is why Scheherazade can be seen as a political hero, a liberator in the Muslim world. "Father," she says to the distraught Vizier. "I would like you to marry me to King Shahrayar, so that I may either succeed in saving the people or perish and die like the rest."[6] She has a scheme in mind that will prove to be successful: to weave spellbinding stories that will captivate the King, leaving him hungry to hear more—and save her life.

To change the mind of a criminal who is intent on killing you by telling him stories is an extraordinary achievement. In order to succeed, Scheherazade has to master three strategic skills: control over a vast store of information, the ability to clearly grasp the criminal's mind, and the determination to act in cold blood. The first skill is of an intellectual nature, requiring a wealth of knowledge, and Scheherazade's encyclopedic erudition is described in the first pages of the book: "Scheherazade had read the books of literature, philosophy, and medicine. She knew poetry by heart, had studied historical reports, and was acquainted with the sayings of men and the maxims of sages and kings. She was intelligent, knowledgeable, wise, and refined. She had read and learned."[7] But knowledge alone does not enable a woman to influence men in power; witness the enormous number of highly educated women involved in social movements in the West today, who are nonetheless unable to keep modern Shahrayars in check. . . .

Our heroine's second talent is of a psychological nature: the ability to change a criminal's mind by using words alone. To use dialogue to disarm a killer is a bold strategy, and in order to succeed, the victim must have a good understanding of the criminal's probable moves and know how to integrate them into unfolding events, as in a game of chess. We have to remember that the King, the aggressor, does not talk to Scheherazade in the beginning. During the first six months of her storytelling, he keeps silent and listens without uttering a word. So Scheherazade has no way of knowing what is going on in his mind, except by watching his facial expressions and body language. How to continue talking in the night without making a fatal psychological miscalculation? Much like a military strategist, who uses his knowledge to foresee future events, Scheherazade has to guess, and guess accurately, because the slightest mistake will be fatal.

Scheherazade's final talent is her cold-blooded capacity to control her fear enough to think clearly and lead the dynamic interaction with the aggressor instead of being led. Scheherazade only survives because she is a super-strategist of the intellect. She would have been killed if she had disrobed like a Hollywood vamp or Matisse's odalisque and stretched out passively in the King's bed. This man is not looking for sex, he is looking for a psychotherapist. He is suffering from acute self-loathing, as we all do when we discover that we have been cuckolded. He is furious because he does not understand the other sex or why his wife betrayed him.

Despite her powerlessness, Scheherazade manages through an accurate reading of a complex situation to change the balance of power and reach the top. This is why, even today, many women like myself who feel totally helpless in politics admire Scheherazade. Some Westerners who misread her story and reduce her to frivolous entertainer might view her as a bad role model for modern women. But I think that if you situate her accurately in her political context, her pertinence as a role model becomes quite clear. She saves not only herself but also an entire kingdom by slowly changing the mind of the chief decision-maker, the King. . . . Ultimately, the King . . . acknowledges that he was completely wrong in being angry with women. "O Scheherazade, you made me doubt my kingly power (*zahadtani fi mulki*) and made me regret my past violence towards women and my killing of young girls."[8]

This last sentence, in which a violent despot acknowledges that dialogue with his wife changed his entire world view, has inspired many famous twentieth-century Arab writers to grant Scheherazade, and by extension, all women, the status of civilizing agents. Peace and serenity will replace violence in men's intentions and deeds, predicted the influential Egyptian thinker Taha Hussein, if they are redeemed by a woman's love. In his *Scheherazade's Dreams (Ahlam Scheherazad)*, published in 1943, the storyteller becomes a symbol for the many innocents who were engulfed by the Second World War—a war that, while instigated by the West, also affected all Arabs and, indeed, the entire planet. Only after listening to his captive for years does Shahrayar realize that she is a repository of a precious secret. If only he can grasp who she is and what she wants, he might achieve emotional growth and serenity:

> *Shahrayar:* Who are you and what do you want?
>
> *Scheherazade:* Who am I? I am the Scheherazade who offered you the pleasure of listening to my tales for years because I was so terrified of you. Now, I have reached a stage where I can give you love because I have freed myself from the fear you inspired in me. What do I want? I want my lord, the King, to have a taste of serenity. To experience the bliss of living in a world free of anxiety.[9]

Redemption, in Taha Hussein's work, starts when a dialogue is established between the powerful and the powerless. Civilization will flourish when men learn to have an intimate dialogue with those closest to them, the women who share their beds. Taha Hussein, who was blind, handicapped, and unfit to take part in wars—just like women—reawakened in the 1940s the symbolism inherent in the medieval Scheherazade tales—that linking humanism with feminism. Any reflection on modernity as a chance to eliminate despotic violence in the Muslim world today necessarily takes the form of a plea for feminism. Regardless of where you are, in Indonesia, Afghanistan, Turkey, or Algeria, when you zap through Muslim television or leaf through the written press, the debate on democracy soon drifts into a debate on women's rights and vice versa. The mysterious bond existing between pluralism and feminism in today's troubled Islamic world was eerily and vividly foreshadowed by the Scheherazade-Shahrayar tales.

In *The Thousand and One Nights,* Shahrayar officially admits that a man should use words instead of violence to settle his disputes. Scheherazade commands words, not armies, to transform her situation, and this adds yet another dimension to the tales as a modern civilizing myth. They are a symbol of the triumph of reason over violence.

Which brings me to emphasize a final point completely missing in Western artists' fantasies of Scheherazade. In the Orient, to use the body alone, that is, sex without a brain, never helps a woman change her situation. The King's first wife failed miserably because her rebellion was limited to body politics—i.e., allowing the slave to mount her. But Scheherazade teaches that a woman can effectively rebel by developing her brain, acquiring knowledge, and helping men to shed their narcissistic need for simplified homogeneity. She teaches that there is a need to confront the different other, and to insist on the acknowledgment and respect of boundaries if dialogue is to be achieved. . . .

Abdesslam Cheddadi, a Moroccan historian and one of the most astute analysts of Islam today, states that the first key message of *The Thousand and One Nights* is that "Shahrayar discovers and becomes convinced that to force a woman to obey marital law is an impossibility."[10] But, adds Cheddadi, as revolutionary as this conviction is, it is less subversive than the tales' second message: If we admit that Shahrayar and Scheherazade represent the cosmic conflict between Day (the masculine as objective order, the realm of the law) and Night (the feminine as subjective order, the realm of desire), then the fact that the King does not kill the queen leaves Muslim men in unbearable uncertainty regarding the outcome of battle. "By allowing Scheherazade to stay alive, the King suspends the law he established himself,"[11] writes Cheddadi. . . .

Street storytellers in medieval Baghdad were often branded as instigators of rebellion and, much like leftist journalists today, censored and banned from talking in public. . . . "In the Orient, persecution of *quççaç* [street storytellers] will come to an end with their total extinction . . . when they are replaced by the preachers (*mudhakkirun* or *wu'az*). It is the only way to establish a clear boundary between what ought to be considered as true and authentic and what pertains to the world of fiction, forgery, and lies."[12]

It goes without saying that the conflict between Truth and Fiction in the Muslim world is justified by another conflict, which brings us back to the conflict between Shahrayar and Scheherazade: If Truth is the realm of the law and its constraints, Fiction is the world of entertainment and pleasure. And to make the whole matter totally indigestible for fanatics, be they traditional or modern, Scheherazade, as Cheddadi reminds us, has an unsettling characteristic: "Scheherazade is introduced to us, from her first appearance in the book, with the credentials of a perfectly accomplished Faquih, a Muslim religious authority."[13] Her knowledge includes much history and an impressive mastery of the sacred literature, including the Koran, *Shari'a,* and the texts of various schools of religious interpretation. It is this strange combination of enormous knowledge—learned from reading over one thousand books—and a seemingly unpretentious goal to stick to the world of the night and fiction, that makes Scheherazade especially suspect, and explains another strange phenomenon: For centuries, the Arab elite scorned her tales and did not bother to put them in writing. . . .

Algerian-born Bencheikh, a contemporary expert of the Scheherazade tales, wonders if the vilification of the tales before modern times by labeling them "*Khurafa*" (loosely meaning "delirium of a troubled brain") was not due to the fact that women were often described as more astute than men.[14] In the logic of the tales, the judge is wrong and the victim is right. . . . "It is the world turned upside down. It is a world where the judge . . . does not escape his victim."[15] It is a world where the values are those of the Night. Remember the constant refrain that closes each of the tales:

> Morning overtook Scheherazade (*wa adraka shahrazad aç-çabah*) and she lapsed into silence (*fasakatat 'ani l'kalami l'mubah*).

Modernity has brought Scheherazade to the center stage of the twentieth-century Arab intellectual scene, because long ago, in ninth-century Baghdad, she clearly articulated key philosophical and political questions that our political leaders still cannot answer today:

Why should an unjust law be obeyed? Because men have written it?

If Truth is so evident, why are imagination and fiction not allowed to flourish?

The miracle in the Orient is that it is Scheherazade's excessive thoughtfulness, together with her interest in wider philosophical and political issues, that made her explosively attractive.

1. Introduction to *The Arabian Nights,* translated from Arabic into English by Hussain Haddawy, based on text edited by Muhsin Mahdi (New York: Norton, 1990), p. xi.
2. Ibid., p. 3.
3. Ibid., p. 5.
4. Haddawy, op cit., p. 11.
5. Ibid., p. 9.
6. Ibid., p. 11.
7. Ibid.

8. "The Story of the Birds," which I have translated here, does not exist in al-Madhi's version of *The Thousand and One Nights,* but does exist in one of the cheapest and most popular versions of Scheherazade's tales, found in Morocco's souks (Beirut: al maktaba ach-cha'biya), vol. 2, 43.

9. Hiam Aboul-Hussein and Charles Pellat, *Cheherazade, Personnage littéraire* (Algiers: Société Nationale d'édition et de Diffusion, 1976), 114.

10. Abdesslam Cheddadi, "Le conte-cadre des Mille et Une Nuits comme récit de Commencement," Contribution au "IV Colloquio de Escritorres Hispano-Arabe," Alméria, Spain, April 26–29, 1988, 4.

11. Ibid., p. 12.

12. Ibid., p. 4.

13. Ibid.

14. Jamel Ed din Bencheikh, *Les 1001 Nuits ou la Parole Prisonnière* (Paris: Editions Gallimard, 1998), 26.

15. Ibid., 34.

. . .

The seemingly impossible tasks assemble. Sort, practically on an unconscious level; find economic sustenance, learn how to move safely in the face of danger, pay attention to the cadences of emotional life; take water, go to the source, repair relationships, know what you know; listen to the stirrings of nature, remember the culture, face mortality and choose life—this is an old wife's wisdom.

(Carol Gilligan, from *The Birth of Pleasure*)

. . .

A WOMAN'S SIDE OF THE STORY
Leila Ahmed

FROM: *A Border Passage from Cairo to America—A Woman's Journey*

It is easy to see now that our lives in the Alexandria house and even Zatoun were lived in woman's time, woman's space. And in woman's culture.

And the women had, too, I now believe, their own understanding of Islam, an understanding that was different from men's Islam, "official" Islam. For although in those days it was only Grandmother who performed all the regular formal prayers, for all the women of the house, religion was an essential part of how they made sense of and understood their own lives. It was through religion that one pondered the things that happened, why they had happened, and what one should make of them, how one should take them.

Islam, as I got it from them, was gentle, generous, pacifist, inclusive, somewhat mystical—just as they themselves were. Mother's pacifism was entirely of a piece with their sense of religion. Being Muslim was about believing in a world in which life was meaningful and in which all events and happenings were permeated (although not always transparently to us) with meaning. Religion was above all about inner things. The outward signs of religiousness, such as prayer and fasting, might be signs of a true religiousness but equally well might not. They were certainly not what was important about being Muslim. What was important was how you conducted yourself and how you were in yourself and in your attitude toward others and in your heart.

What it was to be Muslim was passed on not, of course, wordlessly but without elaborate sets of injunctions or threats or decrees or dictates as to what we should do and be and believe. What was passed on, besides the very general basic beliefs and moral ethos of Islam, which are also those of its sister monotheisms, was a way of being in the world. A way of holding oneself in the world—in relation to God, to existence, to other human beings. This the women passed on to us most of all through how they were and by their being and presence, by the way *they* were in the world, conveying their beliefs, ways, thoughts, and how we should be in the world by a touch, a glance, a word—prohibiting, for instance, or approving. Their mere responses in this or that situation—a word, a shrug, even just their postures—passed on to us, in the way that women (and also men) have forever passed on to their young, how we should be. And all of these ways of passing on attitudes, morals, beliefs, and knowledge—through touch and the body and in words spoken in the living moment—are by their very nature subtle and evanescent . . . they do not leave a record in the way that someone writing a text about how to live or what to believe leaves a record. Nevertheless, they leave a far more important and, literally, more vital living record. Beliefs, morals, attitudes passed on to and impressed on us through those fleeting words and gestures are written into our very lives, our bodies, our selves, even into our physical cells and into how we live out the script of our lives.

It was Grandmother who taught me the *fat-ha* (the opening verse of the Quran, and the equivalent of the Christian Lord's Prayer) and who taught me two or three other short *suras* (Quranic verses). When she took me up onto the roof of the Alexandria house to watch for angels on the night of the twenty-seventh of Ramadan, she recited the *sura* about that special night, a *sura* that was also by implication about the miraculousness of night itself. Even now, I remember its loveliness. It is still my favorite *sura*.

I remember receiving little other direct religious instruction, either from Grandmother or from anyone else . . . the most memorable exchange [was] with my mother on the subject of religion—when, sitting in her room, the windows open behind her onto the garden, the curtain billowing, she quoted to me the verse in the Quran that she believed summed up the essence of Islam: "He who kills one being (*nafs*, self, from the root *nafas*, breath) kills all of humanity, and he who revives, or gives life to, one being revives all of humanity." It was a verse that she quoted often, that came up in any important conversation about God, religion, those sorts of things. It represented for her the essence of Islam.

I happened to be reading, when I was thinking about all this, the autobiography of Zeinab al-Ghazali, one of the most prominent Muslim women leaders of our day. Al-Ghazali founded a Muslim Women's Society that she eventually merged with the Muslim Brotherhood, the "fundamentalist" association that was particularly active in the forties and fifties. Throughout her life, she openly espoused a belief in the legitimacy of using violence in the cause of Islam. In her memoir, she writes of how in her childhood her father told her stories of the heroic women of early Islam who had written poetry eulogizing Muslim warriors and who themselves had gone to war on the battlefields of Islam and gained renown as fearless fighters. Musing about all this and about the difference between al-Ghazali's Islam and my mother's pacifist understanding of it, I found myself falling into a meditation on the seemingly trivial detail that I, unlike al-Ghazali, had never heard as a child or a young girl stories about the women of early Islam, heroic or otherwise. And it was then that I suddenly realized the difference between al-Ghazali and my mother and between al-Ghazali's Islam and my mother's.

The reason I had not heard such stories as a child was quite simply that those sorts of stories (when I was young, anyway) were to be found only in the ancient classical texts of Islam, texts that only men who had studied the classical Islamic literary heritage could understand and decipher. The entire training at Islamic universities—the training, for example, that al-Ghazali's father, who had attended al-Azhar University, had received—consisted precisely in studying those texts. Al-Ghazali had been initiated into Islam and had got her notions as to what a Muslim was from her father, whereas I had received my Islam from the mothers, as had my mother. So there are two quite different Islams, an Islam that is in some sense a women's Islam and an official, textual Islam, a "men's" Islam.

And indeed it is obvious that a far greater gulf must separate men's and women's ways of knowing, and the different ways in which men and women understand religion, in the segregated societies of the Middle East than in other societies—and we know that there are differences between women's and men's ways of knowing even in nonsegregated societies such as America. For, beside the fact that women often could not read (or, if they were literate, could not decipher the Islamic texts, which require years of specialist training), women in Muslim societies did not attend mosques. Mosque going was not part of the tradition for women at any class level (that is, attending mosque for congregational prayers was not part of the tradition, as distinct from visiting mosques privately and informally to offer personal prayers, which women have always done). Women therefore did not hear the sermons that men heard. And they did not get the official (male, of course) orthodox interpretations of religion that men (or some men) got every Friday. They did not have a man trained in the orthodox (male) literary heritage of Islam telling them week by week and month by month what it meant to be a Muslim, what the correct interpretation of this or that was, and what was or was not the essential message of Islam.

Rather they figured these things out among themselves and in two ways. They figured them out as they tried to understand their own lives and how to behave and how to live, talking them over together among themselves, interacting with their men, and returning to talk them over in their communities of women. And they figured them out as they listened to the Quran and talked among themselves about what they heard. For this was a culture, at all levels of society and throughout most of the history of Islamic civilization, not of reading but of the common recitation of the Quran. It was recited by professional reciters, women as well as men, and listened to on all kinds of occasions—at funerals and births and celebratory events, in illness, and in ordinary life. There was merit in having the Quran chanted in your house and in listening to it being chanted wherever it was chanted, whereas for women there was not merit attached to attending mosque, an activity indeed prohibited to women for most of history. It was from these together, their own lives and from hearing the words of the Quran, that they formed their sense of the essence of Islam.

Nor did they feel, the women I knew, that they were missing anything by not hearing the exhortations of sheikhs, nor did they believe that the sheikhs had an understanding of Islam superior theirs. On the contrary. They had little regard, the women I knew, for the reported views and opinions of most sheikhs. Although occasionally there might be a sheikh who was regarded as a man of genuine insight and wisdom, the women I knew ordinarily dismissed the views and opinions of the common run of sheikhs as mere superstition and bigotry. And these, I emphasize, were not Westernized women. Grandmother, who spoke only Arabic and Turkish, almost never set foot outside her home and never even listened to the radio. The dictum that "there is no priesthood in Islam"—meaning that there is no intermediary or interpreter, and no need for an intermediary or interpreter, between God and each individual Muslim and how that Muslim understands his or her religion—was something these women and many other Muslims took seriously and held on to as a declaration of their right to their own understanding of Islam.

No doubt, particular backgrounds and subcultures give their own specific flavors and inflections and ways of seeing to their understanding of religion, and I expect that the Islam I received from the women among whom I lived was therefore part of their particular subculture. In this sense, then, there are not just two or three different kinds of Islam but many, many different ways of understanding and of being Muslim. But what is striking to me now is not how different or rare the Islam in which I was raised is but how ordinary and typical it seems to be in its base and fundamentals. Now, after a lifetime of meeting and talking with Muslims from all over the world, I find that this Islam is one of the common varieties—perhaps even *the* common or garden variety—of the religion. It is the Islam not only of women but also of ordinary folk generally, as opposed to the Islam of sheikhs, ayatollahs, mullahs, and clerics. . . . an Islam that stresses moral conduct and emphasizes Islam as a broad ethos and ethical code and as a way of understanding and reflecting on the meaning of one's life and of human life more generally.

This variety of Islam (or, more exactly perhaps, these familial varieties of Islam, existing in a continuum across the Muslim world) consists above all of Islam as essentially an aural and oral heritage and a way of living and being—and not a textual, written heritage, not something studied in books and learned from men who studied books. This latter

Islam, the Islam of the texts, is a quite different, quite other Islam: it is the Islam of the arcane, mostly medieval written heritage in which sheikhs are trained, and it is "men's" Islam. More specifically still, it is the Islam erected by that minority of men who over the centuries have created and passed on to one another this particular textual heritage: men who, although they have always been a minority in society as a whole, have always been those who made the laws and wielded (like the ayatollahs of Iran today) enormous power in their societies. The Islam they developed in this textual heritage is very like the medieval Latinate textual heritage of Christianity. It is as abstruse and obscure and as dominated by medieval and exclusively male views of the world as are those Latin texts. Imagine believing that those medieval texts on Christianity represent today the only true and acceptable interpretation of Christianity.

Aurally what remains when you listen to the Quran over a lifetime are its most recurring themes, ideas, words, and permeating spirit, reappearing now in this passage, now in that: mercy, justice, peace, compassion, humanity, fairness, kindness, truthfulness, charity, mercy, justice. And yet it is exactly these recurring themes and this permeating spirit that are for the most part left out of the medieval texts or smothered and buried under a welter of obscure and abstruse "learning." One would scarcely believe, reading or hearing the laws these texts have yielded, particularly when it comes to women, that the words "justice," "fairness," "compassion," "truth" ever even occur in the Quran. No wonder non-Muslims think Islam is such a backward and oppressive religion: what these men made of it is largely oppressive. I am sure, then, that my foremothers' lack of respect for the authority of sheikhs was not coincidental. Rather, I believe that this way of seeing and understanding was quite common among ordinary Muslims and that it was an understanding passed on from mothers and grandmothers to daughters and granddaughters. Generations of astute, thoughtful women, listening to the Quran, understood perfectly well its essential themes and its faith. . . .

Leaving no written legacy, written only on the body and into the scripts of our lives, this oral and aural tradition of Islam no doubt stretches back through generations and is as ancient as any written tradition.

One could even argue that an emphasis on an oral and aural Islam is intrinsic to Islam and to the Quran itself, and intrinsic even in the Arabic language. Originally, the Quran was an aural, and only an aural, text recited to the community by the Prophet Muhammad. And it remained throughout his life, and indeed for several years after his death, only an aural text. Moreover, a bias in favor of the heard word, the word given life and meaning by the human voice, the human breath (*nafas*) is there, one might say, in the very language itself. . . . Here and now in this body, this breath (*nafas*) this self (*nafs*) encountering the word, giving it life. Word that, without that encounter, has no life, no meaning. Meaning always only here and now, in this body, for this person. Truth only here and now, for this body, this person. Not something transcendent, overarching, larger, bigger, more important than life—but here and now and in this body and in this small and ordinary life.

We seem to be living through an era of the progressive, seemingly inexorable erasure of the oral and ethical traditions of lived Islam and, simultaneously, of the ever-greater dissemination of written Islam, textual, "men's," Islam (an Islam essentially not of the Book but of the Texts, the medieval texts) as *the* authoritative Islam. Worse still, this seems to be an era of the unstoppable spread of fundamentalist Islam, textual Islam's narrower and more poorly informed modern descendant. It is a more ill-informed version of old-style official Islam in that the practitioners of that older Islam usually studied many texts and thus at least knew that even in these medieval texts there were disagreements among scholars and many possible interpretations of this or that verse. But today's fundamentalists, literate but often having read just a single text, take it to be definitive and the one and only "truth." . . .

What we are living through now seems to be not merely the erasure of the living oral, ethical, and humane traditions of Islam but the literal destruction and annihilation of the Muslims who are the bearers of those traditions. In Algeria, Iran, Afghanistan, and, alas, in Egypt, this narrow, violent variant of Islam is ravaging its way through the land.

> If a day won't come
> When the monuments of institutionalized religion are in ruin
> . . . then, my beloved,
> then we are really in trouble.
> (Rumi)

It has not been only women and simple, unlearned folk who have believed, like the women who raised me, that the ethical heart of Islam is also its core and essential message. Throughout Muslim history, philosophers, visionaries, mystics and some of the civilization's greatest luminaries have held a similar belief.

. . .

PLEASE LISTEN TO THE WOMEN OF IRAQ
Zainab Salbi

When Saba, an 18-year-old daughter of a Women for Women International-Iraq staff member, was shot on the way to school in December 2007, it cost the family about $800 just to get her the blood and the basic medicine she needed while at an Iraqi hospital for one day. The young woman stayed in the hospital for about 24 hours wrapped in a blood-soaked blanket. She remains paralyzed from the neck down today. When Saba narrates the story, her eyes are filled with tears. "I am left paralyzed for what? I have nothing to do with politics. I have nothing to do with anything. I was simply trying to finish my studies and to live my life." Saba's nights are now filled with nightmares. And Saba's cries echo those of so many women in Iraq, 2 million of whom are estimated to be widows and mothers to about 6 million orphans in the country—this out of a population of 27 million. . . .

There is no way to talk about a future stable, economically prosperous, and democratic Iraq without listening to what women have to say. It is time to listen to what Iraqi women are saying about their economic, political, and social reality and the future of the country. We cannot talk about the building of strong nations, any nations, if we don't make sure we support strong women. Strong women lead to strong nations. And there can't be talk about building a strong Iraq if women continue to be killed, oppressed, and suppressed from expressing their views on the future of the country. It is time to hear what women have to say.

. . .

At the age of 20, Meena, who had become a lawyer in order to fight for women's rights, gathered her most trusted women friends to found the Revolutionary Association of the Women of Afghanistan (RAWA). One of RAWA's founding principles was to work for democracy and the right to vote for both men and women. In RAWA, the members learned to practice democracy by deciding issues through collective discussion and consensus. RAWA's mission was to struggle for equality and justice for women, which to them meant freedom from poverty and violence.

After the Soviet invasion, Meena and other RAWA members joined the resistance against the Soviets. As the Afghan resistance grew, the United States, Britain, and many other nations ignored the groups of Afghan democrats and instead chose to support the same violent fundamentalist extremists, opposed to women's education, Meena had learned to fear from her university days. These "warlords" became the West's proxy armies against the Soviets. Afghanistan, a pawn in the Cold War, became the locus of a devastating war, and was torn to shreds. At least a million Afghan children were orphaned, the countryside was infested with land mines, and five million Afghans fled their homeland.

Among these refugees were Meena and many other RAWA members. RAWA shifted most of its schools and medical clinics to vast refugee camps in Pakistan. On February 4, 1987, Meena was abducted, tortured, and strangled by men aligned with a criminal warlord Gulbaddin Hekmatyar working with the pro-Soviet Afghan secret service.

(Melody Ermachild Chavis, from *Meena, Heroine of Afghanistan*)

• • •

BEHIND BARS

Fadwa Tuqan (translated by Hatem Hussaini)

My mother's phantom hovers here
her forehead shines before my eyes
like the light of stars
She might be thinking of me now,
dreaming
    (Before my arrest
    I drew letters in a book
    new and old
    I painted roses
    grown with blood
    and my mother was near me
    blessing my painting)
I see her
on her face silence and loneliness now
and in the house
silence and loneliness
My satchel there on the bookshelf
and my school uniform
on the hanger
I see her hand reaching out
brushing the dust from it
I follow my mother's steps
and listen to her thoughts
yearn to her arms and the face of day

                    . . .

Research reveals that fathers, especially, tend to become deeply disturbed by any behavior in their sons that is not typically "masculine." This kind of father provides a role model that fits the masculine mystique even though he may not be violent, at least not uncontrollably violent—he may use physical punishment to discipline his son. He does not express much emotion. He doesn't cry. He is very concerned with dominance, power, being tough. His taste in movies runs to John Wayne and Sylvester Stallone. . . . Whatever his actual behavior may be, he is likely to indulge in callous sexual talk about women. He may feel that a high level of involvement in childcare is unmanly. As a result, his son is likely to be less empathic. This kind of father is probably typical of a large number of basically decent American men who reinforce in their sons just those qualities that serve to desensitize them and make them more prone to commit violent acts or condone them.

(Myriam Miedzian, from *Boys Will Be Boys:
Breaking the Link between Masculinity and Violence*)

. . .

SHE CANNOT BE LOST TO ME
Karin Lofthus Carrington

Since wars begin in the minds of men, it is in the minds of men that
the defense of peace must be constructed.
—UNESCO Motto

DISASTER IN THE WHEATLANDS

Smoke from the hotbox eddied beneath the locomotive. The Great Northern's west bound Empire Builder, pounding hard for lost time in North Dakota's bronzed wheat lands, ground to an emergency stop just beyond Michigan City. A few miles back, the Empire Builder's second section was coming in out of the east. A flagman ran the few hundred yards back to Michigan City to flag it, but he never made it. Section 2 hit the Michigan City curve with its exhaust drumming, plowed slam-bang into Section 1.

The observation car was smashed. Seconds earlier, two servicemen in it had seen Section 2 coming around the bend, and jumped through the window glass. There was nothing that could be done for the other 34 in the car. All were dead—20 servicemen and women, 14 civilians.

Outside the tangled wreckage, a sailor from a forward car held his baby in his arms, clawed wildly at acetylene-torch crews cutting into the mangled steel. Just before the crash, his wife had entered the observation car.

It was the worst railroad wreck of 1945. (*Time Magazine*, August 20, 1945)

I was two years old, traveling on a Great Northern train from New York to the West Coast with my mother and father on August 9, 1945. I was falling asleep with the help of my newly commissioned father when my mother left our sleeping compartment, blowing a kiss to us and continuing on to the observation car to get my blue blanket that we had left behind. Within minutes that end car on the Great Northern Empire Builder was telescoped into the twilight sky by the impact of the engine from the train's second section. The most modern and sophisticated of train cars stood on end for a few seconds before crashing down on the engine, killing my mother and everyone else in the car instantly and sending scalding steam into that compartment and out into the surrounding area in a great white cloud.

Though I was, of course, not aware of it at the time, it later became significant to me that on the same day as the accident that killed my mother, the United States dropped an atomic bomb on Nagasaki, Japan, massacring 74,000 women, children, and men and wounding 60,000 others. Two days earlier, when the war's first atomic bomb was dropped on Hiroshima killing 202,000 people, my mother had turned 27. The day after the accident, August 10, 1945, World War II unofficially ended. Our attention was elsewhere on that day. It was the day my mother's body was removed from the wreckage of the train and identified by my father. It was also the day I made a sacred, secret covenant with my mother—a covenant that would inform and shape my life experience, seeding my unconventional understanding of the significance and necessity for sustained connection to "mother" and all that she represents throughout our lives.

Seeking to understand the connection I felt between my personal loss and the war, I came to see that there is a strong parallel between the uncontrollable release of energy from the fission of heavy nuclei in the atomic explosion and what happens to the psyche in the face of life-altering trauma. Trauma, particularly violent death and loss, is also an uncontrollable release of energy in the psyche, a blow to the core of our psychological organization that deconstructs the world as we know it, shattering the authentic flow of our life and development.

The psychologist Winnicott describes this flow as "going on being." After the psychological devastation caused by violent trauma, there is no going back to organic "going on being." What psychologists describe as the holding environment—what keeps us safe, connected, and trusting in our world—is destroyed, and those affected are in a kind of psychological free fall. Winnicott says that the interrupted continuity produces gaps or breaks that he called "threats of annihilation." During normal uninterrupted psychological development, we grow through one holding environment into the next. For example, at birth we leave the holding environment of the womb, coming into the world where the arms of the mother become our new holding environment. We then move from the arms of the mother into the world, one holding step at a time.

On August 9, 1945, what held me and what held the world was blown sky high. There was no step-by-step gradual progression into the next stage of development, not for me or for the world. Our connection to source—earth, mother—and our own "going on being" was fractured. What healing and recovery there might be would take decades, and the mark of that day will remain forever on the world and on my psyche.

For years after these two nearly simultaneous violent explosions on separate continents remained merged in my psyche and I would wake up twisted in my sheets, whimpering, with a recurring dream. In the dream I am a prisoner of war, taken captive by enemy soldiers and separated from my mother. I am as terrified by the separation from mother as by the threat of being the enemy's captive. The soldiers were interrogating me and trying to get me to tell them my secret.

I have come to see that the secret the soldiers in my dream were after was not about my imaginary friend—though she did represent a connection with imagination and humanity. Instead they wanted to know or to remember the secret of connection represented by the covenant I had made with my mother. In the aftermath of her death, I made a sacred, unconscious, and thus unspoken covenant with her. I would hold to her loyally, connected in my heart and memory to all that she represented and held for me until, in the magical thinking shared by children and those in grief, she came back to me. During war in particular, soldiers are required to forget this essential connection to mother and source in order to carry out their killing missions. Yet something in them has a ghostly kind of half-life memory of that connection which can haunt them. Their interrogation of me in the dreams I have come to understand as their desperate need to remember the connection to mother and their humanity.

As a psychologist looking back on that time in my life, I see that my mother died when I was in the middle of a particularly critical developmental stage, called rapprochement, which extends from 18 to 36 months, during which a child is called to "differentiate." Differentiation, in modern psychological terms, involves separating from the mother and moving more independently into the world. Theory suggests that ideally the child is able to go back and forth between mother and the world in their transition toward increased independence and autonomy. Analytic theory holds that with the more articulated separation of rapprochement, a child becomes aware of both her *deep dependence on the mother* and of greater *vulnerability in her expanding world*. Thus, rapprochement is traditionally treated as a developmental crisis for the individual—an overwhelming separation from Mother, a trauma that fractures the individual into a conscious and unconscious self. Because of the abrupt loss of my mother and my subsequent covenant of remembrance, I was more focused on a sustained connection to mother as I differentiated, rather than on the separation emphasized by psychological theory.

In reflection I see that those who survived Nagasaki and Hiroshima also sustained the wound of an interrupted rapprochement—one that separated them violently from the past that had held them for centuries and fractured their world into a before and after, a past and a present felt to be irreconcilable. No doubt survivors held loyally to the memory of lost loved ones and the wholeness of their life before Fat Man and Little Boy, even as the New Deal was introduced to induce amnesia.

I too was called to move into the new life. To forget the past. But for me the movement forward was only possible through the remembering and sustaining of an unconscious but embodied connection with the spirit of my mother. My father's urgent and desperate need to leave the past behind threatened to eclipse my mother's existence. He remarried 9 months after my mother's death. No one ever spoke about my birth mother, and when I asked about her, people changed the subject. I became a reminder to everyone of the past and felt for much of my life to be an "outsider" in our "new family."

Our entire extended family and community colluded in the denial, shunning the past and those who spoke of it. I am told that in both Hiroshima and Nagasaki survivors of the atomic bomb attacks were shunned because they were a reminder to everyone else of the past—a past either too painful to remember or necessary to deny for Japan to move forward and rebuild.

In a polarized world, one that splits the individual from (m)other, the past from the present, life from death, denial serves progress and the future by separating everyone from both the vulnerability and grief that connection with the past represents. What is denied however resides in the unconscious, like the long half-life of radioactive material, and will ultimately take a toll on the individual and society.

These individual and collective responses to the vulnerability of loss and grief, and modern psychology's emphasis on the urgent need to disconnect from mother in order to get on with independent life, are fertile soil for war, violence, and despair. If in order to be empowered one must "leave the past behind" and separate from mother and the dependence and vulnerability she represents, then humanity and the world become destabilized, out of balance and unsustainable. The separate individual in this dated paradigm is threatened by unity and by the mother who represents wholeness—a wholeness that contains both strength and vulnerability, both interdependence and dependence, both past and present. This union of opposites, interrupted by a false imperative for the developing individual in rapprochement, is the matrix of life. In some sense the result of a separating consciousness that fractures this matrix *is* our modern world—a world without any connection to the unifying and sustaining source of life that mother and mother earth represent.

The distortion of rapprochement as a time of separation from the essential part of ourselves that mother represents, rather than a time of differentiation within a field of sustained connection with that part of ourselves, is also the seeding ground for soldiering, heroics, and war.

Rapprochement in this sense can be seen as the birthplace of the heroic attitude or archetype in psychological development. The hero is awakened in part as a defense against feelings of susceptibility and defenselessness in the world without the mother. In separating from her, the developing child feels both his/her dependence on (m)other as well as his vulnerability and partial helplessness in the world.

To compensate for feelings of dependence and vulnerability awakened when we differentiate from Mother, the hero classically behaves in polarized ways. He may alternatively become the protector and savior of (m)other in a sentimental, though sincere way and/or he may become dominating and even willing to kill (m)other. He demonstrates through both his protection and dominance that he is not only separated from her, but is more powerful and no longer needs her love and holding. The hero is then tough enough to accomplish his mission. Dr. Stanley Kelleman, a somatic psychologist in Northern California, told his students during the '80s a story of one final training maneuver in a particular branch of the armed services, in which a soldier was asked to drive his bayonet into a simulated figure that bore the face of his mother. This training maneuver was the final threshold in the training and demonstrated the soldier's readiness for battle.

A soldier/hero defends his "Mother Country" but may also kill, rape, and mutilate mothers who are the civilians in enemy territory. Rape in war is fed by the need to prove dominance, deny vulnerability, and by the rapist's need to empower himself. For example, in Eastern Democratic Republic of Congo, a 2007 study by the Canadian-based humanitarian organization Social Aid for the Elimination of Rape (SAFE) reports that every DRC woman is raped by an average of 2.8 men, most of them soldiers. The acts of rape are often brutal and mutilating as part of the war effort. The Congo is perfecting rape as a weapon of war. And the total mutilation of women's genitals and wombs is the ultimate destruction of "mother." These atrocities against women go unpunished, even unacknowledged by the current government of Congo. And the rapists say that they have been trained to rape as a way to get the courage and energy to succeed in their mission. What, we must ask, has become of the relationships between the rapists and their mothers, wives, or daughters which connected them to their humanity?

The soldier/hero is, in the extreme, torn between mother worship (fighting for the Mother Land) and matricide. Men's ambivalence toward (m)other also permeates modern culture in more or less subtle ways, and contributes to the place of women as alternatively revered mothers/goddesses or as disposable property—easy rape targets, whores, and collateral damage not only in war but also in the collective psyche.

The "separated hero" in his determination to demonstrate his independence from the (m)other and defend against any feelings of vulnerability in the world, reassures himself of his power, autonomy, and agency by dominating women through his protective or attacking behavior. In the process, women protect their vulnerability through defiance or subservience, and men's connection to their vulnerability and tenderness is lost. And in a sense, so is our humanity.

In the prepatriarchal Hermitic tradition, healing depended upon a return to source, to origins. This is why pilgrimages are significant in all wisdom traditions. Mother is the embodiment of our origins—of the great connective matrix of life. The classic heroic dilemma is played out between the need to protect that matrix and the need to dominate and/ or destroy it. It is time to let go of the heroic myth, the heroic archetype, our heroic mentality. Our survival requires a re-visioning of the tasks of rapprochement as a time to differentiate and still maintain our connection to (M)other. We must develop the capacity to become at once both strong *and* vulnerable individuals who sustain our connection to source.

In August 2006, I made a pilgrimage to Michigan City, North Dakota, the town where my mother was killed. It was a time of remembrance at many levels. The night of her death, my father and I took refuge in St. Lawrence Catholic Church. I visited that church and found two prominent images of Mary in the vestry. One was a stained glass window of her walking with open, welcoming arms. The other was a pieta, a rendering of Mother Mary mourning her crucified son whom she holds in her arms.

Mary, or a figure representing the great mother, the source of life and heartfelt compassion, is revered in most world religions. She is a holy symbol too of comfort, peace, and the compassionate connection between life and death, past and present, vulnerability and courage, so often split or denied in hero-dominated cultures. A return to the undivided but differentiated source that Mother embodies—a new rapprochement with her—is urgently needed in our world. This rapprochement, which includes remembering and return, will make all the difference in healing the violence, wounds, and disconnection in our individual and collective lives and giving us a vision for peace in the world. May it be so.

. . .

Yes, we have a lot of work to do to have harmony and peace. We have many goals set before us but we can accomplish them by working together. Together we have gifts to bring by teaching what is sacred. We are all in this "leaky canoe" together so we need to be a united force to be reckoned with and we will keep on keeping on until our "hearts are on the ground."

Aho! (Bless you, Walk in beauty)

(Agnes Baker Pilgrim,
from "Joining Prayers")

. . .

SERENITY

Gabriela Mistral (translated by Susan Griffin)

When I sing to you
all that is evil on earth ends:
all is sweet as your forehead:
the ditch and the bramble.

Whenever I sing to you
I feel the end of cruelty:
with ways soft as your eyelids,
the lion and the jackal!

. . .

ACCEPTANCE SPEECH, NOBEL PEACE PRIZE

Shirin Ebadi

In the name of the God of Creation and Wisdom.

This year, the Nobel Peace Prize has been awarded to a woman from Iran, a Muslim country in the Middle East.

Undoubtedly, my selection will be an inspiration to the masses of women who are striving to realize their rights, not only in Iran but throughout the region—rights taken away from them through the passage of history. This selection will make women in Iran, and much further afield, believe in themselves. Women constitute half of the population of every country. To disregard women and bar them from active participation in political, social, economic and cultural life would in fact be tantamount to depriving the entire population of every society of half its capability. The patriarchal culture and the discrimination against women, particularly in the Islamic countries, cannot continue forever. . . .

As you are aware, the honour and blessing of this prize will have a positive and far-reaching impact on the humanitarian and genuine endeavours of the people of Iran and the region. The magnitude of this blessing will embrace every freedom-loving and peace-seeking individual, whether they are women or men.

Today coincides with the 55th anniversary of the adoption of the Universal Declaration of Human Rights; a declaration which begins with the recognition of the inherent dignity and the equal and inalienable rights of all members of the human family, as the guarantor of freedom, justice and peace. And it promises a world in which human beings shall enjoy freedom of expression and opinion, and be safeguarded and protected against fear and poverty.

Unfortunately, however, this year's report by the United Nations Development Programme (UNDP), as in the previous years, spells out the rise of a disaster which distances mankind from the idealistic world of the authors of the Universal Declaration of Human Rights. In 2002, almost 1.2 billion human beings lived in glaring poverty, earning less than one dollar a day. Over 50 countries were caught up in war or natural disasters. AIDS has so far claimed the lives of 22 million individuals, and turned 13 million children into orphans.

At the same time, in the past two years, some states have violated the universal principles and laws of human rights by using the events of 11 September and the war on international terrorism as a pretext. The United Nations General Assembly Resolution 57/219, of 18 December

2002, the United Nations Security Council Resolution 1456, of 20 January 2003, and the United Nations Commission on Human Rights Resolution 2003/68, of 25 April 2003, set out and underline that all states must ensure that any measures taken to combat terrorism must comply with all their obligations under international law, in particular international human rights and humanitarian law. However, regulations restricting human rights and basic freedoms, special bodies and extraordinary courts, which make fair adjudication difficult and at times impossible, have been justified and given legitimacy under the cloak of the war on terrorism.

The concerns of human rights' advocates increase when they observe that international human rights laws are breached not only by their recognized opponents under the pretext of cultural relativity, but that these principles are also violated in Western democracies, in other words countries which were themselves among the initial codifiers of the United Nations Charter and the Universal Declaration of Human Rights. It is in this framework that, for months, hundreds of individuals who were arrested in the course of military conflicts have been imprisoned in Guantánamo, without the benefit of the rights stipulated under the international Geneva conventions, the Universal Declaration of Human Rights and the [United Nations] International Covenant on Civil and Political Rights.

Moreover, a question which millions of citizens in the international civil society have been asking themselves for the past few years, particularly in recent months, and continue to ask, is this: why is it that some decisions and resolutions of the UN Security Council are binding, while some other resolutions of the council have no binding force? Why is it that in the past 35 years, dozens of UN resolutions concerning the occupation of the Palestinian territories by the state of Israel have not been implemented promptly, yet, in the past 12 years, the state and people of Iraq, once on the recommendation of the Security Council, and the second time, in spite of UN Security Council opposition, were subjected to attack, military assault, economic sanctions, and, ultimately, military occupation?

Allow me to say a little about my country, region, culture and faith.

I am an Iranian. A descendent of Cyrus the Great. The very emperor who proclaimed at the pinnacle of power 2,500 years ago that ". . . he would not reign over the people if they did not wish it." And [he] promised not to force any person to change his religion and faith and guaranteed freedom for all. The Charter of Cyrus the Great is one of the most important documents that should be studied in the history of human rights.

I am a Muslim. In the Koran the Prophet of Islam has been cited as saying: "Thou shalt believe in thine faith and I in my religion." That same divine book sees the mission of all prophets as that of inviting all human beings to uphold justice. Since the advent of Islam, too, Iran's civilization and culture has become imbued and infused with humanitarianism, respect for the life, belief and faith of others, propagation of tolerance and compromise and avoidance of violence, bloodshed and war. The luminaries of Iranian literature, in particular our Gnostic literature, from Hafiz, Mowlavi [better known in the West as Rumi] and Attar to Saadi, Sanaei, Naser Khosrow and Nezami, are emissaries of this humanitarian culture. Their message manifests itself in this poem by Saadi:

The sons of Adam are limbs of one another
Having been created of one essence.
When the calamity of time afflicts one limb
The other limbs cannot remain at rest.

The people of Iran have been battling against consecutive conflicts between tradition and modernity for over 100 years. By resorting to ancient traditions, some have tried and are trying to see the world through the eyes of their predecessors and to deal with the problems and difficulties of the existing world by virtue of the values of the ancients. But, many others, while respecting their historical and cultural past and their religion and faith, seek to go forth in step with world developments and not lag behind the caravan of civilization, development and progress. The people of Iran, particularly in the recent years, have shown that they deem participation in public affairs to be their right, and that they want to be masters of their own destiny.

This conflict is observed not merely in Iran, but also in many Muslim states. Some Muslims, under the pretext that democracy and human rights are not compatible with Islamic teachings and the traditional structure of Islamic societies, have justified despotic governments, and continue to do so. In fact, it is not so easy to rule over a people who are aware of their rights, using traditional, patriarchal and paternalistic methods.

Islam is a religion whose first sermon to the Prophet begins with the word "Recite!" The Koran swears by the pen and what it writes. Such a sermon and message cannot be in conflict with awareness, knowledge, wisdom, freedom of opinion and expression, and cultural pluralism.

The discriminatory plight of women in Islamic states, too, whether in the sphere of civil law or in the realm of social, political and cultural justice, has its roots in the patriarchal and male-dominated culture prevailing in these societies, not in Islam. This culture does not tolerate freedom and democracy, just as it does not believe in the equal rights of men and women, and the liberation of women from male domination (fathers, husbands, brothers . . .), because it would threaten the historical and traditional position of the rulers and guardians of that culture.

One has to say to those who have mooted the idea of a clash of civilizations, or prescribed war and military intervention for this region, and resorted to social, cultural, economic and political sluggishness of the South in a bid to justify their actions and opinions, that if you consider international human rights laws, including the nations' right to determine their own destinies, to be universal, and if you believe in the priority and superiority of parliamentary democracy over other political systems, then you cannot think only of your own security and comfort, selfishly and contemptuously. A quest for new means and ideas to enable the countries of the South, too, to enjoy human rights and democracy, while maintaining their political independence and territorial integrity of their respective countries, must be given top priority by the United Nations in respect of future developments and international relations.

The decision by the Nobel Peace Committee to award the 2003 prize to me, as the first Iranian and the first woman from a Muslim country, inspires me and millions of Iranians and nationals of Islamic states with the hope that our efforts, endeavours and struggles toward the realization of human rights and the establishment of democracy in our respective countries enjoy the support, backing and solidarity of international civil society. This prize belongs to the people of Iran. It belongs to the people of the Islamic states, and the people of the South for establishing human rights and democracy.

In the introduction to my speech, I spoke of human rights as a guarantor of freedom, justice and peace. If human rights fail to be manifested in codified laws or put into effect by states, then, as rendered in the preamble of the Universal Declaration of Human Rights, human beings will be left with no choice other than staging a "rebellion against tyranny and oppression." A human being divested of all dignity, a human being deprived of human rights, a human being gripped by starvation, a human being beaten by famine, war and illness, a humiliated human being and a plundered human being is not in any position or state to recover the rights he or she has lost.

If the twenty-first century wishes to free itself from the cycle of violence, acts of terror and war, and avoid repetition of the experience of
the twentieth century—that most disaster-ridden century of humankind,
there is no other way except by understanding and putting into practice
every human right for all mankind, irrespective of race, gender, faith,
nationality or social status.

In anticipation of that day. With much gratitude.

. . .

PRAYER OF THE VIRGIN OF GUADALUPE

Know for certain I am your merciful Mother, the Mother of all creation,
of those who cry to me, of those who have confidence in me. I hear their
weeping and sorrows, their necessities and misfortunes. Listen and let it
penetrate your heart. Do not be troubled and weighed down with grief.
Do not fear any illness or vexation, anxiety or pain. Am I not your
Mother? Are you not under my shadow and protection? Am I not your
fountain of life? Are you not in the folds of my mantle, in the crossing
of my arms? Is there anything else you need?

CHAPTER 7

Compassion and the Interdependence of Peace

May it be that God will bring about friendship between you
and those whom you hold to be your enemies.
—The Qur'an, 60:7

If you want to see the heroic,
look at those who can love
in return for hatred.
If you want to see the brave,
look for those who can forgive.
—Bhagavad Gita

Most religions teach compassion. Yet when talk about national security
gets serious, the power of this emotion to change events is usually un-
derestimated if not dismissed. But though at times compassion may be
consigned to a region of fantasy where only unrealistic hopes and goals
dwell, it is firmly based in reality. Indeed, empathy is hard-wired into
human nature. Cognitive scientists have discovered that cells in the nervous system called "mirror neurons," part of an assembly of nerves, fire
in sympathy with and imitation of actions and emotions we observe.
(That is why we want to laugh when others laugh or often begin to cry
whenever we see someone weeping.) In fact, empathy and the capacity
to mirror are crucial to the learning process.

From an evolutionary perspective, it makes sense that compassion
would become crucial to human nature. Given that as human beings we
belong to a larger ecological system in which we are interdependent
both within and between human societies and with nature, our own
survival depends on a large measure of mutual care. Compassion has a

gravitas that we neglect at our peril, especially now when global warming threatens the survival of the planet. And since essential resources such as water are affected by climate change, and environmental crisis also threatens to become a major cause of violence and warfare, sustainability and peace are inseparable.

While the globalization of a handful of corporations increases, creating greater and greater disparities in wealth, the understanding that we are all interconnected becomes more and more important. Even for citizens of the most wealthy and powerful nations, security and peace can only be achieved with compassion and cooperation. The idea that peace is linked to shared prosperity and well-being is not new. When, after World War II, to prevent a third world war between European nations, the Marshall Plan and a series of efforts that eventually led to the European Union were launched, this approach proved successful in creating a lasting peace.

Reaching out to aid other nations and peoples who are suffering helps to break down boundaries that separate humanity between groups labeled *us* and *them*. Speaking of those divisions, Daniel Goleman tells us, whenever empathy is silenced, "the gulf that divides Us from Them" grows. Whenever we designate anyone as Them and not Us, he goes on to say, "we close off our altruistic impulses."

Difference is often cited as the reason for designating another group as *them*. Yet by itself difference does not create enemies. Governments and leaders play a critical role in determining whether or not those who are different are considered enemies. As the great Polish poet, Czeslaw Milosz, describes in his depiction of the street where he was raised, people of different religions and ethnic groups can live together peacefully in cities, villages, or even on the same street as friends and neighbors. It is only after they are manipulated, exhorted, or even compelled by governing bodies and leaders that they conjure enemies from these differences and hence commit atrocities.

Along with compassion, forgiveness can play a significant role in ending conflicts. To harbor resentments and nurture rage over conflicts that have occurred in the past impedes mutual compassion and thus peace. (Indeed, the word *terror* gained its first political meaning when the French Revolution became obsessed with revenge.) Yet when crimes have not been subjected to justice, forgiveness can feel like denial. And, as Goleman also points out, quoting from psychologist Ervin Staub's work, forgiveness may not help "when the perpetrators fail to acknowledge what they have done, show no regret, and express no empathy for survivors." In this respect, Yoko Ono's moving request for forgiveness, which acknowledges the harm we have done to others in the name of the "War on Terror," can be taken as a model of genuine compassion.

Because the effects of trauma are so profound and long lasting, the process of recovery is very complex. It is important, for instance, in any discussion of forgiveness, to draw a clear line between individual victims and nations or groups. Individual victims of violence are not always able to forgive their perpetrators. If some survivors find healing from forgiveness, releasing them further from the hold of a horrifying past, others, in particular the victims of perpetrators with malicious intent or without conscience, experience the request to forgive their perpetrators as another violation, a further betrayal of trust. Recognizing the great difficulties in any process of healing the effects of violence, the commission established to confront the past under apartheid in South Africa used the word *reconciliation* instead of forgiveness.

Forgiveness may provide a powerful force for personal and social transformation, but it begins as a delicate bloom, one that can only be invited, never forced.

Finally, compassion, which is part of human nature, answers a need within us all, not only to receive but to give. This need is less allied with guilt than with joy and beauty. Wherever care, celebration, and community come together, the heart opens and we remember our souls.

Susan Griffin and Karin Lofthus Carrington

. . .

COMPASSION AS THE PILLAR OF WORLD PEACE
His Holiness the Fourteenth Dalai Lama

According to Buddhist psychology, most of our troubles are due to our passionate desire for and attachment to things that we misapprehend as enduring entities. The pursuit of the objects of our desire and attachment involves the use of aggression and competitiveness as supposedly efficacious instruments. These mental processes easily translate into actions, breeding belligerence as an obvious effect. Such processes have been going on in the human mind since time immemorial, but their execution has become more effective under modern conditions. What can we do to control and regulate these "poisons"—delusion, greed, and aggression? For it is these poisons that are behind almost every trouble in the world.

As one brought up in the Mahayana Buddhist tradition, I feel that love and compassion are the moral fabric of world peace. Let me first define what I mean by compassion. When you have pity or compassion for a very poor person, you are showing sympathy because he or she is poor; your compassion is based on altruistic considerations. On the other hand, love towards your wife, your husband, your children, or a close friend is usually based on attachment. When your attachment changes, your kindness also changes; it may disappear. This is not true love. Real love is not based on attachment, but on altruism. In this case your compassion will remain as a humane response to suffering as long as beings continue to suffer.

This type of compassion is what we must strive to cultivate in ourselves, and we must develop it from a limited amount to the limitless. Undiscriminating, spontaneous, and unlimited compassion for all sentient beings is obviously not the usual love that one has for friends or family, which is alloyed with ignorance, desire, and attachment. The kind of love we should advocate is this wider love that you can have even for someone who has done harm to you: your enemy.

The rationale for compassion is that every one of us wants to avoid suffering and gain happiness. This, in turn, is based on the valid feeling of "I," which determines the universal desire for happiness. Indeed, all beings are born with similar desires and should have an equal right to fulfill them. If I compare myself with others, who are countless, I feel that others are *more* important because I am just one person whereas others are many. Further, the Tibetan Buddhist tradition teaches us to view all sentient beings as our dear mothers and to show our gratitude by loving them all. For, according to Buddhist theory, we are born and reborn countless numbers of times, and it is conceivable that each being has been our parent at one time or another. In this way all beings in the universe share a family relationship. . . .

The principles discussed so far are in accordance with the ethical teachings of all world religions. I maintain that every major religion of the world—Buddhism, Christianity, Confucianism, Hinduism, Islam, Jainism, Judaism, Sikhism, Taoism, Zoroastrianism—has similar ideals of love, the same goal of benefiting humanity through spiritual practice, and the same effect of making their followers into better human beings. All religions teach moral precepts for perfecting the functions of mind, body, and speech. All teach us not to lie or steal or take others' lives, and so on. The common goal of all moral precepts laid down by the great teachers of humanity is unselfishness. The great teachers wanted to lead their followers away from the paths of negative deeds caused by ignorance and to introduce them to paths of goodness. . . .

There are many different religions to bring comfort and happiness to humanity in much the same way as there are particular treatments for different diseases. For all religions endeavour in their own way to help living beings avoid misery and gain happiness. And, although we can find causes for preferring certain interpretations of religious truths, there is much greater cause for unity, stemming from the human heart. Each religion works in its own way to lessen human suffering and contribute to world civilization. Conversion is not the point. For instance, I do not think of converting others to Buddhism or merely furthering the Buddhist cause. Rather, I try to think of how I as a Buddhist humanitarian can contribute to human happiness.

While pointing out the fundamental similarities between world religions, I do not advocate one particular religion at the expense of all others, nor do I seek a new "world religion." All the different religions of the world are needed to enrich human experience and world civilization. . . .

Each religion has its own distinctive contributions to make, and each in its own way is suitable to a particular group of people as they understand life. The world needs them all.

There are two primary tasks facing religious practitioners who are concerned with world peace. First, we must promote better inter-faith understanding so as to create a workable degree of unity among all religions. This may be achieved in part by respecting each other's beliefs and by emphasizing our common concern for human well-being. Second, we must bring about a viable consensus on basic spiritual values that touch every human heart and enhance general human happiness. This means we must emphasize the common denominator of all world religions—humanitarian ideals. These two steps will enable us to act both individually and together to create the necessary spiritual conditions for world peace.

We practitioners of different faiths can work together for world peace when we view different religions as essentially instruments to develop a good heart—love and respect for others, a true sense of community. The most important thing is to look at the purpose of religion and not at the details of theology or metaphysics, which can lead to mere intellectualism. I believe that all the major religions of the world can contribute to world peace and work together for the benefit of humanity if we put aside subtle metaphysical differences, which are really the internal business of each religion. . . .

Whether we will be able to achieve world peace or not, we have no choice but to work towards that goal. If our minds are dominated by anger, we will lose the best part of human intelligence—wisdom, the ability to decide between right and wrong. Anger is one of the most serious problems facing the world today.

· · ·

FROM THEM TO US
Daniel Goleman
FROM: *Social Intelligence: The New Science of Human Relationships*

It was during the last years of apartheid in South Africa, the system of complete segregation between the ruling Dutch-descended Afrikaaners and the "colored" groups. Thirty people had been meeting clandestinely for four days. Half were white business executives, half black community organizers. The group was being trained to conduct leadership seminars together, so they could help build governance skills within the black community.

On the last day of the program they sat riveted to a television set while President F. W. de Klerk gave a now-famous speech that heralded the coming end of apartheid. De Klerk legalized a long list of previously banned organizations and ordered the release of many political prisoners.

Anne Loersebe, one of the black community leaders there, was beaming: as each organization was named, she pictured the face of someone she knew who could now come out of hiding.

After the speech the group went through an ending ritual in which each person had a chance to offer parting words. Most simply said how meaningful the training had been, and how glad they were to have been there.

But the fifth person to speak, a tall, emotionally reserved Afrikaaner, stood and looked directly at Anne. "I want you to know," he told her, "that I was raised to think you were an animal." And with that, he broke into tears.[1]

Us-Them restates I-It in the plural: the underlying dynamics are one and the same. As Walter Kaufmann, the English translator of Martin Buber, put it, with the words "Us-Them," "the world is divided in two: the children of the light and the children of the darkness, the sheep and the goats, the elect and the damned."[2]

The relationship between one of Us and one of Them by definition lacks empathy, let alone attunement. Should one of Them presume to speak to Us, the voice would not be heard as fully or openly as would that of one of Us—if at all.

The gulf that divides Us from Them builds with the silencing of empathy. And across the gulf we are free to project onto Them whatever we like. As Kaufmann adds, "Righteousness, intelligence, integrity, humanity and victory are the prerogatives of Us, while wickedness, stupidity, hypocrisy, and ultimate defeat belong to Them." . . .

"Hatred," said Elie Wiesel, the Nobel Peace Prize winner and Holocaust survivor, "is a cancer that is passed from one person to another."[3] Human history chronicles an endless stream of horrors perpetuated by one group that turns viciously against another—even when that other group has far more similarities to than differences from themselves. Northern Irish Protestants and Catholics, like Serbs and Croatians, have battled over the years, though genetically they are each other's closest biological brothers and sisters.

We confront the challenge of living in a global civilization with a brain that primarily attaches us to our home tribe. As a psychiatrist who grew up amid the ethnic turmoil of Cyprus put it, groups that are so much alike move from Us to Them via the "narcissism of minor differences," seizing on small features that set the groups apart while ignoring their vast human similarities. Once the others are set at a psychological distance, they can become a target for hostility.

This process is a corruption of normal cognitive function: categorization. The human mind depends on categories to give order and meaning to the world around us. By assuming that the next entity we encounter in a given category has the same main features as the last, we navigate our way through an ever-changing environment.

But once a negative bias begins, our lenses become clouded. We tend to seize on whatever seems to confirm the bias and ignore what does not. Prejudice, in this sense, is a hypothesis desperately trying to prove itself to us. And so when we encounter someone to whom the prejudice might apply, the bias skews our perception, making it impossible to test whether the stereotype actually fits. Openly hostile stereotypes about a group—to the extent they rest on untested assumptions—are mental categories gone awry.

A vague sense of anxiety, a tinge of fear, or mere uneasiness at not knowing the cultural signals of Them can be enough to start the skewing of a cognitive category. The mind builds its "evidence" against the other with each additional disquiet, each unflattering media deception, each feeling of having been treated wrongly. As these incidents build, apprehension becomes antipathy, and antipathy morphs into antagonism.[4]

Outright anger primes prejudice even in those whose biases are slight. Like a match on tinder, antagonism catalyzes the switch from Us *and* Them (the mere perception of difference) to Us *versus* Them, active hostility.

Anger and fear . . . amplify the destructiveness of a budding bias. When flooded by these strong emotions, the prefrontal area of the brain becomes incapacitated, as the low road hijacks the high. This sabotages the ability to think clearly, thereby foiling a corrective answer to that essential question, does he really have all the bad traits I ascribe to Them? And if the damning view of Them has already been accepted, even in the absence of anger or fear that question is no longer asked.

Implicit Bias

Us-and-Them comes in many forms, from rabid hatred to unflattering stereotypes so subtle they elude even those who hold them. Such ultra-subtle prejudices hide in the low road, in the form of "implicit" biases, automatic and unconscious stereotypes. These quiet biases seem capable of driving responses—such as the decision of who to hire from a pool of equally qualified applicants—even when they do not fit our consciously held beliefs.[4]

People who show not the least outward sign of prejudice and who espouse positive views toward a group can still harbor hidden biases, as revealed by clever cognitive measures. For instance, the Implicit Association Test offers you a word and asks you to match it to a category as quickly as you can.[5] Its scale for hidden attitudes about whether women are as qualified as men for careers in science asks you to match words like "physics" and "humanities" to either "women" or "men."

We can make such a match most quickly when an idea fits the way we already think about something. Someone who believed that men are better at science than are women would be quicker when matching "men" and science-related words. These differences are counted in mere tenths of seconds and are discernible only by computer analysis.

Such implicit biases, faint as they are, seem to skew judgments about people in a target group, as well as choices such as whether to work with someone, or judgments of a defendant's guilt.[6] When there are clear rules to follow, implicit biases have less effect—but the fuzzier the standards in a situation, the more powerful they become.

One cognitive scientist, a woman, was shocked to find that a test of implicitly held biases revealed that she unconsciously endorsed a stereotype against women scientists—like herself! So she changed the decor in her office, surrounding herself with photos of famous women scientists like Marie Curie.

Could that make a difference in her attitudes? It just might.

At one time psychologists saw unconscious mental categories like implicit attitudes as fixed; because their influence works automatically and unconsciously, the assumption was that their consequences were inevitable. . . .

But more recent research has shown that automatic stereotypes and prejudices are fluid—implicit biases do not reflect a person's "true" feelings but can shift.[7] At the neural level, this fluidity may reflect the fact that even the low road remains an eager learner throughout life. . . .

Many methods have been proven to reduce implicit bias, if only for the time being. When people were told that an IQ test showed they had high intelligence, their negative implicit biases vanished—but when they were told the test showed they had low intelligence, the biases strengthened. Implicit bias against blacks diminished after people were given positive feedback by a black supervisor.

Social demands can do it: people who are put in a social setting where a prejudiced view is "out of step" register less implicit bias, too. Even the explicit resolve to ignore a person's membership in a target group can reduce hidden prejudice.[8] . . .

A very different, and rather novel, way to neutralize prejudice a bit was discovered in Israeli experiments where people's sense of security was activated via subtle methods, like bringing to mind loved ones. Feeling momentarily more secure shifted prejudiced participants to a positive stance toward groups like Arabs and ultra-Orthodox Jews, both of whom had been among their initial targets of bias. When told they could spend time with an Arab or an ultra-Orthodox Jew, they were far more willing than they had been just minutes before.

No one claims that such a fleeting sense of security can resolve long-standing historical and political conflict. Still, that demonstration adds to the case that even hidden prejudice can be lessened.[9]

Closing the Hostile Divide

Exactly what might repair Us-Them divides has been hotly debated for years among psychologists who study intergroup relations. But much of that debate has now been resolved by the work of Thomas Pettigrew, a social psychologist who has been studying prejudice ever since soon after the American civil rights movement destroyed legal barriers between races. Pettigrew, a native of Virginia, was one of the first psychologists to plumb the heart of racial hatred. He began as a student of Gordon Allport, a social psychologist who argued that friendly and sustained contacts erode prejudice.

Now three decades later, Pettigrew has led the largest analysis of studies ever on what kinds of contact change hostile groups' views about each other. Pettigrew and his associates tracked down 515 studies dating from the 1940s to 2000 and combined them into a single massive statistical analysis, with responses from an astonishing 250,493 people from thirty-eight countries. The Us-Them divides in the studies ranged from black-white relations in the United States to a multitude of ethnic, racial, and religious animosities around the world, as well as biases against the elderly, disabled, and mentally ill.[10]

The strong conclusion: emotional involvement, like friendships and romances between individuals from either side of a hostile divide, make people far more accepting of each other's groups. For instance, having had a childhood playmate from another group typically inoculates people against prejudice later in life—as was found in one study of African-Americans who played with whites as children (though their schools were segregated at the time). The same effect operated under apartheid among those rural Afrikaner housewives who had become friends with their African domestic workers.

Significantly, studies that track the time course of across-the-divide friendships show that the closeness itself leads to a reduction in prejudice. But mere casual contact on the street or at work does relatively little, if anything, to change hostile stereotypes.[11] Pettigrew argues that the essential requirement for overcoming prejudice is a strong emotional connection. Over time the warmth each person feels towards the other generalizes to all of Them. For instance, when people had good friends across tense ethnic divides in Europe—Germans with Turks, French with North Africans, British with West Indians—the friends had far less prejudice toward the other group as a whole.[12]

"You may still hold a general stereotype about them, but it's not connected to strong negative feelings anymore," Pettigrew told me.

But what of implicit bias, the subtle stereotypes that slide under the radar of even those who profess to hold no bias? Don't they matter too? Pettigrew is skeptical.

"Groups often hold stereotypes about themselves that are widespread in their culture," he observed. "For instance, I'm a Scot; my parents were immigrants. Scots are stereotyped as skinflints. But we turn that around, saying we're just being thrifty. The stereotype remains, but the emotional valence has changed."

Tests for implicit bias look at each person's cognitive categories, which in themselves are but cool abstractions, devoid of feeling. What counts about a stereotype, Pettigrew argues, is the feeling tone that goes with it: simply holding a stereotype matters less than do the emotions attached.

Given the intensity, even violence, of some intergroup tensions, worrying about implicit bias may be a luxury reserved for places where prejudice has largely dwindled to subtleties rather than expressions of outright hatred. When groups are in open conflict, emotions are what we count; when they are getting along, the mental residues of outright prejudice matter to the extent that they foster subtle acts of prejudice.

Pettigrew's research shows that holding negative feelings toward a group predicts hostile actions far more strongly than does holding an unflattering stereotype of Them.[13] Even after people from hostile groups form friendships, some of the original stereotypes remain. But their feelings warm up—and that makes the difference: "Now I like them, even if I still hold on to the general stereotype." Pettigrew speculates, "The implicit bias may stay, but if my emotions shift, my behavior will, too."

Forgiving and Forgetting

But what can be done to heal the hatred of peoples when they *have* shed blood? In the aftermath of intergroup violence, prejudice and animosity inevitably metastasize.

Once hostilities have ceased, over and above harmonious relations there are good personal reasons to speed the process. One is biological: holding on to hatred and grudges has grave physiological consequence. Studies of people posthostility reveal that every time they merely think of the group they hate, their own body responds with pent-up anger; it floods with stress hormones, raising their blood pressure and impairing their immune effectiveness. Presumably, the more often and intensely this sequence of muted rage repeats, the more risk of long lasting biological consequence.

One antidote lies in forgiveness.[14] Forgiving someone we've held a grudge against reverses the biological reaction: it lowers our blood pressure, heart rate, and levels of stress hormones and it lessens our pain and depression.[15]

Forgiveness can have social consequences, like making friends with former enemies. But it need not take that form. Especially while wounds are still fresh, forgiveness does not require condoning some offensive act, forgetting what happened, or reconciling with the perpetrator. It means finding a way to free oneself from the claws of obsession about the hurt.

For a week psychologists coached seventeen men and women from Northern Ireland, both Catholic and Protestant, on forgiveness. Each of them had lost a family member to sectarian violence. During that week the bereaved aired their grievances and were helped to find new ways to think about the tragedy—most resolving not to dwell on their hurt but to honor the memory of their loved ones by dedicating themselves to a more hopeful future. Many intended to help others go through the same ritual of forgiveness. Afterward, the group not only felt less hurt emotionally, but also reported a substantial drop in physical symptoms of trauma like poor appetite and sleeplessness.[16]

Forgive perhaps, but don't forget—at least not entirely. There are larger lessons for humanity to learn from acts of oppression and brutality. They need to be held in mind as morality tales, reminders to the ages. As Rabbi Lawrence Kushner says of the Holocaust, "I want to remember its horror only to make sure that such a thing never happens to me or to anyone else ever again."[17] . . .

Cultivating the capacity to fight hatred is the subtext of *New Dawn*, a joint project of Dutch philanthropists and American psychologists.[18] "We're giving people an understanding of the influences that led to genocide, and what they can do to see it never repeats," said Ervin Staub, a psychologist at the University of Massachusetts at Amherst and one of the designers of the show.

Staub knows about the dynamics of genocide from a personal experience as well as from his research. As a child, he was one of tens of thousands of Hungarian Jews saved from the Nazis by Swedish ambassador Raoul Wallenberg.

Staub's book *The Roots of Evil* summarizes the psychological forces that spawn such mass murder.[19] The groundwork gets laid during severe social upheavals, like economic crises and political chaos, in places that have a history of division between a dominant group and a less powerful one. The turmoil causes members of a majority group to find appealing the ideologies that scapegoat a weaker group, blaming them for the problem and envisioning a better future that They are preventing. The hatred spreads all the more readily when the majority group has itself been victimized in the past and still feels wounded or wronged. Already seeing the world as dangerous, when tensions rise they feel a need to resort to violence against Them to defend themselves, even when their "self-defense" amounts to genocide.

Several features make such violence more likely: when the targets are unable to speak up to defend themselves, and bystanders—those who reject who could object, or people in nearby countries—say and do nothing. "If others are passive when you first harm the victims, the perpetrators interpret that silence as an endorsement," Staub says. "And once people start the violence, step by step they exclude their victim from the moral realm. Then there's nothing to hold them back."

Staub, working with psychologist Laurie Anne Pearlman, has been teaching these insights—and antidotes to hatred, like objecting openly—to Rwandan groups of politicians, journalists, and community leaders.[20] "We ask them to apply these insights to their own experience of what happened. It's very powerful. We're trying to promote community healing and build the tools to resist the forces of violence."

Their research shows that both Hutus and Tutsis who have gone through such training feel less traumatized by what happened to them and are more accepting of the other group. But it takes more than strong emotional connections and friendship to overcome the Us-Them divide. Forgiveness may not help when the groups continue to live next to each other, Staub finds, and when the perpetrators fail to acknowledge what they have done, show no regret, and express no empathy for survivors. The imbalance widens if the forgiveness is one-sided.

Staub distinguishes forgiveness from reconciliation, which is the honest review of oppression and efforts at making amends like those undertaken by the Truth and Reconciliation Commission in South Africa after the fall of apartheid. In his programs in Rwanda, reconciliation has meant that those on the side of the perpetrators admit what was done, and people on both sides come to see each other more realistically. That paves the way for both people to live together in a new way.

"Tutsis will tell you," Staub finds, "'some Hutus tried to save our lives. I'm willing to work with them for the sake of our children. If they apologize, I can see myself forgive.'"

1. The Afrikaaner and Anne were witnessed by Peter Senge and recounted in Peter Senge et al., *Presence: Human Purpose and the Field of the Future* (Cambridge, Mass.: Society for Organizational Learning, 2004).

2. On Us-Them, see Walter Kaufmann, prologue to Martin Buber, *I and Thou* (1937; New York: Simon & Schuster, 1990), p. 13.

3. Elie Wiesel made these remarks at the sixtieth anniversary of the liberation of Auschwitz. See *Jerusalem Post,* January 25, 2005.

4. For instance, data from the Implicit Association Test suggest that in the United States most whites and about half of blacks are quicker to associate positive terms like "joy" with whites and negative ones like "bomb" with blacks. Even people who espouse antiracist views are often chagrined to find that they, too, are quicker to be positive about whites and negative about blacks.

5. On the Implicit Association Test, see Anthony Greenwald et al., "Measuring Individual Differences in Implicit Cognition: The Implicit Association Test," *Journal of Personality and Social Psychology* 74 (1998), pp. 1464–80.

6. T. Andrew Poehlman et al., "Understanding and Using Implicit Association Test: III. Meta-analysis of Predictive Validity," unpublished manuscript.

7. Irene V. Blair, "The Malleability of Automatic Stereotypes and Prejudice," *Personality and Psychology Review* 202 (2002), pp. 242–61.

8. Intriguingly, people who hold an ongoing resolve to suppress negative stereotypes are able to do so as long as they are aware of the moment they see a person in the target group. But when the exposure to that person is subliminal (a blink, just 33 milliseconds), the implicit bias remains. See Blair, "The Malleability."

9. This study also suggests why demagogues have always stirred fear and anger into the mix with hostility toward Them. A group's sense of security poses a threat to one thing: prejudice.

10. On intergroup studies, see Thomas Pettigrew and Linda Tropp, "A Meta-analytic Test of Intergroup Contact Theory," *Journal of Personality and Social Psychology* (2006, in press).

11. Casual contact counts less than relationships that people feel are important. See Rolf van Dick et al., "Role of Perceived Importance in Intergroup Conflict," *Journal of Personality and Social Psychology* 87, no. 2 (2004), pp. 211–27.

12. On ethnic divides in Europe, see Thomas Pettigrew, "Generalized Intergroup Contact Effects on Prejudice," *Personality and Social Psychology Bulletin* 23 (1997), pp. 173–85.

13. On affect versus cognitive categories, see Pettigrew and Tropp, "Meta-analytic Test."

14. Forgiveness, of course, comes more readily when the offender offers an authentic apology. As one Israeli proposed, a leader on either side of the Israeli

rift with the Palestinians could make a ritual apology like, "You have been through so much because of us. We are sorry. We are sorry because we didn't mean to hurt you, we only wanted to build a nation." That might help the peace process. See Lucy Benjamin, "Impasse: Israel and Palestine," Conference at Columbia University, New York, November 20, 2004.

15. On the physiology of forgiveness, see Fred Luskin, *Forgive for Good* (San Francisco: HarperSanFrancisco, 2001).

16. On forgiveness in Northern Ireland, see ibid.

17. Rabbi Lawrence Kushner was interviewed in Jonathan Cott, *On a Sea of Memory* (New York: Random House, 2005), p. 153.

18. The producer of *New Dawn* is George Weiss, La Benevolencija Productions, Amsterdam. The Rwanda Project has its website at www.Heal-reconcile -Rwanda.org.

19. Ervin Staub, *The Roots of Evil* (New York: Cambridge University Press, 1992).

20. Ervin Staub and Laurie Anne Pearlman, "Advancing Healing and Reconciliation in Rwanda and Other Post-conflict Settings," in L. Barbanel and R. Sternberg, eds., *Psychological Interventions in Times of Crisis* (New York: Springer-Verlag, 2006).

. . .

Today we can actually track scientifically the neural dimensions of our narrow definitions of self. When our resonance circuits are engaged, we can feel another's feelings and create a cortical imprint that lets us understand what may be going on in the other's mind—because it is like ours—and our mind and our brain turn on our mindsight mechanism. We uncap our inner lens and take a deep look into the face of the other to see the mind that rests beneath the visage. But if we cannot identify with someone else, those resonance circuits shut off. We see others as objects, as "them" rather than "us." We literally do not activate the very circuits we need in order to see another person as having an internal mental life.

This shutting off of circuits of compassion may be one explanation for our violent history as a species. Without mindsight, people become objects, rather than subjects themselves with minds like ours worthy of respecting and even knowing.

(Daniel J. Siegel, from *Mindsight: The New Science of Personal Transformation*)

. . .

FALLING BODIES
Alice Walker

He told me
Some of them were holding hands
Leaping from
The flaming
Windows.

To these ones
Leaping, holding hands
Holding
Their own
I open
My arms.

Everything
It is
Necessary
To understand
They mastered
In the last
Rich
Moments
That
They owned.

There is no more
To learn
In life
Than this:
How to
Love and
How not to miss
To waste
The moment
Our understanding
Of this
Is clear.

We are
Each other's
Own
Near and far
Far and wide
(Even if we leap
Into loving
In such haste
It is certain
There will remain
Nothing of us
Left.)

Consider: The pilot
& the
Hijacker
Might
Have been
Holding
Hands.

Those who wish
To make
A war
Of this
Will never believe
It possible.

But how enlightenment
Comes
To others
We may never
Know
Or even
How
Someday
It may come
To us.

. . .

FORGIVE US

Yoko Ono

December 8th is near again. Every year, on this day, I hear from many people from all over the world who remember my husband, John Lennon, and his message of peace. They write to tell me they are thinking of John on this day and how he was shot and killed at the prime of his life, at age 40, when he had so much life ahead of him.

Thank you for your undying love for John and also for your concern for me on this tragic anniversary. This year, though, on December 8th, while we remember John, I would also like us to focus on sending the following messages to the millions of people suffering around the world.

To the people who have also lost loved ones without cause: forgive us for having been unable to stop the tragedy. We pray for the wounds to heal.

To the soldiers of all countries and all centuries, who were maimed for life, or who lost their lives: forgive us for our misjudgments and what happened as a result of them.

To the civilians who were maimed, or killed, or who lost their family members: forgive us for having been unable to prevent it.

To the people who have been abused and tortured: forgive us for having allowed it to happen.

Know that your loss is our loss.

Know that the physical and mental abuse you have endured will have a lingering effect on our society, and the world.

Know that the burden is ours.

As the widow of one who was killed by an act of violence, I don't know if I am ready yet to forgive the one who pulled the trigger. I am sure all victims of violent crimes feel as I do. But healing is what is urgently needed now in the world.

Let's heal the wounds together.

Every year, let's make December 8th the day to ask for forgiveness from those who suffered the insufferable.

Let's wish strongly that one day we will be able to say that we healed ourselves, and by healing ourselves, we healed the world.

With deepest love,

Yoko Ono Lennon

New York City 2006

. . .

Now power properly understood is nothing but the ability to achieve purpose. It is the strength required to bring about social, political and economic change. . . . What is needed is a realization that power without love is reckless and abusive, and love without power is sentimental and anemic. Power at its best is love implementing the demands of justice, and justice at its best is power correcting everything that stands against love.

(Martin Luther King, Jr., from *Where Do We Go from Here: Chaos or Community?*)

· · ·

SUSTAINABILITY, SECURITY, AND PEACE
Fritjof Capra

The Roots of Terrorism

Since September 11, 2001, there has been a striking tendency to portray terrorism as the result of evil forces operating in a vacuum. In reality, the very nature of terrorism derives from a series of political, economic, and technological problems that are all interconnected.[1] To understand the root causes of our vulnerability, we need to understand the conditions that breed hatred and violence, as well as the characteristics of a technological infrastructure that makes large-scale attacks against the United States a highly effective terrorist weapon.[2]

Such an understanding begins with the realization that we live in a complex, globally interconnected world in which linear chains of cause and effect do not exist. To understand this world, we need to think systemically—in terms of relationships, connections, and context.

Thinking systemically means to realize that security, energy, environment, climate, and economy are not separate issues but merely different facets of one global system. It leads us to understand that the root causes of our vulnerability are both social and technological, and that both kinds are consequences of our resource-extractive, wasteful, and consumption-oriented economic system.

America's Image in the World

Any attempt to understand the roots of the new terrorism has to begin with the understanding of America's image in the world. This image is multifaceted. It includes many positive aspects of our society—such as individual liberty, cultural diversity, and economic opportunity—as well as the great enthusiasm for American technology, fashion, sports, and entertainment, especially among the world's youth.

On the other hand, the United States is seen by millions around the world as the leader of a new form of global capitalism that has significantly increased poverty and social inequality. It has generated unprecedented wealth at the very top while forcing billions of people into desperate poverty. Consequently . . . relationships between the rich and the poor are increasingly shaped by fear and hatred, and it is not difficult to see that many of the desperate and marginalized are easily recruited by terrorist organizations.

According to recent estimates by the United Nations Development Program (UNDP), every poor person on earth could have clean water, basic health services, nutrition, and education for about $40 billion a year. This would be by far the most effective way of dealing with the roots of terrorism. Instead, the Bush Administration launched a war in Iraq, which by 2009 had cost over $900 billion, a war that significantly increased the number of potential and actual terrorists.

Now let me turn to the technological roots of our vulnerability. The main thrust of the World Trade Organization's free-trade rules has been to dismantle local production in favor of exports and imports. This puts enormous stress on the environment because of increased transportation and energy use, and has created a highly centralized system of supply lines that is inherently vulnerable.

It is evident that an energy system dependent on gigantic pipelines and refineries, dams, power lines, and nuclear plants is more vulnerable than one powered by decentralized solar technologies. A food system supplied by a few megafarms and long supply lines is much more prone to terrorist attacks than one featuring a multitude of small farms and local farmers' markets.

The Politics of Oil

The vulnerability of our centralized, high-tech infrastructure is exacerbated by misguided energy policies that have decisively shaped U.S.

foreign policy. Successive American governments have perpetuated an unnecessary dependence on oil. In exchange for unlimited access to this so-called strategic resource, the United States has supported undemocratic and repressive regimes in many parts of the world, in particular in the Middle East, which continues to fuel anti-American hatred in populations who are deprived of basic human rights.

Especially relevant here is our relationship with Saudi Arabia.[3] This relationship is based on an extraordinary bargain, concluded in 1945 between President Roosevelt and King Ibn Saud, according to which Saudi Arabia grants the U.S. unlimited and perpetual access to its oil fields (which contain 25 percent of the world's known oil reserves!) in exchange for protection of the Saudi royal family against its enemies, both external and internal. This bargain has shaped American foreign and military policy for almost half a century, during which we have protected a totalitarian regime in Saudi Arabia that blatantly disregards basic human rights and tramples democracy.

The main purpose of the Gulf war in 1991, originally code-named "Desert Shield," was not to drive Iraq out of Kuwait, but to protect Saudi Arabia from a possible attack and to guarantee U.S. access to the Saudi oil fields. Since then, we have maintained and steadily expanded our military presence in the Gulf. In addition we also defend the Saudi regime against its internal enemies. The Saudi Arabian National Guard, which protects the royal family, is almost entirely armed, trained, and managed by the United States.

A shift of energy policy from the current heavy emphasis on fossil fuels to renewable energy sources and conservation is not only imperative for moving toward ecological sustainability, but must also be seen as vital to our security. More generally, we need to broaden the concept of security to include not only energy security but also food security, the security of a healthy environment, social justice, and cultural integrity. A community designed to be secure is also one that is ecologically and socially sustainable.

Ecological Sustainability

Let us now take a closer look at ecological sustainability, so as to really understand its fundamental link to security.

The concept of sustainability was introduced in the early 1980s by Lester Brown, founder of the Worldwatch Institute, who defined a sustainable society as one that is able to satisfy its needs without diminishing the chances of future generations. This definition of sustainability is an important moral exhortation. It reminds us of our responsibility to pass on to our children and grandchildren a world with as many opportunities as the ones we inherited. However, it does not tell us anything about how to actually build a sustainable society. We need an operational definition.

We do not need to invent sustainable human communities from scratch but can model them after nature's ecosystems, which are sustainable communities of plants, animals, and microorganisms. Since the outstanding characteristic of the biosphere is its inherent ability to sustain life, a sustainable human community must be designed in such a manner that its ways of life, businesses, economy, physical structures, and technologies *do not interfere with nature's inherent ability to sustain life.*

A sustainable human community interacts with other living systems—human and nonhuman—in ways that enable those systems to live and develop according to their nature. In the human realm, therefore, sustainability is fully consistent with the respect of cultural integrity, cultural diversity, and the basic right of communities to self-determination and self-organization.

To ecologists, the fundamental link between security and sustainability is not surprising, because sustainability means long-term survival. Over more than three billion years of evolution, nature's ecosystems developed "technologies" and "design principles" that are sustainable in the long run and hence resilient and inherently secure. Natural selection has seen to it that the vulnerable systems are no longer around. Designing a secure society, therefore, means designing it with ecology in mind.

Ecoliteracy

My operational definition of ecological sustainability implies that the first step in our endeavor to build sustainable communities must be to become "ecologically literate," that is, to understand the principles of organization that ecosystems have evolved to sustain the web of life. In the future, ecological literacy, or "ecoliteracy," will become a critical skill for politicians, business leaders, and professionals in all spheres, and should be the most important part of education at all levels—from primary and secondary schools to colleges, universities, and the continuing education and training of professionals.

We need to teach our children and young people, as well as our political and corporate leaders, the basic facts of life:

- that an ecosystem generates no waste, one species' waste being another species' food;
- that matter cycles continually through the web of life;
- that the energy driving these ecological cycles flows from the sun;
- that diversity increases resilience;
- that life, from its beginning more than three billion years ago, did not take over the planet by combat but by cooperation, partnership, and networking.

In the coming decades, the survival of humanity will depend on our ability to understand these basic principles of ecology and to live accordingly.

Ecodesign

Ecoliteracy is the first step on the road to sustainability. The second step is to move from ecoliteracy to ecodesign. We need to apply our ecological knowledge to the fundamental redesign of our technologies and social institutions, so as to bridge the current gap between human design and the ecologically sustainable systems of nature. Ecodesign principles reflect the principles of organization that nature has evolved to sustain the web of life. To practice industrial design in such a context requires a fundamental shift in our attitude toward nature, a shift from finding out what we can *extract* from nature, to what we can *learn* from her.

In recent years, there has been a dramatic rise in ecologically oriented design practices and projects, all of which are now well documented.[4] Let me just concentrate on energy here, since it is most relevant to security and peace.

Energy from the Sun. In a sustainable society, all human activities and industrial processes must be fueled by solar energy like the processes in nature's ecosystems. Hence, the shift to a sustainable society centrally includes a shift from fossil fuels to solar power.

Indeed, solar energy is the energy sector that has seen the fastest growth over the past decade. The use of photovoltaic cells increased by about 17 percent a year in the 1990s, and the recent invention of solar roofing tiles in Japan promises to lead to a further boost of photovoltaic electricity. These "solar shingles" are capable of turning rooftops into small power plants, which is likely to revolutionize electricity generation.

Wind power has grown even more spectacularly. It increased by about 24 percent a year during the 1990s, and in 2001 wind generating capacity increased by an astonishing 31 percent. Since 1995, wind power has increased nearly fivefold, while coal declined by 8 percent. Wind power offers long-term price stability and energy independence. There is no OPEC for wind, because wind is widely dispersed.

The total generating capacity from wind is now 23,000 megawatts worldwide, enough to meet the residential electricity needs of some 23 million people (1 megawatt per 1,000 people). Over the next decade, Europe alone plans to add about three times that amount. Even with this dramatic growth, the development of wind power is only at the beginning.

Hydrogen Fuel Cells. Any realistic solar energy program will have to come up with enough liquid fuel to operate our airplanes, buses, cars, and trucks. Until recently, this has been the Achilles' heel of all renewable-energy scenarios. During the last few years, however, this problem found a spectacular solution with the development of efficient hydrogen fuel cells that promise to inaugurate a new era in energy production—the "hydrogen economy."

A fuel cell is an electrochemical device that combines hydrogen with oxygen to produce electricity and water—and nothing else! This makes hydrogen the ultimate clean fuel. Several companies around the world are now racing to be the first to commercially produce residential fuel cell systems. In the meantime, Iceland has launched a multi-million-dollar venture to create the world's first hydrogen economy. To do so, Iceland will use its vast geothermal and hydroelectric resources to produce hydrogen from seawater, to be used first in buses and then in passenger cars and fishing vessels.

Hypercars. Closely connected with the shift to renewable energy sources is the redesign of automobiles, which may be the ecodesign branch with the most far-reaching industrial consequences. It involves design ideas so radical that they will not only change today's automobile industry beyond recognition but may have equally sweeping effects on the associated oil, steel, and electricity industries.

Amory Lovins and his colleagues at the Rocky Mountain Institute have synthesized these ideas into a conceptual design they call the "hypercar," which combines three key elements:

1. Ultralight, weighing two to three times less than steel cars, with the standard metal auto body replaced by a body made of strong carbon fibers embedded in special moldable plastics—which cuts the car's weight in half!

2. High aerodynamic efficiency.

3. Propulsion by a "hybrid-electric" drive, which combines an electric motor with fuel that produces the electricity for the motor on board.

When these three elements are integrated into a single design, they save at least 70 percent of the fuel used by standard cars, while also making the car safer and more comfortable.

A massive investment in hypercars could easily make us completely independent of foreign oil. In fact, if we increased the fuel efficiency of our light vehicles by a mere 2.7 mpg, we would not need to import any Persian Gulf oil.

The Transition to the Hydrogen Economy

We are at the beginning of a historic transition from the petroleum age to the hydrogen age. Oil is currently cheap in the United States if you look only at the price we pay at the pump. But the military costs to protect each barrel of oil are actually higher than the cost of the oil—and when you factor in the environmental costs, the real price of oil becomes prohibitively high.

As the transition to the hydrogen economy progresses, its energy efficiency will become so superior to oil that even cheap oil will be uncompetitive and thus no longer worth extracting. As the ecodesigners like to point out, the Stone Age did not end because people ran out of stones. Similarly, the Petroleum Age will not end because we will run out of petroleum. It will end because we have developed superior technologies.

The choice is clear. If we continue to favor an economic system dependent on fossil fuels, centralized technologies, and vulnerable supply lines, we need to protect it by a huge worldwide police force at considerable expense and risks to civil liberties. If, on the other hand, we shift to a decentralized world economy, based on renewable energy sources, sustainable agriculture, and regional food systems, we can create communities that no terrorist can threaten and that threaten no other nation. We have the necessary technologies to do so; what we need is the political will and leadership.

1. For a longer version of this essay, see Fritjof Capra, "Trying to Understand: A Systemic Analysis of International Terrorism," October 5, 2001, www.fritjofcapra.net/articles100501.html.

2. See Stephen Zunes, "International Terrorism," September 2001, www.fpif.org/reports/international_terrorism.

3. See Michael Klare, "Asking Why," September 2001, www.fpif.org.

4. See Fritjof Capra, *The Hidden Connections* (New York: Doubleday, 2002), 233ff.

. . .

WILENSKA

Czeslaw Milosz (translated by Madeleine G. Levine)

FROM: *Beginning with My Streets: Essays and Recollections*

A street with a strange name, not homogeneous, changing form every dozen or so steps, ecumenical to boot, Catholic-Jewish. At its beginning (or end) at the Green Bridge, it was wide, lacking a distinctive consistency, for there were no more than a couple of apartment houses at the outlets of the various side streets; it constricted into a narrow throat beyond the intersection with St. George (or Mickiewicz) Boulevard. When I was a child, the foundations of an unfinished building sat there for a long time, until at last a huge edifice was erected, a department store owned by the Jablkowski brothers, the first more or less "universal" store in Wilno, several stories high.

Not far from the Jablkowskis', across from the Helios movie theater, was an amazing haberdashery, the likes of which I never saw anywhere else in the city. Its owners were not Jews but Poles from somewhere far away in Galicia, distinguished from ordinary people by their speech and their exaggerated politeness. The family: two women and a man, a family triangle, it seems. The man smelled of eau de cologne, his slightly curled hair was parted and combed smooth, his hands were white and puffy. They said, "I kiss your hand." And the shop did not remind one at all of what was normally meant by a "shop"; the gleaming parquet floor was polished so that there wasn't a speck of dust on it; the goods were in glass cases.

Next door to this shop was a small bookstore, where every year on the first of September I experienced strong emotions, jostling against the other pupils and buying my new schoolbooks. Without a doubt, one of the most powerful experiences is to only look and touch for a moment, without knowing what is hidden under the colorful dust jackets.

Across the street, as I said before, was the Helios movie theater, remembered along with various films seen there, among them Pudovkin's *Storm over Asia*, which made a powerful impression on me. But this theater also has remained in my memory as a symbol that evokes a vague feeling of disgust and shame that has been pushed away to a level deeper than consciousness. Among Witold's many unsucciessful careers (before he died of tuberculosis at age thirty-six)—his service in the Borderland Defense Corps, for example, his participation in a Jewish fur-trading cooperative, etc.—there was also an attempt at founding a cabaret review. The premiere took place in the hall of the Helios, and I, a fourteen-year-old boy at the time, was unable to defend myself with rational judgment against the bawdy vulgarity of this show; hence the shame—because of Witold, who, like it or not, belonged to the family, and also because of my parents, who even laughed—remained undiminished, spreading like a greasy stain.

On the same side of the street, right behind the movie theater, Rutski's bookstore was to serve as a kind of counterweight much later on. The son of the dignified, dour Mr. Rutski was my colleague at the university and was married to Sitka Danecka; my relations with Sitka, before then, testify optimistically to the diversity of human relationships and the freedom from Form that is possible every now and then. We used to go on kayaking trips together, and we felt so comfortable with each other that we forgot about the difference in our sex. We were not, however, just "colleagues"; we were linked by a much warmer mutual heartfelt caring. Nonetheless, no Form compelled us into erotic intimacies; friendship was more precious.

Beyond Halpern's shop (I think that was his name), where there was dust, semi-darkness, a wealth of dyes, pencils, paper in many colors, notebooks, Wilenska Street, now even narrower, turned into a street of Christian harness makers, cobblers, tailors; there was even a Turkish bakery. From it, or perhaps from another, came my *gymnasium* colleague Czebi-Ogły, who was a Muslim. Next, the façades of the buildings became subdivided into a multitude of little Jewish shops, and after a momentary rise in dignity across from the little square near the Church of St. Catherine (there was a beautiful old store there that carried hunting guns), Wilenska was dominated by impoverished trade all the way to the intersection of Trocka, Dominican, and German Streets.

From a courtyard on Wilenska, in its "artisan" section, one entered a lending library to which Grandmother Milosz had a subscription paid for out of her modest pension. I often turned up there, either delegated by her or to borrow books for myself, when I was twelve, thirteen. Mostly Zeromski, Rodziewiczowna, Szpyrkowna, that is to say, bad literature, and it seems to me that a tolerable intelligence in someone who received such training should not be underrated, with a few points added for the obstacles that he must have had to overcome. In all languages, *belles lettres* are predominantly kitsch and melodrama; however, the accidents of Polish history decreed that fiction had an exceptionally powerful effect on people's minds, as a language and as a sensibility, so I suspect there is in the so-called Polish soul an exceptionally rich underpinning of kitsch. As for me—let's be frank: in the books that I borrowed from the library I was enchanted by such scenes as the death of the beautiful Helen in *Ashes,* who threw herself into a ravine, and perhaps even more so by the ending of a certain story that was translated from the French about the Chouans, or the counter-revolutionaries in the Vendée. The hero's head is sliced off on the guillotine, but that does not put an end to his highly emotional adventures. To this day I can remember the last sentence: "But his head, still rolling, whispered, 'Amelie!'"

. . .

ON FORGIVENESS
Jack Kornfield
FROM: *The Art of Forgiveness, Lovingkindness, and Peace*

Forgiveness is a letting go of past suffering and betrayal, a release of the burden of pain and hate that we carry.

Forgiveness honors the heart's greatest dignity. Whenever we are lost, it brings us back to the ground of love.

With forgiveness we become unwilling to attack or wish harm to another.

Whenever we forgive, in small ways at home, or in great ways between nations, we free ourselves from the past.

It is hard to imagine a world without forgiveness.

Without forgiveness life would be unbearable.

Without forgiveness our lives are chained, forced to carry the sufferings of the past and repeat them with no release.

Consider the dialogue between two former prisoners of war:
"Have you forgiven your captors yet?"
"No, never!"
"Well, then, they still have you in prison, don't they?"
We begin the work of forgiveness primarily for ourselves.

We may still be suffering terribly from the past while those who betrayed us are on vacation.

It is painful to hate. Without forgiveness we continue to perpetuate the illusion that hate can heal our pain and the pain of others.

In forgiveness we let go and find relief in our heart.

Even those in the worst situations, the conflicts and tragedies of Bosnia, Cambodia, Rwanda, Northern Ireland, or South Africa, have had to find a path to reconciliation. This is true in America as well. It is the only way to heal.

Sometimes this means finding the courage to forgive the unforgivable, to consciously release the heart from the clutches of another's terrible acts.

We must discover a way to move on from the past, no matter what traumas it held.

The past is over:
Forgiveness means giving up all hope of a better past.

Forgiveness Does Not Happen Quickly.

For great injustice, coming to forgiveness may include a long process of grief, outrage, sadness, loss, and pain.

True forgiveness does not paper over what has happened in a superficial way. It is not a misguided effort to suppress or ignore our pain. It cannot be hurried. It is a deep process repeated over and over in our heart which honors the grief and betrayal, and in its own time ripens into the freedom to truly forgive.

Forgiveness Does Not Forget, nor Does It Condone the Past.

Forgiveness sees wisely. It willingly acknowledges what is unjust, harmful, and wrong. It bravely recognizes the sufferings of the past, and understands the conditions that brought them about. There is a strength to forgiveness. When we forgive we can also say, "Never again will I allow these things to happen." We may resolve to never again permit such harm to come to ourselves or another.

Finding a way to extend forgiveness to ourselves is one of our most essential tasks.

Just as others have been caught in suffering, so have we.

If we look honestly at our life, we can see the sorrows and pain that have led to our own wrongdoing. In this we can finally extend forgiveness to ourselves; we can hold the pain we have caused in compassion. Without such mercy, we will live our own life in exile.

The pains of our past cannot be released—until we touch them with healing and forgiveness.

> The truth about our childhood is stored up in our body, and although we can repress it, we can never alter it. Our intellect can be deceived, our feelings manipulated, our conceptions confused, and our body tricked with medication. But someday our body will present its bill, for it is as incorruptible as a child who, still whole in spirit, will accept no compromise or excuses, and it will not stop tormenting us until we stop evading the truth. (Alice Miller)

We have all been blinded, we have all suffered.

Pema Chödrön tells this story:

> A young woman wrote about finding herself in a small town in the Middle East surrounded by people jeering, yelling, and threatening to throw stones at her and her friends because they were Americans.
>
> Of course she was terrified, and what happened to her is important. Suddenly she identified with every person throughout history who had ever been scorned and hated. She understood what it was like to be despised for any reason: ethnic group, racial background, sexual preference, gender. Something cracked wide open and she stood in the shoes of millions of oppressed people and saw with a new perspective. She even understood her shared humanity with those who hated her. This sense of deep connection, of belonging to the same family, is the awakening of the great heart of compassion.

In the Babemba tribe of South Africa, when a person acts irresponsibly or unjustly, he is placed in the center of the village, alone and unfettered. All work ceases, and every man, woman, and child in the village gathers in a large circle around the accused individual. Then each person in the tribe speaks to the accused, one at a time, each recalling the good things the person in the center of the circle has done in his lifetime. Every incident, every experience that can be recalled with any detail and accuracy, is recounted. All his positive attributes, good deeds, strengths, and kindnesses are recited carefully and at length. This tribal ceremony often lasts for several days. At the end, the tribal circle is broken, a joyous celebration takes place, and the person is symbolically and literally welcomed back into the tribe.

The Sufi master Pir Vilayat Khan teaches us:

> Overcome any bitterness that may come because you were not up to the magnitude of the pain entrusted to you.
>
> Like the mother of the world who carries the pain of the world in her heart, you are sharing in a certain measure of that cosmic pain, and are called upon to meet it in joy instead of self-pity.

. . .

GOOD FRIDAY WORLD
Anne Lamott
FROM: *Plan B: Further Thoughts on Faith*

There is the most ancient of sorrows in the world again, dead civilians and young soldiers. None of us knows quite what to make of things, or what to do. Since the war started last week, the days feel like midnight on the Serengeti, dangers everywhere, some you can see, but most hidden. The praying people I know pray for the lives of innocent people and young Americans to be spared, for peace and sanity to be restored on the global field. Everything feels crazy. . . .

What are you supposed to do, when what is happening can't be, and the old rules no longer apply . . . ?

A friend called today and said that since the war has begun, she finds herself inside a black hole half the time. "What if we gave fifty percent of our discretionary budget to the world's poor," she said, "and then counted on the moral power of that action to protect us?" Good Lord: What can you say in the face of such innocence?

"You didn't stop taking those meds, did you?" I asked.

This made her laugh. "I just don't feel like I can get through the day. Even though I know I will."

Like her, I am depressed and furious. I often feel like someone from the Book of Lamentations. The best thing I've heard lately is the Christian writer Barbara Johnson's saying that we're Easter people, living in Good Friday world.

I don't have the right personality for Good Friday, for the crucifixion: I'd like to skip ahead to the resurrection. In fact, I'd like to skip ahead to the resurrection vision of one of the kids from our Sunday school, who drew a picture of the Easter Bunny outside the tomb: everlasting life, and a basket full of chocolates. *Now* you're talking.

In Jesus' real life, the resurrection came two days later, but in our real lives, it can be weeks, years, and you never know for sure that it will come. I don't have the right personality for the human condition, either. But I believe in the resurrection, in Jesus', and in ours. The trees, so stark and gray last month, suddenly went up as if in flame, but instead in blossoms and leaves—poof! Like someone opening an umbrella. It's often hard to find similar dramatic evidence of rebirth and hope in our daily lives.

What is there to do in such difficult, violent times? I try to follow my own advice to take short assignments, and do shitty first drafts of my work, and most of all, to take things day by day. Today I am going to pray that our soldiers come home soon. I am going to pray for the children of American and Iraqi soldiers, for the innocent Iraqi people, for the POWs, for the humanitarian aid, and for our leaders. I am going to pray for the children and youth in Oakland and East Palo Alto and Palestine and Israel. I am going to pray to forgive one person today—to give up a soupçon of hostility. Forgiveness is not my strong suit.

You can always begin by lighting a candle. Since the United States went to war in Iraq, I've been thinking about A. J. Muste, who during the Vietnam War stood in front of the White House night after night with a candle. One rainy night, a reporter asked him, "Mr. Muste, do you really think you are going to change the policies of this country by standing out here alone at night with a candle?"

"Oh," Muste replied, "I don't do it to change the country, I do it so the country won't change me."

I am going to send checks to people and organizations I trust, including Oakland's progressive representative Barbara Lee, who speaks for me. I will ask her to send the check on to someone who is nurturing children in the inner city, because this nation's black and Hispanic kids will be the hardest hit by the wartime deficit spending. I am going to buy myself a pair of beautiful new socks, and my son some new felt-tip pens.

I am going to walk to the library, because my church is too far away to go to on foot. And it's so beautiful out. The hills of my own town are lush and green and dotted with wildflowers. The poppies have bloomed, and as summer approaches, five o'clock is no longer the end of the world.

I am going to check out a collection of *Goon Show* scripts, and a volume of Mary Oliver poems. Libraries make me think kindly of my mother. I am not sure if this will lead me directly to the soupçon of forgiveness, but you never know. You can take the action, and the insight follows. It was my mother who taught me how to wander through the racks of the Belvedere–Tiburon library, and wander through a book, letting it take me where it would. She and my father took me to the library every week when I was little. One of her best friends was the librarian. They both taught me that if you insist on having a destination when you come into the library, you're shortchanging yourself. They read to live, the way they also went to the beach, or ate delicious food. Reading was like breathing fresh ocean air, or eating tomatoes from old man Grbac's garden. My parents, and the librarians along the way, taught me about the space between words; about the margins, where so many juicy moments of life and spirit and friendship could be found. In a library, you can find small miracles and truth, and you might find something that will make you laugh so hard that you will get shushed, in the friendliest way. I have found sanctuary in libraries my whole life, and there is sanctuary there now, from the war, from the storms of our families and our own minds. Libraries are like mountains or meadows or creeks: sacred space. So this afternoon, I'll walk to the library. . . .

I am going to try to pay attention to the spring, and look up at the hectic trees. Amid the smashing and crashing and terrible silences, the trees are in blossom, and it's soft and warm and bright. I am going to close my eyes and listen. During the children's sermon last Sunday, the pastor asked the kids to close their eyes for a moment—to give themselves a time-out—and then he asked them what they had heard. They heard birds, and radios, dogs barking, cars, and one boy said, "I hear the water at the edge of things." I am going to listen for the water at the edge of things today.

I keep remembering the inhabitants of those islands in the South Pacific where the United States air force set up a base of operations during World War II. The islanders loved the air force's presence, all that loud, blinding illumination from above, a path of klieg lights descending on their land. They believed it was divine, because there was no other way to understand all that energy, and after the air force left, they created a fake runway with candles and torches and pyres, and awaited its return. I am going to pray for the opposite of loud crashing lights, however. I am going to notice the lights of the earth, the sun and the moon and the stars, the lights of our candles as we march, the lights with which spring teases us, the light that is already present. If the present is really all we have, then the present lasts forever. And that, today, will be the benediction.

. . .

Contemporary psychological research shows that some individuals, when they are in a highly agitated state of mind, are oblivious to how they are feeling. Their hearts may be racing, their blood pressure climbing, and they may be sweating profusely, yet they are not aware of being angry or afraid or anxious. About one person in six exhibits this pattern. Being so unaware of their own pain, is it possible that they could understand or empathize with what someone else may be feeling? Being unable to empathize, how can they live complete lives?

When we practice mindfulness, one of the qualities that we are developing is empathy. As we open to the full range of experiences within ourselves, we become aware of what we perceive in each moment, no longer denying some feelings while clinging to others. By coming to know our own pain, we build a bridge to the pain of others, which enables us to step out of our self-absorption and offer help. And when we actually understand how it feels to suffer—in ourselves and in others—we are compelled to live in a way that creates as little harm as possible.

With empathy acting as a bridge to those around us, a true morality arises within. Knowing that someone will suffer if we perform a harmful action or say a hurtful word, we find we do these things less and less. It is a very simple, natural and heart-full response. Rather than seeing morality as a set of rules, we find a morality that is an uncontrived reluctance to cause suffering.

(Sharon Salzberg, from *A Heart as Wide as the World*)

. . .

A TASK
Czeslaw Milosz

In fear and trembling, I think I would fulfill my life
Only if I brought myself to make a public confession
Revealing a sham, my own and of my epoch:
We were permitted to shriek in the tongues of dwarfs and demons
But pure and generous words were forbidden
Under so stiff a penalty that whoever dared to pronounce one
Considered himself as a lost man.

. . .

THE TABLE OF PEACE
Terry Tempest Williams
FROM: *The Open Space of Democracy*

And I know that what is popularly called politics is only a tiny part
of what causes history to move.
—W. H. Auden

In the fall of 2002, I was living in Italy. There was a growing fear that
America was going to wage war in Iraq. . . .

The European Social Forum had just held its meetings in Florence,
where issues ranging from health and the environment to international
trade to the possibility of a war in Iraq were discussed. It ended with
this gesture of movement, much of it along the banks of the Arno River,
creating a river of another sort, a river of humans engaged in a diverse
dialogue of peace.

Train after train stopped and emptied itself of the working middle
class. Men, women, and children from Italian towns and villages gathered
to participate with citizens from all over Europe. Massimo Sottani, a former mayor of Regello whom I had met in the village where I was staying,
had invited me to join him with his family and friends. "It is not only our
right and obligation to participate in civic life, it is in our best interest," he
said as we stood outside the station waiting for more of his friends. . . .

At one point, an elderly Florentine man who held memories of Mus-
solini stepped out on his balcony above the wave of people and draped
a white bedsheet over the railing in support of peace. As participants
waved to the old man, the crowd spontaneously began singing "*Ciao,
Bella, Ciao,*" the song of the partigianos, the Italian resistance against
the fascists in World War II. Neighbor after neighbor repeated the gesture, draping white sheets and pillow cases over their balconies until the
apartment walls that lined the streets appeared as great sails billowing in
the breeze. . . .

Looking over my shoulder from the rise on the bridge, all I could see
was an endless river of people walking, many hand in hand, all side by
side, peacefully, united in place with a will for social change. Michelan-
gelo was among them, as art students from Florence raised replicas of
his *Prigioni* above their heads, the unfinished sculptures of prisoners
trying to break free from the confines of stone. Machiavelli was among
them, as philosophy students from Rome carried his words: "There is
nothing more difficult to take in hand, more perilous to conduct, or

more uncertain in its success than to take the lead in the introduction of a new order of things." Leonardo da Vinci was among them, his words carrying a particularly contemporary sting: "And by reason of their boundless pride . . . there shall be nothing remaining on the earth or under the earth or in the waters that shall not be pursued and molested or destroyed."

The hundreds of thousands of individuals who walked together in the name of social change could be seen as the dignified, radical center walking boldly toward the future. As an American in Florence, I wondered, how do we walk with the rest of the world when our foreign policies seem to run counter to the rising global awareness of a world hungry for honest diplomacy?

A week before the manifestation in Florence, I attended a dinner at Sandro Bennini's home where I had the good fortune of meeting Massimo Sottani.

We knocked on the large wooden door and waited. Sandro Bennini, the baker in the village of Donnini, had invited us to dinner. Four of us, staying at a friend's home just down the road, accepted.

Sandro opened the door and with a wide, sweeping gesture of his hand welcomed us inside. He was dressed in tails, a full black tuxedo with a gardenia over his heart.

In an instant, we could see that all furniture had been moved out of the living room and replaced with an enormous square table lavishly set for forty people, ten on each side. Two three-tier bronze candelabra were lit casting shadows on a centerpiece of stuffed roosters, grapes, olives, figs, pomegranates, and mushrooms, all familiar to a Tuscan household.

At each place setting of bone china, silver, and crystal goblets, there was a parchment scroll with burned edges tied neatly with a white satin ribbon. Once opened, it proclaimed the six-course menu to come: Deep-fried seasonal vegetables; cream of pumpkin soup; tiny squash-filled crepes; *lesso ritatto* (Tuscan specialty); roast of wild boar with herbs; gelato; and biscotti with espresso.

The house filled with guests, stunned by the elaborate celebration. Like us, most had anticipated a casual gathering. None of us were appropriately dressed. Our postures corrected what our clothes could not.

"Welcome, my friends," Sandro said. "I invite you to sit down at this Table of Peace. With the heart, anything is possible." He smiled and then said, "Tonight I share with you my gifts of bread and song." And then with both hands extended the width of the table, he said with great gusto, "*Godere*. Enjoy."

Chianti was poured, toasts were made with glasses raised high. A pianist emerged as waiters appeared with the first bowls of soup. Suddenly, Sandro the Baker became Sandro the Tenor and so began this evening in Tuscany where we were invited to a feast of Italian arias that lasted well into the next day.

In that candlelit night of magic, Sandro Bennini held back nothing. He sang for hours, offering us his passion for food and music, his gifts of drama and decorum, and shared them relentlessly with his eyes closed and his hands over his heart.

The village priest sang songs of lost Florentine virgins alongside Sandro. An Italian named Marco stood on top of his chair and blew kisses to all saying this was a night to remember that all bad love affairs eventually turn good through the memory of time. And wine. A German tourist who had visited Sandro's bakery earlier that day fell asleep and was snoring in time with the music, rising and falling with each bel canto. The former mayor of Regello, Massimo Sottani, was sitting next to me. He whispered the story of a gold-leaf triptych painted by Masaccio that has hung in his village's church since 1421. He spoke about how the eyes of the painting had presided over births and deaths and daily masses, that the Uffizi Gallery begged for it to be housed in Florence but the people of Cascia said no. The triptych belonged to the village.

What I learned in Italy is that beauty is not optional. It resides at the core of each conversation, around each dinner table. Beauty nourishes our soul alongside food. It allows us to remember not only what is possible, what we are capable of creating as human beings, but what is necessary. Each of us bears gifts and we can share them within the embrace of our own communities, even around the Table of Peace.

We, Americans of puritanical origins, have much to learn. Why do we hold back both our gifts and our passions in the name of what is proper? Modesty in its extreme is nothing more than clothed repression, in the end, covering what we all know is there—our longing to share our inward and outward beauty. How can there be shame in this desire to expose the best of who we are? If we choose to hide or minimize our gifts, how can we ever embrace hope?

In times of war, it seems to me the only appropriate action is to bare our hearts fearlessly with love and generosity, sharing the gifts that we have been given, whatever they may be, freely with those around us.

Sandro Bennini, through his gifts of bread and song, baked and sung world peace heroically around his own dinner table. It didn't matter if the meal was served on time, though it was. It didn't matter if he sometimes sang off key, which he did. What mattered was the beauty of his intention, to bring people together in his village who had never met before and in so doing, celebrate the exuberant, joyous, tender unpredictability of humanity. In the sanctuary of his home, anything was possible, because all hearts were open.

. . .

THE COURAGE TO WAIT
Pema Chödrön

If the justified aggression of men and women just like us is the cause of war, then how do we ordinary folks go about finding peace? When we feel aggression in any of its forms—resentment, discrimination, jealousy, complaining, and so forth—it's hard to know what to do. We can apply all the good advice we've heard and given people. But often all that doesn't seem to help us.

Traditionally, it's taught that patience is the antidote to aggression. When I heard this the first time, it immediately caught my interest. I thought, if patience is really the antidote to aggression, maybe I'll just give it a wholehearted try. In the process I learned about what patience is and about what it isn't. I would like to share with you what I've understood and to encourage you to find out for yourself how patience can dissolve the mean-heartedness that results in us harming one another.

Most importantly, I learned about patience and the cessation of suffering—I learned how patience is a way to de-escalate aggression and its accompanying pain. This is to say that when we're feeling aggression—and I think this would go for any strong emotion—there's a seductive quality that pulls us in the direction of wanting to get some resolution. We feel restless, agitated, ill at ease. It hurts so much to feel the aggression that we want it to be resolved. Right then we could change the way we look at this discomfort and practice patience. But what do we usually do? We do exactly what is going to escalate the aggression and the suffering. We strike out, we hit back. Someone insults us and, initially, there is some softness there—if you can practice patience, you can catch it—but usually you don't even realize there was any softness. You find yourself in the middle of a hot, noisy, pulsating, wanting-to-get-even state of mind. It has a very unforgiving quality to it. With your words and actions, in order to escape the pain of aggression, you create more aggression and pain.

I recently read a letter from a U.S. soldier in Iraq. He wrote about the so-called enemy fighters, the unknown people who are so filled with pain and hate that they sit in the dark waiting to kill foreign soldiers like him. When they succeed, and his friends' bodies are blown into unrecognizable pieces, he just wants revenge. He said that each day he and his fellow U.S. soldiers were also becoming men who wait in the darkness hoping to kill another human being. As he put it, "We think that by striking back we'll release our anger and feel better, but it isn't working. Our pain gets stronger day by day." Amid the chaos and horror of war, this soldier has discovered a profound truth: if we want suffering to lessen, the first step is learning that keeping the cycle of aggression going doesn't help. It doesn't bring the relief we seek, and it doesn't bring happiness to anyone else either. We may not be able to change the outer circumstances, but we can always shift our perspective and dissolve the hatred in our minds.

So when you're like a keg of dynamite just about to go off, patience means just slowing down at that point—just pausing—instead of immediately acting on your usual, habitual response. You refrain from acting, you stop talking to yourself, and then you connect with the soft spot. But at the same time you are completely and totally honest with yourself about what you are feeling. You're not suppressing anything; patience has nothing to do with suppression. In fact, it has everything to do with a gentle, honest relationship with yourself. If you wait and don't fuel the rage with your thoughts, you can be very honest about the fact that you long for revenge; nevertheless you keep interrupting the tortuous story line and stay with the underlying vulnerability. That frustration, that uneasiness and vulnerability, is nothing solid. And yet it is so painful to experience. Still, just wait and be patient with your anguish and with the discomfort of it. This means relaxing with that restless, hot energy— knowing that it's the only way to find peace for ourselves or the world.

Patience has a quality of honesty, and it also has the quality of holding our seat. We don't automatically react, even though inside we *are* reacting. We let all the words go and are just there with the rawness of our experience.

Fearlessness is another ingredient of patience. If you want to practice patience that leads to the cessation of suffering, to the de-escalation of aggression, it means cultivating a fearlessness that is both compassionate and brave. Because at this point you're getting to know anger and how it easily breeds violent words and actions, and this can be decidedly unnerving. You can see where your anger will lead before you do anything. You're not repressing it, you're just sitting there with the pulsating energy—going cold turkey with the aggression—and you get to know the naked energy of anger and the pain it can cause if you react. You've followed the tug so many times, you already know. It feels like an undertow, that desire to say something mean, to seek revenge or slander, that desire to complain, to just somehow spill out that aggression. But you slowly realize that those actions don't get rid of aggression, they increase it. Instead you're patient—patient with yourself—and this requires the gentleness and courage of fearlessness.

Developing patience and fearlessness means learning to sit still with the edginess of the discomforting energy. It's like sitting on a wild horse, or maybe even more like a wild tiger that could eat you up. There is a limerick effect: "There was a young lady of Niger who smiled as she rode on a tiger. They came back from the ride with the lady inside, and the smile on the face of the tiger." Sitting with our uneasiness feels like riding on that tiger.

When we stick with this process we learn something very interesting: there is no resolution for these uncomfortable feelings. This resolution that human beings seek comes from a tremendous misunderstanding: we think that everything can become predictable and secure. There is a basic ignorance about the truth of impermanence, the truth of the fleeting groundless nature of all things. When we feel powerful energy, we tend to be extremely uncomfortable until things are fixed in some kind of secure and comforting way, either on the side of "yes" or the side of "no," the side of "right" or the side of "wrong." We long for something that we can hold on to.

But the practice of patience gives us nothing to hold on to. Actually, the Buddhist teachings, in general, give us nothing to hold on to. In working with the patience and fearlessness, we learn to be patient with the fact that not only us but everyone who is born and dies, all of us as a species, are naturally going to want some kind of resolution to this edgy, moody energy. And there isn't any. The only resolution is temporary and ultimately just causes more suffering. We discover that joy and happiness, a sense of inner peace, a sense of harmony and of being at home with yourself and your world come from sitting still with the moodiness of the energy until it rises, dwells, and passes away. It never resolves itself into something solid. We stay in the middle. The path of touching in on the inherent softness of the genuine heart is sitting still, being patient with that kind of unformed energy. And we don't have to criticize ourselves when we fail, even for a moment, because we're just completely typical human beings; the only thing that's unique about us is that we're brave enough to go into these things more deeply and explore beneath our surface reaction of trying to get solid ground under our feet.

Patience is an enormously supportive and even magical practice. It's a way of completely shifting the fundamental human habit of trying to resolve things by either going to the right or to the left, labeling things "good" or labeling them "bad." It's the way to develop fearlessness, the way to contact the seeds of war and the seeds of lasting peace—and to decide which ones we want to nurture.

Patience and curiosity also go together. You wonder, "Who am I?" Who am I at the level of my neurotic patterns? Who am I beyond birth and death? If you wish to look into the nature of your own being, you need to be inquisitive. The path is a journey of self-reflection, beginning to look more closely at what's going on in our mind and heart. The meditation practices give us suggestions on how to look, and patience is an essential component for this looking. Aggression, on the other hand, prevents us from seeing clearly; it puts a tight lid on our curiosity. Aggression is an energy that is determined to resolve the situation into some kind of solid, fixed, very hard pattern where somebody wins and somebody loses. There is no room for open-ended curiosity or wonder.

If you have already embarked on this journey of self-reflection, you may be at a place that everyone, sooner or later, experiences on the spiritual path. After a while it seems like almost every moment of your life you're there, where you realize you have a choice. You have a choice whether to open or close, whether to hold on or to let go, whether to hold your seat or strike out. That choice is presented to you again and again and again.

Perhaps each one of us has made the discovery that behind resistance—definitely behind aggression and jealousy—behind any kind of tension, there is always a soft spot that we're trying to protect. Someone's actions hurt our feelings and before we even notice what we're doing, we armor ourselves in a very old and familiar way. So we can either let go of our solid story line and connect with that soft spot or we can continue to stubbornly hold on, which means that the suffering will continue.

· · ·

BUDDHIST MEDITATION ON COMPASSION

May I be happy
May I be peaceful
May I be free from suffering
May I be at ease
May I be joyful
May I be filled with loving kindness

May those I love be happy
May those I love be peaceful
May those I love be free from suffering
May those I love be at ease
May those I love be joyful
May those I love be filled with loving kindnes

May my enemies be happy
May my enemies be peaceful
May my enemies be free from suffering
May my enemies be at ease
May my enemies be joyful
May my enemies be filled with loving kindness

May all beings be happy
May all beings be peaceful
May all beings be free from suffering
May all beings be at ease
May all beings be joyful
May all beings be filled with loving kindness

. . .

IN MY SOUL
Rabia of Basra (translated by Daniel Ladinsky)

In
my soul
there is a temple, a shrine, a mosque, a church
where I kneel.

Prayer should bring us to an altar where no walls or names exist.

Is there not a region of love where the sovereignty is
illumined nothing,

where ecstasy gets poured into itself
and becomes
lost,

where the wing is fully alive
but has no mind or
body?

In
my soul,
there is a temple, a shrine, a mosque,
a church

that dissolve, that
dissolve in
God.

CHAPTER 8

Paths to Transformation

I felt my legs were praying.

—Abraham Heschel, on marching at Selma with Martin Luther King

By presenting new and deeper ways to frame the problem of violence against civilians that the world faces today, we have provided several starting points for significant change. For this reason, we have chosen to end this anthology with a selection of essays that present a variety of practical paths to transformation. This selection is neither exhaustive nor even representative of the rich variety of paths toward peace but instead provides some examples for what can be done.

Realizing that despair and cynicism prevent so many from working for social and political change, we have chosen to begin this chapter with an essay on hope. Since one of the justifications for tolerating poverty, injustice and violence is the contention that unjust or terrible as they may be, certain conditions are simply inevitable, it is crucial to realize that change is possible, as history has shown us many times, when in the eighteenth century, for instance, the seemingly invincible power of monarchies gave way to democracy or in the next century when the slave trade in Britain and then slavery in America were abolished.

Because this volume addresses the psychological and spiritual issues that underlie and cause violence as well as meet and heal its consequences, we have emphasized ways to change consciousness in this chapter, too. To change hearts and minds is crucial to lay the groundwork for even the most practical political changes. To cite one example, though international law forbids targeting or killing civilians, the practice continues today because these laws have not been enforced. In order for that to happen, civilians all over the world must come to recognize that from birth we have the right to be free from violent attack, and that any movement to protect civilians must be founded on the recognition that this is a universal right, not one that belongs to the citizens of one country alone.

We have also included traditional nonviolent protest in this chapter. Protest in fact shifts consciousness in many profound ways. Marches, sits-ins, and picket lines help to create communities that support change through friendship and communication. Those who participate in any political action feel empowered and thus enabled to work on change in still other ways. Protest also exposes the public to perspectives underrepresented in the press, which can create a transformative chain reaction in consciousness. And, as Abraham Heschel said so eloquently, protest is also a form of prayer.

We have also included many direct methods of changing consciousness—approaches such as citizen diplomacy that facilitate understanding between those defined as enemies, ways of fostering psychological healing in communities that have suffered violence, and processes that can open the mind to new possibilities.

Many crucial ways to organize citizens—signing petitions, donating money, even speaking up, or lending support to those who are devoting their lives, and (as with Marla Rusikoff) at times even giving their lives—are not included here. But with the few examples we do include, we hope to incite the imagination and inspire creative participation in the great turning that will allow the end of terror and the beginning of a new and mutual concord.

Susan Griffin

. . .

HOPE IN THE DARK
Rebecca Solnit

On January 18, 1915, eighteen months into the first world war, the first terrible war in the modern sense—slaughter by the hundreds of thousands, poison gas, men living and dying in the open graves of trench warfare, tanks, barbed wire, machine guns, airplanes—Virginia Woolf wrote in her journal, "The future is dark, which is on the whole, the best thing the future can be, I think." Dark, she seems to say, as in inscrutable, not as in terrible. We often mistake the one for the other.

People imagine the end of the world is nigh because the future is un-imaginable. Who twenty years ago would have pictured a world without the USSR and with the Internet? We talk about "what we hope for" in terms of what we hope will come to pass, but we could think of it another way, as why we hope. We hope on principle, we hope tactically and strategically, we hope because the future is dark, we hope because it's a more powerful and more joyful way to live. Despair presumes it knows what will happen next. But who, two decades ago, would have imagined that the Canadian government would give a huge swathe of the north back to its indigenous people, or that the imprisoned Nelson Mandela would become president of a free South Africa?

Twenty-one years ago this June, a million people gathered in Central Park to demand a nuclear freeze. They didn't get it. . . . Many went home disappointed or burned out. But in less than a decade, major nuclear arms reductions were negotiated. . . . Since then, the issue has fallen off the map, and we have lost much of what was gained. The United States never ratified the Comprehensive Test Ban Treaty. . . .

It's always too soon to go home. And it's always too soon to calculate effect. I once read an anecdote by someone in Women Strike for Peace, the first great antinuclear movement in the United States in 1963, the one that did contribute to a major victory: the end of aboveground nuclear testing with its radioactive fallout that was showing up in mother's milk and baby teeth. She told of how foolish and futile she felt standing in the rain one morning protesting at the Kennedy White House. Years later she heard Dr. Benjamin Spock—one of the most high-profile activists on the issue then—say that the turning point for him was seeing a small group of women standing in the rain, protesting at the White House. If they were so passionately committed, he thought, he should give the issue more consideration himself.

Unending Change

A lot of activists expect that for every action there is an equal and op-posite and *punctual* reaction, and regard the lack of one as failure. After all, activism is often a reaction: Bush decides to invade Iraq, we create a global peace movement in which 10 to 30 million people march on seven continents on the same weekend. But history is shaped by the groundswells and common dreams that single acts and moments only represent. It's a landscape more complicated than commensurate cause and effect. Politics is a surface in which transformation comes about as much because of pervasive changes in the depths of the collective imagination as because of visible acts, though both are necessary. And though huge causes sometimes have little effect, tiny ones occasionally have huge consequences.

The world gets better. It also gets worse. The time it will take you to address this is exactly equal to your lifetime, and if you're lucky you don't know how long that is. The future is dark. Like night. There are probabilities and likelihoods, but there are no guarantees.

As Adam Hochschild points out, from the time the English Quakers first took on the issue of slavery, three quarters of a century passed before it was abolished in Europe and America. Few if any working on the issue at the beginning lived to see its conclusion, when what had once seemed impossible suddenly began to look, in retrospect, inevitable. And as the law of unintended consequences might lead you to expect, the abolition movement also sparked the first widespread women's rights movement, which took about the same amount of time to secure the right to vote for American women, that has achieved far more in the subsequent 83 years, and is by no means done. Activism is not a journey to the corner store; it is a plunge into the dark.

Writers understand that action is seldom direct. You write your books. You scatter your seeds. Rats might eat them, or they might just rot. In California, some seeds lie dormant for decades because they only germinate after fire. Sharon Salzberg, in her book *Faith*, recounts how she put together a book of teachings by the Buddhist monk U Pandita and consigned the project to the "minor-good-deed category." Long afterward, she found out that when Burmese democracy movement's leader, Aung San Suu Kyi, was kept isolated under house arrest by that country's dictators, the book and its instructions in meditation "became her main source of spiritual support during those intensely difficult years." Emily Dickinson, Walt Whitman, Walter Benjamin, and Arthur Rimbaud, like Henry David Thoreau, achieved their greatest impact long after their deaths, long after weeds had grown over the graves of the bestsellers of their times. Gandhi's Thoreau-influenced nonviolence was as important in the American South as it was in India, and what transpired with Martin Luther King's sophisticated version of it has influenced civil disobedience movements around the world.

At the port of Oakland, California, on April 7, several hundred peace activists came out at dawn to picket the gates of a company shipping arms to Iraq. The longshoreman's union had vowed not to cross our picket. The police arrived in riot gear and, unprovoked and unthreatened, began shooting wooden bullets and beanbags of shot at the activists. Three members of the media, nine longshoremen, and fifty activists were injured. I saw the bloody welts the size of half grapefruits on the backs of some of the young men—they had been shot in the back. Told that way, violence won. But the violence inspired the union dockworkers to form closer alliances with antiwar activists and underscored the connections between local and global issues.

Victories of the New Peace Movement

It was a setup for disappointment to expect that there would be an acknowledged cause and effect relationship between the antiwar actions and the Bush administration. On the other hand . . .

- We will likely never know, but it seems that the Bush administration decided against the "Shock and Awe" saturation bombing of Baghdad because we made it clear that the cost in world opinion and civil unrest would be too high. We millions may have saved a few thousand or a few hundred thousand lives.

- Many people who had never spoken out, never marched in the street, never joined groups, written to politicians, or donated to campaigns, did so. . . . New networks and communities and websites and listserves and jail solidarity groups and coalitions arose.

- In the name of the so-called war on terror . . . we [were] encouraged to fear our neighbors, each other, strangers, (particularly middle-eastern, Arab, and Moslem people), to spy on them, to lock ourselves up, to privatize ourselves. By living out our hope and resistance in public together with strangers of all kinds, we overcame this catechism of fear, we trusted each other; we forged a community that bridged all differences.

- We achieved a global movement without leaders. . . . What could be more democratic than millions of people who, via the grapevine, the Internet, and various groups from churches to unions to direct-action affinity groups, can organize themselves?

- We succeeded in doing what the anti-Vietnam War movement infamously failed to do: to refuse the dichotomies. We were able to oppose a war on Iraq without endorsing Saddam Hussein. We were able to oppose a war with compassion for the troops who fought it. . . . We were not *against* the U.S. and *for* Iraq; we were against the war. . . . We are not just an antiwar movement. We are a peace movement.

- Questions the peace and anti-globalization movements have raised are now mainstream. . . . Activists targeted Bechtel, Halliburton, Chevron, and Lockheed Martin, among others, as war profiteers. . . . The actions worked not by shutting the places down in any significant way but by making their operations a public question. . . . Representative Henry Waxman publicly questioned Halliburton's ties to terrorist states, and the media closely questioned the Bush administration's closed-door decision to award Halliburton, the company vice-president Cheney headed until he took office, a $7 billion contract to administer Iraqi oil.

The Angel of Alternate History

What is best [in American history has been] called forth by what is worst. The abolitionists and the Underground Railroad, the feminist movement and the civil rights movement, the environmental and human rights movements were all called into being by threats and atrocities. There's plenty of what's worst afoot nowadays. But we need a progressive activism that is not one of reaction but of initiation. . . . We need to extend the passion the war brought forth into preventing the next one, and toward addressing all the forms of violence besides bombs. We need a movement that doesn't just respond to the evils of the present but calls forth the possibilities of the future. We need a revolution of hope.

While serving on the board of Citizen Alert, a Nevada nonprofit environmental and antinuclear group, I once wrote a fundraising letter modeled after *It's a Wonderful Life*. Frank Capra's movie is a model for radical history, because what the angel Clarence shows the suicidal George Bailey is what the town would look like if he hadn't done his best for his neighbors. This angel of alternate history shows not what happened but what didn't, and that's what's hardest to weigh. Citizen Alert's victories were largely those of what *hadn't* happened to the air, the water, the land, and the people of Nevada. And the history of what the larger movements have achieved is largely one of careers undestroyed, ideas uncensored, violence and intimidation uncommitted, injustices unperpetrated, rivers unpoisoned and undammed, bombs undropped, radiation unleaked, poisons unsprayed, wildernesses unviolated, countryside undeveloped, resources unextracted, species unexterminated.

I was born during the summer the Berlin Wall went up, into a country in which there weren't even words, let alone redress, for many of the practices that kept women and people of color from free and equal citizenship, in which homosexuality was diagnosed as a disease and treated as a crime, in which the ecosystem was hardly even a concept, in which extinction and pollution were issues only a tiny minority heeded, in which "better living through chemistry" didn't yet sound like black humor, in which the U.S. and USSR were on hair-trigger alert for a nuclear Armageddon. . . . It was a world with more rainforest, more wild habitat, more ozone layer, and more species; but few were defending those things then. An ecological imagination was born and became part of the common culture only in the past few decades, as did a broader and deeper understanding of human diversity and human rights.

The world gets worse. It also gets better. And the future stays dark.

History is full of small acts that changed the world in surprising ways. I was one of thousands of activists at the Nevada Test Site in the late 1980s. . . . We didn't shut down our test site, but our acts inspired the Kazakh poet Olzhas Suleimenov, on February 27, 1989, to read a manifesto instead of poetry on live Kazakh TV—a manifesto demanding a shutdown of the Soviet nuclear test site in Semipalatinsk, Kazakhstan.

The Soviet Test Site was indeed shut down. Suleimenov was the catalyst, and though we in Nevada were his inspiration, what gave him his platform was his poetry in a country that loved poets. Perhaps Suleimenov wrote all his poems so that one day he could stand up in front of a TV camera and deliver not a poem but a manifesto. And perhaps Arundhati Roy wrote a ravishing novel that catapulted her to stardom so that when she stood up to oppose dams and destruction of the local for the benefit of the transnational, people would notice. Or perhaps these writers opposed the ravaging of the earth so that poetry, too—poetry in the broadest sense—would survive in the world.

Not Left but Forward

This is earth. It will never be heaven. There will always be cruelty, always be violence, always be destruction. There is tremendous devastation now. In the time it takes you to read this, acres of rainforest will vanish, a species will go extinct, women will be raped, men shot, and far too many children will die of easily preventable causes. We cannot eliminate all devastation for all time, but we can reduce it, outlaw it, undermine its source and foundation: these are victories.

Nearly everyone felt, after September 11, 2001, along with grief and fear, a huge upwelling of idealism, of openness, of a readiness to question and to learn, a sense of being connected and a desire to live our lives for something more, even if it wasn't familiar, safe, or easy.

That desire is still out there. It's the force behind a huge new movement we don't even have a name for yet, a movement that's not a left opposed to a right, but perhaps a below against above, little against big, local and decentralized against consolidated. If we could throw out the old definitions, we could recognize where the new alliances lie; and those alliances—of small farmers, of factory workers, of environmentalists, of the poor, of the indigenous, of the just, of the farseeing—could be extraordinarily powerful against the forces of corporate profit and institutional violence. Left and right are terms for where the radicals and conservatives sat in the French National Assembly after the French Revolution. We're not in that world anymore, let alone that seating arrangement. We're in one that for all its ruins and poisons and legacies is utterly new. Anti-globalization activists say, "Another world is possible." It is not only possible, it is inevitable; and we need to participate in shaping it.

Hope, the opposite of fear, lets us . . . live according to our principles as long as we're here. . . . Zapatista spokesman Subcommandante Marcos adds, "History written by Power taught us that we had lost . . . We did not believe what Power taught us. We skipped class when they taught conformity and idiocy. We failed modernity. We are united by the imagination, by creativity, by tomorrow. In the past, we not only met defeat but also found a desire for justice and the dream of being better. We left skepticism hanging from the hook of big capital and discovered that we could believe, that it was worth believing, that we should believe—in ourselves. Health to you, and don't forget that flowers, like hope, are harvested."

And they grow in the dark. "I believe," adds Thoreau, "in the forest, and the meadow, and the night in which the corn grows."

· · ·

NONVIOLENT COMMUNICATION: A LANGUAGE OF COMPASSION

Marshall B. Rosenberg

Introduction

I have been preoccupied most of my life with two questions. What happens to disconnect us from our compassionate nature, leading us to behave violently and exploitatively? And conversely, what allows some people to stay connected to their compassionate nature under even the most trying circumstances?

My preoccupation with these questions began in childhood, around the summer of 1943, when our family moved to Detroit, Michigan. The second week after we arrived, a race war erupted over an incident at a public park. More than forty people were killed in the next few days. Our neighborhood was situated in the center of the violence, and we spent three days locked in the house. . . .

When the violence ended and school began, I discovered that a name could be as dangerous as any skin color. When the teacher called my name during attendance, two boys glared at me and hissed, "Are you a kike?" I had never heard the word before and didn't know it was used by some people in a derogatory way to refer to Jews. After school, the same two boys were waiting for me: they threw me to the ground, kicked and beat me.

Since that summer in 1943, I have been examining the two questions I mentioned. What empowers us, for example, to stay connected to our compassionate nature even under the worst circumstances? I am thinking of people like Etty Hillesum, who remained compassionate even while subjected to the grotesque conditions of a German concentration camp. As she wrote in her journal at the time:

> I am not easily frightened. Not because I am brave but because I know that I am dealing with human beings, and that I must try as hard as I can to understand everything that anyone ever does. And that was the real import of this morning: not that a disgruntled young Gestapo officer yelled at me, but that I felt no indignation, rather a real compassion, and would have liked to ask, "Did you have a very unhappy childhood, has your girlfriend let you down?" (Etty Hillesum, from *Etty: A Diary 1941–1943*)

While studying the factors that affect our ability to stay compassionate, I was struck by the crucial role of language and our use of words. I have since identified a specific approach to communicating—both speaking and listening—that leads us to give from the heart, connecting us with ourselves and with each other in a way that allows our natural compassion to flourish. I call this approach Nonviolent Communication, using the term *nonviolence* as Gandhi used it—to refer to our natural state of compassion when violence has subsided from the heart. While we may not consider the way we talk to be "violent," words often lead to hurt and pain, whether for others or ourselves. In some communities, the process I am describing is known as Compassionate Communication; the abbreviation NVC is used . . . to refer to Nonviolent or Compassionate Communication.

A Way to Focus Attention

NVC is founded on language and communication skills that strengthen our ability to remain human, even under trying conditions. It contains nothing new; all that has been integrated into NVC has been known for centuries. The intent is to remind us about what we already know—about how we humans were meant to relate to one another—and to assist us in living in a way that concretely manifests this knowledge.

NVC guides us in reframing how we express ourselves and hear others. Instead of being habitual, automatic reactions, our words become conscious responses based firmly on an awareness of what we are perceiving, feeling, and wanting. We are led to express ourselves with honesty and clarity, while simultaneously paying others a respectful and empathetic attention. In any exchange, we come to hear our own deeper needs and those of others. NVC trains us to observe carefully, and to be able to specify behaviors and conditions that are affecting us. We learn to identify and clearly articulate what we are concretely wanting in a given situation. The form is simple, yet powerfully transformative.

As NVC replaces our old patterns of defending, withdrawing, or attacking in the face of judgment and criticism, we come to perceive ourselves and others, as well as our intentions and relationships, in a new light. Resistance, defensiveness, and violent reactions are minimized. When we focus on clarifying what is being observed, felt, and needed rather than on diagnosing and judging, we discover the depth of our own compassion. Through its emphasis on deep listening—to ourselves as well as others—NVC fosters respect, attentiveness, and empathy, and engenders a mutual desire to give from the heart.

Although I refer to it as "a process of communication" or a "language of compassion," NVC is more than a process or a language. On a deeper level, it is an ongoing reminder to keep our attention focused on a place where we are more likely to get what we are seeking.

There is a story of a man on all fours under a street lamp, searching for something. A policeman passing by asked what he was doing. "Looking for my car keys," replied the man, who appeared slightly drunk. "Did you drop them here?" inquired the officer. "No," answered the man, "I dropped them in the alley." Seeing the policeman's baffled expression, the man hastened to explain, "But the light is much better here."

I find that my cultural conditioning leads me to focus attention on places where I am unlikely to get what I want. I developed NVC as a way to train my attention—to shine the light of consciousness—on places that have the potential to yield what I am seeking. What I want in my life is compassion, a flow between myself and others based on a mutual giving from the heart.

When we give from the heart, we do so out of a joy that springs forth whenever we willingly enrich another person's life. This kind of giving benefits both the giver and the receiver.

The use of NVC does not require that the persons with whom we are communicating be . . . motivated to relate to us compassionately. If we stay with the principles of NVC, stay motivated solely to give and receive compassionately, and do everything we can to let others know this is our only motive, they will join us in the process, and eventually we will be able to respond compassionately to one another. I'm not saying that this always happens quickly. I do maintain, however, that compassion inevitably blossoms when we stay true to the principles and process of NVC.

The NVC Process

FOUR COMPONENTS OF NVC

1. Observations
2. Feelings
3. Needs
4. Requests

To arrive at a mutual desire to give from the heart, we focus the light of consciousness on four areas—referred to as the four components of the NVC model.

First, we observe what is actually happening in a situation: what are we observing others saying or doing that is either enriching or not enriching our life? The trick is to be able to articulate this observation without introducing any judgment or evaluation—to simply say what people are doing that we either like or don't like. Next, we state how we feel when we observe this action: are we hurt, scared, joyful, amused, irritated? And thirdly, we say what needs of ours are connected to the feelings we have identified. An awareness of these three components is present when we use NVC to clearly and honestly express how we are.

For example, a mother might express these three pieces to her teenage son by saying, "Felix, when I see two balls of soiled socks under the coffee table and another three next to the TV, I feel irritated because I am needing more order in the rooms which we share in common."

She would follow immediately with the fourth component—a very specific request: "Would you be willing to put your socks in your room or in the washing machine?" This fourth component addresses what we are wanting from the other person that would enrich our lives or make life more wonderful for us.

Thus, part of NVC is to express these four pieces of information very clearly, whether verbally or by other means. The other aspect of this communication consists of receiving the same four pieces of information from others. We connect with them by first sensing what they are observing, feeling, and needing; then we discover what would enrich their lives by receiving the fourth piece—their request.

As we keep our attention focused on the areas mentioned, and help others do likewise, we establish a flow of communication, back and forth, until compassion manifests naturally: what I am observing, feeling, and needing; what I am requesting to enrich my life; what you are observing, feeling, and needing; what you are requesting to enrich your life.

NVC PROCESS

- The concrete actions we *observe* that affect our well-being
- How we *feel* in relation to what we observe
- The *needs,* values, desires, etc., that create our feelings
- The concrete actions we *request* in order to enrich our lives

When we use this process, we may begin either by expressing ourselves or by empathetically receiving these four pieces of information from others. Although we will learn to listen for and verbally express each of these components . . . it is important to keep in mind that NVC is not a set formula, but adapts to various situations as well as personal and cultural styles. While I conveniently refer to NVC as a "process" or "language," it is possible to experience all four pieces of the process without uttering a single word. The essence of NVC is to be found in our consciousness of these four components, not in the actual words that are exchanged.

Applying NVC in Our Lives and World

When we use NVC in our interactions—with ourselves, with another person, or in a group—we become grounded in our natural state of compassion. It is therefore an approach that can be effectively applied at all levels of communication and in diverse situations:

- Intimate relationships
- Families
- Schools
- Organizations and institutions
- Therapy and counseling relationships
- Diplomatic and business negotiations
- Disputes and conflicts of any nature

Some people use NVC to create greater depth and caring in their intimate relationships. . . . Still others use this process in the political arena. A French cabinet member visiting her sister remarked how differently the sister and her husband were communicating and responding to each other. Encouraged by their descriptions of NVC, she mentioned that she was scheduled the following week to negotiate some sensitive issues between France and Algeria regarding adoption procedures. Though time was limited, we dispatched a French-speaking trainer to Paris to work with the cabinet minister. The minister later attributed much of the success of her negotiation in Algeria to her newly acquired communication techniques.

In Jerusalem, during a workshop attended by Israelis of varying political persuasions, participants used NVC to express themselves regarding the highly contested issue of the West Bank. Many of the Israeli settlers who have established themselves on the West Bank believe that they are fulfilling a religious mandate by doing so, and they are locked in conflict not only with Palestinians but with other Israelis who recognize the Palestinian hope for national sovereignty in this region. During a session, one of my trainers and I modeled empathic hearing through NVC and then invited participants to take turns role-playing each other's position. After twenty minutes, a settler announced her willingness to consider relinquishing her land claims and moving out of the West Bank into internationally recognized Israeli territory if her political opponents could listen to her in the way she had just been listened to.

Worldwide, NVC now serves as a valuable resource for communities facing violent conflicts and severe ethnic, religious, or political tensions. The spread of NVC training and its use in mediation by people in conflict in Israel, the Palestinian Authority, Nigeria, Rwanda, Sierra Leone, and elsewhere have been a source of particular gratification for me. [Several years ago,] my associates and I were . . . in Belgrade for three highly charged days training citizens working for peace. When we first arrived, expressions of despair were visibly etched on the trainees' faces, for their country was then enmeshed in a brutal war in Bosnia and Croatia. As the training progressed, we heard the ring of laughter in their voices as they shared their profound gratitude and joy for having found the empowerment they were seeking.

I [presented] Nonviolent Communication to about 170 Palestinian Muslim men in a mosque at Dheisheh Refugee Camp in Bethlehem. Attitudes toward Americans at that time were not favorable. As I was speaking, I suddenly noticed a wave of muffled commotion fluttering through the audience. "They're whispering that you are American!" my translator alerted me, just as a gentleman in the audience leapt to his feet. Facing me squarely, he hollered at the top of his lungs, "Murderer!" Immediately, a dozen other voices joined him in chorus: "Assassin!" "Child-killer!" "Murderer!"

Fortunately, I was able to focus my attention on what the man was feeling and needing. In this case, I had some cues. On the way into the refugee camp, I had seen several empty tear gas canisters that had been shot into the camp the night before. Clearly marked on each canister were the words *Made in U.S.A.* I knew that the refugees harbored a lot of anger toward the U.S. for supplying tear gas and other weapons to Israel.

I addressed the man who had called me a murderer:

I: Are you angry because you would like my government to use its resources differently? *(I didn't know whether my guess was correct—what was critical was my sincere effort to connect with his feeling and need.)*

He: Damn right I'm angry! You think we need tear gas? We need sewers, not your tear gas! We need housing! We need to have our own country!

I: So you're furious and would appreciate some support in improving your living conditions and gaining political independence?

He: Do you know what it's like to live here for twenty-seven years the way I have with my family—children and all? Have you got the faintest idea what that's been like for us?

I: Sounds like you're feeling very desperate and you're wondering whether I or anybody else can really understand what it's like to be living under these conditions. Am I hearing you right?

He: You want to understand? Tell me, do you have children? Do they go to school? Do they have playgrounds? My son is sick! He plays in open sewage! His classroom has no books! Have you seen a school that has no books?

I: I hear how painful it is for you to raise your children here; you'd like me to know that what you want is what all parents want for their children—a good education, opportunity to play and grow in a healthy environment . . .

He: That's right, the basics! Human rights—isn't that what you Americans call it? Why don't more of you come here and see what kind of human rights you're bringing here!

I: You'd like more Americans to be aware of the enormity of the suffering here and to look more deeply at the consequences of our political actions?

Our dialogue continued, with him expressing his pain for nearly twenty more minutes, and me listening for the feeling and need behind each statement. I didn't agree or disagree. I received his words, not as attacks, but as gifts from a fellow human being willing to share his soul and deep vulnerabilities with me.

Once the gentleman felt understood, he was able to hear me as I explained my purpose for being at the camp. An hour later, the same man who had called me a murderer was inviting me to his home for a Ramadan dinner.

. . .

NONVIOLENCE: WEAPON OF THE BRAVE,
WEAPON OF THE FUTURE[1]

Michael N. Nagler

In the summer of 1960, Vinoba Bhave, already considered a saint by many, was passing through the Chambal Valley in Madhya Pradesh on one of his *padayatra* or "walking pilgrimages." He was told the area was "infested" with dacoits, or hereditary bandits, but Bhave, instinctively shunning the dehumanizing imagery, said no, it was not "infested with dacoits" but "inhabited by virtuous people." Armed police had not been able to cope with these people—call them what you will—and an ugly confrontation was brewing. Drawing on the authority people like himself enjoy in India, he sent word to the bandits that if they come forward and turned themselves in to him he would see that they were dealt with fairly by the law. They would have to accept penalties, but no further punishment would be visited on themselves or their families, as they had feared. Surprisingly (to some), scores of these men came and laid their arms at his feet, forestalling a bloody confrontation with the authorities.[2]

Vinoba was regarded by many as Gandhi's foremost disciple. Most of his work after the Mahatma's passing was on land reform, but here, where he applied *Satyagraha* (literally, "clinging to truth") directly to conflict, it raises the fascinating question, could nonviolence, in an appropriate form, be the answer to terrorism? Could it be used by ordinary people, the vast majority of us, who are not in Vinoba's spiritual category and do not even live in a culture that recognizes what Gandhi called "the greatest power at the disposal of humanity"?

What Is Satyagraha?

When Gandhi discovered the power of taking on suffering in order to win over an opponent—nominally the basis of Christianity and Western Civilization—the idea was so unusual that a new term had to be coined for it, especially since the term that would otherwise come to mind, "passive resistance," failed to convey the active vitality of their method and could lead to fatal confusion: passive resistance did not, in the usage of the time, rule out the use of violence. Satyagraha, as mentioned, literally means clinging to truth. But "truth" (*satya*) has broader meanings in the Indian languages than it does in English. It means, to be sure, truth as opposed to falsehood; but it also means "the real" as opposed to the unreal or nonexistent—and it also means "the good." There is a profound optimism at the bottom of this belief, that the world cannot be based on evil (in fact, in the West also this would be rejected as the Manichaean heresy). Evil exists, Gandhi would explain, but it exists only to the extent that we support it—by our belief in its power, by our fascination with its violence, by our fear. Withdraw that support and good would reemerge: how could it not? This vision would have the utmost consequences for the tremendous work he would go on to launch later in India:

> The world rests upon the bedrock of satya or truth. *Asatya* meaning untruth also means non-existent, and satya or truth also means that which is. If untruth does not so much as exist, its victory is out of the question. And truth being that which is can never be destroyed. This is the doctrine of Satyagraha in a nutshell.[3]

Obviously, in Gandhi's conception Satyagraha is a kind of force—indeed, the only kind that ultimately exists and works in the world. Its field of operations is the minds and hearts of people, but it is no less a scientific reality for that. It is not hit-or-miss (more on this below). To understand it as an abstract, moral category, is misleading. Gandhi had this to say about how it works:

> What Satyagraha does in such cases is not to suppress reason but to free it from inertia and to establish its sovereignty over prejudice, hatred, and other baser passions. In other words, if one may paradoxically put it, it does not enslave, it compels reason to be free."[4]

No matter how brutal and dehumanized we human beings become as the result of the propaganda we have been exposed to, the capacity for what Gandhi calls "reason" in this context (meaning a kind of humane awareness) is always there, however buried. At least one friend of mine owes her very existence to this fact. Lilian Kshensky's parents-to-be were Polish Jews who joined the underground in Warsaw during WWII. One night the Gestapo raided their apartment and found documents that would have spelled their death; but just at that moment their little boy went up to the Gestapo captain and started playing with the shiny buttons on his uniform! His parents were horrified, but when the captain looked down at the child he stopped talking, and, after a long moment that must have seemed like eternity he said, in a totally changed voice, "I have a little boy at home just his age, and I miss him very much." Then he quietly added, "Your son has saved your life" and ordered his men out of the apartment.

Lily, an important peace activist today, was born ten years later. Satyagraha is a way to do consciously what the Kshenskys' little boy did in all his innocence: to reawaken another's humane awareness. By acting humanly ourselves we reawaken the dormant humanity of the other. Interestingly enough, there is now strong scientific evidence that this effect is embedded in our central nervous system. Scientists have found that we all possess "mirror neurons" that respond to another's mental states, a bit like a biological tuning fork that picks up outside vibrations.[5] If I cry, or exhibit anger—or overcome it—whatever you may or may not feel consciously a part of you is mirroring my response.

That this awakening will happen is not in doubt. Whether it will happen visibly, whether your act of Satyagraha will "work" in that immediate sense, depends on many factors—just as the effects of violence do. This does not mean that Satyagraha is easy, or that it always accomplishes what we want. But it does mean two important things: that whenever we use it, *some* good will eventually result; and that there is a science to maximizing that effect. Satyagraha is not luck, or grace—it's *predictable.*

Basic Principles

More and more people are coming to believe that, as Gandhi claimed, there is *no* situation where Satyagraha cannot be applied, with beneficial results. The specific application will be somewhat different, but there are certain basic principles that most scholars and activists agree give it its power:

- Means and ends are not separable: we can never use destructive means like violence to bring about constructive ends like democracy and peace.
- Nonviolence is always directed against the evil, *not* the person doing it. In Christian terms, we "hate the sin, but not the sinner." The clearest sign that "soul-force" is at work is when your opponent ends up being your ally, even your friend. Indeed, activists often discover that the more they can bring themselves

to accept the person opposing them, the *more* effectively they can overcome his or her wrongdoing.

- We believe that there is no irreducible conflict between human groups that cannot be resolved through understanding, and if necessary "forcing reason to be free."
- We believe that our actions have consequences well beyond the immediate, visible results we aim at. In fact, as history has shown many times, our efforts may fail to deliver the immediate results we wanted but succeed in doing more than we dreamed of.

In 1953, at the height of the Korean War, there was a huge surplus of food in the United States but a famine in China. The Fellowship of Reconciliation launched a campaign to deluge the White House with miniature grain bags and a quote from Isaiah: "If thine enemy hunger, feed him." We (the author included) never heard anything from the White House and concluded that we had been a failure yet again. But 25 years later, thanks to the Freedom of Information Act, we found out that the Joint Chiefs of Staff at that time were trying to press President Eisenhower to let them start bombing mainland China—an act of folly which could quite conceivably have precipitated World War III. The President was able to say, "Gentlemen, 35,000 Americans think we should be feeding the Chinese. This is hardly the time to start bombing them!" Disaster averted. As Gandhi historian B. R. Nanda explains,

> The fact is that Satyagraha was not designed to seize any particular objective or to crush the opponent, but to set in motion forces which would ultimately lead to a new equation; in such a strategy it [is] perfectly possible to lose all the battles and still win the war.[6]

There is an incredibly simple truth at the heart of all this: violence is destructive, nonviolence is constructive. At some level nonviolence will *always* lead to integration and community, while violence must promote hatred and disunity. With violence, we can lurch from crisis to crisis, exactly as we are doing today. We can never grow toward a regime of stable peace and creativity. That only nonviolence can do for us. I find it convenient to say that an action "works" when it accomplishes its short-term, obvious effects while it works (without quotes) in the sense that it changes situations under the surface and thus can produce effects later on, the connection not always being obvious. Using these terms, we can formulate an important law:

Nonviolence sometimes "works" and always works,

while by contrast,

Violence sometimes "works" and never works.

This explains why Gandhi, after fifty years of experimentation with Satyagraha in every walk of life, could declare that he "knew of no single case in which it had failed." Where it seemed to fail he concluded that he or the other satyagrahis (people offering Satyagraha) had failed in some way or other to live up to its steep challenge.

The bitter legacy of the many wars that were "won" only to lead to further cycles of destruction—WWI, Kosovo, no doubt Afghanistan and Iraq today—is not the fate of struggles that are won by nonviolence. As the American Friends Service Committee pointed out in a cogent booklet of 1955 called *Speak Truth to Power,* India and Algeria both gained independence from European colonial powers at about the same time, but while India did it with largely nonviolent means, Algeria did not. Yes, both countries became politically free, but enormously greater casualties were suffered in the Algerian conflict: the Algerians lost nearly 900,000 people while vastly greater India lost only a few thousand. Furthermore, relations would remain strained between Algeria and France almost to the present day, while India and Britain immediately entered an era of cooperation and mutual benefit.

Peace scholar Kenneth Boulding has proposed very useful language for elucidating the difference: Satyagraha struggles are based on *integrative power;* military struggles are based on *threat power.* As Boulding puts it, "Integrative power, then, involves bringing the dissident back into the community. Sanctions alone, threat alone, will not do this. If we think of power merely in terms of threat power, we will get nowhere."[7]

Needless to say, Satyagraha struggles are enormously less costly than ordinary military. The current year's budget for Nonviolent Peaceforce, perhaps the largest operation of the dozen or so organizations doing Third Party Nonviolent Intervention (TPNI—see more below) is $3.8 million, or *one fifth* the cost of a single F-16 fighter.

To be fair, however, Satyagraha is in one way much *more* costly than violence. It takes a lot of courage to face hostility with as much love as we can muster, to face it without weapons. While combat soldiers are undeniably brave, theirs is a physical courage, often based on a (false) sense of security derived from weapons. They are not noted for the courage to refuse orders that go against their conscience, or otherwise resist the social pressures of the crowd. As a high-ranking military officer quipped recently about retired generals who were at last speaking out against the war in Iraq, "These are men who are willing to risk their lives, but not their careers." A satyagrahi must not only be willing to endure physical attacks, if necessary at the risk of life itself, but *also* face the misunderstanding and hatred of a world which has not yet realized what Satyagraha is and what motivates someone to offer it. As Gandhi pointed out, a real satyagrahi must be prepared to go it alone.

The Application

Now we can sketch out how Satyagraha could be used in the confrontation with terrorism.

Vinoba Bhave gives us the first step: stop dehumanizing "terrorists." We have to stop superimposing on them images of disease and impurity. They do not cease to be human beings because they are desperate and hate us.

Similarly, we must *take their concerns seriously*. As a friend of mine said right after the 9/11 attacks, "terrorism cannot be condoned, but it can be understood." Johann Galtung, renowned peace scholar and expert practitioner of group conflict resolution, has determined after much research that what the Muslim world really needs, at the end of the day, is respect for their religion. Would it hurt us to grant it?

People who have committed crimes—be they called "terrorists" or soldiers—should be brought to justice; but we can go Vinoba one better. We can go to reparations and reconciliation, in other words restorative justice. This is, any day, better than even measured, "just" punishment.

We should, finally, not shun the fact that none of the parties involved in the present violence will go along with any of these changes unless we, the members of global civil society, bring them to it by determined nonviolent persuasion. This will unavoidably demand struggle and self-sacrifice. But we are suffering already, and will suffer much more if the cycles of violence go unchecked. And *this* kind of suffering, undertaken voluntarily, is qualitatively different from what we're undergoing now. "Unearned suffering," said Martin Luther King, "is redemptive." In other words, it actually works.

1. This chapter is adapted from *Hope or Terror: Gandhi and the Other 9/11* (Berkeley & Minneapolis: Metta & the Nonviolent Peaceforce, 2006).

2. Vasant Nargolkar, *The Creed of Saint Vinoba* (Bombay: Bharatiya Vidya Bhavan, 1995), 127f.

3. *CWMG,* op. cit., 235.

4. Pyarelal, *The Epic Fast* (Ahmedabad: Navajivan, 1932), 35.

5. Cf. Natalie Angier, "Why We're So Nice: We're Wired to Cooperate," *New York Times,* July 23, 2002.

6. *India News,* October 1, 1994, 11.

7. Kenneth E. Boulding, *The Three Faces of Power* (Newbury Park, CA: Sage), 250.

. . .

I contemplate a mental and therefore a moral opposition to immoralities. I seek entirely to blunt the edge of the tyrant's sword, not by putting up against it a sharper-edged weapon, but by disappointing his expectation that I would be offering physical resistance. The resistance of the soul that I should offer instead would elude him. It would at first dazzle him and at last compel recognition . . . which . . . would not humiliate him but uplift him.

(Mohandas Gandhi, from "Ahimsa or the Way of Nonviolence")

. . .

CANDLES IN BABYLON
Denise Levertov

Through the midnight streets of Babylon
between the steel towers of their arsenals,
between the torture castles with no windows,
we race by barefoot, holding tight
our candles, trying to shield
the shivering flames, crying
"Sleepers Awake!"
               hoping
the rhyme's promise was true,
that we may return
from this place of terror
home to a calm dawn and
the work we had just begun.

. . .

ON CITIZEN DIPLOMACY
Dulce Murphy

Since the beginnings of recorded history, citizen diplomacy has been part of international relations. But until recently it has not been named as such, much less studied as a significant aspect of foreign affairs. I've been involved in such activity since 1980 at a time when the Soviet Union and the United States were engaged in the Cold War. Politically and culturally concerned citizens like myself, primarily from the United States and Great Britain, were motivated to take action then. Many of our actions, which began as naïve attempts at making change through personal contacts, led to speaking out about misunderstood ideologies among citizens of many divergent cultures.

Today, citizen diplomacy has become a strong force, practiced by both lay people and professionals. Dissertations on the subject are becoming more common as the importance and success of what we have named Track Two Diplomacy makes its way into school curricula all over the world.

Citizen diplomacy originated with the development of a series of "Track Two" interventions. Joseph Montville, former career diplomat in the U.S. State Department and now Chairman of the Board of Track Two: An Institute for Citizen Diplomacy, coined the term in 1981. He distinguished traditional diplomatic activities (track one diplomacy) from "unofficial, informal interaction between members of adversarial groups or nations with the goals of developing strategies, influencing public opinions and organizing human and material resources in ways that might help resolve the conflict."

Why is citizen diplomacy so effective? Our experience with formal diplomacy is that the actions of governments often have a limited ability to solve problems. By contrast, citizens have a strong psychological investment in protecting their political, cultural, economic survival and their human rights. When confronting governments, leaders, and conflicts, citizens who are affected by a crisis often refuse to stand by and watch a dangerous situation unfold. Although citizen diplomacy does not replace formal diplomacy, it complements the efforts of governments by building trust and mutual understanding based on face-to-face relationships among citizens of different cultures, regions, and religions. When ideology is put on hold by creative human contact, humanity gets a chance to speak.

Direct diplomacy among citizens can overcome negative stereotypes and in this way bridge the psychological distances between groups and nations in conflict. The early Esalen Institute Soviet-American Exchange Program, with which I began my own work in citizen diplomacy, was able to make strong human connections with Soviet citizens, win their trust, and establish enduring good faith relationships. This allowed both of us to speak about our own shortcomings as well as those of the other. This process helped to prepare Soviets psychologically for the dramatic transformation to come.

The seed for Esalen's Track Two diplomacy was planted when Michael Murphy, co-founder of Esalen Institute, was invited to go to the Soviet Union in 1971 to meet some of the people featured in Shelia Ostrander and Lynn Schroeder's book *Psychic Discoveries Behind the Iron Curtain*. Although I was intrigued, it wasn't until 1980 that I took my first trip there, the year the United States boycotted the Olympics in Moscow. Little did I know that it would change my life—I fell in love with a country. Perhaps it was this state of mind that allowed me to see clearly the possibilities for an understanding between the people of two super powers that might transform the Cold War, decrease mutual aggression, and perhaps even challenge the Iron Curtain.

After more than sixty trips to the former Republics of the Soviet Union, I still feel deeply connected. I have devoted much of my working life since that time to improving the relationship between our two countries and, along the way, have made many deep and lasting friendships.

In 1980 the Esalen-Soviet American Exchange Program, which began during a threatening turn of the Cold War, was established as The Russian-American Center. In the spring of 2004, we changed the organization's name to Track Two: An Institute for Citizen Diplomacy to signify the expansion of its mandate to include other countries, teaming with our Russian colleagues to that end. There is no Communist-Capitalist rivalry now with spillover into other countries, and the end of the Cold War has allowed the forces of reconciliation to have an impact in Germany, Eastern Europe, South Africa, Central America, China, and other parts of the world. We have participated in one of the most successful good works of modern times, and we continue to address problems and opportunities shared by the peoples of Russia, the United States, and areas of the world in conflict. Track Two has worked with the Soviet Union and Russia for more than thirty years by promoting interaction between governmental and non-governmental organizations, as well as individuals, of these countries.

Our projects with Russia continue, and our Islamic Outreach program is becoming a major project for both Track Two and Esalen's Center for Theory and Research. We are joining with people concerned about terrorism around the world. Responding to this post-Cold War situation, Track Two is working with groups promoting better relations between American, European, Russian, Islamic, and Asian cultures, as well as with individuals seeking to strengthen Russia's democratic institutions.

Esalen's Soviet-American Exchange Program—the earlier incarnation of Track Two—played an important role in bringing an end to the Cold War. By nurturing a network of deep human relationships, by holding annual conferences, and other meetings that built upon those relationships, by creating and maintaining the Luchkov Library of Psychological Literature at Moscow State University, by signing one of the first agreements between an American private-sector group and the USSR Ministry of Health, by participating in the first live interactive satellite communication (later to be known as space bridges), and by hosting Boris Yeltsin's first visit to the United States, we created crucial communications between the two countries that served the needs of the 1980s.

In 1988 we introduced eminent Soviet writers to International Pen, an organization that monitors government censorship and freedom of expression around the world. At that time it was headed first by Susan Sontag and later by Norman Mailer. The Soviets did indeed join International Pen, a central event of Soviet Glasnost. Esalen and Track Two consider this to be one of their most important contributions to the Soviet Union's opening to free speech and democracy.

In 1989 I found myself in New York City with an entourage of Soviets and Americans. Somehow, someway, the Esalen Soviet project had been asked to bring Boris Yeltsin to the United States on his first trip to our continent. Leon Aron wrote in his magisterial biography of Yeltsin, "Little, if anything, could match for Yeltsin the trip's sense of discovery or the impact it would have on him in the long run." Aron's description of Yeltsin's visit to a Houston supermarket is well known. Yeltsin was overwhelmed by the "wonders" of what he encountered—rows of fresh vegetables, meat, staples, bright colors and reasonable prices. The experience was a real shocker for him, and because of it, he made changes in his life and ultimately his country. He had been told that the United States had planted false evidence of prosperity in certain East and West Coast cities, and that the middle of the country was impoverished and riddled with crime. The Houston supermarket experience helped change his mind.

I had the privilege of being with Yeltsin while he was in New York City. The first excursion was a trip on the subway—an embarrassment to me, as the Moscow subway system at that time was known as one of the cleanest, safest, and most attractive in the world. We were on our way to Wall Street and ultimately the New York Stock Exchange. Here we were with this odd group of people from Esalen, a group dedicated to new modes of healing and raising consciousness and Yeltsin's own eclectic group of organizers and handlers. As we were invited to wander the floor of this very American institution, I found myself shoulder to shoulder with Boris as we both looked on in amazement, neither of us having experienced anything like it in our lives. The experience was captured by several American as well as foreign television stations. My close observation of Boris that day changed my own thinking and the way I would view citizen diplomacy. I became more hopeful about the future and the importance of so many Americans and Soviets devoting their lives to this work.

Supplementing official summitry, for years Track Two has sponsored countless meetings of groups of different professionals, from psychologists to astronauts. By letting the commonality of their professional—and human—interests speak louder than the differences between their nations and cultures, the members of the Track Two network have spanned the globe with bonds of growing friendship and mutual understanding. Track Two diplomacy flies beneath the radar of official treaties, age-old enmities, hardened ideologies, and partisan politics. When people with similar interests can talk face-to-face about the things that interest them, the faces of the enemy (the title of a book and video by Sam Keen, born of Track Two diplomacy) are replaced by human faces and real communication.

There is impressive evidence that Esalen's Track Two work contributed significantly to the transformation of the Soviet Union and Russia's relationship with the United States. Now, relations between Islam and the West are strained. The American relationship with Europe has been frayed by disagreements over Iraq and the Middle East in general, as well as Russia and China. Indeed, we in the United States may be more in need of building friendship and understanding through citizen diplomacy than at any time in the past century.

The so-called "wars" we are asked to fight may be un-winnable without new thinking and new practices like citizen diplomacy. We are not fighting along established geo-political battle lines. We are struggling for hearts and minds, commitment, understanding, and intelligence. There are plenty of opportunities for highly focused, inter-cultural citizen-led efforts that are not seen or sometimes understood by official, high level diplomacy.

Rooted in the context of Esalen's explorations of human potential, Track Two will continue to give voice to the growing constituency of individuals who feel disheartened and powerless vis-à-vis governments that don't get it. Citizen diplomacy aims to fill the moral and intellectual voids of official peacemaking leadership. Our major goal is to re-humanize relations that are dysfunctional.

Track Two has developed a set of principles that we believe can be applied to today's and tomorrow's complicated relationships with Islam, with Iran, and with China over the longer term:

- Dream the dream, even if it is "impossible." You must have an overarching goal, but no cherished outcome.
- You can do things that governments can't. It's important not to give power away to the leaders.
- Know that everyone wants something greater to emerge.
- Believe your instincts, not your government, or your media, or your conditioning.
- Find allies. Develop personal connections and trust. We all have friends in curious places. Respect the importance of community. Collegiality is crucial.
- Diversity is essential. Don't be afraid to gather people who don't like one another.
- Get good people together. A small group can make a difference.
- It is important to create a safe space and have expert facilitation.
- Become engaged, and then see the possibilities. Do your homework, but adopt beginner's mind. Don't imagine that you can complete a strategic plan and come in with the right answers.
- Be prepared to be surprised by what you find.
- Listen carefully. Listen to what wants to happen. Listen for a conspiracy of opportunities.
- Tolerate ambiguity. Don't jump to conclusions too quickly.
- Unexpected benefits are as important as the expected ones.
- Aim for a balance between surrender and action.

- Work from a non-adversarial place. This means:
  - Never stimulate factionalism.
  - Conduct bi-national or multi-national, not unilateral planning of projects.
  - If you have an axe to grind, you might be ground down.
  - Don't do it for them lest you end up doing it to them.
  - Instead of facing each other, sit shoulder to shoulder and face "the problem" together.
  - Always speak from equality.
  - You cannot condescend.
- Practice empathy. In whatever way possible, become the other. When we humanize the other, we humanize ourselves.
- Show up and keep showing up. Perseverance furthers. The antidote to the biggest force is gentle contact. Large institutions are like inertial masses resting on frictionless surfaces. Lean against them long enough, and they will move. Hurl yourself against them expecting immediate results, and you will only bloody yourself.
- Always ask: Who is doing this? The internal work you do on yourself prepares for the external work you do in the world. Beware of ego. You must be willing to be anonymous.
- Engaging in this work is an adventure. Enjoying it is a matter of attitude.
- Find the acupuncture points. Look for the best leverage points. Look for where self-interest aligns with common interest.
- Think outside of the box! Exercise creativity on the spot and in real time.
- Conduct a multi-pronged approach with several simultaneous agendas.
- When you do exchanges, pick topics that both sides are good at: e.g., movies, environmental issues, astronauts and cosmonauts.
- Look for metaphors and symbols of transformation, e.g., teenagers from two countries climbing a mountain as an example of citizen "summitry."
- Be a catalyst for others. Give away all that you have so that others may spread the work.

- In all things, practice care and give a damn. But also care in a less Teutonic, warmer way, for example, observing the birthdays of close foreign colleagues.
- Success brings its challenges. Beware of grandiosity when playing on a very big stage.
- You are bound to fail from time to time, but failure is an essential part of success. Venture capitalists in the 1990s looked for leaders who had already had at least one failure. Your failures can be turned into later successes through learning.

Meta-rule: You can't know which of the above principles will best apply in each new situation.

The principles of citizen diplomacy continue to serve us well to develop the trust and good will as citizen diplomats in many fields and in many countries, just as we did in the Soviet Union, when we promoted mutual understanding between Russians and Americans.

· · ·

A NEW WORLD DIPLOMACY
Václav Havel

We all know that our civilization is in danger. The population explosion and the greenhouse effect, holes in the ozone and AIDS, the threat of nuclear terrorism and the dramatically widening gap between the rich North and the poor South, the danger of famine, the depletion of the biosphere and the mineral resources of the planet, the expansion of commercial television culture and the growing threat of regional wars—all this combined with thousands of other things represents a general threat to mankind.

The large paradox at the moment is that man—a great collector of information—is well aware of all this, yet is absolutely incapable of dealing with this danger to himself. Traditional science, with its usual coolness, can describe the different ways we might destroy ourselves, but it cannot offer us truly effective and practicable instructions on how to avert them. . . .

What is needed is something different, something larger. Man's attitude toward the world must be radically changed. We have to abandon the arrogant belief that the world is merely a puzzle to be solved, a machine with instructions for use waiting to be discovered, a body of information to be fed into a computer in the hope that, sooner or later, it will spit out a universal solution.

It is my profound conviction that we have to release from the sphere of private whim and rejuvenate forces such as a natural, unique, and unrepeatable experience of the world, an elementary sense of justice, the ability to see things as others do, a sense of transcendental responsibility, archetypal wisdom, good taste, courage, compassion, and faith in the importance of particular measures that do not aspire to be a universal, and thus an objective or technical, key to salvation. Things must once more be given a chance to present themselves as they are, to be perceived in their individuality. We must see the pluralism of the world, and not bind it by seeking common denominators or reducing everything to a single common equation.

We must try harder to understand rather than to explain. The way forward is not in the mere construction of universal systemic solutions, to be applied to reality from the outside; it is also in seeking to get to the heart of reality through personal experience. Such an approach promotes an atmosphere of tolerant solidarity and unity in diversity based on mutual respect, genuine pluralism, and parallelism. In a word, human uniqueness, human action, and the human spirit must be rehabilitated.

The world, too, has something like a spirit or soul. That, however, is something more than a mere body of information that can be externally grasped and objectified and mechanically assembled. Yet this does not mean that we have no access to it. Figuratively speaking, the human spirit is made from the same material as the spirit of the world. Man is not just an observer, a spectator, an analyst, or a manager of the world. Man is a part of the world, and his spirit is part of the spirit of the world. We are merely a peculiar node of Being, a living atom within it, or, rather, a cell that, if sufficiently open to itself and its own mystery, can also experience the mystery, the will, the pain, and the hope of the world.

The world today is a world in which generality, objectivity, and universality are in crisis. This world presents a great challenge to the practice of politics, which, it seems to me, still has a technocratic, utilitarian approach to Being, and therefore to political power as well. After they have gone through the mill of objective analysis and prognosis, original ideas and actions, unique and therefore always risky, often lose their human ethos and therefore, *de facto,* their spirit. Many of the traditional mechanisms of democracy created and developed and conserved in the modern era are so linked to the cult of objectivity and statistical average that they can annul human individuality. We can see this in political language, where cliché often squeezes out personal tone. And when a personal tone does crop up, it is usually calculated, not an outburst of personal authenticity.

It is my impression that sooner or later politics will be faced with the task of finding a new, post-modern face. A politician must become a person again, someone who trusts not only a scientific representation and analysis of the world, but also the world itself. He must believe not only in sociological statistics, but in real people. He must trust not only an objective interpretation of reality, but also its soul; not only an adopted ideology, but also his own thoughts; not only the summary reports he receives each morning, but also his own instincts.

Soul, individual spirituality, firsthand personal insight into things, the courage to be oneself and go the way one's conscience points, humility in the face of the mysterious order of Being, confidence in its natural direction, and, above all, trust in one's own subjectivity as the principal link with the subjectivity of the world—these, in my view, are the qualities that politicians of the future should cultivate.

Looking at politics "from the inside," as it were, has if anything confirmed my belief that the world of today—with the dramatic changes it is going through, and in its determination not to destroy itself—presents a great challenge to politicians.

It is not that we should simply seek new and better ways of managing society, the economy, and the world as such. The point is that we should fundamentally change how we behave. And who but politicians should lead the way? Their changed attitude toward the world, toward themselves, and toward their responsibility can in turn give rise to truly effective systemic and institutional changes.

You have certainly heard of the "butterfly effect." It is a belief that everything in the world is so mysteriously and comprehensively interconnected that a slight, seemingly insignificant wave of a butterfly's wings in a single spot on this planet can unleash a typhoon thousands of miles away.

I think we must believe in this effect in politics. We cannot assume that our microscopic yet truly unique everyday actions are of no consequence simply because they apparently cannot resolve the immense problems of today. That would be an *a priori* nihilistic assertion, and an expression of the arrogant, modern rationality that believes it knows how the world works.

But what do we really know about it?

Can we say that a casual conversation between two bankers and the Prince of Wales over dinner in Davos tonight will not sow a seed from which a wonderful flower will one day grow for the whole world to admire?

In a world of global civilization, only those who are looking for a technical trick to save that civilization need feel despair. But those who believe, in all modesty, in the mysterious power of their own human Being, which mediates between them and the mysterious power of the world's Being, have no reason to despair at all.

. . .

ON COURAGE AND RESISTANCE
Susan Sontag

Allow me to invoke not one but two, only two, who were heroes—among millions of heroes. Who were victims—among tens of millions of victims.

The first: Oscar Arnulfo Romero, Archbishop of San Salvador, murdered in his vestments, while saying mass in the cathedral on March 24, 1980—twenty-three years ago—because he had become "a vocal advocate of a just peace, and had openly opposed the forces of violence and oppression." (I am quoting from the description of the Oscar Romero Award, being given today to Ishai Menuchin.)

The second: Rachel Corrie, a 23-year-old college student from Olympia, Washington, murdered in the bright neon-orange jacket with Day-Glo striping that "human shields" wear to make themselves quite visible, and possibly safer, while trying to stop one of the almost daily house demolitions by Israeli forces in Rafah, a town in the southern Gaza Strip (where Gaza abuts the Egyptian border), on March 16, 2003. Standing in front of a Palestinian physician's house that had been targeted for demolition, Corrie, one of eight young American and British human-shield volunteers in Rafah, had been waving and shouting at the driver of an oncoming armored D-9 bulldozer through her megaphone, then dropped to her knees in the path of the supersized bulldozer . . . which did not slow down.

Two emblematic figures of sacrifice, killed by the forces of violence and oppression to which they were offering nonviolent, principled, dangerous opposition.

Let's start with risk. The risk of being punished. The risk of being isolated. The risk of being injured or killed. The risk of being scorned. We are all conscripts in one sense or another. For all of us, it is hard to break ranks; to incur the disapproval, the censure, the violence of an offended majority with a different idea of loyalty. . . .

To fall out of step with one's tribe; to step beyond one's tribe into a world that is larger mentally but smaller numerically—if alienation or dissidence is not your habitual or gratifying posture, this is a complex, difficult process. It is hard to defy the wisdom of the tribe, the wisdom that values the lives of members of the tribe above all others. It will always be unpopular—it will always be deemed unpatriotic—to say that the lives of the members of the other tribe are as valuable as one's own. . . .

The perennial destiny of principles: While everyone professes to have them, they are likely to be sacrificed when they become inconveniencing. Generally a moral principle is something that puts one at variance with accepted practice. And that variance has consequences, sometimes unpleasant consequences, as the community takes its revenge on those who challenge its contradictions—who want a society actually to uphold the principles it professes to defend. . . .

At the center of our moral life and our moral imagination are the great models of resistance. . . . What models, what stories? A Mormon may resist the outlawing of polygamy. An antiabortion militant may resist the law that has made abortion legal. They, too, will invoke the claims of religion (or faith) and morality against the edicts of civil society. . . .

Courage has no moral value in itself, for courage is not, in itself, a moral virtue. Vicious scoundrels, murderers, terrorists may be brave. To describe courage as a virtue, we need an adjective: we speak of "moral courage," because there is such a thing as amoral courage, too. And resistance has no value in itself. It is the *content* of the resistance that determines its merit, its moral necessity.

Let's say: resistance to a criminal war. Let's say: resistance to the occupation and annexation of another people's land. . . .

Here is what I believe to be a truthful description of a state of affairs that has taken me many years of uncertainty, ignorance and anguish to acknowledge.

A wounded and fearful country, Israel, is going through the greatest crisis of its turbulent history, brought about by the policy of steadily increasing and reinforcing settlements on the territories won after its victory in the Arab-Israeli war of 1967. The decision of successive Israeli governments to retain control over the West Bank and Gaza, thereby denying their Palestinian neighbors a state of their own, is a catastrophe—moral, human, and political—for both peoples.

The Palestinians need a sovereign state. Israel needs a sovereign Palestinian state. Those of us abroad who wish for Israel to survive cannot, should not, wish it to survive no matter what, no matter how. We owe a particular debt of gratitude to courageous Israeli Jewish witnesses, journalists, architects, poets, novelists, professors—among others—who have described and documented and protested and militated against the sufferings of the Palestinians living under the increasingly cruel terms of Israeli military subjugation and settler annexation.

Our greatest admiration must go to the brave Israeli soldiers, represented here by Ishai Menuchin, who refuse to serve beyond the 1967 borders. These soldiers know that all settlements are bound to be evacuated in the end.

These soldiers, who are Jews, take seriously the principle put forward at the Nuremberg trials in 1945–46: namely, that a soldier is not obliged to obey unjust orders, orders that contravene the laws of war—indeed, one has an obligation to disobey them.

The Israeli soldiers who are resisting service in the Occupied Territories are not refusing a particular order. They are refusing to enter the space where illegitimate orders are bound to be given—that is, where it is more than probable that they will be ordered to perform actions that continue the oppression and humiliation of Palestinian civilians. Houses are demolished, groves are uprooted, the stalls of a village market are bulldozed, a cultural center is looted; and now, nearly every day, civilians of all ages are fired on and killed. There can be no disputing the mounting cruelty of the Israeli occupation of the 22 percent of the former territory of British Palestine on which a Palestinian state will be erected. These soldiers believe, as I do, that there should be an unconditional withdrawal from the Occupied Territories. They have declared collectively that they will not continue to fight beyond the 1967 borders "in order to dominate, expel, starve and humiliate an entire people."

What the refuseniks have done—there are now more than one thousand of them, more than two hundred and fifty of whom have gone to prison—does not contribute to telling us how the Israelis and Palestinians can make peace, beyond the irrevocable demand that the settlements be disbanded. . . .

It simply declares: enough. Or: there is a limit. *Yesh gvul*. It provides a model of resistance. Of disobedience. For which there will always be penalties.

None of us have yet to endure anything like what these brave conscripts are enduring, many of whom have gone to jail. To speak for peace at this moment in this country is merely to be jeered (as in the recent Academy Awards ceremony), harassed, blacklisted (the banning by one powerful chain of radio stations of the Dixie Chicks); in short, to be reviled as unpatriotic. . . .

The usual way of heralding people who act on principle is to say that they are the vanguard of an eventually triumphant revolt against injustice.

But what if they're not? What if the evil is really unstoppable? At least in the short run. And that short run may be—is going to be—very long indeed.

My admiration for the soldiers who are resisting service in the Occupied Territories is as fierce as my belief that it will be a long time before their view prevails.

But what haunts me at this moment—for obvious reasons—is acting on principle when it isn't going to alter the obvious distribution of force, the rank injustice and murderousness of a government policy that claims to be acting in the name not of peace but of security. . . .

The force of arms has its own logic. If you commit an aggression and others resist, it is easy to convince the home front that the fighting must continue. Once the troops are there, they must be supported. It becomes irrelevant to question why the troops are there in the first place.

The soldiers are there because "we" are being attacked or menaced. Never mind that we may have attacked them first. They are now attacking back, causing casualties. Behaving in ways that defy the "proper" conduct of war. Behaving like "savages," as people in our part of the world like to call people in that part of the world. And their "savage" or "unlawful" actions give new justification to new aggressions. And new impetus to repress or censor or persecute citizens who oppose the aggression the government has undertaken.

Let's not underestimate the force of what we are opposing. The world is, for almost everyone, that over which we have virtually no control. Common sense and the sense of self-protectiveness tell us to accommodate to what we cannot change.

It's not hard to see how some of us might be persuaded of the justice, the necessity of a war. Especially of a war that is formulated as a small, limited military action that will actually contribute to peace or improve security; of an aggression that announces itself as a campaign of disarmament—admittedly, disarmament of the enemy, and, regrettably, requiring the application of overpowering force. An invasion that calls itself, officially, a liberation. . . .

Every violence in war has been justified as a retaliation. We are threatened. We are defending ourselves. The others, they want to kill us. We must stop them.

And from there: We must stop them before they have a chance to carry out their plans. And since those who would attack us are sheltering behind noncombatants, no aspect of civil life can be immune to our depredations.

Never mind the disparity of forces, of wealth, of firepower, or simply of population. How many Americans know that the population of Iraq is 24 million, half of whom are children? (The population of the United States, as you will remember, is 290 million.) Not to support those who are coming under fire from the enemy seems like treason. . . .

The dramaturgy of "acting on principle" tells us that we don't have to think about whether acting on principle is expedient, or whether we can count on the eventual success of the actions we have undertaken.

Acting on principle is, we're told, a good in itself.

But it is still a political act, in the sense that you're not doing it for yourself. You don't do it just to be in the right, or to appease your own conscience; much less because you are confident your action will achieve its aim. You resist as an act of solidarity. With communities of the principled and the disobedient: here, elsewhere. In the present. In the future.

Thoreau's going to prison in 1846 for refusing to pay the poll tax in protest against the American war on Mexico hardly stopped the war. But the resonance of that most unpunishing and briefest spell of imprisonment (famously, a single night in jail) has not ceased to inspire principled resistance to injustice through the second half of the twentieth century and into our new era. . . .

The likelihood that your acts of resistance cannot stop the injustice does not exempt you from acting in what you sincerely and reflectively hold to be the best interests of your community.

Thus: It is not in the best interests of Israel to be an oppressor.

Thus: It is not in the best interests of the United States to be a hyperpower, capable of imposing its will on any country in the world, as it chooses.

What is in the true interests of a modern community is justice.

It cannot be right to systematically oppress and confine a neighboring people. It is surely false to think that murder, expulsion, annexations, the building of walls—all that has contributed to reducing a whole people to dependence, penury and despair—will bring security and peace to the oppressors. . . .

Those brave Israeli Jews who, in fervent and active opposition to the policies of the present government of their country, have spoken up on behalf of the plight and the rights of Palestinians are defending the true interests of Israel. . . .

Beyond these struggles, which are worthy of our passionate adherence, it is important to remember that in programs of political resistance the relation of cause and effect is convoluted, and often indirect. All struggle, all resistance is—must be—concrete. And all struggle has a global resonance.

If not here, then there. If not now, then soon. Elsewhere as well as here.

To Archbishop Oscar Arnulfo Romero.

To Rachel Corrie.

And to Ishai Menuchin and his comrades.

. . .

Tribunals may well ensure accountability and show there will be no impunity. That is fine as far as it goes. But you need something other than retributive justice for healing. In and of itself, the judicial process is handicapped. It alone cannot be effective in reconciling a society divided by hatred.

What we found with our Truth and Reconciliation Commission was that it was enormously therapeutic and cleansing for victims to tell their stories. In a judicial process you have to prove guilt of the perpetrator by cross-examining witnesses on specific acts. The court must be objective and, legally speaking, equally hostile to the victim and the perpetrator.

In our commission, the sympathy for the dignity of the victim was assumed. And instead of being proven guilty beyond the shadow of a doubt, the perpetrator had to confess in order to get amnesty. That was the beginning, not the end, of the process. This combination of storytelling and confession put it all out in the open. With full disclosure, people feel they can move on.

(Archbishop Desmond Tutu from "War Crimes Tribunal May End Impurity but They Can't Heal Hatred")

• • •

THE COURAGE TO LOVE
Adelaide Donnelley

Like everyone else my reaction to the attack of 9/11 was one of fear, anger, and disorientation at the enormity of what had happened. But gradually, as the weeks went on, I came to believe that the best way to respond to such horrifying violence was to work, in whatever way I could, to bring empathy and understanding to my community and to the larger world. Searching for models of a nonviolent approach, I came across a man from the North-West Frontier Province of India (now Pakistan) who devoted his life to transforming violence using Islamic teachings as his guide. Badshah Khan was a member of the Pashtun tribe and a colleague of Gandhi's. Like Gandhi, he believed in the power of love to transform human relations. "It is my innermost conviction that Islam is work, faith and love," Khan once said. "Without love, the name 'Muslim' is sounding brass and tinkling cymbal."

The son of a wealthy landowner and village official, Khan was born into a more privileged home than many of his countrymen. But privilege is no protection against tragedy. In 1915, shortly after the birth of a second son, an influenza epidemic broke out, and his son fell ill. Khan and his wife watched helplessly as the child's condition worsened. One day his wife, in desperation, cried, "Allah, spare my son's life. Give his sickness to me." Later that afternoon the boy began to recover. Two days later Khan's young wife died. Beside himself with grief, Khan retreated to a small country mosque to fast and pray. Gradually, as he sat in silence, Khan found his grief subsiding and his heart filling with love. When he emerged several days later he committed himself to manifesting that love—using the Koran as his guide—through service to God and mankind. For the next seventy years, his activities and words never wavered from that goal.

Though Khan selflessly devoted himself to service, he was not free from negative emotions. At times, when his children were young, he became impatient and overbearing. Occasionally he even struck them in frustration. Alarmed at his angry and prideful tendencies, Khan realized that he must first transform himself before he could ask the same of his Pashtun countrymen. After an intense period of self-reflection and inner struggle, he left his two young sons with his parents and went from village to village, working to help others quell their violent tendencies and find new ways to resolve conflict. "Violence will always breed hatred," Khan told each person he met, "Nonviolence breeds love."

In 1929, feeling moved to take stronger measures, Khan created a nonviolent army of "soldiers" out of a hundred thousand sharp-shooting Pashtuns. Feeling that everyone was a child of God, Khan encouraged women to participate equally with men—an action that further alienated more rigid Mullahs.

Devoted to Khan, this improbable army of tribesmen and women committed themselves to transforming their own personal violence. They also set about eradicating social inequity in their communities and liberating their homeland from British rule. In response, the British treated Khan and his movement with a cruelty not shown to other followers of nonviolence in India. "The brutes must be ruled brutally," a British report on the Pashtuns exclaimed. Despite this treatment, the Pashtun army carried no weapons, for Khan believed that nonviolence was "the only form of force which can have a lasting effect."

During this period Khan was introduced to the work of Gandhi, who, at the time, was conducting his own experiment with nonviolence in India. Over time, the two became friends, and Gandhi was deeply impressed by the young Pashtun—Khan's ability to transform his warring tribesmen into soldiers for nonviolence was a confirmation of all Gandhi believed. As their friendship deepened, they traveled together urging nonviolence and self-rule for India. At the same time, they protested the proposed partition of India, an act both felt would threaten Hindu-Muslim unity. Challenging British imperial control in the area, Khan was repeatedly imprisoned (he spent 40 of his 99 years in prison).

With the partition of India and the jockeying for power in newly-formed Pakistan, Khan was increasingly marginalized by those in power. Threatened by his popularity, the new leaders repeatedly jailed him and ultimately disempowered his Pashtun followers. But despite what he suffered personally, Khan never wavered from his belief in nonviolence. Whether in jail or out, he continued to work to make his thoughts and actions an indivisible whole.

It was a testament to the force of love Khan radiated, that on the day of his funeral in 1988—for the first time since the Soviet Occupation—Afghanistan opened its borders. On that day, thousands of grieving Pashtuns crossed over the Khyber Pass, carrying Khan's coffin to his home in Jalalabad. Thousands more who stayed behind in Afghanistan joined the mourners in spirit, and a cease-fire was declared so that all could pay tribute to his life. In death, as in life, Khan united people in a spirit of peace.

During the current situation, not only in Iraq but Afghanistan and much of the Mideast, it is crucial for the world to remember what Khan accomplished in the North-West Frontier Province. At a time when our present day world is experiencing so much conflict, it is important to know that in the midst of one of the most vengeful and feuding climates in history, the light of love was still able to shine.

· · ·

In addition to anger, for a long time I experienced a lot of guilt about having survived. How come I survived when so many didn't?

Through the practice of mindfulness, my survivor's guilt, to a large extent, is being transformed into an intense sense of responsibility. Though in a technical sense I was ordained as a Zen Buddhist monk by Bernie Glassman, I have come to feel that I was also ordained by all those who have died. I feel an intense responsibility to everyone who's ever died in war, in any war. For every American soldier who died, for every South Vietnamese soldier who died, for every civilian who died, for every Vietcong soldier who died—for every person who's ever died in that war or any war, I feel an intense responsibility, because they are in me. An intense responsibility because I have been given the awareness, through the death of these people, through their sacrifice, that war and violence are never a solution.

(Claude Anshin Thomas, from *At Hell's Gate: A Soldier's Journey from War to Peace*)

. . .

THE GREATEST DANGER

Joanna Macy

How do we live with the fact that we are destroying our world?

Because of social taboos, despair at the state of our world and fear for our future are rarely acknowledged or expressed directly. The suppression of despair, like that of any deep recurring response, contributes to the numbing of the psyche. Expressions of anguish or outrage are muted, deadened as if a nerve had been cut. This refusal to feel impoverishes our emotional and sensory life. Flowers are dimmer and less fragrant, our loves less ecstatic. We create diversions for ourselves as individuals and as nations in the fights we pick, the aims we pursue, and the stuff we buy.

Of all the dangers we face, from climate chaos to permanent war, none is so great as this deadening of our response. For psychic numbing impedes our capacity to process and respond to information. The energy expended in pushing down despair is diverted from more crucial uses, depleting the resilience and imagination needed for fresh visions and strategies.

Zen poet Thich Nhat Hanh was asked, "What do we most need to do to save our world?" His answer was this: "What we most need to do is to hear within us the sounds of the Earth crying."

Cracking the Shell

How to confront what we scarcely dare to think? How to face our grief and fear and rage without "going to pieces"?

It is good to realize that falling apart is not such a bad thing. Indeed it is as essential to transformation as the cracking of outgrown shells. Anxieties and doubts can be healthy and creative, not only for the person but for the society, because they permit new and original approaches to reality.

What disintegrates in periods of rapid transformation is not the self, but its defenses and assumptions. Self-protection restricts vision and movement like a suit of armor, making it harder to adapt. Going to pieces, however uncomfortable, can open us up to new perceptions, new data, and new responses.

In our culture, despair is feared and resisted because it represents a loss of control. We're ashamed of it and dodge it by demanding instant solutions to problems. We seek the quick fix. This cultural habit obscures our perceptions and fosters a dangerous innocence of the real world.

Acknowledging despair, on the other hand, involves nothing more mysterious than telling the truth about what we see and know and feel is happening to our world. When corporate-controlled media keep the public in the dark, and power-holders manipulate events to create a climate of fear and obedience, truth-telling is like oxygen. It enlivens and returns us to health and vigor.

Belonging to All Life

Sharing what is in our heartmind brings a welcome shift in identity, as we recognize that the anger, grief, and fear we feel for our world are not reducible to concerns for our individual welfare or even survival. Our concerns are far larger than our own private needs and wants. Pain for the world—the outrage and the sorrow—breaks us open to a larger sense of who we are. It is a doorway to the realization of our mutual belonging in the web of life.

Many of us fear that confrontation with despair will bring loneliness and isolation. On the contrary, in letting go of old defenses we find truer community. And in community, we learn to trust our inner responses to our world—and find our power.

You are not alone! We are part of a vast, global movement: the epochal transition from empire to Earth community. This is the Great Turning. And the excitement, the alarm, even the overwhelm we feel, are all part of our waking up to this collective adventure.

As in any true adventure, there is risk and uncertainty. Our corporate economy is destroying both itself and the natural world. Its effect on living systems is what David Korten calls the Great Unraveling. It is happening at the same time as the Great Turning, and we cannot know which way the story will end.

Great Uncertainty

Let's drop the notion that we can manage our planet for our own comfort and profit—or even that we can now be its ultimate redeemers. It is a delusion. Let's accept, in its place, the radical uncertainty of our time, even the uncertainty of survival.

In primal societies, adolescents go through rites of passage, where confronting their own mortality is a gateway to maturity. In analogous ways, climate change calls us to recognize our own mortality as a species. With the gift of uncertainty, we can grow up and accept the rights and responsibility of planetary adulthood. Then we know fully that we belong, inextricably, to the web of life. Then we can serve it and let its strength flow through us.

Uncertainty, when accepted, sheds a bright light on the power of intention. That is what you can count on: not the outcome, but the motivation you bring, the vision you hold, the compass setting you choose to follow.

Our intention and our resolve can save us from getting lost in grief. During a recent visit to Kentucky, I learned what is happening to the landscape and culture of Appalachia: how coal companies use dynamite to pulverize everything above the underground seams of coal; how bulldozers and dragline machines 20-stories high push away the "overburden" of woodlands and top soil, filling the valleys. I saw how the activists are held steady by sheer intention. Though the nation seems oblivious to this tragedy, these men and women persist in the vision that Appalachia can, in part, be saved. They hold to their resolve that future generations may know slopes of sweetgum, sassafras, magnolia, the stirrings of bobcat and coon, and, in the hollows, the music of fiddle and fresh flowing streams. They seem to know—and, when we let down our guard, we too know—that we are living parts of the living body of Earth.

This is the gift of the Great Turning. When we open our eyes to what is happening, even when it breaks our hearts, we discover our true [dimensions]; for our heart, when it breaks open, can hold the whole universe. We discover how speaking the truth of our anguish for the world brings down the walls between us, drawing us into deep solidarity. And that solidarity, with our neighbors and all that lives, is all the more real for the uncertainty we face. When we stop distracting ourselves trying to figure the chances of ultimate success or failure, our minds and hearts are liberated into the present moment. And this moment together [is] alive and charged with possibilities.

. . .

THANKS BUT NO THANKS
Bokara Legendre

In one of his many lives, Buddha was a hare that lived peacefully in a mountain forest eating grass and leaves. His friends were an ape, a jackal, and a young otter whom he taught to eschew evil and do good in the way of giving alms to the poor and spending holy days fasting. However, he was distressed that as a rabbit, he had nothing much of worth to offer. After much thought, he decided to offer himself.

One day hopping about the woods he met a Brahman traveler and was inspired to say to him, "Kindle a fire for your dinner." Once the fire was roaring, the rabbit shook the dust off his fluffy coat and jumped in, finally content that he was giving himself as a meal to the Brahman and dying in the flames of compassion and purification.

Although this may seem a bit extreme, scientists actually have proven that we are hardwired to be compassionate and kind. When sensors are connected to various parts of the human brain and films of compassionate acts shown the subjects, the pleasure center in the brain lights up at the sight of altruistic behavior. We enjoy being helpful and philanthropic.

Since what makes us happy is apparently seeing other living beings more comfortable or happier, why is it that institutions find it infinitely easier to raise money for bricks and mortar than for people or animals? Build a monastery and the money for architecture comes easily. Try to raise funds for the people who teach, live, and work there, and few are interested in giving. The Metropolitan Museum attaches a bronze plaque bearing the donor's name to the door of a multimillion dollar room. For a higher donation, one can have a marble plaque. Donors are lined up to present plaque-bearing rooms. However, I'm told, few want to fund operating expenses that include salaries for museum and maintenance staff. The same is true for organizations such as theaters and churches. Donors prefer something concrete—odd, when you think we see from the plaque-bearing seat a marvelous play in the theater; animals peeking through the iron bars in the zoo; flowers in the garden.

Why do so many of us make the mistake of thinking that immortality lies in stone or wood? I think it's because we see a material thing manifested and imagine that it is durable, wishing to be so ourselves, imagining generations of people thanking us and admiring us, even celebrating us for our largesse. I thought that way myself. And now I see the error of my ways.

For my first foray into Buddhist building, I contributed to a modest meditation cottage at an institution with which I had a long connection. It was in fact a "cottage small by a waterfall," a wooden yurt destined for a circle of zafus facing away from its lovely view. I felt quite puffed up with pleasure over this fine new sacred space, and looked forward to the promised (but yet undetermined) day of its initiation. I thought they would have a little meditation ceremony and thank me.

What was held instead was a gala occasion complete with a parade of Tibetan flags, Chinese flute players, and general feasting to honor the installation of a special bowl in the stream. The date of this opening celebration was not divulged to me, and it occurred while I was briefly away on a trip. I discovered later that it had been great fun, and there was no mention of me.

Chastened, but, as yet, unenlightened, I figured there had been some mistake—an unusual slight I had best overlook. I was given a second chance at minor immortality when I presented a much-desired statue of the founding priest of a local Buddhist monastery to the shrine room. Again, I anticipated a moment of tribute and thanks, only to discover the statue behind the ladies room door, as I entered it on my way from a day's sitting in the zendo. Returning to my cushion, what could I do but laugh at the possibly unintended comment on my grandiosity.

Worried that I was doing "it" wrong, and not a little hurt, I conferred with a Buddhist priest about my expectations in giving to spiritual institutions and my disappointment at their distinct lack of fulfillment. He assured me two oversights was not a rule, and then urged me to present *his* monastery with a much-needed piece of boring equipment. He promised I would be properly celebrated for this munificence. Naturally I bit this bone to my starving vanity with a vice-like grip.

On the appointed day it was raining. We met in the monastery parking lot, each gripping a black umbrella. We slogged through the red mud and puddles to a shack in which the machinery whirred. He lit a bunch of Tibetan incense sticks, planted them in the sloshy muck outside the door, recited a short incomprehensible chant, and we rushed back to our respective cars.

I recognized that philanthropy to Buddhist institutions is for me a Buddhist lesson—a few short raps with the master's stick for my need to be important. I come away noticing the mysterious ways of spiritual teaching which always give me what I need, not what I want. For me, there will be no bells and whistles where spiritual giving is concerned. . . .

Giving (whether cash or physical help) to individuals—human and animal—is the most satisfying and heart-warming experience because afterward I see a life made a tiny bit happier. I think Bill Gates has got the secret. I notice that his money is going to save individual lives, not to building monuments. Just to remind myself what the secret is again—bricks and mortar crumble. Give support to the people, and they will build the supports they need. Caregivers can create a hospital in a tent. It's not zoos that are needed to protect animals . . . from poachers and overcrowding, but guards who will protect their habitats so the animals can stay at home and be wild.

I decided I was just getting too materialistic with the buildings and things. Helping the people instead of the places might be the answer. . . . Bill Gates has spent thirty billion dollars on a program based on two simple concepts: "every life is equally valuable" and "to whom much has been given much is expected." This last is the basis that started America off in its splendid role as the world's most generous country of personal philanthropists, the Rockefellers and the Carnegies leading the way. Traditionally, the privilege of money came with the duty to give it away. As a nation, however, we are not very philanthropic. According to a recent *New York Times* piece, our government's bilateral philanthropy stands about equal with Portugal's. We are not a kind nation, but we are a nation of kind people.

Recently, philanthropy has famously become a means of social climbing. Individuals may rise from just about any social strata to the highest reaches of society in this country by presenting a vast something and having it named for them. A lot gets done this way. Art investments have been an important rung in the social ladder. A good example is Robert and Ethel Scull. He was a taxi fleet owner from Brooklyn who started buying [works by] Robert Rauschenberg, Jasper Johns, and Andy Warhol when those artists were virtually unknown. Indeed, Rauschenberg and Johns were surviving by designing the windows in Tiffany's. Soon the Sculls' house became the center of hip New York society, and the day I met the Sculls, Ethel was deciding whether to wear a real Courrèges or a fake to be immortalized (and encased) in plaster by Bob Motherwell. They had arrived. And so had the artists.

But what about the beggars outside Tiffany's . . . ? Or the ragged men in the subway? Or on the park bench? To how many people can one dole dollars all day, and how many of them are just saving up to buy drugs? These are the questions everyone is faced with. What percentage of one's income is enough? What percentage of one's time is enough? Over- whelmed, I often do nothing or the wrong thing. Sometimes, as in the case of [Hurricane] Katrina, one is so overwhelmed with the enormity of the need, I feel like [a deer] caught in the headlights. What can I give? I guess everything, but I'm just not there yet.

My own hang-ups with helping seem to center on being thanked. I'm coming around, as a matter of self-preservation, to the view that the lesson I came to philanthropy to learn is: love anonymity, because if I love whatever life brings me, without expectations, I will be happy. I did not learn this exclusively through giving to spiritual institutions. Life is chockablock with proof that one is unimportant. Buddhists do seem to have it right with the idea that it's all emptiness. No thing. No fuss.

Life is just so heartbreakingly full of . . . desperation [that] I know now I have to keep my sense of humor in the face of the suffering and continue my own hopelessly foible-filled attempts at alleviating even the tiniest bit. Although the Buddha gave up all his goods and chattel in one life and burned himself up for dinner in another, I don't believe anyone formally thanked him, and I don't believe he cared.

. . .

Many of us find it difficult to consider giving money to people we've never met, living in distant countries we've never visited. This obviously doesn't get any easier during periods of economic uncertainty, when many people are justifiably anxious about their own economic prospects. While I don't seek to diminish in any way the challenges that attend tough economic times, we should remember that even in the worst of times, our lives remain infinitely better than those of people living in extreme poverty. I'm hoping that you will look at the larger picture and think what it takes to live ethically in a world in which 18 million people are dying unnecessarily each year.

(Peter Singer, from *The Life You Can Save: Acting Now to End World Poverty*)

. . .

THE GENERATION OF TRUST
Tyrone Cashman

As the First World War, the result largely of a serious miscalculation, had sunk into a senseless bloodbath where tens of thousands of young men had for months been slaughtering each other for the sake of gaining a few yards of territory, an urgency was felt in the Wilson administration that somehow a workable exit strategy be found. According to anthropologist Gregory Bateson, it was a public relations man, George Creel, who proposed that the Germans might surrender if they were offered soft armistice terms. He proposed a set of soft terms, assuring territorial integrity and requiring no reparations. These were then drawn up into Fourteen Points by an *inquiry* of 150 advisors applying them to issues likely to arise in a peace conference. Ten months later these Points became the basis of the terms of German surrender.

It is well known that, once the Germans had lain down their arms, the English, French, and Italian leaders, dragging the American President along, turned around and drafted the Treaty of Versailles imposing crushing reparations on Germany. These not only broke the economy of Germany, but literally de-moralized the nation and its political processes.

As Bateson points out, the most important thing among all mammals, not just humans, is our relationship with each other. The ethics of talk within a war are different from the ethics of talk *about* war. Pursuing a war requires spying, camouflage, cryptic codes, and intentional deceit. Pursuing peace talks requires negotiations with a certain good faith. Just as hostilities require constant suspicion, so discussions about ending hostilities must be done honorably, with assumptions of basic trust. Without this, there is no longer any natural limit to violence.

The deception of Versailles, and the crushing monetary reparations, followed by the further impoverishment of the global Great Depression, crushed the morale and distorted the moral sensibility of the German people. The perpetrators of that great betrayal, the victorious countries, also were *de*-moralized. Those who were observers at the Versailles event could see that the seeds of another, perhaps more horrible, war were being sown.

The Second World War came right on schedule, guided into place by arrogance, cowardice, fear, and complacency on one side and rage, bitterness, and hatred on the other. European wars up to this time had been limited wars. After the Versailles Treaty there were no longer limits. Blitzkriegs and concentration camps with mass murder of non-combatants were not only thinkable but done by one side, and carpet bombing of civilian men, women, and children was calmly planned and carried out by the other.

The question of this essay is: Is there any way back from such horror? Anthropologists of communication have looked at what is required to rebuild a context of trust, starting from a position equal to total war.

Focusing on how evolution solved the risky situation of extremely well-armed predators of large mammals, the wolves, who live and hunt in packs, Bateson notes that in order for a wolf pack to live in safety, each male must trust the other not to kill him. In wolves, a built-in social ethos prevents most internecine killing. It has two central elements. Competition for food and for females soon sorts out which male wolf is going to be the alpha. Skirmishes among wolves new to a pack quickly clarify which wolves are one's superior in fighting and which are one's inferior. Each wolf ends up knowing who he can intimidate and who can intimidate him. If he keeps to his place in the hierarchy he will not be hurt. But skirmishes continue to happen to reinforce the structure of the hierarchy in everyone's mind. The real question is, what keeps such skirmishes from being lethal? What is it that keeps a wolf pack at strength for the risky team effort of bringing down a moose or caribou? It is a complex set of signals that prevent the dominant wolf in a fight from killing the subdominant one—*if* he makes the right moves. When one wolf is wounded, or sees that he will very soon be wounded by his opponent during a fight, he will suddenly let go of all defensive posture and throw himself on the ground with his throat entirely exposed to the winner. Utterly defenseless, the loser might have his throat ripped out in an instant. And the winning wolf does leap upon him and grab his throat and growl fiercely. But instead of ripping out the throat, he only holds it tight in his teeth and growls for many minutes.

There is a message here. In species that do not have symbolic language, there is no way to indicate the idea of "no" or "not" except by a gesture that would normally do something, but is held back from doing it. When canines play, they nip at each other and growl—which are aggressive gestures. But in play, puppies do not *really* bite. They just play bite—a little bite or nip that does not harm the other. So, too, the alpha wolf lets the other wolf know that he will not kill him, even though he could. This violent play makes it clear that it is entirely due to the intention of the other that one is not being killed. This develops loyalty and trust, up and down the hierarchy, the essential social glue in a hunting team.

Anthropologist Terrence Deacon has commented in a similar way on the trust-creating ritual of the Yanomamo people in South America. Their ethnographer, Napolean Chagnon, reports that these forest tribes are in continual state of guerilla warfare with each other, with sneak attacks to kill unwary men, or capture unwary women, who go outside the protective palisade of their villages. Their food source is slash-and-burn horticulture. When, after a few years, the soil of their gardens is depleted they must create new fields farther away, and move their villages. But with hostile neighboring tribes it is too dangerous to make such a large move. Because of this, a ritual of mutual trust-building must be created.

The neighboring hostile tribe is invited to a feast inside the protective palisade of the tribe that has to move. The home tribe hides their weapons out of reach, and the men lie down in their hammocks defenseless. Then the outside tribe comes into the village, armed to the teeth. One after another, each warrior makes a very convincing attack with axe or bow and arrow on each of the home village men, but holds back the blow just inches from the head or throat of the victim. The home village men lie calmly through this.

Then the ritual is reversed, and the outside villagers lie down in the hammocks while the home village men go through their vicious but mock attacks. If this ritual has been successfully completed, with each man encountering each other man without serious wounding or killing, a feast is presented. Stories are told about how some other neighboring tribe is the common enemy of both these tribes, and plans are made on how to attack them together. Mutual trust is thus created, and the home tribe can safely create new gardens and move their village.

We are one of the mammal species that have evolved ways to re-engender trust, once it has been lost.

It seems that the Allies in the Second World War began such a process, perhaps without fully realizing it. The War in both the European theatre and the Pacific theatre of WWII ended, not with an armistice, but with Unconditional Surrender. Versailles had rendered a negotiated peace impossible.

The Japanese of Okinawa were convinced that when the Americans took the island they would rape and kill and torture in ways that no one could imagine. Anyone agreeing to Unconditional Surrender knows that all such eventualities are possible. Because of this fear, large numbers of Japanese civilians leapt from the high Okinawan cliffs to their deaths to keep from being taken prisoner by the Americans.

But the American soldiers who moved into occupy Okinawa were mostly peaceful. And when General MacArthur took over in Tokyo as the virtual dictator of the nation of Japan, the people were astonished to find that he treated them with dignity and honored their practices and ways of governing.

In Europe, similarly, because much was destroyed, the Unconditional Surrender was followed by humanitarian aid from the U.S. for two years. But, after two years, when it was clear that Europe was not going to be able to rebuild due to drained treasuries, Secretary of State Marshall conceived of the Plan to help Europe rebuild itself. Many billions of dollars flowed to the countries of Europe, including Germany. Aid was also offered to the Soviet Union, but Stalin did not accept it, and forbade the East Bloc countries to accept it. The Plan worked in Western Europe with such extreme success that the countries of Europe rebuilt quickly to levels of agricultural and industrial production exceeding their pre-war levels.

In effect, what the Allies did at the end of the Second World War was to reverse the Versailles formula. They demanded Unconditional Surrender and then reacted without vengeance or punishment but instead with help and support. The First World War was ended with a seductively acceptable negotiated armistice followed by betrayal and revenge.

If the subsequent healing of relationships with Germany and Italy and Japan did not grab the surprised attention of the world, it was certainly because the escalating competition with the Soviet Union and the East Bloc countries, together with McCarthyism in the U.S., thoroughly distracted America's attention.

One of the Marshall Plan's central institutions was the Organization of European Economic Cooperation. It was Europeans who were going to organize and rebuild Europe, said Marshall, with the help of American aid. But, cooperation and trade between European countries was a requirement of the Plan. Here were the seeds of what came to be the European Union. The Organization of European Economic Cooperation (OEEC) was the training ground for structures and bureaucrats who would later put together the European Community. This matured into the OECD of today. Another organization, the European Coal and Steel Community, was put in place, and Germany joined it in 1951. This organization was the taproot of the European Economic Community.

Working independently and parallel with this effort was the lone political visionary, the religiously motivated Catholic, Robert Schuman, whose tireless efforts toward his vision of a united Europe overcame a mountain of skepticism. In addition, quietly working to bring the youth in all the European countries together to get to know each other over summer work projects, was an organization of reconciled Protestants and Catholics, the Le Mouvement Chrétien pour la Paix.

Out of situations of enormous suspicion and hatred arising from millions of families having lost sons in military deaths in the First War, followed by extreme betrayal in the Peace Treaty, came a War larger and more horrible than any known before. Then, out of that War, with all its mass murders and mass bombings by both sides of the conflict, have come levels of cooperation and healthy competition hard to believe by those who had lived through the horrors of the early forties. History is not simply, "a nightmare from which we do not wake up." Trust can be rebuilt after it is utterly shattered. There are ways to do it.

We have proved it can be done. The orgasmic pleasure of hatred and violence can be redirected into the pleasures of cooperation, of a sense of security and of economic well-being that will arise from intelligent cooperation.

. . .

PRAYER

Carolyn Forché

Begin again among the poorest, moments off, in another time and
place.
Belongings gathered in the last hour, visible invisible:
Tin spoon, teacup, tremble of tray, carpet hanging from sorrow's
balcony.
Say goodbye to everything. With a wave of your hand, gesture to all
you have known.
Begin with bread torn from bread, beans given to the hungriest, a
carcass of flies.
Take the polished stillness from a locked church, prayer notes left
between stones.
Answer them and hoist in your net voices from the troubled hours.
Sleep only when the least among them sleeps, and then only until
the birds.
Make the flatbed truck your time and place. Make the least daily
wage as your value.
Language will rise then like language from the mouth of a still river.
No one's mouth.
Bring night to your imaginings. Bring the darkest passage of your
holy book.

. . .

It's time for the quiet voices to get loud.

We soft-spoken peace lovers must raise our voices and let it be known that we can lovingly and aggressively reach across those invisible lines that divide us into competing groups.

We must work hard to understand who our "enemies" are. We have to listen hard in order to articulate, loudly and clearly, the truths we have come to understand.

We can and must pursue peace with furious energy and focus.

(Cathy Schwartzman Lawrence, from "Loud Peace")

• • •

HINDU PRAYER FOR PEACE
(translated by Mohandas Gandhi)

I desire neither earthly kingdom
nor even freedom from birth and death.
I desire only the deliverance
from grief of all those afflicted by misery
Oh Lord lead us from the unreal to the real;
from darkness to light,
from death to immortality.
May there be peace in celestial regions
May there be peace on earth,
May the waters be appeasing,
May herbs be wholesome,
and may trees and plants bring peace to all.
May all beneficent beings bring peace to us.
May thy wisdom spread peace all through the world.
May all things be a source of peace to all and to me.

Contributor Biographies

JENNIFER ABRAHAMSON is a journalist who has worked as a humanitarian spokesperson for the United Nations in Africa. Her latest book, *Sweet Relief*, is about Marla Ruzicka, who founded the Campaign for Innocent Victims in Conflict (www.civicworldwide.org). When at age 24, Marla was killed by a roadside bomb, she was working in Iraq to prevent civilian deaths.

EQBAL AHMAD was a Pakistani writer and anti-war activist who taught all over the world, including the United States, before returning to Pakistan where he wrote a weekly column for the oldest English language journal, *Dawn*.

LEILA AHMED is the first professor of Women's Studies in Religion at Harvard Divinity School. Born and raised in Egypt, she is the author of *Women and Gender in Islam* and *A Border Passage: from Cairo to America*.

TAHA MUHAMMAD ALI is a leading figure in contemporary Palestinian poetry. He has published six volumes of poems, including *So What: New and Selected Poems (with a Story) 1971–2005*.

ST. THOMAS AQUINAS was a twelfth-century Italian Catholic priest who was the foremost proponent of natural theology and author of the *Summa Theologica*. He was a masterful theologian, an influential philosopher, and considered to be the model teacher for the priesthood.

HANNAH ARENDT, eminent philosopher and a German Jewish survivor of the Holocaust, is the author of many classic works, including *The Origins of Totalitarianism*.

REZA BARAHENI, founder of modern literary criticism in Iran, was imprisoned in 1973, tortured and beaten. The author of more than fifty books, he currently lives and teaches in Canada.

NATHAN D. BAXTER, formerly dean of Washington National Cathedral, is the 10th Bishop of the Episcopal diocese of Central Pennsylvania.

ERNEST BECKER, the eminent cultural anthropologist and interdisciplinary scientific thinker and writer, won the Pulitzer Prize in 1974 for *The Denial of Death*.

CLAUDIA BERNARDI is a native of Argentina. Her work as an artist, teacher, and human rights activist has carried her to many war-torn regions, from Ethiopia to El Salvador (www.wallsofhope.org).

WENDELL BERRY has worked on a hillside farm in Kentucky for more than three decades. An outspoken social and environmental critic, he is the author of more than thirty books of poetry, fiction, and essays.

FRITJOF CAPRA, physicist and systems theorist, is a founding director of the Center for Ecoliteracy in Berkeley (www.ecoliteracy.org). He is the author of several international bestsellers, including *The Tao of Physics* and *The Hidden Connections: A Science for Sustainable Living*.

KARIN LOFTHUS CARRINGTON is a psychotherapist, consultant, writer, and teacher whose work focuses on the interrelationship of depth psychology, spirituality, and social conscience. She has taught at John F. Kennedy and Pacifica Graduate Universities and is the co-editor of the volume *Same Sex Love and the Path to Wholeness*.

TYRONE CASHMAN, an early pioneer in large-scale implementation of renewable energy systems, is presently researching and writing on the evolutionary foundations of science, ethics, and religion.

MELODY ERMACHILD CHAVIS is the author of *Altars in the Streets*. She has worked as a part of the defense teams of twenty-five prisoners on California's death row and for others on federal death row. She is devoted to the abolition of the death penalty.

PEMA CHÖDRÖN is a Buddhist teacher and head abbot at Gampo Abbey, Cape Breton, Nova Scotia, the first Tibetan monastery for Westerners. She has written many books, including *Practicing Peace in Times of War*.

DEEPAK CHOPRA is acknowledged as one of the world's greatest leaders in the field of mind-body medicine. He is the Director of the Chopra Center for Wellbeing (www.chopra.com).

HIS HOLINESS THE FOURTEENTH DALAI LAMA, Tenzin Gyatso, is both the head of state and the spiritual leader of Tibet. He was awarded the Nobel Peace Prize in 1989.

MAHMOUD DARWISH was a prominent Palestinian poet and writer of prose. He published over thirty volumes of poetry and eight books of prose.

MIKE DAVIS is an American social commentator, urban theorist, historian, and political activist, now a professor in the Department of History at the University of California, Irvine.

JOAN DIDION is a distinguished writer, highly esteemed as a journalist, essayist, and novelist. She was awarded the National Book Award in 2005 for *The Year of Magical Thinking*.

SUSAN DOMINUS is a journalist with the *New York Times* where she writes the Metro Column.

ADELAIDE DONNELLEY has worked as a psychologist, photographer, and writer. Her book, *Sorrow Mountain*, tells the story of a Tibetan nun imprisoned by the Chinese for twenty years.

ARIEL DORFMAN, the renowned Argentine-Chilean novelist, playwright, essayist, academic, and human rights activist, was forced out of Chile during the Pinochet coup. He teaches literature and Latin American studies at Duke University.

SHIRIN EBADI is an Iranian lawyer, human rights activist, and founder of the Children's Rights Support Association in Iran. She was awarded the 2003 Nobel Peace Prize for her pioneering efforts for democracy and women's and human rights in Iran.

JAN EGELAND was the United Nations Undersecretary-General for Humanitarian Affairs and Emergency Relief Coordinator from June 2003 to December 2006. He is currently Secretary General of the Norwegian Red Cross.

RIANE EISLER, founder of the Center for Partnership Studies (www.partnershipway.org), is best known for her international bestseller *The Chalice and The Blade: Our History, Our Future*. Her latest work is *The Real Wealth of Nations: Creating a Caring Economics*.

DANIEL ELLSBERG, advisor to the Department of Defense under Nixon, and now a lecturer and activist on the dangers of the nuclear era, was the subject of the 2010 Academy Award–nominated documentary, *The Most Dangerous Man in America*. He is the author of *Secrets*, an account of his decision to release the Pentagon Papers to the *New York Times*.

JODIE EVANS served as part of Governor Jerry Brown's administration and organized his campaign for president in 1992. She has organized movements for ecology, feminism, and civil rights as a founding member of Code Pink for Peace (www.codepink4peace.org).

MORGAN FARLEY is a psychotherapist and writer whose work has been nominated for a Pushcart Prize and a Discovery Award.

THE FIQH COUNCIL OF NORTH AMERICA is an association of Muslims who interpret Islamic law on the North American continent. Its eighteen members issue religious rulings, resolve disputes, and answer questions relating to the Islamic faith.

CINDY FOLKERS, a radiation and health specialist, has written and presented on the health hazards of radiation exposure and sustainable alternatives to nuclear power. She holds a master's degree in environmental science from Johns Hopkins University.

CAROLYN FORCHÉ is an American poet, editor, and human rights advocate. Her powerful collection of poetry, *The Country between Us*, made many North American readers aware of the U.S. supported violations of human rights in Latin America. Her anthology *Against Forgetting* has become an indispensable classic.

SIGMUND FREUD, the founder of psychoanalysis, is known for his theories of the unconscious mind. He is considered to be one of the major thinkers of the twentieth century.

ERICH FROMM was an internationally renowned Jewish-German-American psychologist and philosopher, associated with the Frankfurt School of Critical Theory. His works included *Escape from Freedom* and *The Art of Loving*.

MOHANDAS GANDHI was the great political and spiritual leader for India, when India was still under the rule of the British Empire. Through his pioneering philosophy Satyagraha—the resistance of tyranny through mass civil disobedience—he led India to its independence.

CAROL GILLIGAN is an American feminist, ethicist, and psychologist who is currently a professor at New York University. She is best known for her 1982 work, "In a Different Voice."

DANIEL GOLEMAN, the former behavioral and brain science editor for the *New York Times,* is the author of numerous best-selling books, including *Emotional Intelligence, Social Intelligence,* and more recently, *Ecological Intelligence* (www.danielgoleman.info).

MIRIAM GREENSPAN is a psychotherapist, writer, and public speaker. She is the author of *Healing through the Dark Emotions: The Wisdom of Grief, Fear, and Despair.*

SUSAN GRIFFIN, author of *Woman and Nature: The Roaring Inside Her,* *A Chorus of Stones* (a finalist for the Pulitzer Prize), and *Wrestling with the Angel of Democracy,* has received many awards, including a Guggenheim Fellowship (www.susangriffin.com).

THE MOST REVEREND FRANK T. GRISWOLD, III was the twenty-fifth Presiding Bishop and Primate of the Episcopal Church in the United States of America.

HAFIZ was a twelfth-century Persian mystic and poet. His lyrical poems, known as *ghazals,* are noted for their beauty and for bringing to fruition the love, mysticism, and Sufi themes that had pervaded early Persian poetry.

MARTHA HARRELL is a Jungian analyst and faculty member of the CG Jung Institute of New York where she teaches alchemy. She is a former faculty member of the Yale School of Medicine.

VÁCLAV HAVEL is a prominent Czech writer and dramatist, the ninth and last president of Czechoslovakia (1989–1992), and the first president of the Czech Republic (1993–2003).

CHRIS HEDGES was awarded the Pulitzer Prize in 2002 as part of the team of reporters at *The New York Times* for coverage of global terrorism. He was foreign correspondent for nearly two decades reporting for *The Christian Science Monitor* and National Public Radio. His books include *Collateral Damage, American's War against Iraqi Civilians,* with Laila Al-Arian.

JUDITH HERMAN is a psychiatrist, researcher, teacher, and author who has focused on the understanding and treatment of incest and traumatic stress. She is a professor of clinical psychiatry at Harvard University Medical School.

JAMES HILLMAN is an American psychologist, writer, and international lecturer as well as a private practitioner. His magnum opus, *Re-visioning Psychology*, written in 1975, was nominated for the Pulitzer Prize.

JANE HIRSHFIELD, distinguished poet, critic, and translator, has written many books of poetry including *After* (2006), and *Given Sugar, Given Salt* (2001), the latter a finalist for the National Book Critics Circle Award.

TERRI JENTZ, the author of *Strange Piece of Paradise*, a finalist for the 2006 National Book Critics Circle Award, the LA Times Book Award, and the Edgar Allan Poe Award, is an essayist and screenwriter.

MARTIN LUTHER KING, JR., the American clergyman, activist, and prominent leader in the African American Civil Rights Movement, was awarded the Nobel Peace Prize in 1964 and posthumously awarded the Presidential Medal of Freedom in 1977. He is remembered and revered throughout the world for his courageous and visionary leadership.

AARON KIPNIS, the author of *Knights without Armor*, teaches at Pacifica Graduate Institute. He is an advisor to several organizations, including the California Youth Authority and the Harvard School of Education.

HENRY A. KISSINGER is a German-born American political scientist, diplomat, and recipient of the Nobel Peace Prize. He served as National Security Advisor and later concurrently as Secretary of State under Presidents Nixon and Ford.

JACK KORNFIELD was trained as a Buddhist monk in Thailand, Burma, and India and has taught around the world since 1974. He holds a Ph.D. in clinical psychology from Harvard. He is a co-founder of the Insight Meditation Society and The Spirit Rock Center (www.spiritrock.org). His most recent book is *The Wise Heart*.

STANLEY KUNITZ was a distinguished American poet, author of many volumes. He served as U.S. Poet Laureate twice, in 1974 and again in 2000.

GEORGE LAKOFF, author of *Moral Politics: How Liberals and Conservatives Think*, has published several volumes that have made major contributions to the science of cognition and linguistics. He is a professor of cognitive linguistics at the University of California at Berkeley.

ANNE LAMOTT, author of several novels and nonfiction works including *Plan B: Further Thoughts on Faith*, is well known for her engagingly authentic, wise, and often humorous voice. She is also a progressive political activist, public speaker, and teacher.

CATHY SCHWARTZMAN LAWRENCE is currently Associate Cantor at Temple Ner Tamid in Bloomfield, New Jersey, and teaches on the voice faculty of the Brooklyn Youth Chorus Academy. She has also performed as an opera singer and as a folk singer.

BARBARA LEE has been a member of the United States House of Representatives since 1998, representing California's 9th congressional district. She was the only person in Congress to vote against authorizing the war in Iraq.

BOKARA LEGENDRE is a painter, writer, and performance artist who has produced and hosted a series of television and radio interview programs and has worked as a reporter for a variety of publications including the *New York Times*.

DENISE LEVERTOV, the eminent poet, who wrote and published twenty books of poetry, including *Candles in Babylon*. Among her many awards and honors, she received the Shelley Memorial Award, the Robert Frost Medal, a grant from the National Institute of Arts and Letters, and a Guggenheim Fellowship.

FEDERICO GARCÍA LORCA, the revered Spanish poet and dramatist, was killed by Nationalist partisans at the age of 38 at the beginning of the Spanish Civil War.

HELENE SHULMAN LORENZ is a philosopher and psychological thinker, as well as a journalist, filmmaker, theater director, and cultural activist. She collaborates with the Center for the Theater of the Oppressed in Los Angeles (www.theateroftheoppressed.org).

JOANNA MACY, the respected environmental and spiritual leader, is an eco-philosopher, Buddhist scholar, and teacher of both general systems theory and deep ecology (www.theworkthatconnects.org).

IGNACIO MARTÍN-BARÓ, a Spanish-born priest trained in psychology, known for his radical work with campesinos, was killed by a Salvadoran death squad in 1989.

HERMAN MELVILLE wrote *Moby Dick* in 1851, a book that is considered by some to be the greatest novel in American literature.

FATEMA MERNISSI, a Moroccan feminist writer, sociologist, and the best-selling author of *Scheherazade Goes West* is currently a lecturer at Mohammed V University where she is a research scholar at the University Institute for Scientific Research (www.mernissi.net).

THEODOR MERON, one of the world's most distinguished authors on international humanitarian law, and Chares L. Denison Professor of Law at New York University, was the president of the International Criminal Tribunal for the former Yugoslavia.

MYRIAM MIEDZIAN, the author of several books, holds a doctorate in philosophy and a master's degree in social work.

CZESLAW MILOSZ was a Polish poet, writer, academic, translator, and a member of the Polish resistance in World War II. In 1980, he won the Nobel Prize in literature.

GABRIELA MISTRAL, Chilean poet, educator, diplomat, and feminist was the first Latin American to win the Nobel Prize in literature in 1945.

JOAN MIURA was incarcerated as a child of "Foreign Enemy Ancestry" at the Tulare, Tule Lake, and Topaz internment camps mandated by President Franklin Delano Roosevelt under U.S. Executive Order 9066. She is a consultant and administrator who lives in Northern California.

ROBIN MORGAN, editor of *Sisterhood Is Powerful* and *Ms.* magazine and a former child actor, is a radical feminist activist, writer, and poet. She is a founding member of Global Sister (www.globalsister.org).

DULCE MURPHY, the former president of Esalen's Russian-American Exchange Center, now called TRACK TWO: An Institute for Citizen Diplomacy (www. trackii.com), has worked extensively with Russia and the Soviet Union since 1980.

MICHAEL N. NAGLER is professor emeritus of classics and comparative literature at the University of California, Berkeley, where he founded the Peace and Conflict Studies Program. He has consulted for the U.S. Institute of Peace as well as many other organizations.

ELIZABETH NEUFFER was an award-winning journalist and fellow of the Council of Foreign Relations who covered conflicts in Afghanistan, Rwanda, and Bosnia. She was killed in an automobile accident while working in Iraq in 2003.

SAM NUNN is an American lawyer and politician who served for twenty-four years as a senator from Georgia. He is currently co-chairman and chief executive officer of the Nuclear Threat Initiative.

MARY OLSON is a health advocate who joined the staff of the Nuclear Information and Resource Service (www.nirs.org) in 1991. She now serves as NIRS Southeast Regional Coordinator based in Asheville, North Carolina.

YOKO ONO is an artist, writer, filmmaker, and musician, known for her groundbreaking avant-garde work, including collaborations with her late husband, John Lennon. An activist for peace, she has also made significant contributions to the fight against AIDS (imaginepeace.com).

AMOS OZ is an Israeli writer, novelist, journalist, and a professor of literature at Ben-Gurion University. Since 1967, he has been a prominent advocate of a two-state solution to the Israeli-Palestinian conflict.

WILLIAM J. PERRY was Secretary of State under President Bill Clinton and is currently the Michael and Barbara Berberian Professor at Stanford University. He serves as the co-director of the Nuclear Risk Reduction Initiative and the Preventative Defense Project.

AGNES BAKER PILGRIM is the chairperson of the International Council of 13 Indigenous Grandmothers and the oldest living member of the Takilma Siletz nation of southern Oregon.

SAMANTHA POWER is the author of the Pulitzer Prize-winning *A Problem from Hell: America and the Age of Genocide*. She is currently affiliated with the Carr Center for Human Rights Policy at Harvard University's Kennedy School of Government and is a member of the National Security Council.

RABIA OF BASRA (c. 717–801), a central figure in the Sufi poetic tradition, is the most popular and influential of the female Islamic saints.

TARIQ RAMADAN is a Swiss Muslim academic and professor of Islamic studies at Oxford University, who advocates a reinterpretation of Islamic texts and emphasizes the heterogeneous nature of Islamic society.

ROBERT H. RESSLER is an evolutionary psychologist and singer-songwriter working on a book about the original meaning and modern significance of the Garden of Eden story. His CD of songs about the story, *Behind the Fig Leaf*, was released in 2010.

RAINER MARIA RILKE (1875–1926) is considered one of the German language's greatest poets. His two most famous verse sequences are *Sonnets to Orpheus* and *Duino Elegies*.

YANNIS RITSOS, one of the most celebrated Greek poets of the twentieth century, was a member of the Greek resistance during World War II. During the 1960s under the Greek dictatorship, he was repeatedly imprisoned and forced into exile.

THEODORE ROETHKE, the late poet and professor, was awarded the Pulitzer Prize for poetry in 1954 for his book *The Waking*.

MARSHALL B. ROSENBERG is an American psychologist and creator of the nonviolent communication technique and process. He founded and directs the Center for Nonviolent Communication (www.cnvc.org).

LENKE ROTHMAN was a well-known Swedish artist and writer, born in Hungary who survived Auschwitz and Bergen Belsen, an experience that was often the subject of her work.

NELLY SACHS, the German poet and dramatist whose experience of the Holocaust transformed her into an eloquent spokesperson for the grief of her fellow Jews (a close friend of the artist Lenke Rothman) and was awarded the Nobel Prize in 1966.

ZAINAB SALBI is an Iraqi American writer, activist, and social entrepreneur. She co-founded Women for Women International (www.womenforwomeninternational.org).

SHARON SALZBERG is a renowned meditation teacher who has been practicing and studying Buddhism for more than thirty years. She is the author of several books on meditation, including the best-selling *Lovingkindness: The Revolutionary Art of Happiness*.

NATHAN SCHWARTZ-SALANT is a distinguished Jungian analyst and writer. Taken together, his many books and essays have changed the way we understand the human psyche. He practices in New York City.

SHANTIDEVA, born as a Brahmin in eighth-century India, was a prominent Buddhist scholar and author of the famous *Bodhicaryavatara*. (Pema Chödrön has written a commentary on this text, called *No Time to Lose*.)

VANDANA SHIVA, India-based physicist, philosopher, ecofeminist, environmental activist, and author of numerous books, is a founding member of the International Forum on Globalization and Women's Environment and Development Organization and is a member of the World Future Council (www.worldfuturecouncil.org). In 1993, she received the Right Livelihood Award.

GEORGE P. SHULTZ, currently at the Hoover Institute, served as U.S. Secretary of Labor and later as Secretary of the Treasury under the Nixon administration and as Secretary of State under President Ronald Reagan.

DANIEL J. SIEGEL is a clinical professor of psychiatry at the UCLA School of Medicine where he is also director of the Mindful Awareness Research Center. He is the author of *The Developing Brain* and *Mindsight: The New Science of Personal Transformation*.

PETER SINGER is an Australian philosopher who is the Ira W. DeCamp Professor of Bioethics at Princeton University and Laureate Professor at the Center for Applied Philosophy and Public Ethics at the University of Melbourne.

HUSTON SMITH, a preeminent scholar in religious studies, author of *World's Religions*, formerly Professor of Philosophy at the Massachusetts Institute of Technology, and now distinguished adjunct at Syracuse University, was the subject of a five-part series hosted by Bill Moyers on PBS called *The Wisdom of Faith with Huston Smith*.

REBECCA SOLNIT is a writer and an activist. Her book *Savage Dreams*, focusing on the protest movement against nuclear testing, was nominated for a National Book Critics Circle Award. In 2003, her book *River of Shadows: Eadweard Muybridge and the Technological Wild West* was awarded the National Book Critics Circle Award in Criticism.

SUSAN SONTAG, the author of several classic books including *On Photography* and *Regarding the Pain of Others,* was a renowned American essayist, novelist, social critic, filmmaker, and activist.

WILLIAM STAFFORD, the well-loved American poet and pacifist, won the National Book Award in 1963 and was the Poet Laureate of the United States in 1970.

HOWARD TEICH is an American psychologist, consultant, and writer who has developed solar and lunar psychology as an organizing principle for consciousness. His latest work is *The Psychology of Light: Healing the Divided Soul.*

JASMINA TEŠANOVIĆ is a feminist, political activist, translator, publisher, and filmmaker who lives in Sarajevo where she witnessed and survived the Bosnian war.

CLAUDE ANSHIN THOMAS is an American Zen Buddhist monk and Vietnam War veteran. He is a vocal advocate of nonviolence and an international speaker, teacher, and writer.

FADWA TUQAN was a major voice for both Palestinians in the Middle East and women within the Muslim world. Winning many awards, her poetry is widely translated and internationally admired.

ARCHBISHOP DESMOND TUTU is a South African cleric and activist who was Bishop of Lesotho and became the first black General Secretary of the South African Council of Churches. He was awarded the Nobel Peace Prize in 1984 and the Presidential Medal of Freedom in 2009.

ALICE WALKER, who won the Pulitzer Prize and the American Book Award for her novel *The Color Purple*, is an internationally honored, essential writer of our time. An activist and social visionary, she has been a participant in most of the major movements for planetary change.

RABBI ARTHUR WASKOW is director of the Shalom Center and the author of more than twenty books on Jewish thought and practice, on the Abrahamic traditions and on U.S. public policy. For similar work by him on the intersections of Jewish tradition and contemporary issues see his books *Seasons of Our Joy* and *Godwrestling—Round 2,* and The Shalom Center website at www.theshalomcenter.org.

IDA B. WELLS-BARNETT was an African American civil rights activist and an early women's rights advocate during the women's suffrage movement. Fearless in her opposition to lynching, Wells documented hundreds of these atrocities.

LAWRENCE WESCHLER, once a staff writer for the *New Yorker*, is the author of more than ten books, including the luminous *Vermeer in Bosnia*.

TERRY TEMPEST WILLIAMS is best known for her book *Refuge*. Her most recent work, *Finding Beauty in a Broken World*, documents and reflects on, among other events, her adoption, with her husband, of a remarkable 20-year-old young man who had survived the Hutu/Tutsi genocide.

SPOJMAI ZARIAB was born in Kabul in 1949. Considered one the most important Afghan voices of our times, her last book was recently translated into French and published by L'Inventiare in France as *Ces murs qui nous écoutant* (These Walls That Listen).

Credits

CHAPTER I

SUSAN GRIFFIN, *A Chorus of Stones: The Private Life of War* (New York: Doubleday, 1992), 12–13. Copyright 1992 by Susan Griffin.

CHRIS HEDGES, "The Truth of War." Excerpted from the Aurora Forum, The Truth of War Panel, October 26, 2006, Stanford University, Stanford, CA. Used by permission of The Aurora Forum.

YANNIS RITSOS, "Afternoon." Edmund Keeley, trans. From *Yannis Ritsos, Repetitions, Testimonies, Parentheses.* Copyright 1991, Princeton University Press. Reprinted by permission of Princeton University Press and Edmund Keeley.

GEORGE P. SHULTZ ET AL., "A World Free of Nuclear Weapons." From George P. Shultz, William J. Perry, Henry A. Kissinger, Sam Nunn, "A World Free of Nuclear Weapons," *Hoover Digest,* 2007: 1. Copyright 2007 by the Board of the Leland Stanford Junior University. Reprinted with permission from the Hoover Institution on War, Revolution and Peace.

MIKE DAVIS, "The First Car Bomb." Excerpted from *Buda's Wagon: A Brief History of the Car Bomb* (New York: Verso, 2007), 1–3 and 4–5. Copyright 2007 by Mike Davis.

CINDY FOLKERS AND MARY OLSON, "Radiation and Children: The Ignored Victims" (Nuclear Information and Resource Service [NIRS], August 2004). Copyright 2004 by Cindy Folkers and Mary Olson. Reprinted by permission of Cindy Folkers and Mary Olson, NIRS.

JENNIFER ABRAHAMSON, "An Injured Child." Excerpted from *Sweet Relief: Maria Ruzicka's Fight for Civilian Victims of War.* Copyright 2006 by Jennifer Abrahamson. Reprinted with permission of Gallery, a Division of Simon & Schuster, Inc. All rights reserved.

SAMANTHA POWER, "Remarks at the Stockholm International Forum on Genocide Prevention," January 26, 2004. Used by permission of Samantha Power.

HUSTON SMITH, "On Religion and Terrorism." Excerpted from "Huston Smith on Terrorism: An Interview with Kaisa Pahakka," *Journal of Transpersonal Psychology* 34(1)(2002): 1–11. Used by permission.

TARIQ RAMADAN, "The Spiritual Source of Islam." Excerpted from "Birth and Education" in *In the Footsteps of the Prophet: Lessons from the Life of Muhammad* (New York: Oxford University Press, 2007), 12–14. Reprinted by permission of Oxford University Press, Inc.

EQBAL AHMAD, *Terrorism: Theirs and Ours* (New York: Seven Stories Press, 2001), 11–26. Copyright 2001 by Eqbal Ahmad. Reprinted with the permission of Seven Stories Press, www.sevenstories.com.

VANDANA SHIVA, "Solidarity Against All Forms of Terrorism." Excerpted from Smitu Kothari, Bindia Thapar, Kamia Bhasin, eds., *Voices of Sanity: Reaching Out for Peace* (Delhi: Lokayan, 2001), 89–92. Copyright 2001 by Vandana Shiva. Reprinted with permission by Vandana Shiva.

IDA B. WELLS-BARNETT, "Lynched for No Offense." Excerpted from *On Lynchings* (Amherst, NY: Humanity Books, 2002). Essay first published in 1892.

THE FIQH COUNCIL OF NORTH AMERICA, "Fatwa Issued on July 28, 2005." Copyright 2009 FCNA, Fiqh Council of North America, an independent 501(c) (3) nonprofit organization.

NATHAN D. BAXTER, "Invocation for the National Day of Prayer and Remembrance for 9/11." From The Very Reverend Nathan D. Baxter, Bishop, Diocese of Central Pennsylvania, "Invocation for an Interfaith Service Prayer and Remembrance." Copyright September 11, 2002, by Nathan D. Baxter. Reprinted with permission by Nathan D. Baxter.

CHAPTER 2

JUDITH HERMAN, "The Aftermath of Violence: Trauma and Recovery." Excerpted from *Trauma and Recovery: The Aftermath of Violence—From Domestic Abuse to Political Terror* (New York: Basic Books, 1992), 20–23. Copyright 1992, 1997 by Basic Books, a member of the Perseus Books Group. Reprinted by permission of Basic Books.

IGNACIO MARTÍN-BARÓ, excerpted from "War and Mental Health" in *Writings for a Liberation Psychology* (Cambridge: Harvard University Press, 1996).

ROBIN MORGAN, "Ghosts and Echoes: Reflections after 9/11." Excerpted from "Ghosts and Echoes" in her "Letters from Ground Zero" as fully reprinted in *The Demon Lover: The Roots of Terrorism*, 2nd edition (New York: Washington Square Press/Simon & Schuster, 2001). Copyright 2001 by Robin Morgan, www. RobinMorgan.us. Reprinted with permission of Robin Morgan.

CHAPTER 4

MARTIN LUTHER KING, JR., "Eulogy for the Martyred Children." Excerpted from Clayborne Carson and Kris Shepard, eds., *A Call to Conscience: The Landmark Speeches of Dr. Martin Luther King, Jr.* (New York: IPM, 2001), 98. Copyright 2001 by The Heirs to the Estate of Martin Luther King, Jr. "Eulogy for the Young Victims of the Sixteenth Street Baptist Church Bombing," copyright 2000 by The Heirs to the Estate of Martin Luther King, Jr.

CHAPTER 5

TAHA MUHAMMAD ALI, "There Was No Farewell" in *So What: New and Selected Poems 1971–2005 (Arabic Edition)*, Peter Cole, Yahya Hijazi, and Gabriel Levin, trans. (Port Townsend, WA: Copper Canyon Press, 2008), 61. Copyright 2006 by Taha Muhammad Ali. English translation copyright 2006 by Peter Cole, Yahya Hijazi, and Gabriel Levin. Reprinted by permission of Copper Canyon Press, www.coppercanyonpress.org.

ARIEL DORFMAN, excerpted from "The Half-Life of a Despot," *New York Times*, December 12, 2006, Section A, p. 31. Copyright December 12, 2006, The New York Times. All rights reserved. Used by permission and protected by the Copyright Laws of the United States. The printing, copying, redistribution, or retransmission of the material without express written permission is prohibited.

HANNAH ARENDT, excerpted from "Lying in Politics" in *Crises of the Republic* (New York: Harcourt Brace Jovanovich, 1972), 37. Copyright 1972 by Hannah Arendt.

DANIEL ELLSBERG, *Secrets: A Memoir of Vietnam and the Pentagon Papers* (New York: Viking, 2002), 289. Copyright 2002 by Daniel Ellsberg.

LAWRENCE WESCHLER, excerpted from *A Miracle, a Universe: Settling Accounts with Torturers* (Chicago: University of Chicago Press, 1998), 4. Copyright 1990 by Lawrence Weschler. Used by permission of Lawrence Weschler.

THEODOR MERON, "Rape as a War Crime." From "Rape as a Crime under International Humanitarian Law," *The American Journal of International Law* 87(3)(July 1993): 424–428. Reprinted by permission.

ELIZABETH NEUFFER, excerpted from "Justice Delivered" in *The Key to My Neighbor's House: Seeking Justice in Bosnia and Rwanda* (New York: Picador, 2002), 251. Copyright 2001, 2002 Elizabeth Neuffer.

THE MOST REVEREND FRANK T. GRISWOLD, "Facing into Truth." Sermon preached at Trinity Cathedral, Cleveland, Ohio. Copyright September 29, 2002. Reprinted by permission of Bishop Frank T. Griswold.

CHAPTER 6

REZA BARAHENI, excerpted from "Masculine History" in *The Crowned Cannibals* (New York: Vintage Books, 1977).

FATEMA MERNISSI, "The Mind as Erotic Weapon." Excerpted from *Scheherazade Goes West: Different Cultures, Different Harems* (New York: Washington

CHAPTER 8

TEXT
10/13 Sabon

DISPLAY
Sabon (Open Type)

COMPOSITOR
Westchester Book Group

PRINTER AND BINDER
Maple-Vail Book Manufacturing Group